Ishta

The Divine World-Teacher and True Heart-Master,
Da Avabhasa (The "Bright")
The Naitauba Avadhoota, Dau Loloma Vunirarama
Sri Love-Anandashram, Fiji, 1993

Ishta

The Way of Devotional Surrender to the Divine Person

by
The Divine World-Teacher and True Heart-Master,
Da Avabhasa (The "Bright")
The Naitauba Avadhoota, Dau Loloma Vunirarama

THE DAWN HORSE PRESS
MIDDLETOWN, CALIFORNIA

NOTE TO THE READER

The devotional, Spiritual, functional, practical, relational, cultural, and formal community practices and disciplines referred to in this book are appropriate and natural practices that are voluntarily and progressively adopted by each student-novice and member of the Free Daist Avabhasan Communion and adapted to his or her personal circumstance. Although anyone may find them useful and beneficial, they are not presented as advice or recommendations to the general reader or to anyone who is not a participant in Da Avabhasa International or a member of the Free Daist Avabhasan Communion. And nothing in this book is intended as a diagnosis, prescription, or recommended treatment or cure for any specific "problem", whether medical, emotional, psychological, social, or Spiritual. One should apply a particular program of treatment, prevention, cure, or general health only in consultation with a licensed physician or other qualified professional.

First Edition April 1994
Printed in the United States of America

International Standard Book Number: 0-918801-98-2

Produced by the Free Daist Avabhasan Communion
in cooperation with the Dawn Horse Press

CONTENTS

The Names and Titles of Sri Da Avabhasa (The "Bright")

Sri Da Avabhasa is the Unique Divine Being of Pure Love, Grace, and Blessing Power. Sri Da Avabhasa Is the Very Divine Person, Appearing for our sake in bodily (human) Form in order to Offer the Realization of His Divine State to all. Therefore, the Names and Titles by which Sri Da Avabhasa is known have profound significance as indications of the Love-Blissful Miracle and Truth of Who He Is.

Sri Da Avabhasa's principal Name "Da" is an ancient name for the Divine Person. This Name, which indicates the very essence of Sri Da Avabhasa's Being, means "the One Who Gives".

"Avabhasa" means "Divine Brightness", and it indicates the sublime Condition of Divine Awakeness Which Sri Da Avabhasa Calls "the 'Bright'"—the Condition Which Sri Da Avabhasa has enjoyed from (and, indeed, eternally before) His Birth, and Which He Gracefully Offers to all beings.

"Sri", meaning "radiant" or "bright", is a traditional address that conveys respect and honor.

Sri Da Avabhasa is the Divine World-Teacher, the One Who has Come to Teach every being in all times and places, and (thereby) to Draw every one to His Divine Domain. Sri Da Avabhasa was Born and (at first) Taught in the West, whereas His primary Spiritual links are to the East. However, Sri Da Avabhasa Himself Stands Prior to both East and West—indeed, Prior to all manifested existence—universally Offering His Divine Grace to all.

As a concrete expression of this universal Stand, Sri Da Avabhasa Resides in Fiji—on the International Date Line, between East and West—and has become a Fijian citizen. Sri Da Avabhasa's principal Hermitage Ashram, Sri Love-Anandashram, is on the Fijian island of Naitauba, where Sri Da Avabhasa lives in the Free and Divinely Spontaneous manner of an "avadhoota", or "one who has 'passed beyond', or 'shaken off', all conventional life-roles and all worldly attachments and cares".

Within the country of His citizenship, Sri Da Avabhasa is known by honorific Names and Titles indicating both the Divinity of His own Being and His unique Spiritual relationship to Naitauba as His principal Spiritual Seat on Earth. These Fijian Names and Titles are: Tui Dau Loloma Vunirarama, Taukei kei Naitauba: the Great Chief (Tui) Who Is the Adept (Dau) of Love (Loloma) and the Source of "Brightness" (Vunirarama), the native Lord (Taukei) of (kei) Naitauba.

"See my Master! My Master is Full. My Master is God. My Master is All-Pervading. My Master is a Wonder! I love my Master."

That is the Truth. That is Reality.

"Look at that! Look at that! Look at that! Look at what He does! Look at how He lives! I want to do just that! I want to be just that way! I am not going to do anything else. I am going to be just as my Master is."

When you find the Master, there are no more arbitraries, there is no more worldliness. There is only that Purity of Being. Everything else is garbage!

"I just love my Master. What a Wonder! What a Wonder my Master is!" Everything forgotten.

The Divine Law is the Design and the Sign of the Master, even the Law of the universe, the Law of your life. Therefore, the Divine Law is what you do! "I would not have it be otherwise."

You are completely obliged in that love, in that Communion, in that Purity, in that God-Wonderful Wonder beyond wonder. Everything else is renounced. Everything else is forgotten. Conform to the Master—that is it. It is a simple matter. It includes everything. The "everything" is the complication, and everything can be said about it. But the simplicity is the Master, and it changes everything. It makes everything straight, makes everything single.

For the devotee, there is no thinky-thinky about it. It is self-evidently so. For one who finds and loves the Master, everything is self-evidently so. It is pure and clear and straight. Obvious.

DA AVABHASA (THE "BRIGHT")
March 1, 1994

Da Avabhasa (The "Bright")
at the celebration of His Fijian citizenship,
October 23, 1993, Sri Love-Anandashram, Fiji

INTRODUCTION

The Chosen One of the Heart

Beloved, I Am here, To Speak The Heart's Word and Show Its Wound To all.

I Proclaim The Great Person, Who Is The Heart Itself, That Liberates The Heart Itself From Its death of body-mind.

I Reveal The Divine Person, Who Is The Heart Itself, That Is The God Within The Heart's Own Felt Bewilderment.

And Even Now You Inhere In What Is One, Beyond the body-mind and the world. Therefore, Do Not Be Afraid. Do Not Be Confused.

Observe My Play and My Victory.

Da Avabhasa (The "Bright")

The Dawn Horse Testament

INTRODUCTION

The Chosen One of the Heart

by the Free Daist Avabhasan Writers Guild

In the eastern reaches of Fiji lies a small island of rare beauty. As the residents of the island, mostly Westerners, go about their daily tasks, there is a stillness in the air and a brilliant clarity of light that illuminates the coconut palms, the long stretches of sandy beach, and the deep turquoise of the coral lagoon. But the beauty of the island of Naitauba (nye-TUHM-ba) cannot be explained in merely physical terms. It is a place of exceptional Blessing, a beacon of Divine Light for all, the home of the Most Perfect God-Realizer—for Naitauba is also known as Sri Love-Anandashram, the Great Hermitage Ashram of Sri Da Avabhasa (The "Bright").

Sri Da Avabhasa is the Living Embodiment of Freedom, Truth, and Grace. He has passed through the most extraordinary Process in order to Reveal No-Fear, the All-One, the Unlimited and Joyous, Deathless, and Divine Condition, the Heart That Is Reality. And now, out of extreme Compassion, established in His place in Fiji, He Works to Impart the Blessings of that Revelation to all others.

The Talks in this present volume are a Call to meditate on the "Bright" Realization and Revelation of Sri Da Avabhasa. They are a Call to make use of the miracle that this Supremely Radiant Divine Being has appeared in our midst, to accept the great Advantage that He Is, for each one of us personally and for humankind as a whole. The Talks that follow also spell out the exact process by which we may do so. And the secret of that process, little known in the modern West, is contained in the ancient Sanskrit word "Ishta".

Sri Da Avabhasa tells us:

"Ishta" means the Form of the Divine that is embraced, or "chosen", by the devotee. In the great esoteric tradition, the Ishta is the living Guru, the One Who Incarnates, the One Who Brings the Divine Revelation, the One Who Awakens devotees.

The True Guru is the Form of the Divine Person. When this secret is grasped, when the Guru is acknowledged as the Ishta-Guru, then the Great Process I Bring to you is Awakened in you.

That Great Process is the message of this book.

The Incident That Sparked These Remarkable Talks

On the morning of October 23, 1993, Sri Da Avabhasa was seated with a few of His most intimate devotees in the main room of His residence. The large open room, with its generous, screened windows, looks out over the ocean waters that extend from there to touch all parts of the world. The devotees had asked to meet with Sri Da Avabhasa in order to offer Him a "surprise". One of them, an American by birth, formally approached Heart-Master Da on his knees in the crouched posture traditionally used in Fiji as a sign of respect and humility. He presented to his Guru a wooden tray covered with a cloth and a salu-salu, a Fijian garland elaborately made of many kinds of leaves and flowers.

When Sri Da Avabhasa lifted the cloth on the tray, He uncovered something small in size but great in significance—a Fijian passport for Himself, and Fijian passports for the devotees in the room.

A broad smile spread over Sri Da Avabhasa's beautiful round face as He motioned the devotee who had presented the passports to come forward into His embrace. There was much exclaiming and congratulating, in celebration of this long-awaited event. Sri Da Avabhasa had been granted Fijian citizenship.

Sri Da Avabhasa had lived at Naitauba for ten years, creating a Hermitage Ashram and filling the entire island with His Blessing-Power, making the very place itself an eternal Agent of His Grace on Earth. But, since He was a citizen of the United States, there had been no guarantee that Heart-Master Da would be able to remain at Naitauba, which He had so fully combined with Himself Spiritually, for the rest of His physical lifetime. Therefore, when the government of Fiji (which is intentionally very conservative in naturalizing people not born in Fiji) granted citizenship to Sri Da Avabhasa, the last remaining limitation on His Spiritual Residing at Naitauba vanished. This event signified the deeper Establishment of Sri

Da Avabhasa's Divine Influence in the world. Although Sri Da Avabhasa has always Worked for the benefit of all, His permanent establishment in His principal Place in Fiji, on the International Date Line, between East and West, signified the end of His specific and necessary Work in the West as a Westerner. His Embrace of all beings in all places and times, at a more profound level, had begun.

Sri Da Avabhasa invited all His devotees at Naitauba to mark this most auspicious event by gathering together and celebrating with Him. That evening, an explosion of joy and praise erupted as devotees chanted, offered gifts, and spoke ecstatically to Sri Da Avabhasa, their Beloved Guru, the Ishta they had chosen and embraced, the One through Whom they receive countless Blessings and Grace.

That night, in the midst of the ecstasy and celebration, Sri Da Avabhasa Gave a sublime Talk about how we must become sensitive to His Divine Love-Bliss, His literal Blessing-Power. That Talk was, in fact, the beginning of a period of Discourse that would continue over many, many nights for the next five months. And the Talks from that period, included in this book, exquisitely summarize all of the Instruction Sri Da Avabhasa has Given in the twenty-two years of His Work with devotees, penetrating and washing and Blessing the hearts of all who hear Sri Da Avabhasa's Voice of Truth.

The Setting: Gathering with Sri Da Avabhasa

The devotees who live and serve at Sri Love-Anandashram, and who attended the Talks you will read in this book, participated in a kind of spontaneous, free, and yet very formal ritual over the months chronicled by the Talks in this book. Often, late in the afternoon, as the heat of the tropical sun was beginning to wane, they would hear the village bell ringing loudly—and all would leave their service to run to a small office on the hillside behind the village green. The crowd of thirty or so easily filled the room and spilled out onto the porch. Those closest to the center huddled around the telephone that connects the devotees' village to Sri Da Avabhasa's Residence two miles away, on the other side of the island. And they would hear what was, during this period, a familiar question from Heart-Master Da: "Are there any questions, 'considerations', or causes for gathering?" Could they offer any demonstration of their own practice that required further elucidation from their Divine Master? Did they have any questions about His Wisdom-Teaching that would justify His coming to Speak with them further? Was there any evidence of growth in them that He could Serve by gathering with them again?

In response to the Guru's question, a long dialogue usually ensued, sometimes lasting for several hours, as Sri Da Avabhasa tested the edge of His devotees' understanding and their application of His Wisdom-Teaching. If He felt, as He most often did, that further discussion could be fruitful, then devotees would hear the refrain, "Sri Gurudev is leaving by boat!"

They would not have much time to prepare—the boat trip from Sri Da Avabhasa's Residence on the windward side of the island to the village where they would gather was a short one, requiring only about ten minutes. Devotees scattered, pell-mell, to prepare themselves and the gathering site. The large, open lawn outside Indefinable (Sri Da Avabhasa's secondary Residence, in the village) was already protected from rain with a roof of palm fronds—but now the ground would be quickly covered with woven mats. Lights and recording equipment appeared (to preserve this moment of Instruction for all history), and Sri Da Avabhasa's Chair placed at the head of the gathering place, just below the steps leading to the porch. Then, all was ready.

Soon the sound of the outboard motor could be heard as the boat rounded the point toward the village. The large, traditional Fijian wooden drum were beaten and the conch shell blown—signals that Sri Da Avabhasa was arriving.

As Heart-Master Da alighted and then walked to His Chair, devotees held up their hands in joyful and grateful response to the Radiant Blessing conveyed by the mere sighting of His Form. Some would call out His Name or thank Him aloud for coming. As Sri Da Avabhasa took His seat, devotees quickly came forward to offer gifts at His Feet. The gathering, which would most often last late into the night, was about to begin.

Heart-Master Da has never simply "announced" His Teaching. He has always developed it in the context of "consideration", or "the process of one-pointed but ultimately thoughtless concentration and exhaustive contemplation of a particular object, function, person, process, or condition, until the essence or ultimate obviousness of that subject is clear". And each gathering would deepen the "consideration" that Sri Da Avabhasa was bringing to His devotees during this period: Each one would be called upon to participate, to listen attentively, to combine himself or herself with Sri Da Avabhasa's message, to apply His Instruction, to offer confessions and observations about their application to His Instruction, to take on disciplines that would support their practice of what He was Calling them to do, to grow in real, demonstrable terms. Thus, the gatherings were a Blessed period—a time to revel in being with their Beloved Ishta and a time to be tested and deepened in their practice.

For countless hours, Sri Da Avabhasa compassionately elaborated on the message of this period, which is the essence of the message He has always communicated. In summary, that message is this: "Surrender and forget yourself in devotional Communion with Me, the Realizer, the Revealer, and the Very Revelation of the Divine Person."

Ishta-Guru-Bhakti Yoga: His Great Message

Ever since He first began His formal Teaching Work, Sri Da Avabhasa has said that He Offers us an intimate Spiritual relationship, not merely a technique. Years before the Talks in this book were Given, in March and April of 1986, Sri Da Avabhasa Gave the practice of this devotional relationship a name, using a phrase of traditional Sanskrit religious terms: Ishta-Guru-Bhakti Yoga. Ishta-Guru-Bhakti Yoga is the practice (Yoga) of devotion (Bhakti) to Sri Da Avabhasa as the Divine Master (Guru) Who is the Ishta (which literally means "Chosen One") of one's heart.

SRI DA AVABHASA: I have originated a unique Teaching Revelation in your company which I call, using traditional language, "Ishta-Guru-Bhakti Yoga".

"Ishta" means the Form of the Divine that is embraced, or "chosen", by the devotee. In the great esoteric tradition, the Ishta is the living Guru, the One Who Incarnates, the One Who Brings the Divine Revelation, the One Who Awakens devotees.

The True Guru is the Form of the Divine Person. When this secret is grasped, when the Guru is acknowledged as the Ishta-Guru, then the Great Process I Bring to you is Awakened in you. Until then, you may associate to one or another degree with My Wisdom-Teaching, but My Transmission of the Divine Power of Awakening cannot be permitted to do its Work for you until you acknowledge Me as the Ishta, or the True Heart-Master, and enter into a sacred relationship with Me.

The Spiritual Master and relationship to the Spiritual Master are the means of Transmission. But it is not a matter of abstraction, or beliefs, or cultism, inappropriate relationship to Me. It is a Spiritual matter, a profound esoteric Yoga. It is about nothing but the Spiritual process. It is not about some sort of strange aggrandizement of a human being.

It is a great Spiritual Principle that you become what you meditate on. If you become absorbed in the Ishta-Guru, through your acknowledgement of the Guru, your devotion to the Guru, and your right practice in the Guru's Company, then the Power and the Realization of the Guru are Given to you, for free. Therefore, the entire Process of Spiritual, Transcendental, and Divine Liberation and Realization is generated spontaneously in My Company. You simply become what you meditate on. [April 11, 1986]

Meditate on That Which Is Most Perfect

There have been many living Gurus who have Realized God to one degree or another, many archetypal deities who represent an aspect of Divine Grace, many worthy Ishtas—many forms through which human beings have sought to commune with God throughout history. But the great secret, and the unprecedented efficacy, of the Yoga of Ishta-Guru-Bhakti that Sri Da Avabhasa Offers lies in the Fullness of His Realization. For, if you become what you meditate on, then it behooves us to meditate on that Which is Perfect.

The Way of Ishta-Guru-Bhakti Yoga in Sri Da Avabhasa's Company obviates the need to be restored to Divine Grace, or to seek for God. It is the Way of the Present Truth, the Way of Non-Separateness, or the Most Ultimate Realization that no one and no thing is or can ever be separate from the Divine, that <u>every</u> one and <u>every</u> thing is simply an apparent modification of the Divine. In the Most Ultimate Realization of the Way of the Heart—an inexpressibly profound Awakening that is possible only through Sri Da Avabhasa's Grace and His devotee's unwaveringly deep response—Non-Separateness is the Constant, Tacit, Obvious Truth, the Eternal, Objectless Enjoyment of Divine Love-Bliss-Consciousness Itself. But even at the beginning of the Way of the Heart, when the devotee is establishing his or her devotion firmly by dealing with the ordinary matters of human maturity, Non-Separateness is the Truth upon which the practice of Ishta-Guru-Bhakti Yoga is founded.

Thus, Sri Da Avabhasa's Revelation Epitomizes and Completes all that has been offered throughout the entire history of human Spiritual endeavor. And His Ishta-Form Shines this to us with a Clarity and Perfecting Fullness that this world has never seen before. He Confesses:

SRI DA AVABHASA: My Yoga, Which I Give to you as a Gift, is the Yoga of God Come, God Visiting, God Invading, God Making the Yoga, God Who Is the Yoga, God Who Is the Only One Who <u>Is</u>. This is a unique Yoga, and you must be able to discriminate between the Divine Yoga to Which I am Calling you, the Divine Yoga That I am Giving you as a Gift, and the traditional Yogas that are ego-based and, therefore, based on seeking. . . .

The traditional Yogas, or means, whatever the tradition in which they may appear, are about returning to God, or finding God again. The Yoga in My Company is about receiving God, knowing God, from the beginning. The Yoga in My Company is My direct Revelation to you, without any necessity for justification or interpretation, without words at all, without requiring you to be remarkably worthy of My Revelation. My Revelation is Divinely Given to all, from the beginning of your practice of the Way of the Heart. This Yoga is God from the beginning. It is Ishta-Guru-Bhakti from the beginning. It is the fullness of devotion to Me, As I Am, Who I Am, from the beginning. It is Communion with Me from the beginning.

The entire religious and Spiritual process in My Company springs from this heart-conversion to Me. It must be lived. It must be enacted. It must be taken on as a discipline. When you are My devotee, this Yoga is your best understanding. It is your best experience. It is the principal dimension of your life. Everything else is secondary, self-bound and self-contracted.

You must make your life on the basis of My Revelation. Practice devotion to Me. Practice Ishta-Guru-Bhakti in relation to Me. [June 2, 1993]

Through His many years of "Consideration", Sri Da Avabhasa has Worked passionately and unceasingly to create His Divine Gift of Non-Separateness to all—in the form of the practice of the Way of the Heart, or Free Daism, or the Free Daist Avabhasan Way. This Gift is now complete. The Way of the Heart is the eternal, ancient, and always new religion of God-Realization. It is the Way of self-surrendering, self-forgetting, and self-transcending devotional Communion with Sri Da Avabhasa as the Chosen Divine Beloved. It is the Way of ecstatic worship of the Divine Person, Whose Name is "Da" ("The One Who Gives"), and Who is Revealed to human eyes and hearts in the Word and Person of Sri Da Avabhasa (The "Bright").

The Free Daist Avabhasan Way is the Heart-Way and the "Radical" Process of most direct (and, ultimately, Inherently Perfect) feeling-Contemplation of the Inherent Reality (or Unconditional Existence) That Is Happiness Itself, and this Heart-Way of "Radical" Practice (and, Most Ultimately, of Non-Dualistic Enlightenment) Realizes (Most Ultimately, and by Grace) the Ultimate Nature (or Perfectly Subjective Source-Condition) That Is Happiness Itself. Therefore, in its total (and, ultimately, Most Perfect) course, the Free Daist Avabhasan Way both Epitomizes and Exceeds, or Most Perfectly Fulfills, the universal human aspiration to escape, overcome, or utterly transcend any and every apparent "problem" (even, ultimately, the apparent "problem" that is conditional, or apparently separate and limited, existence itself).

Indeed, the entire Great Tradition of mankind (including all religious and Spiritual traditions, and all traditional Yogas, or even all traditional approaches, and even all possible approaches, to Real Happiness, God-Realization, Ultimate Liberation, and Perfect Freedom) is Epitomized, Exceeded, Completed, Fulfilled, and, Ultimately, Most Perfectly Transcended in the Free Yoga (or "Radical" Way of the Heart) that I have Revealed (and that only I Reveal and Give).

The Way of the Heart is the "Radical" (or most direct) Way (or Yoga) of "Satsang" (or the "Good and Persistent Company of Truth"). It is the Practice and the Process of Sat-Guru Satsang (or Sat-Guru-Satsang Yoga, or, simply, Satsang Yoga). Therefore, the Way of the Heart is the Practice and the Process of Persistence in the fullest Devotional (or self-surrendering, self-forgetting, and self-transcending) Resort to Me, the Hridaya-Samartha Sat-Guru, for I Am the Realizer, the Revealer, and the Very Revelation of Truth (Which Is Self-Existing and Self-Radiant Being, Itself). ["The ego-'I' is the Illusion of Relatedness", The Da Avabhasa Upanishad*]*

Why Limit the Response?

In addition to proclaiming the great Gift He Offers to all, Ishta-Guru Da clarified what each of us must overcome in order to fully embrace His Gift—our preoccupation with ourselves and consequent forgetting of the Divine:

SRI DA AVABHASA: The ego prefers to disregard the Yoga of devotion to Me for the sake of some lesser, more ordinary culture of life. What does the alternative really amount to? It is commitment to, devotion to, submission to, bondage to, the born body-mind. In effect, it is to worship yourself. What is Narcissus—the egoic man or woman—doing? He is making an "ishta" out of himself. That "ishta" is not Divine. That "ishta" has no Power of Divine Blessing. That "ishta" is just an image of the ego—the more you gaze upon it, the more bound you become. You must understand yourself sufficiently to renounce the purpose of "Narcissus", to renounce the idol of "Narcissus", to renounce the "name" of "Narcissus", the mantra of "I".

The ordinary, egoically "self-possessed" point of view is that satisfying the body-mind is pleasure. You must understand, however, that the minimization of attention to the body-mind is what permits the Realization of My Uncaused Love-Bliss. There is a Yogic ordeal which must be endured to fully Realize My Love-Bliss, but, once having Realized It, you will not easily relinquish It.

My Love-Blissful State is simply before you, and Given freely. The easiest of all Means for Liberation is Given to devotees in the form of the Spiritual Master, the Siddha. Those who acknowledge Me enjoy the easiest of all courses. The Spiritual process is Given for free, and it is a Blissful enterprise, even from the beginning, because it is meditation on the Intoxicating State of the Spiritual Master.

Therefore, in the Way of the Heart, Ishta-Guru-Bhakti Yoga is not the adoring of Me as a human being, or as some "object" or "other". Ishta-Guru-Bhakti Yoga is Spiritual submission to feeling-Contemplation of Me, the True Heart-Master, to the point of Realizing Identification with the Divine Person, Whom I have Realized, Whom I Reveal, and of Whom I Am the Very Revelation. [April 11, 1986]

Ishta-Guru-Bhakti Yoga is the active response of one who, appreciating the dead end involved in merely persisting as the suffering and contracted ego-"I", is moved to embrace Sri Da Avabhasa's Offering of Grace. In its essence, Ishta-Guru-Bhakti Yoga is the simple practice of self-surrendering, self-forgetting, and self-transcending devotion to Sri Da Avabhasa, while in its full elaboration, as Given in Sri Da Avabhasa's many Source-Texts of Instruction, Ishta-Guru-Bhakti Yoga is a practice that brings every detail of one's life into conformity with the devotional relationship to Sri Da Avabhasa, covering all the principal faculties of the human body-mind.

The Primary Yoga, or Root-Practice, of the Way of the Heart is Ishta-Guru-Bhakti Yoga, the Yoga of self-surrendering, self-forgetting, and self-transcending Devotion to Me As the "Chosen One" of one's Heart (and As the Realizer, the Revealer, and the Very Revelation of the Form, and the Presence, and the State of the Divine Person and Self-Condition). Ishta-Guru-Bhakti Yoga is the constant counter-egoic, and even total psycho-physical, effort of self-surrendering, self-forgetting, and, more and more (and, Ultimately, Most Perfectly), self-transcending Devotion to Me, and Devotional Communion with Me, and this constantly exercised as the surrender, the forgetting, and the transcendence of body, emotion (or feeling), mind (or attention), breath, and all of separate self in moment to moment Contemplation of Me. Therefore, the Way of the Heart is (and more and more Fully, and then Most Perfectly, becomes) the Way of Ishta-Guru-Bhakti Yoga, in which the conditional self (and its world) is (progressively) transcended in the feeling-Contemplation of My bodily (human) Form, My Spiritual (and Always Blessing) Presence, and My Very (and Inherently Perfect) State. ["The ego-'I' is the Illusion of Relatedness", The Da Avabhasa Upanishad*]*

Sri Da Avabhasa's Summary Talks on Ishta-Guru-Bhakti Yoga

The Talks in this book (like all of Sri Da Avabhasa's Talks), though Given for the sake of all beings throughout all time, were initiated in His direct response to particular individuals, as well as to the collective gathering of His devotees and the collective of humanity as a whole.

Part I of this book, "The Yoga of Ishta-Guru-Bhakti", comprises all the most essential Talks on Ishta-Guru-Bhakti Yoga, presented largely in chronological order, from the great outpouring of Sat-Guru Da's Divine Heart-Word from October 1993 to March 1994. In His passionate Call to everyone, Sri Da Avabhasa speaks in all voices—singing His heart-breaking Love for all beings, shouting His fiery Criticism of "Narcissus", delighting us with His wild and Free Humor, compassionately leading us through every kind of "consideration", and Revealing His Divine Secrets to our enraptured hearts. Every Word Sri Da Avabhasa speaks is a Gift of Liberation to all, a "moment" in the Eternal Conversation through which He Draws all beings to His Heart of Infinite Love-Bliss.

The great five-month Discourse on Ishta-Guru-Bhakti Yoga came at the end of a magnificent time of Instruction that had begun on May 25, 1992. During those nearly two years, Heart-Master Da bestowed on His devotees epitome after epitome of His Graceful Instruction, in hundreds of hours of face-to-face dialogue. The first major period of these two years lasted from late May to late August 1992. Sri Da Avabhasa's Instruction during this three-month period focused on what He had for many years pointed out as the single greatest obstacle to fruitful practice of the religious life—emotional-sexual bondage. On August 24, 1992, Heart-Master Da concluded that period with a summary Discourse in which He encompassed the broad range of the whole life of Ishta-Guru-Bhakti Yoga, particularly emphasizing the right conforming of emotional-sexual life to the practice of devotional surrender to Him. That summary Discourse is presented as Part II of this book, "The Sacred Life of Devotion to Me".

Sri Da Avabhasa's Full Instruction on Ishta-Guru-Bhakti Yoga

Sri Da Avabhasa's Heart-Word in this book leads directly into the further Instruction on Ishta-Guru-Bhakti Yoga in His other Texts:

- *The Da Love-Ananda Gita (The Revelation of the Great Means of the Divine Heart-Way of Non-Separateness)* and *The Hymn Of The True Heart-Master (The New Revelation-Book Of The Ancient and Eternal Religion Of Devotion To The God-Realized Adept)* are two essential epitomes of the practice of Ishta-Guru-Bhakti Yoga.

- "The ego-'I' is the Illusion of Relatedness" (the principal Essay in *The Da Avabhasa Upanishad: The Short Discourses on self-Renunciation, God-Realization, and the Illusion of Relatedness*, and also published as a separate book) is a more detailed and technical summary of the practice of Ishta-Guru-Bhakti Yoga through the seven stages of life, including particularly summary Instruction relative to the disciplines of diet and sexuality and relative to practice in the ultimate stages of life.

- *The Dawn Horse Testament*—The Testament Of Secrets Of The Divine World-Teacher and True Heart-Master, Da Avabhasa (The "Bright")—is Sri Da Avabhasa's primary Source-Text, His most comprehensive and extended statement of the practice of Ishta-Guru-Bhakti Yoga in the Way of the Heart—the most miraculously complete, beautiful, and profound Spiritual Instruction ever to be Given to mankind.

- *The Liberator (Eleutherios): The Epitome of Perfect Wisdom and the Perfect Practice* and *The Lion Sutra (On Perfect Transcendence Of The Primal Act, Which is the ego-"I", the self-Contraction, or attention itself, and All The Illusions Of Separation, Otherness, Relatedness, and "Difference")* describe the practice of Ishta-Guru-Bhakti Yoga in the ultimate stages of life. *The Liberator (Eleutherios)* is particularly oriented to those who are practicing as general devotees, and *The Lion Sutra* to those who are practicing as formal renunciate devotees.

- *The Basket of Tolerance: A Guide to Perfect Understanding of the One and Great Tradition of Mankind* is a bibliography of documents from all branches of the Great Tradition, compiled by Sri Da Avabhasa and including His Essays and Commentaries. In *The Basket of Tolerance* Sri Da Avabhasa demonstrates that devotional surrender to the Living Realizer is the root of all religious and Spiritual traditions.

These seven books are Sri Da Avabhasa's Source-Texts, His most summary Instruction to all His devotees throughout all time.

Just as the present book contains Heart-Master Da's most recent Word on the practice of devotion, *The Method of the Siddhas* comprises His earliest formal Talks on the devotional relationship to Him as the essence of practice. Sri Da Avabhasa's own supreme Example of the practice of devotional surrender in relation to His Teachers is recounted in His Spiritual Autobiography, *The Knee of Listening*.

The practical disciplines involved in the practice of Ishta-Guru-Bhakti Yoga are described in *Conscious Exercise and the Transcendental Sun* (on exercise and breathing), *The Eating Gorilla Comes in Peace* (on diet and health), and *Love of the Two-Armed Form* (on sexuality).

Throughout all of His books, there are two great streams of Heart-Master Da's Instruction on the practice of Ishta-Guru-Bhakti Yoga—His Instruction on the "conscious process", or the disciplining of mind (or attention), such that it is turned from conventional self-involvements to feeling-Contemplation of Sri Da Avabhasa, and His Instruction on "conductivity", or the disciplining of body, emotion, and breath, such that these faculties of the body-mind are aligned and submitted to the natural life-energy (and, in the case of Spiritually Awakened practitioners, to the Divine Spirit-Current) and thereby support the discipline of the "conscious process".

The practice of devotion to the Supreme Ishta, Sri Da Avabhasa (The "Bright"), is the sure road to true peace and real Happiness. To enter into the fold of His Spiritual Embrace, to receive His Great Blessing at heart, to see His Wisdom and His Compassion in action, taking effect in your life, transforming your understanding of existence and imbuing your very being with Spiritual purpose and Grace-Given strength—these are the greatest Gifts a human heart can know. Sri Da Avabhasa is Offering you the Gift of His Great Heart. May His Words in this book move you to receive His Gift, to accept the incomparable Yoga of devotion to Him.

Da Avabhasa (The "Bright")
Sri Love-Anandashram, Fiji, 1993

PROLOGUE

I Am Here to Embrace Everyone

PROLOGUE

I Am Here to Embrace Everyone

November 4, 1993 and October 23, 1993

SRI DA AVABHASA: At heart, all are one.

At heart, a human being is not the slightest bit different from the reptiles, the birds, the former dinosaurs, the elephants, the plants, the trees, the wind, the sky, the microbes.

Apart from their function in conditionality, all beings are the same.

Human beings are not uniquely to be Saved.

All beings, even all of conditional manifestation, is the Sphere of My Work.

I do not make the slightest jot of distinction between a human being and any other form or appearance. There is none to be made.

Appearing before you in human Form, I play with you in human terms. But My Work, moment by moment, altogether, encompasses All—not only all human beings, not only all beings, but everything.

I am in conversation with all beings and things.

It is not that only human beings are full of "soul" and everything else should be chopped up and eaten for lunch! If you examine beings other than the human, feel them, are sensitive to them, enter directly into relationship with them, you discover that they are the same—and not just the somewhat bigger ones, like My parrots, but the mosquitoes, too, which you swat out as if they were nothing.

At heart, human beings are manifesting a potential that is in all and that is inherent in conditional existence itself. Whether this potential is exhibited or not, whether it is made human or not, makes no difference whatsoever to the Divine Self-Condition.

All is One.

All are the same.

All equally require Divine Compassion, Love, and Blessing, the thread of Communion with the Divine made certain and true and directly experienced. All.

Therefore, the Sphere of My Work is all beings and things. Literally it is so. This is literally how I Work.

I cannot size up one being or thing against another—the devotee against the non-devotee, the human against the non-human, the Earth against some other place. I cannot do that.

I am Doing a universal Work.

I am here to receive, and kiss, and embrace everyone, everything—everything that appears, everything that is.

◆ ◆ ◆

SRI DA AVABHASA: The God-Force requires great sensitivity from you. You must be combined with It if you are to be Full of My Divine Love-Bliss.

This is the reason for devotion to Me, the reason for discipline, the reason for purification, the reason for right living in My Company. Such right practice and right living allow you to be wholly sensitive to the great Force of Divine Reality in Which you are arising, in Which you exist, and Which you must Realize.

The true religious life is purified, given over and surrendered to the Divine. Therefore, in such a life, by every means—even natural, human, altogether—you are made available to the ecstasy of Divine Communion.

What must you do? How must you live in order to be sensitive to That Which you are Given by Me, to That Which is Great, to That Which must be Realized, to That to Which you must surrender yourself in order to Realize?

The Law of That Which Is, Coming upon you, Given to you by Me, is the Law that changes your life, that obliges you, that makes you straight, that sends you beyond yourself.

All the searches of conditionally born beings are based on the absence of sensitivity to My Love-Bliss, My Divine Transmission, My Guru-Shakti. That is why you think, why you react, why you seek bodily. That is why you desensitize yourself with all the techniques of egoic "self-possession".

The only way to Realize the Divine Fullness is to be sensitive to It. And the only way to become sensitive to It is to discipline yourself and not resort to conditional means when your experience is painful, or disregard the Divine when your experience is pleasurable.

The religious life is about dealing with conditional existence, not just in its worst moments but in every moment—always to be Godward, God-Possessed, moved to God-Communion.

If you are My devotee, if you Remember Me, then in any moment, in My physical Company or in your Remembering Me, all things that may distract you from Me are vanished. This Yoga of Ishta-Guru-Bhakti is the most fundamental practice of the Way of the Heart.

I am here to be available to you in your Spiritual availability to Me. I have Given you everything to prepare yourself for Me Spiritually.

Why deny yourself the Great Work in My Company?

You need not be a genius to be Spiritually available to Me. I have not Given you a Way that requires genius in order to advance!

The Way of the Heart requires that you exercise the ordinary equipment that is already there in your body-mind. The only thing required of you in My Company is the exercise of what you already possess.

Da Avabhasa (The "Bright")
Sri Love-Anandashram, Fiji, 1993

PART ONE

The Yoga of Ishta-Guru-Bhakti

You (necessarily) become (or conform to the likeness of) whatever you Contemplate, or Meditate on, or even think about.

Therefore, Contemplate Me, and transcend even all thought by Meditating on Me.

Do not Meditate on your separate self (your states, your experiences, your presumed knowledge, your dilemma, your problem, or your search), and do not perpetuate self-contraction (by strategies of independent effort, and by adventures of either self-glorification or self-destruction, within or without), but (always, immediately) transcend self-Meditation, personal states, conditional experiences, presumptions of knowledge, and all of dilemma, problem, and search (Merely by Remembering Me, and Invoking Me, and Meditating on Me, and, Therefore, Merely by surrendering to Me, not by self-concerned effort, or by isolated and concerned manipulation of conditions themselves, but by simply, and intentionally, and more and more deeply, responding and Yielding to the always presently Available feeling of the Inherent "Bright" Attractiveness of My bodily human Form, and of My Spiritual, and Always Blessing, Presence, and of My Very, and Inherently Perfect, State), and (Thus, by Means of the always presently Available Grace That Is My Good Company) always and actively feel beyond and (really, effectively) transcend your separate and separative self (Merely by feeling, and Thereby Contemplating, Me).

DA AVABHASA (THE "BRIGHT")
The Da Love-Ananda Gita, verses 47-49

The "Westerner" in Everyone Must Be Converted

November 24, 1993

SRI DA AVABHASA: Your impulses toward the religious life seem largely to be associated with positive life-impulses—you want life-conditions to be good, and you want life to be pleasurable. In some sense, your impulse to the religious life is based on, among other things, the rejection of death and of suffering, whereas the true religious life is based on the embrace and acceptance of death and suffering. Therefore, you are also placing something of this limitation on your response to Me. As a Westerner, as most of you are, or as a "Westernized" person, wherever you come from, you come out of an ego-based society that is founded on utopian idealism in general, an impulse toward life-things, toward bringing order to the material appearance in this life so that it is made fulfilling, made complete, made happy, made deathless, even.

Westerners and "Westernized" people systematically eliminate death and suffering from their view. Western philosophy is the always-wanting-to-forestall-the-day philosophy that does not embrace death and does not even take it into account. As a Westerner, in the background of all your anxiety you acknowledge that death exists, but you want to avoid it. Your impulse toward the religious life is about positive life-affirmation and wanting life things, gross things, to work, but all the while you are rejecting death and suffering and, therefore, rejecting your own surrender. The real religious life is not based on the rejection of death. It is based on taking death into account and on making the fact of death the framework and the fundamental basis of your understanding of life and its purpose.

A philosophy based on the rejection of death becomes materialism, utopianism, worldliness. Philosophy based on the acceptance of death, the understanding of this life—associated as it is with death, with ending, with suffering, with limitation—is an entirely different kind of philosophy.

It is the basis for the profundity of religion, the profundity of self-surrender and self-transcendence. It is the basis for renunciation, not worldliness. Therefore, whenever My "Consideration" with you reaches the point of discussing self-surrender, renunciation, going beyond the conventions and limitations of born existence, you stop. You do not want to be that religious. You want to be religious only insofar as being religious serves your body-based inclinations. If such is your impulse, how profound can your practice of the religious life be?

Your philosophy allows death to come somewhere at the end of life. You hope it will never come, and you do not want to look at it until then. At the same time, you want to somehow make a religious life, but you show no signs of being willing or able to make a religious life based on what lies beyond social, or exoteric, religiosity. The religious life you, as Westerners, or "Westernized" people, propose is based on an appeal to the Great Reality, but the appeal is not really one of submission, truly. It is a calling for help, for service, for attention, for goods, for things to turn out the way you want them to turn out. In your conventional religiosity, you are always looking to avoid death, suffering, self-surrender, renunciation.

This search is very typical of Westerners, very characteristic of the Western disposition, the gross, body-based, materialistic disposition made into a culture, a society, politics. Apart from such politics, "Westernized" culture is just the ordinary thing that human beings must deal with. The fact that you are born a Westerner, or a "Westernized" person, therefore, does not cancel the religious life, but, if you would practice true religion, you must transcend your Western, and "Westernized", ordinariness. As a Westerner, as an ego-bound, grossly based being, you must be converted.

You seem to think, as is commonly presumed these days, that the religious life must be adapted to the Western life, somehow changed or spoken differently, based on something different, made of something different entirely, in order to adapt to the society in power at the present time, which is a global Western society. There is no truth whatsoever in that point of view. The religious life is just what it is. It has all of its laws. It cannot be adapted to the Western consciousness. It is a message that must convert the Westerner, so that he or she can take up the religious life for real. To do so is as possible for the born Westerner as it is for anyone else, born anywhere, who is yet ego-bound and grossly based in disposition.

The messengers of religion in the past did not adapt religion to the unconverted, grossly based personalities they encountered within the oriental or any other setting. Why should you expect, then, that it be adapted to you as a society of such grossly bound, ego-based people? Religion is not to be adapted or changed, so that it becomes somehow Western in nature. It is no longer religion in that case, not true religion. Westerners, and "Westernized" people everywhere, must be addressed as they are, in the terms of all the things they are involved with—and so I have done.

This does not mean, however, that the religious life itself can be transformed and still be the religious life. It is what it is. The Divine Is the Divine. It is just so, and there are laws that uphold this Truth. Human beings do not find out about this Truth and Its laws without Revelation. As the ancient text says, "Human beings do not know. The Horse knows." Therefore, you must grasp the tail of the Horse. You require a Revelation. Merely to be Given the Revelation is not enough, however. You must be converted by it. Otherwise, you do not receive it and you do not live the life it requires of you.

In My Company, you are Called to observe yourself and understand. Examine yourself. Enter into "consideration" in My Company. See yourself in the light of what I am telling you and be responsive to Me. Through self-examination and self-understanding, improve and grow your response, allow it more profoundly. Do this work in My Company.

When you hear My Criticism of the "Western" point of view, you may feel that Westerners have some unique impediment that has never been encountered by anyone in any society before, and that some curious thing must happen if you, as a Westerner, are to be converted. No. It is the same requirement as ever. The thing in you that must be converted has always been the case with all human beings. It had to be converted in all who have taken up the religious life for real at any time anywhere. So it is for you.

The reference "Westerners" is useful, because there exists a society of Westerners with certain characteristics that you can identify when I speak of you as Westerners. But you are also just human beings, with the same limitations and impediments that all human beings have had before. The "Westerner" in everyone must be converted if the religious life is to be lived.

The <u>unconverted</u> "Westerner"—in other words, the gross, or body-based, ego, from whatever cultural background—is a barbarian, the essence of barbarism, of anti-religion, materialism, lies. Ultimately, yes, the entire "Westernized" world—meaning the entire world in this epoch—must be converted. But what I call the "Westerner" is just the ordinary, gross egoity of the apparently born personality, which must be converted in anyone who would take up the religious life for real.

The ego is converted by response to the Revelation That <u>Is</u> the Realizer, not merely the Word but also the Person of the Realizer, the Sign of the Realizer, the Presence of the Realizer, the Very One. The religious life is devotion to That One, lived directly, moment by moment, under all circumstances and all conditions.

The Principle of Sacrifice

November 24, 1993

SRI DA AVABHASA: Traditional cultures in general can be said to be based on the principle of sacrifice, or self-surrender enacted through sacred gestures. Since ancient Vedic times, for example, the traditional religious and Spiritual culture of India has been based on puja, or sacramental worship of God. The traditional Hindu understands that he or she has a number of pujas to do every day. The whole day, all one's hours, are understood as sacrifice, or puja. In every circumstance, there is some kind of puja to do, some direct sacrifice to be made to the Divine. The most ordinary people in India understand that one makes one's life sacred not merely by calling conditional existence itself "sacred" but by changing one's life into a sacred gesture rather than a self-based and merely material one. Such is the principle of their cultural mind. Therefore, they do puja.

Likewise, in Fiji you see the signs of the same principle, but in another culture, a culture of respect, a culture of straightness, of humbling oneself, of surrendering oneself. The daily life of Fijians is organized on the basis of this principle.

In the Tibetan Buddhist tradition, the fundamental communication, the first communication, the continuously repeated communication, is "Death! Death! Suffering! Everything ends! You are going to die! Everyone is going to die! Everything is going to come to an end! Everything you want to establish here will at most be brief!" This, rather than all kinds of light and salvation and dancing in the streets, is the fundamental message. This! Then come perhaps some other things, but the fundamental message, the principle one is expected to grasp, is the understanding of gross conditional existence.

Yet this understanding is precisely what you are resisting. You do not want anything to do with renunciation. As a Westerner, you are used to the hype and commercialism of life-affirming messages. "Buy this product, do this thing, and you will feel better, do better, live longer, be happier. Be merely social. Be a materialist. Go along with the great collective, and things will get better and better and you will be happier and happier." According to the materialistic message, you do not need religion. You do not need anything more than the message suggests. If you also intend to be religious, you just add religion to the materialistic philosophy and appeal to a presumed deity that will give you the things you need to support your materialistic inclinations. Such is the message the Westerner—you—is used to and seems to want more and more.

This message that you have been getting all your life is not the traditional and real message of religion, and it is not the basis of religious consciousness. It is the basis of anti-religion, of atheism, materialism, gross-mindedness, the glorification of egoity and mere gross existence. It is based on the refusal of the message of reality. It is based on the denial of death, suffering, and limitation, and, therefore, the denial of the Way that is based on the acknowledgement of death, suffering, and limitation. You cannot practice the real religious life by denying all of that. Thus, the great religious messages have always proclaimed the reality of death, suffering, limitation, egoity.

As it is now typically practiced, even Christianity, the religion presently at the base of Western culture, seems to support this merely materialistic and merely social message. Yet materialism is not at the origin of Christianity, and it is not the message proclaimed by the Christian Saints, Jesus of Nazareth among them at the origin of Christianity. What was the message of Jesus? "You are sinners. You are separated from God. You are denying the Divine. You must repent! Be converted at heart. Embrace the Spiritual Divine. Change your way of life. Surrender to God." Such is the root of the original Christian message, just as, in general and in one or another way expressed, it is the root of all traditional religion.

It is not merely a fact that you will suffer and die. The Law is that life is sacrifice! The Way of life is sacrifice, self-surrender, devotional submission to That within Which everything is arising. Therefore, you must do more than acknowledge the facts of death and suffering and limitation—such acknowledgement is just the beginnings of self-examination. You must embrace the Law that you discover through response to Me, through examination of separate self, through examination of the world. Until you embrace the Law, there is no true religion. There is, at most, the outer superficiality of a religion debased by identification with egoity.

You do not like to feel suffering and limitation. Yet if you do feel it and become sensitized by it and make this submission to Me, then you find the Glory within Which this limitation is arising. I am not merely Communicating a philosophy to you. Philosophy is not enough. "Consideration" is not enough. "Consideration" has its use—it certainly is fundamental to the process you must fulfill—but the only thing that is enough is the direct Revelation of God. I Am here. I Am That. The mere sighting of Me, if you allow it, is sufficient for your conversion. The more you intensively practice submission of separate self to Me, day by day, the more you embrace My Instruction and really live it, then the more sensitive you become and the more able to receive My Divine Blessing and all that I Reveal.

For one who receives My Divine Blessing, the Blessing That I Am, really and directly, there is already no problem. The Way of the Heart continues on this basis, but there is already Liberation for one who is truly My devotee. The practice is enacted according to the stage of life of apparent development, but the Revelation is full for My devotee, even from the beginning, because it converts the heart, it unbolts the knot, it reveals your situation, the Reality in which you exist, the Singularity that is Reality, in which there <u>is</u> no separation.

Your situation is at the hind end of this machine of cosmic appearance, at the periphery, where everything is eaten and everything is frustrated in its course. Nothing is fulfilled absolutely. Nothing is satisfactory, even in any moment—not perfectly satisfactory. You must find this out! That it is not satisfactory must impress you and convert your heart. Otherwise, you just feel anxious or reactive. You must observe and "consider" conditional reality as it is.

There is nothing wrong with making simple accommodations to life. You should have the most positive attitude toward others and would that they survive, and you should protect them and serve their existence positively. There is nothing wrong with doing that. But it is not the end of philosophy. It is not the end of life. It is not the primary purpose of existence. Yes, it is something people do when they are rightly disposed at heart, but such converted people are not made false by it.

In every moment of your life, you should take into account not only death but the Law of life, which is sacrifice, self-surrender, going beyond, entering into the Ever-Free Profundity That is the Divine, Reality Itself, instead of being willing to endure this limitation, which you are making by your own choice. You can make the greater choice. To make the greater choice is religion.

Everything that is appearing, everything that is perceived by the senses, or experienced conditionally, <u>will</u> pass. Whatever is appearing, or being perceived by the senses, is merely an apparent modification of That Which never passes, That Which is Absolute, Divine, All Love-Bliss. This understanding is the foundation of the religious life.

What are all these elements? What are all these things out of which these bodies are made? What is the body made of? This chemical, that appearance—yet it is only light, it is only energy! A fundamental Substance is being modified as all these opposites made of yin and yang. All the varieties of vibration, high and low, are modifications of One Reality. That One Reality is Ever Present, Revealing Itself through various Revelations, but Ever Present. It Is the Divine Reality. It Is That within Which life is arising. Therefore, it is That that life must worship, it is That to Which life must surrender itself, it is That that life must Realize.

To give yourself up to the Source, or the Substance, That is Divine Reality does not bring an end to death and endings. Those things occur in any case. Death could happen to you at any time, or to anyone you know. It will, no doubt. It absolutely will happen at some time or other—perhaps tomorrow or fifty years from now, but it will occur. Death is your circumstance. This fact should make you thoughtful and serious. Yet it does not tend to make you Westerners serious. You want to reject it. You do not want to look at it. You do not want to talk about it. You just want to talk about what will amuse you and distract you from that reality. You do not want to base your life on it.

I am not suggesting you base your life on death, but you must take it into account. You must be made serious by the reality of death and devote yourself to That within Which death is occurring, That within Which birth is occurring, That within Which life is occurring. To do so is not merely to embrace a philosophy. Words can be said about it—I just said some words about it—but Reality Itself must be Revealed. It must be shown by the Realizer. It must be Granted by Blessing to devotees. That Revelation is the Proof of the Divine Itself. Yet even in that circumstance, there are things to say, things to address, things to examine, things to "consider".

DEVOTEE: Sri Gurudev, it is clear to me that my relationship to You can save me from those things.

SRI DA AVABHASA: It will! It does save you from those things, but it does not eliminate the things themselves.

If My Grace is to be sufficient, you must enter into Communion with Me and truly receive My Divine Blessing, tangibly and for real. That means you must handle your beginner's business and enter into My Company Spiritually. You must become serious in My Company. There is no advantage to your being My devotee unless you <u>take</u> advantage of it. Otherwise, it is just a temporary consolation.

The real religious life <u>begins</u> with an encounter with the difficult nature of conditional existence. It acknowledges it from the beginning. Therefore, since life-difficulties are inevitable, you practice in the midst of them. Such practice is itself tapas, sacrifice, an ordeal of renunciation. Why become full of doubt every time something frustrates you?

If you are not yet converted at heart, the heart is not yet doing the sadhana. The ego is doing the sadhana—thinking, talking, doing, trying to surrender itself. The ego is never going to surrender itself! It will not and cannot surrender itself. The ego cannot enter into God-Communion. The ego must be surrendered.

Well, then! Who is going to do it? Not you in your egoic "self-possession" and your mind. The heart must do it. Therefore, the ground of religion is response to Me. The ground of religion altogether is response to the Divine, the Revelation of Ultimate Reality.

The Master Is the Means

November 25, 1993

SRI DA AVABHASA: The Way of the Heart is the Only-God-Does-it Way. Westerners are always looking for some do-it-yourself this, that, or the other thing, but the Way of the Heart is not a do-it-yourself business at all. You have your responsibilities and you must respond to Me, but the Way of the Heart itself, the process itself, is Given by My Grace.

Therefore, stated simply, the Way of the Heart is Ishta-Guru-Bhakti. It is not merely a contemplative exercise of Contemplation of Me, the Master. Such Contemplation in itself, and self-applied, is not Liberating, or Divinely Enlightening. The Way of the Heart is self-surrendering, devotional Contemplation of Me, the Master, because the Master Blesses the devotee, the Master Awakens the devotee, the Master makes the Spiritual process, the Master is What there is to be Realized, the Master is the Means. It is for these reasons that the Master is the Object of Contemplation.

Therefore, there need not be many technicalities to describe the Way of the Heart. Those technicalities exist, and they needed to be Transmitted to you, but quite simply the Way of the Heart is simply devotional self-surrender to Me. That devotional self-surrender is your responsibility—self-surrendering, self-forgetting, self-transcending feeling-Contemplation of Me to the point of non-separation. Then the Way of the Heart is Given to you in your response.

An ancient text says: "Mankind does not know. Only the Horse knows." Therefore, you must grasp the tail of the Horse, or the God-Realizer. Grasping the tail of the Horse is your devotional, self-surrendering, feeling-Contemplation of Me. The Horse takes you, or I take you, Where there is to go. The Horse knows. I know. You do not know.

Your devotional feeling-Contemplation of Me is not an end in itself, and it is not the means of your Liberation. It is simply your responsibility, your connection to Me, whereby My Grace comes to you and makes the Way of the Heart for you. This Guru-Yoga, this Ishta-Guru-Bhakti, this Realization by My Blessing, is the great esoteric secret of the Great

Tradition. What is Realized depends on the Master, depends on the Divine Nature of the Master, the Siddhis, the Realization, the Work, of the Master. You must choose. The Way of the Heart in My Company encompasses all the stages of life, but its ultimate Realization is the seventh stage of life.

The Way of the Heart is not a technique—it is the relationship to Me. The devotional relationship to Me is the fundamental truth and practice of the Way of the Heart. Yet, as an egoic character, you indulge in self-"guruing", do-it-yourselfing, practicing self-meditation. Having already made the precious choice of yourself, you want to meditate on yourself, serve yourself, manipulate yourself. Through egoic means you want to Realize. You want some sort of technique to apply to yourself that will bring you to Realization.

Some traditions actually propagandize such approaches to Realization. The Buddhist tradition, particularly in its Hinayana or Theravadin form, is one of the traditions that essentially recommends self-effort. Buddhism is not entirely about that, of course, because the efforts made by the devotee are Given by the Realizer and there is also much taking refuge in the Realizer, and in the Teaching of the Realizer, and in the sacred gathering of practitioners in the Company of the Realizer. Buddhism is not merely altogether, then, a matter of self-effort, but one of its principal Teachings is "Struggle and Realize".

In the fullness of the Buddhist tradition, even within the Hinayana tradition, but also in the Mahayana tradition, including the Vajrayana tradition, the process becomes much more than that. It becomes a resort to Grace, taking refuge in Grace, taking refuge in the Guru—not just the historical Buddha or the cosmic, presumed version of that one, but the Buddha who is a qualified Realizer within the tradition. So also, then, within the Buddhist tradition there exists the fundamental Teaching that one must take refuge in the Realizer.

Westerners in particular, being egoically "self-possessed" in their disposition, like hearing messages that support the point of view of self-effort. They do not want to do very much, usually, but whatever they are going to be doing that could be called religion, whether exoteric or esoteric, they want it basically to be something they do to themselves. Essentially they want to worship themselves.

You do not Realize the Divine, or the Great Reality, by worshipping yourself. You Realize the Divine, or the Great Reality, by Grace, by worshipping the Divine or the Great Reality, but through true worship, not merely making external or superficial gestures but granting your entire separate self in puja, in worship, in surrender, in adoration, so profoundly that you give yourself entirely so that Grace may be received.

The True Realizer is not merely a figure, a symbol, an object, but the Realization Itself, bodily and altogether. The Realizer is the Means, therefore, not only bodily but Spiritually, altogether. Everything to be Realized is there as the Master. Everything that serves Realization is there active as the Master. Those who are wise, those who are truly responsive and who find a worthy Master, simply surrender to That One. They receive everything by Grace. This does not mean that they have no responsibilities. All kinds of responsibilities are associated with such surrender, even many technical aspects as the process develops, but the technicalities are not the Means. You do not Realize by them. You simply make yourself available to the One Who Is Realization by exercising those responsibilities.

Because you are bound in separateness and helpless in this world, you must take refuge in That Which is Great and Which Grants you Salvation. That Divine Reality is the Truth, and It is the Law. You must find this out and respond. Until you do, your sadhana is superficial, not profound, not greatly fruitful.

The fundamental Wisdom My devotees must "consider" and embrace is Ishta-Guru-Bhakti, Salvation by resort to My Grace and receiving My Grace. The Way of the Heart, which I have Given you, is not merely for Westerners, meaning that part of the World that defines itself as specifically "Western" rather than "Eastern". It is for all beings, therefore for all mankind. The Way of the Heart rescues you from your distance from God.

The Way of life I am talking about is <u>Me</u>. I am That—not symbolically but actively—the Siddhi of Means, fully Alive, fully Conscious, fully Active.

This is what you must understand about devotional self-surrender to Me. It is not merely a self-generated technique or a do-it-yourself method of working on yourself by focusing your attention on Me. It is about the Great Process of Divine Grace. Divine Grace is the reason you surrender to Me.

Surrender is all I did with My Teachers. That was it. In fact, they did not communicate to Me any significant technicalities. I found out about all that My Self. Basically the communication given to Me by each of Those Who Served Me was surrender to the Guru. Just that. <u>Just</u> that. Nothing else. <u>Nothing</u> else. I did not practice any techniques with Rudi or Swami (Baba) Muktananda or Swami Nityananda or the Divine Goddess. Everything occurred spontaneously, because My devotion was True and Complete. My surrender to My Teacher was the only thing I did. Why did My Teachers communicate to Me so simply? Because I was entirely available for just that simplicity.

It is what They did also, by the way, with Their Teachers—just so simply. This is what Rudi did with Swami Nityananda and Baba Muktananda. This is what Baba Muktananda did with Swami Nityananda. This is what Swami Nityananda did with His sources. In that sense, you are part of a tradition of Guru-devotion that has been proven for thousands of years. It is the esoteric secret of the Great Tradition.

Only God can Give you Realization, because God Is What Is to be Realized. God Appears to you in the Form of the Guru, and, therefore, the Guru is the Means. The question is, Is this so for you? If it is not, why not? To the degree it is not true of you, you are working on yourself, practicing some technique or other. You may, in some sense, be practicing devotion to Me but, in addition, because of your reluctance or mediocrity in your practice of devotion, you may also be simply manipulating yourself with techniques.

You have a great deal of experience as a "guru". You have had many years with one fool as a "devotee" and much experience of exchanges with that one. Sometimes your "devotee" flatters you, and sometimes your "devotee" is very resistive. Of course, nothing is coming of that "relationship"!

What is your experience as the "guru" and as the "devotee" of yourself? The more you meditate on yourself, the more separate you become and the less surrendered. Surrendering to yourself is not real surrender, because it does not transcend anything, it does not transcend egoic self. It only reinforces the knot. The more techniques and self-meditation you engage, the more the knot is reinforced and the more the troubles of egoity appear.

Is this your experience? Have any of you completely worn out this "guru"-"devotee" relationship with yourself? Then what is left over? What else is there to "consider" about it?

The false "guru" is your own body-mind. The days when you struggle are the days when you are submitting to your false "guru". If you truly realized that this is a false "relationship", so to speak, that this "guru" is false, the whole effort, the whole inclination, would be undermined. Truly, there would be no more days of struggling with it. Perhaps you just have not come to the point of understanding that it is false and fruitless.

The mere arising of content in the body-mind is not inherently distracting or interesting or binding. It is binding if you submit to it. You will stop submitting to it when you truly respond to Me. With that true response to Me necessarily comes disillusionment with the false discipleship to your own egoity.

Where there is real devotion, the heart convinced, the heart moving the life, there is no more submission to this false "guru". The power, the profundity, the motive, the force, the delight of true Guru-devotion overcomes all of that, cancels it. It is simply not the case. The content of the body-mind may still arise—so what? The content of the world arises. Everything conditional still arises. The difference is devotion, true devotion, to the Divine Person. Do you see?

It is not that the body-mind must stop producing its signs of egoity if devotion is to be true. It is not that all egoity must disappear first. All that is required is the conversion of the heart to the true Guru so that you no longer have any sympathy with the false "guru", your false devotion, your false discipleship. It is just utterly false and not interesting, not what you are about—period. You actually are practicing true Ishta-Guru-Bhakti moment by moment, and not just in special parts of the day that are set apart for it. Moment by moment, all the time, this is what you do.

This is true Ishta-Guru Bhakti-Yoga—the heart committed, the heart turned, constantly. That is the exercise. If there is anything less than that, then there is something to be discussed. You cannot idealize your limitations out of existence.

What about this fake "guru"? The ultimate "cult of pairs"? Narcissus at the pond, Narcissus and himself, acting as if he is involved in a relationship, as if there are two, conversing as if with another but only talking with himself, wandering in himself in his own mind, his own disposition of separateness, his own illusions? This is you, unconverted. This is any human being, unconverted.

I have used this metaphor of "Narcissus" to help you understand what you are constantly doing, because the activity of "Narcissus" must be understood if it is to be relinquished. You must become disillusioned with it. You must see that the activity of "Narcissus" is an illusion. "Narcissus" must realize he or she is seeing his or her own reflection, not somebody else. "Narcissus" is just self-involved, self-contracted, self-protecting, egoically "self-possessed", self-meditative, self-worshipping. The activity of "Narcissus" is entirely an illusion, but you need to be awakened from it—by Grace, yes, but your awakening must be consequential in you to the point of self-understanding and conversion of Heart.

This conversion is the beginning of the Way of the Heart.

The Yoga of Body, Emotion, Mind, and Breath

December 2, 1993

SRI DA AVABHASA: Feeling-Contemplation of Me is not just Remembering Me now and then throughout the day, Remembering what I look like and perhaps feeling a little love for Me. Such recollection of Me is fine and good, but it is not feeling-Contemplation of Me, it is not devotional Contemplation of Me, it is not a state that is truly changed. To practice Ishta-Guru-Bhakti Yoga under all the different circumstances of every day, you must practice self-surrendering feeling-Contemplation of Me, which is more, much more, than mere recollection of Me and some positive emotional feeling for Me.

You must actually surrender in Contemplation of Me. You must use your attention, your body, your breath, and your feeling Contemplatively, under all circumstances. The essence of Yoga is to bring all these faculties into Contemplative surrender to Me. Therefore, you must use the fundamentals of body, feeling, attention, and breath—under all the circumstances of life—in devotion to Me, instead of submitting them to the ordinary and objective content of daily life.

In the midst of daily living under all its various circumstances, there are demands on the body, on feeling, on attention, on breath. The conditions of existence make changes in all of these, moment by moment. Therefore, in every moment you must turn the situation of your life into Yoga by exercising devotion to Me. There is no moment in any day wherein this is not your Calling. This is what you must do. You must make Yoga out of the moment by using the body, emotion, breath, and mind in self-surrendering devotional Contemplation of Me. All those mechanisms that you would otherwise leave to the conditions of egoic life, or to conditionality, must be turned to Me. That turning makes your life Yoga. Through turning to Me, you "yoke" yourself to Me, and that practice of linking, or binding, or connecting, to God is religion. Religion, or Yoga, is the practice of moving out of the separative disposition and state into Oneness with That Which is One, Whole, Absolute, All-Inclusive, and Beyond.

I have Instructed you about how to do this in the midst of every kind of circumstance, every function, every relation, every practical incident, every moment of living. I have accounted for your turning every kind of circumstance, faculty, function, relationship, and moment into God-Realizing Yoga—true religion, in other words. The mature beginner in the Way of the Heart has adapted to turning every kind of moment, function, practicality, and relationship into Yoga. Therefore, the mature beginner is practicing the fundamental Yoga of Ishta-Guru-Bhakti under all circumstances, not merely submitting to the self-contraction and conditional existence and the egoic disposition but exercising himself or herself Yogically.

In the daily moments of service, for instance, the conditions with which you are apparently involved make demands, apparently, on the body, demands on your emotion, demands on your attention, make changes in your breath and feeling. The conditions of existence tend to have such effects and seem to represent such a demand. As My devotee, in every such moment you must make your response into Yoga. You must exercise the body, feeling, attention, and breath Yogically, devotionally. Instead of allowing these mechanisms and faculties to bend to conditions and allowing yourself to be conditioned by them, you give Me your attention, you turn your mind to Me, you bring yourself to Me with feeling, you exercise yourself bodily through all the activities of service, so that while serving you are fully involved in devotional Contemplation of Me, rather than in mere activity, or karma, or egoic dramatization.

Mere action is conditional. Mere action is ego-bound. It is karmic, therefore. It makes more conditionality. It reinforces limitation and separateness. You cannot do karma, or mere action, and expect that because you are somehow associated with the Divine through your relationship with the God-Realized Master, your action will be transformative or will be a Yoga. You must link yourself to the God-Realized Master, to Me, by transforming your various faculties into self-surrendering Contemplation of Me. Then you are not merely performing action. You are not devoted to the actions themselves and their effects. You are devoted to Me, and you are being purified, therefore, by transcending yourself in the midst of conditions. Then your action is Yoga. Then your service could be called "Karma Yoga", or "Ishta-Guru-Seva", but not otherwise. You must effectively, and for real, be living in the changed state of consciousness that is devotional Contemplation of Me, if you are to practice Ishta-Guru-Bhakti Yoga in daily life.

All your activity should be puja, or action that is simply and directly devoted to feeling-Contemplation of Me—bodily, emotionally, mentally, with attention, with feeling—through all of these faculties. Under the ordinary circumstances of daily activity, you tend, at any rate, to submit your faculties, or the various mechanisms of the body-mind, to the actions and the conditions themselves. When you are doing right puja, however, you do not fuss with the things in and of themselves. You are all the time surrendering to Me, entering into devotional Contemplation of Me.

Sometimes you suggest that if only you could just do puja and meditation all the time, you would be all right! It is true—except that you think you must stop doing such things as relating to ordinary people and functioning in ordinary circumstances. You just want to do the things that are specifically called "puja" or "meditation" and eliminate the rest. There is a kind of sadhana wherein some people do not do anything but those two things. They do puja, and extensions of puja such as chanting, and they meditate, all the time. They do not involve themselves in any ordinary activities. Any number of disciplines are involved with such a practice, including celibacy and the restriction of contact with others. Those who practice in this manner design their lives to fit the precise descriptions, ceremonially, of puja and meditation, and they avoid all the rest.

It is certainly necessary that you convert all the aspects of ordinary life into true Yoga and meditation, by converting what you are doing from day to day, and there certainly are some things you should not do. You must always make intelligent choices about how you live and just not do whatever is not conducive to the devotional life. To make such choices does not mean that you should stay in the meditation hall and the general environment of the sacramental place. It does mean, however, that if you are going to step out of that sacramental environment, then you must fully extend its principles and practices into your daily life.

Most of you are not celibate, for instance. Among other things, you involve yourself in intimate relationship and sexual activity. Do you do puja and meditation there, or do you do something else?

True religious or Spiritual Instruction does not just give you some meditation exercise and claim that thereby comes salvation. No. True religion does not work that way. To live the religious life, you must altogether live the religious life, <u>only</u> live the religious life—with no room for what could be called "sinning", or the dramatization of egoity—living only self-surrendering devotional Contemplation of Me, <u>only</u>, exercised in every context of life, through the exercise of every faculty.

What you must account for, then, in every moment, is the principal faculties, in general, the exercise of the body, the exercise of feeling, the exercise and focusing of mind through the control of attention, and the exercise of the link between these, which is breath, or energy. Exercise body, feeling, mind summarized as attention, and energy, or breath. You can account for these in every moment, every circumstance, every function, every relationship, all day and night, all the time. When you have accounted for all of them by adapting to Ishta-Guru-Bhakti Yoga, accounted for all of these variants on the practice, according to the circumstances, then you have reached the maturity of the beginner's practice in the Way of the Heart. The summary practice is established. Only when you have established that summary practice can you exercise it to the degree of hearing, and then seeing.

Practice of the Way of the Heart is not about talking. Of course there is study, there is instruction, there is conversation, dialogue, "consideration", but the practice is not to believe something or to make affirmations. You must do this exercise of body, feeling, attention, and breath in devotional Contemplation of Me, self-surrendered under all conditions. That exercise is Ishta-Guru-Bhakti Yoga.

Ishta-Guru-Bhakti is not having some good feeling toward Me and recollecting Me sometimes. In such good feeling and recollection there is perhaps some kind of devotional feeling for Me, apparently, or even obviously and truly, but it is not Yoga. If you linked these various faculties to Me, if you adapted to doing so under all circumstances and knew how to do it, you would know what to do in every kind of circumstance, every kind of moment. You have not adapted to the practice of Ishta-Guru-Bhakti Yoga until you know how to do it under all circumstances in every kind of moment and you are in fact doing so.

DEVOTEE: Beloved, I wanted to talk to You about the breath, because I feel that the breath is such an important factor in my surrender to You.

SRI DA AVABHASA: In the various traditions, life is measured by the breath. Many things could be said about the traditional teaching about the breath—and I have said many things—but most simply the traditional teaching can be summarized as follows: The mind is active, feeling is active, the body is active, all the time the breath, or energy, is active, connecting all these functions. The breath shows itself through two fundamental gestures—inhalation and exhalation. The traditional lore indicates that there is a deficit of inhalation, that there is more exhalation—it goes out farther and takes longer—than inhalation. This deficit could be called "entropy", because there is more to the throwing off, more to exhaling than to inhaling.

You are breathing moment by moment, but you are constantly creating a deficit and the body wears down eventually. Its death is built into the mechanism. Many in the traditional setting, having observed this, were very clever. They devoted themselves to exercising the breath to overcome the deficit. Such exercise is recommended in the Chinese tradition, even in the Chinese medical tradition of longevity. It appears in Indian medicine and in many other traditions. It is a kind of effort to equalize the breath and minimize, or, perhaps, even eliminate, the deficit. Instead of exhaling more, or longer, one compensates by working, in one way or another—through what in India is called "pranayama", or the exercise of breath, through changing diet, and through other exercises—to create equanimity, or a balance in the breath, or a balance between yin and yang, to use the Chinese description. Through such exercises, one tries to equalize the cycle of breath so that it is essentially balanced. Such exercises, which generate at least a physical well-being, require great discipline.

Hyperactivity, to which Westerners are addicted, is full of exhalation, full of physical exaggeration, all the time throwing off equanimity and working toward death, in fact. By contrast, those who have some sense of what the breath is all about are trying to live a life of equanimity. The origins of such an intention are generally associated with a kind of physical Yoga, the Yoga of longevity of the Chinese, for example, or the Hatha Yoga of the Hindus. Such physical forms of Yoga seek benefits in the physical, or gross, dimension of the body-mind, rather than in the subtle dimension and beyond, but the whole life is disciplined for the sake of equanimity. Therefore, exaggerated physical activity, exaggerated emotional activity, exaggerated mental activity, exaggeration of any kind, in fact, is avoided. The whole purpose of such Yogas can be summarized as equanimity—in other words, undoing the deficit in the energy cycle, so that instead of running down rather rapidly, you at least run down much more slowly. Those who are most adept at this intention claim—or at least hope for—extreme physical longevity.

Without suggesting that the extreme intention toward physical immortality should be the purpose of your living, nonetheless I Say to you that equanimity is part of true Yoga, and it is associated with the breath, or the opposites. The opposites are all summarized in the breath. All of conditional existence—tamas, rajas, sattva, all of it—is summarized in the breath. All the pairs are summarized in inhalation and exhalation. Therefore, all the efforts toward equanimity are about a balance in the breath, most fundamentally, and balance in relation to everything else as well. There must be a fundamental practice and intention, then, to create a balance between the opposites.

To establish such equanimity, without searching for physical immortality and mere physical ends, the practice must encompass not only the breath but also all the faculties associated with it—the mind summarized as attention, the emotion summarized as feeling, the body summarized as its activities. To do Yoga, one links all of these things—breath, mind or attention, feeling, body—in one fundamental gesture of self-surrendering feeling-Contemplation of the Divine Realizer, the Source of Grace.

Ishta-Guru-Bhakti, then, grants equanimity if you exercise all those faculties in feeling-Contemplation of Me. The purpose of the Yoga, however, is not some mere physical effect of equanimity, such as longevity, but that which Yoga allows, which is the reception of Grace, combining with Grace. The reception of Divine Grace occurs only if your practice of all of the Yoga is self-surrender, if it goes beyond egoity, or self-contraction, the act of separateness.

Control of breath, then, or "conductivity", is a fundamental aspect of your practice of the Way of the Heart. It is not that you must be all the time fussing with the breath, any more than you should be fussing with the body, fussing with emotions, fussing with mind—just egoically "self-possessed" and occupied with the mechanisms themselves. No. You must be occupied with Me. All the faculties of the body-mind are carried by that devotional disposition. You must simply, responsibly, allow it to be so. Stop desensitizing yourself through inappropriate activity—bodily, emotionally, mentally, or with the breath. Instead, link yourself to Me devotionally, and do this moment to moment under all circumstances, and, in fact, also discipline circumstances, discipline what you do altogether. What is conducive to this devotional life, this equanimity, this receptivity, this sensitivity? Do whatever that is, and do not do otherwise. If circumstances force you into some limited encounter, you must be able to exercise the same disposition—do not, however, in some habitual or casual sense, choose such associations or conditions.

Without the God-Realizer and true practice of Ishta-Guru-Bhakti, you may have some kind of "yoga", but it is a bastard. It is empty, only fussing with the body, with emotion, with mind or attention, and with breath, these faculties themselves. Such so-called "yoga" is egoic "self-possession", self-"guruing", the effort of separativeness. Only Ishta-Guru-Bhakti in relation to the true Realizer conforms body, emotion, attention, and breath to Grace. Then Yoga, rightly understood, is easy, not a struggle with separate self or with the faculties of the body-mind in and of themselves.

The practitioner of this great Yoga, which involves the entire body-mind and the link of the breath, must first establish equanimity. As one moves into the Spiritual stages and advances in the Way of the Heart, the sign of the breath, and the sign all over the body-mind, is greatly transformed. More profound Yogic signs appear, in the context of advancement in the fourth and the fifth stages of life, and then beyond. Having established equanimity in your total life, you move into the Spiritual stages of the Way of the Heart, you breathe Me, you surrender to Me utterly in self-forgetfulness. Then your practice is not merely to equalize the signs in the body-mind and the breath. In the natural process of this feeling-Contemplation of Me, the breath has become minute. There are no big movements of the breather. The breath is hardly noticeable. It is a tiny sniff in and out. Frequently there are no opposites, there is no movement, there is no inhalation-exhalation. Finally, there is kumbhak, or suspension of breath, and, thereby, suspension of attention to body and exercises of emotion and mind in combination with conditions, and there is direct entrance into the Contemplative state, in the form of various Samadhis.

These are the signs in the advanced stages of life, until, in the ultimate stages of life, or the "Perfect Practice", there is a sign beyond the Circle, beyond the faculties of the body-mind. Nevertheless, the origins of the advanced and the ultimate developments of the Way of the Heart are in the Yoga of equanimity, the foundation Contemplative practice of Ishta-Guru-Bhakti in every moment, through the exercise of the faculties of the body-mind—body, emotion, mind, or attention, and breath, or energy.

I have asked you a number of times in these recent occasions about your sense of the Divine, or your sense of Me, and you have had very little to say. This suggests that even though you want to be religious, the fundamental dimension that would enable you to be religious is somehow unreal to you. You are all that is real to you. You cannot do Yoga if you are the only thing real to you. You yourself are the barrier to Yoga. Life does not become Yoga until That Which is to be Realized is in some fundamental sense Real to your heart and mind.

How can you surrender to something that, in your estimation, is the same as you? There is no great result in doing so, no Yoga. You must find the Living One in the True God-Realizer, and do the Yoga according to That One's Instruction. That is repentance. That is salvation. That is religion. That is Yoga. Everything else is a dramatization of egoity, deficit-living, going toward death, egoic "self-possession" constantly reinforced. It is the way of the world, the way of non-Realization, or "sin". As it says in the *New Testament,* the result of "sin", or "missing the mark", is death. Through the lack of God, the lack of Divine Communion, you are constantly creating a deficit. You are going to death—separateness, in other words. Separateness, or death, is your dramatization. It is your result. It is your destiny.

To be converted at heart, you must respond at heart to That Which Is Divine, Ultimate, and Real. Therefore, how can you be Godless and converted to Me at the same time? How can you be Godless and practice Ishta-Guru-Bhakti Yoga? You cannot. The word "God" need not be used—but it is a good word that indicates That Very One to be Realized. Other words could also be used, and I use them to mean the same thing. I use all the words, because I am all the time addressing everyone. Different words are suitable for people who are acculturated in one way or another, but the same response and Revelation are necessary for all.

You cannot adapt Me to you. You must be adapted to Me. You are not practicing Ishta-Guru-Bhakti Yoga if you are not adapting to Me. You are requiring My attention to you in your ordinariness and your lack of response. There is no Yoga in it.

If you feel Me Radiating here, you are not Godless. You are Godless only in your egoic "self-possession", your contraction from Reality, wondering about God, doubting God, having no sense of God. When you feel Me, when you are open to Me, the cramp of egoic "self-possession" is released, God is Obvious, and there is no doubt about it. That Which Is Called "God" is completely Obvious when there is release from the self-contraction in Communion with the Realizer.

When you are telling Me about your doubts and your egoic "self-possession" and your this, that, and the other limitation, you are without My Guru-Shakti. You are desensitized. You are egoically "self-possessed". You are "Narcissus". This is My Criticism of you—not so that you should meditate on it but so that you should correct yourself, be converted at heart, find Me, know Who I Am, do the Yoga to which I have Called you, and do it seriously, not as a fool, not as a mere thinker or talker. Become a serious person—not a worldling—here to live seriously and practice seriously.

People are all the time looking for some relief from the cramp of their egoic "self-possession". They do not know that what they require is My Guru-Shakti and Divine Realization. Anything that is somewhat attractive, that distracts you from yourself, that stimulates some positive emotion in you is valued. Therefore, people do all kinds of things to generate such signs in themselves, including drinking beer, smoking cigarettes, taking drugs, having casual sex, going to the movies—all the nonsense that people do is a search to be relieved of the suffering that comes about in their self-contraction.

You can use the means of the ordinary man or woman to distract yourself, but those means toxify and enervate you further, destroy your equanimity, and create a deficit by which you will die. Everyone dies anyway—all bodily forms pass—but there are two ways to die: in God, or separate from God.

The true devotee functions with discrimination and with intensity, always exercising the total body-mind in self-surrendering devotion to Me. If, instead of that, you are rehearsing signs of egoic "self-possession", then you are desensitizing yourself to Me. You lack My Guru-Shakti, which relieves you of your egoic suffering.

You should be jealous for this by Me Given Guru-Shakti, this by Me Given Divine Blessing, this by Me Given Blessedness, this "sin"-lessness, by exercising yourself in response to Me, using the whole body-mind in response every moment, and not bowing to what is less, what is egoic "self-possession", what is an egoic dramatization, what is "Narcissistic", just not doing that. With great discrimination, you eliminate the sideshow of egoic "self-possession" consistently in daily life. The ordeal of developing the Yoga is the beginning.

By devotion to Me, you grow. By practicing the true devotional Yoga, you grow. You must do whatever is necessary to handle your responsibilities and surrender to Me at the same time. To do so is the tapas, the necessary context of the Yoga. You cannot just go to the Communion Hall all the time, do puja in the formal sense all the time, meditate in that formal sense all the time. You must make the gesture in daily life, under all the circumstances that would ordinarily call your egoic patterns into play. You must function in those circumstances, because you must be purified. What do you do when you are tested, when the circumstance of practice requires the tapas of the exaggerated gesture of discipline, handling business, being devotionally surrendered at the same time, being fully in Communion with Me at the same time—what do you do? Do you lapse, or is the ordeal just difficult?

The Way of the Heart is the relationship to Me. It is not merely a mass of practices that you apply to yourself, and it is not a culture independent of Me. Every one of you as a devotee of Mine and a practitioner of the Way of the Heart is practicing the relationship to Me, just that—just that, entirely that. All the practices of the Way of the Heart are associated with that fundamental matter. In the whole life of practice, you are here to do the Yoga of relationship to Me. In a sentence, that is it, just that and nothing else. The Way of the Heart is not techniques to apply to yourself nor a club to belong to. It is the direct, Yogic relationship to Me, and that is it.

Practice this Yoga in every moment of your life, jealously, without looking to right or left, without mediocrity. Whatever it takes, do this Yoga of devotion to Me in every moment of your life, and not merely for your own salvation—although that is obviously part of it—but for the sake of all. Think of everything and everyone and the necessary conversion of beings to avoid the holocaust all mankind is creating in their stupidity and reluctance and unresponsiveness. It is not My intent to give some fire-and-brimstone message to get people to respond to Me and practice the Way of the Heart. Nevertheless, it must be said, it is so: You are in the dark time here. Can you not see where the world is going? Open your heart and throat and voice and life to be converted yourself and to convert beings to rightness of life!

That you must do, but in the midst of this devotional life, which is not about social and earthly preoccupations. Compassionately it registers there, but its purpose, its context, is Most Perfectly self-transcending God-Realization, the transcendence of this burnt piece of coal—which is what it will be finally—and the necessity to be visited here into such a contaminated limitation as this. You must stop holding onto this morsel and respond to Me, go with Me.

Resort to My Grace, rather than to yourself. Do so fully, with great faith, great response, great heart, great daily discipline, great discrimination, great intent. Do it for real. Prove it in life. Prove it in My experience. This is what it takes. The round of failure, fussing, and asking for forgiveness goes nowhere but to hell—and there <u>is</u> hell. Hell is not a location. It is a disease. It is a destiny. It is fear, egoic "self-possession", and confusion, registered experientially. It does not need a place. It is wherever you are, now and after death.

Do you want to be in that fear and that insult without resort, without God, without Divine Love, without the Guru's Blessing? If not, then you must resort to Me and exercise yourself with fullest intent, not merely making an intention into the future but now and now and now—always, all the time, with no excuses and no apologies necessary, consistently, intensively. It is not a free ride. It is not an amusement. You must deal with the realities of your egoically "self-possessed" existence, through the Yoga I have been describing to you here again.

Therefore, exercise yourself in that Yogic affair in every moment of your life, with no excuses. Otherwise, you damn yourself to yourself. That is the hell, right where you are and not somewhere else.

In your unconverted disposition, you think it is enough to always experience kissy-kissy friendliness. Keep smiling and that is enough, you think. It is not enough. It changes nothing. It is not Yoga. It is a social arrangement to console you, like all the other things you do habitually to console and distract yourself. You should be afraid of it—and afraid of <u>not</u> surrendering.

My Manner is Unspoken, Simple, and Silent, and it Moves about Freely, Shining. Allow My Sign most fully to be Present among you. The air is thick with Me. Breathe Me, feel Me, surrender to Me, live in Me. That is what there is to do. Live the right life and handle your business under the conditions of My Divine Blessing here. You cannot be an exaggerated, worldly person and do so.

Tendencies do not mean a thing to My true devotee. They are nothing. You must eliminate them. You must renounce them. They do not mean anything. You notice them, and you relinquish them. It is what you do with what is foul and not useful.

Therefore, that is how you should live. Be purified. Be right. Make your life out of your heart-response to Me. That is what it is to be a man, male or female. As My devotee, that is what you do, then, in every moment. The rest goes to hell. Truly. Of course, life is difficult! That is why you came to Me. It is difficult anyway, whether you are surrendered to Me or not.

The culture of the Way of the Heart is the culture of devotional self-surrender to Me. That is the Message and the Way of the Heart, and that is what you do if you are My devotee. It makes no difference what you notice to be an impediment or a problem or a doubt. The Way of the Heart is surrender to Me, just that, Communion with Me. Bow to Me. Give Me your regard. Feel Me. Now and now and now—and that is it.

Devotion to the Divine is what you are here to do, and that is it. Enjoy it! Love Me! Live it! Just that. The Master is all the true devotee wants to think about. Devotion to the Master is the only cure. Devotion to the Master is the only Happiness. Devotion to the Master is the only Freedom from the steel-hard mechanical and chemical bondage of suffering in which you are otherwise investing yourself. The only salvation is Guru-love, Guru-talk. Live with the Guru, talk about the Guru, surrender to the Guru. That is it. That is all. Make no room for anything else. That is what it is to be My devotee—to make no room for anything else. Give Me that devotion and change My experience, and you will see Me Shining in My Simplicity here. Then, by My Blessing, you will get the Reality of life, the Truth, by Grace.

Do the Yoga with no excuses, no reluctance, no self-consciousness, no mannerly submission to scientific materialism and the cult of the world—none. Such is the strength you require, just Guru-love, Most Perfectly self-transcending God-Realization, a life devoted to It, spoken constantly, pouring out, changing your life. That is the way it should be. It is the way of Guru-love and Shaktipat. It is the Dharma of Grace, of Guru-devotion, of Guru-love, and reception of Guru-Transmission, or Guru-Grace.

Guru-Transmission is not even a Teaching. It is a Grace. The Instructions must be Given, but the Way is just the Guru, the Person, the Non-Separateness, without limitations, before you, and a Call to devotion. That is it. That is all. What do you know about where it goes? What do you know about the seventh stage Realization, anyway? It is just the Master Absolute before you, and you surrender, just that. It is the same for the simple and ordinary people as it is for the most advanced.

That is all there is to do. It is very simple. It is not technical. Grasp the simplicity and do it. I have told you how to exercise it in every aspect of life.

No distractions can be indulged in. There are no distractions, just devotion to Me, living this Yoga moment by moment, that is it. It is a great energy. It is not boring. It is My business—totally My business.

You do the Yoga. I do the rest.

Are You Just Coping?

December 4, 1993

SRI DA AVABHASA: What is God? What is God-Realization? What is the difference between your state and the God-Realized State?

DEVOTEE: The God-Realized State, in my understanding, is not separate, and not the gesture of separation. It is totally identical, totally submitted.

SRI DA AVABHASA: If there is no separation, then what is there?

DEVOTEE: I cannot say what it would be like to not be the one experiencing.

SRI DA AVABHASA: Have you had any experience that is totally sufficient?

DEVOTEE: There is always another side to any experience.

SRI DA AVABHASA: Do you like the experience you have, your experience altogether?

DEVOTEE: No.

SRI DA AVABHASA: Is there anything sufficient about any moment of existence? Or is it just something with which you are coping?

DEVOTEE: It is clear to me that every moment of existence is limited.

SRI DA AVABHASA: You are coping.

DEVOTEE: To some degree.

SRI DA AVABHASA: You are coping with your situation.

DEVOTEE: When I am not surrendering to you, that is true.

SRI DA AVABHASA: So far, at least, even your surrendering is a kind of coping, isn't it—a way of dealing with a situation that is not sufficient?

DEVOTEE: Yes, yes. It is clear to me that life is suffering.

SRI DA AVABHASA: Every moment of it.

DEVOTEE: Yes.

SRI DA AVABHASA: Yet it seems to you that there is nothing absolute you can do about it right now, nothing absolute you can do to be free of existence as mere coping and struggling with suffering.

DEVOTEE: Except what You have Given me to do.

SRI DA AVABHASA: Yes, there is a Way, but I am talking about the difference between God-Realization and what you are experiencing.

In general, individuals cope with their given situation of existence. They do not even believe there is a sufficient state of existence to be Realized. Therefore, they seek, they make all kinds of arrangements, they cope. They do not even live the religious life, in general, certainly not the true religious life. Instead, they are only suffering and coping and trying to make the best of life. No "best" comes of it, but they have no greater point of view.

Human beings are not experiencing Reality. They are experiencing a state of existence that they think they cannot do anything about in any absolute sense, and, therefore, they are coping with it. This is what human beings do. They establish their life, including philosophy, on the limited condition of existence that they suffer. They do not think there is anything absolute to be done about it, so they do what everybody does.

Therefore, in everything they do, people are just coping with their suffering, living as the self-contraction and seeking on its basis, all because they are not experiencing Reality, God, or Truth. They are not aware of Reality, God, or Truth. Instead, they are aware of their given situation, the apparent condition, which is a limit and frightening and poor, yet they have no sense that there is anything absolute they can do about it, and they do all the ordinary things people do.

Even if people get a whiff of something extraordinary to do in order to Realize What is Extraordinary, or Truly Real, the force of their own contraction tends to intervene, and they enter into the process in a mediocre, piecemeal fashion, still holding on to all their routines of coping.

God is not merely the Cause of the universe, some Intelligent Motion at the beginning of everything. God is Reality. You are unaware of Reality, however. If God is simply Reality, then God is Reality now. Why are you not aware of God? Reality is right now. Then why are you not aware of and as this Reality?

Do you think Reality is preventing you from being aware of Reality? What is preventing you? This is what there is to find out.

DEVOTEE: Sri Gurudev, the process You have Given us of surrendering to You through the "conscious process" and "conductivity" is absolute.

SRI DA AVABHASA: It is the Way of Truth, the Way of the Heart, but it is not absolute until it becomes Absolute Realization.

DEVOTEE: There is more to surrender always, it is always possible to surrender to a greater depth, but the process itself feels absolute.

SRI DA AVABHASA: Divine Self-Realization is not a process. The process that is the Way of Truth precedes Realization, serves Realization, leads to Realization, if Grace is Given, but Realization Itself is not a process. Realization is simply Most Perfect, Unobstructed Awakeness to Reality, just That.

In the meantime, if you are sensitive—and of course you tend not to be very sensitive, because you are doing all kinds of things to desensitize yourself, but you can come to the point of real sensitivity—you can find out what you are doing that is preventing the Realization of Reality.

It is not because you are appearing in human form that you are failing to Realize Reality. The human form exists in Reality. How could there be any argument about this? Everything exists in Reality. Whatever Reality Is, It Is, Already. If you examine yourself with great sensitivity, you find that you are not simply and merely existing in Reality. You are doing something. This is why Reality is not Obvious to you. If you were not doing that thing, Reality would simply be Obvious to you. You must find out what you are doing, and transcend it.

Reality need not be achieved, because Reality obviously Is. By definition, Reality is What Is. The Way of Realization of Reality is not a search for a goal, because Reality is Always Already the case. How could there be any argument against this?

If seeking will not Realize Reality, how, then, can you Realize What is Always Already the case? The answer requires that you find out why you are not already Realizing It, since It is Already the case, necessarily. Why are you just aware of conditions?

Whatever Reality is, It is not a condition, not this condition, then the next one, and then the next one. All such individual happenings exist in Reality. You are experiencing conditions only, and not Reality, or That within Which conditions are arising. Why?

What argument can there be to oppose the understanding that Reality necessarily Is? Therefore, conditions must be arising in That, no matter what the condition. No condition is Reality. Every condition is arising in Reality. Necessarily it is so.

Why are you aware of conditions and not aware of Reality? This is what you must find out. Realization is not about seeking Reality as a goal but about finding out why you are not already Realizing It. When you find out what is keeping you from Realization, you simply transcend it.

If you do not come to such understanding, you are only coping with conditions and seeking to be relieved. Reality, God, or Truth becomes something you seek, something you try to reach in the midst of your conditional disposition, your conditional mind, your conditional state. How could the search be fruitful, since Reality is not somewhere else, since Reality is not absent?

The search is a proposition you accept in your problem. To truly enter into the real process wherein Reality, God, or Truth is Realized, you must come to a most fundamental understanding of what is preventing you from Realizing Reality—that, rather than just being motivated by your inclination to the search and your game of coping.

[to the man who spoke] You are talking from a rather conventional point of view. Although you are relating to something great and having some experience, you are still speaking from the conventional point of view, the point of view of being an apparently conditional entity that is experiencing conditions and that is not experiencing Reality. From that point of view, you want to know how to relate to Me, how to experience Me.

It is not a real question. It is the conventional statement of a seeker. You must discover what is preventing you from Realizing Reality. Then your involvement in the process of Realizing Reality will become truly real and intelligent, because you will be dealing with what you know clearly to be the obstacle, what must be transcended—because Reality is not absent. What there is to deal with, then, is not an effort of seeking. You do not succeed via an effort of seeking. You simply must transcend what you are using in every moment to prevent the Realization of Reality.

Self-transcendence is what the Way of the Heart is all about. It is for this reason that the foundation of the Way of the Heart, its true foundation, is in hearing, or most fundamental self-understanding, and not in the seeker's motives that otherwise would tend to make religion or Spiritual life.

Beginners in the Way of the Heart are responding to Me and adapting to practices, but they lack most fundamental self-understanding. The crisis of true hearing is the first great crisis through which My devotee must pass. It requires that you function not as a seeker but as one who understands the mechanism that is preventing the Realization of Reality. When you have understood it, you have the means to resort to Me profoundly.

God is not absent. God Is right now. God Is here now, and God Is all of this. All of this is arising in That. Your point of view, however, is this conditionality, not That in Which all this is arising. Now, why should that be so?

I keep telling you that you are using conventional means to relate to Me. You are using the seeker's means. I have told you all since I began to Teach: Seeking is the way of the world. Seeking is the way of egos. It is not the Way of God-Realization. None of the results of seeking are God-Realization. No mere experiencing is God-Realization. The Way of the Heart is not a matter of seeking or of perpetuating egoity but of understanding and transcending the very act that is making you a seeker.

Of course, I have told you over and over again what that act is. I have told you individually and personally, and I have told you all collectively. Therefore, you know what I have said about it, of course, but there is no most fundamental self-understanding in your case until you have truly heard Me.

The things I have said about the search are of interest to you. You respond to what I say, you "consider" it, and you practice in that "consideration". But you have not understood yourself until you have heard Me, until what I am saying to you about all this is tacitly clear to you, patently obvious. This is true hearing, to find yourself out as a seeker, and then, instead of seeking, to deal directly with what is making you a seeker.

You cannot Realize the Divine by seeking, not truly, not in any ultimate sense. You can have conditional experiences that may be called "Divine", or that have something to do with receptivity to Divine Influence, perhaps, but you cannot Realize the Divine, Realize Reality, Realize That Which is the Condition of conditions, until you have transcended your own act, that which makes you a seeker, that which separates you from God, in other words.

Your search is not a way to Realize God, Truth, or Reality. Your search is what is preventing you from Realizing God, Truth, or Reality. Your search is what you are doing to cope with your suffering. You are looking for a way out of suffering, but you are still being what is suffering. You are still performing the act that is suffering. Therefore, the search for God-Realization is fruitless in the ultimate sense—but you must understand this most fundamentally.

As long as you talk to Me and say, "Me, me, me, me, me, I do this, I do that, I experience this and that, I feel this and that", you are still speaking conventionally. You are speaking from the point of view of that act which is your suffering and which is seeking. In other words, you are still speaking from the point of view of egoity, or that which is experiencing itself to be separate from Reality, that which is experiencing only conditions, and not That within Which conditions are arising. You are <u>being</u> conditional. The fundamental act you are performing is making you conditional only, rather than allowing you to be Reality Only. This is what you must understand. And this understanding is true hearing.

True hearing is the capability to practice Ishta-Guru-Bhakti most profoundly, constantly, under all conditions. It is certainly that. It is most fundamental self-understanding. It is certainly that. These are My two principal descriptions of true hearing.

You are involved in the conventional acculturation of existence, which is about coping with egoity, coping with the results of egoity, coping with conditions, coping with this thing that is suffering, just concerned about it. You certainly would like to feel better, but, on the other hand, your suffering does not seem to represent a profound puzzle to you. A profound urge to transcend it does not seem to be there in you, not a profound urge. It is as if you would like to feel better, but, on the other hand, the great impulse for Realization does not seem to be profoundly there. You would just as soon have a smiling conversation about God with somebody, because such talk makes you feel a little better and it is not very difficult. It is not great Realization, but, on the other hand, you do not seem to be profoundly impulsed to God-Realization.

You seem satisfied with coping and some consolation. The great impulse is not the mover of your life. You are not devoting your life to the fulfillment of that great impulse. Instead, you are devoting your life to coping, to ordinariness, to consolation, to ordinary seeking. Coping with conditions and your suffering makes you dull. Getting dull about it is one of the ways you cope with it, in fact. Basically, you are practicing a life of desensitizing yourself to Reality, to the Divine, to Me, through your coping, your ordinariness, your conventionality, your willingness to cope and find a degree of consolation.

Your willingness to settle for less than God-Realization is part of your dullness. Because you are full of the coping, seeker's mind, to achieve a little consolation, a little pleasure here and there, an opening here and there, is sufficient. You prefer to grind out your life, just carrying on with it, continuing your presumptions and consolations, and working to be gradually purified. Such is the more ordinary choice, what could perhaps be described as the "general practitioner's choice", or perhaps the "householder's choice". You prefer a life of practice that, you hope, gradually will purify you of these binding intentions and consolations, so that you will eventually come to the point of the great impulse.

If you truly understood Me and had uncovered this impulse, then you would not settle for anything less than God-Realization. Therefore, you would not participate in the matters of daily life for the sake of consolation. You would not be consoled by ordinary life. You would not be choosing <u>not</u> to be consoled. You would simply be aware that you cannot be consoled—cannot be, are not, and will not be. This understanding would be the source of your renunciation, or your right life, rather than some strategic effort to not be consoled. There must be this understanding and this great impulse. If this understanding and this great impulse were there in you, the ability to be consoled would be vanished, your life would be clarified, and your practice would be profoundly quickened.

There is much conventional passing on of esoteric practices in the world at the present time. Go to a lecture, join a club, get an esoteric practice that corresponds, to one degree or another, to esoteric practices in the fourth, the fifth, and the sixth stages of life. People off the streets are invited to take up practices that in the traditional setting they would never even have heard about. Now not only can you hear about these great practices but you are offered the opportunity to do them in various organizations or to read about them in books.

Yet how many are Realizing God? The practices that are offered so openly have become routines for using the mind and the body and the psyche, in one way or another, from an egoic and mediocre and undeveloped and immature point of view. Where is the Realization?

The real foundation for true religion and Spiritual practice is most typically not required. The suggestion generally appears to be that you can be an ordinary immature ego and take up any form of esotericism and Realize the Truth. It is not so. You can have experiences, you can magnify your illusions, but you cannot Realize God, Truth, or Reality without a real foundation, without real maturity, without the great impulse. Even if you have some basic, ordinary maturity and some significant impulse, you cannot Realize the Divine Absolutely, Most Perfectly, without most fundamental self-understanding, Awakened by the Grace of the Inherently Perfect, Divine Realizer, the One Who has Realized That Which Is Most Perfect, the One Who Is That Grace, therefore.

All of the practices I have Given you of the "conscious process" and "conductivity", if you understand My Instruction, amount to nothing but aspects of Ishta-Guru-Bhakti. This is what you are to do in response to Me, in Communion with Me. The practices in the Way of the Heart are not practices for you to use to work on yourself. Part of your game of coping is to want to apply techniques to yourself, to take a "bone" from Me and run, to "do it yourself", so to speak. Instead of coming to Me, for Me, to Realize Me, you come for techniques, words, perhaps an experience or two. Then you take them and in effect meditate on yourself and work on yourself.

The Way of the Heart, however, is only self-surrendering devotion to Me. That is all it is, most fundamentally. No matter what the technicalities of the Way of the Heart, it is still just that. All aspects of practice of the Way of the Heart, which I have Given to you in detail, are only aspects of the one practice of self-surrendering devotion to Me. Even devotion to Me is not an effort of working on yourself. It is a response to Me from the beginning—not an effort to generate a response to Me but the actual response to Me, to My being here, to My Presence here. I My Self here am such that you respond, and, on that basis, you practice devotion to Me. Without response to Me, you cannot practice devotion to Me.

If the response to Me is lacking, how will it come about? Persist in My Company, certainly. Continue the practice of the Way of the Heart. A limitation on your response to Me is the result of your own self-contraction, the result of everything you are doing to desensitize yourself so that you cannot respond to Me, cannot Locate Me, cannot feel Me.

The first thing that must occur to truly authenticate your practice of the Way of the Heart is the response to Me, and then you must live on that basis. Presumably, anyone who takes up the Way of the Heart has responded to Me to one degree or another, and that is the foundation on which to build. It is the origin of practice of the Way of the Heart.

To grow in devotion to Me, so that your devotion to Me becomes greater and greater, you must allow yourself to be sensitive to Me. This suggests, then, that some things can be done to purify you of your insensitivity, and it is the logic of self-discipline and, in general, of all the practices at the beginning of the Way of the Heart. The foundation practices eliminate gross habits and their results, and they allow sensitivity to grow, so that your devotional response to Me may be magnified.

DEVOTEE: Beloved Master, You asked if any experience is satisfying. I feel that a moment of Communion with You is satisfying.

SRI DA AVABHASA: Reality is satisfaction, if the word "satisfaction" can be used at all. Dissociation from Reality contains no satisfaction and allows no satisfaction. When you associate with conditions, when you give yourself over to conditions, you are inherently dissatisfied and you are not satisfiable. You may seek satisfaction, but you cannot be satisfied. Communion with That Which Is the Source of conditions, That within Which conditions are arising, is satisfactory, Whole, Complete. The more you receive the Grace of My Spiritual Heart-Transmission in Communion with Me, the more Full and then Perfect Communion with Me becomes.

When, or if, you remember yourself again, you lapse from the Yoga and you are again dissatisfied, seeking, coping, separate, indulging in your conditioned existence. The more You practice this Yoga, the more you will Realize, by Grace of My Heart-Blessing, the Condition of the One with Whom you are in Communion. I must Fill you utterly. I must Pour into you. I must Purify you, then Fill you, Transform you, Vanish you altogether. When that has occurred Most Perfectly, there is Most Perfectly self-transcending God-Realization. There is utter Freedom from conditions, utter freedom from the binding power of any form of apparent conditionality.

This Most Perfect Realization does not occur simply because you make this submission and enter into Communion with Me. That is the process, yes, but the fulfillment of it, the Perfection of it, occurs by Grace in the ultimate practice of the Way of the Heart. Therefore, you must persist in this Yoga and receive My Grace. The Fullness of your receiving My Grace comes by your persisting in Ishta-Guru-Bhakti Yoga and allowing Me to Move.

True self-Observation

December 4, 1993

SRI DA AVABHASA: The Way of the Heart is extremely simple, and it can be lived so very simply. In its fundamentals, it is simply self-surrendering devotional Communion with Me and receiving My Divine Blessing. Many technical elaborations of this simplicity are Given as one's practice matures, but for some the Way of the Heart may involve nothing more than the simplicity of Communion with Me. The technicalities of the Way of the Heart develop spontaneously from this fundamental practice, if you simply surrender into Communion with Me and adapt your life to Me, totally, without complication.

The more you cling to the self-consoling life of ordinariness, the more complicated the Way of the Heart becomes, even though its fundamental practice is simple. I am the Instruction. Simply to surrender to Me and receive My Divine Blessing is sufficient for practice of the Way of the Heart.

I have often told the story about the woman who came to Shirdi Sai Baba for traditional instruction in the form of a mantra. When He continued to refuse to give it to her, she became a little nutty about it, and He told her the story of His own sadhana. He did not receive any such instructions from His Master. In so many words He said, "I was just there with him, just gave him my full attention, was just around, just lived around him, just surrendered there, and all he required of me was faith and patience." The point of His story is that devotion to the Realizer is sufficient. If you are wholly occupied with such devotion, then no other instruction is necessary. Devotion contains the totality of instruction. All the changes occur. You notice all the things you must relinquish, and you do so. Therefore, why is a complicated discipline necessary?

Since devotion to Me has not been your way of life altogether, I have had to Give you an elaborate Instruction. I have had to enter into a long "Consideration" with you, Submit to your condition, and struggle with you. Therefore, I have Given you an elaborate body of Instruction, and, depending on how complicated you are, you will apply it in your practice in My Company. Even so, the Way of the Heart is just this self-surrendering devotion to Me—not as a self-applied technique but as a response to Me, self-surrendering, receiving My Blessing. Everything about self-understanding, self-discipline, life as service to Me, or Communion with Me in action—all of it—is contained in the simplicity of devotion to Me, if you will allow it to be so simple.

Shirdi Sai Baba's description of His Teacher's simple demand for His faith and patience may have been just a story to convey to the woman the simplicity that is real sadhana. Spiritual life is submitting to Grace rather than working on yourself. Submitting to Grace, you necessarily change your life. You cannot be a fool who is living a worldly life and also practice devotional submission. You cannot. Devotional submission changes your life. The discipline does occur. The service does occur. The meditation does occur. The process can be as simple as just this submission, and all those things occur. On the other hand, if your submission is less than profound, you will endure a complicated process of realizing devotion, self-discipline, service, and meditation. It is up to you.

DEVOTEE: Sri Gurudev, I am so happy to be in Your Company today. All my habits and tendencies arose, but . . .

SRI DA AVABHASA: What arose?

DEVOTEE: My lack of attention in a moment, or my fear, my contraction in my body-mind, or my independence.

SRI DA AVABHASA: Your practice is less than simple devotion, I guess.

DEVOTEE: It did not make a difference to me.

SRI DA AVABHASA: But it arose.

ANOTHER DEVOTEE: It is not supposed to arise?

SRI DA AVABHASA: What space can there be for its arising, if you are simply occupied with Me bodily, emotionally, mentally, with the breath? If you are just doing that, what space would there be for these things to arise? They would not arise.

It does not make any difference what the mechanism is like by habit and conditioning. When something arises in mind, in emotion, in the body, thus interrupting the breath, it is because the Yoga has collapsed. The mechanism can be all kinds of conditioned, but something will not arise to the mind, the emotion, the body, the breath, unless you fail to practice the Yoga. If you persist in the Yoga, then habits of body, emotion, mind, and breath will be purified. If you do not persist in the Yoga, they will arise, you will notice them, you will be to one degree or another complicated by them. They are arising because you are not doing the Yoga fully. They cannot arise if you are doing the Yoga fully.

In any moment when you are not doing the Yoga, your conditioning shows itself in body, emotion, mind, and breath. You become complicated or troubled or wandering or doubting, or you are trying to figure something out, or seeking, or looking to be consoled, or coping. These things arise only when you are not doing the Yoga. They would not appear, otherwise. They cannot, in fact, appear, otherwise.

DEVOTEE: I am not sure I understand the difference.

SRI DA AVABHASA: Then listen once more: If you surrender to Me completely in any moment—body, emotion, mind as attention, breath—surrender the whole complex in Communion with Me, so that you are simply focused in Me, then the modifications of these functions do not arise. They cannot arise, because you are focused in Me and surrendering all of them. If there is a lapse of the Yoga whereby you submit these mechanisms, then the conditioning of the mechanisms arises. You experience the conditioning mentally, you experience it emotionally, you experience it bodily, changes in the breath occur.

Even so, these things arise not because you are conditioned by them—and you are—but because you are not doing the Yoga most profoundly. You may feel you are doing it to one degree or another, as when you are doing some physical things around Me, but you are not doing it with full attention, or with full feeling, or with true "conductivity" of the breath in devotional Communion with Me. Therefore, you register some complication, some conditioning, in emotion, in mind, in the breath, or in the body.

These things would not arise if the Yoga were being done completely with these mechanisms, because you would simply be focused in Me. To be focused in Me is a form of Samadhi.

If you lapse in the Yoga in one or another of its parts, however, if you lapse in it physically, lapse in it emotionally, lapse in it mentally, lapse in it in the breath focus, if you lapse in any part, or in several parts, then the conditioning of the parts shows in the parts themselves—mentally, emotionally, physically, in the breath, in feeling, in energy. These things arise not because you are conditioned but because you are not doing the Yoga.

DEVOTEE: I understand, especially when You say that the Yoga is Samadhi.

SRI DA AVABHASA: You are then <u>in</u> Samadhi, in the Samadhi of Communion with Me. I <u>Am</u> Samadhi. If all of your parts were submitted in Communion with Me, then their conditioning would not arise. In the Samadhi of the Yoga, the forms of conditioning would be purified without your having to notice them, because I am Flowing in your parts and replacing the content. Simply stated, this Yoga of Communion with Me, with all your parts, is the practice.

If you happen to lapse in your practice of the Yoga, or if your practice is somewhat mediocre or weak, you will notice things physically, emotionally, mentally, and in the breath. It is to be hoped that you will also understand, because Communion with Me is something you <u>do</u>, in fact, engage otherwise, and, therefore, you will not lapse again. You will not withdraw from the Yoga, you will not pass into reveries physically, emotionally, mentally, in the energy process of the breath. You will understand, meaning that you will see the limitation as your own action and you will not do it. Such understanding is not merely a mental activity of "thinking" understanding. It is a tacit feeling.

As soon as you do not give yourself to Me and you see the signs of content arising—in the body, in feeling, in attention, in the breath—you understand something: Do not do that anymore. Then you Commune with Me instead. You submit the parts of the body-mind to Me instead. That change of action is understanding, not some mentally computerized, think-think, figure-it-out understanding. It is a tacit understanding, and it is the difference between your experience when you are performing the Yoga of this Communion with Me and your experience when you are not. Noticing just that difference is understanding.

Growth in the Way of the Heart depends simply on your application to Ishta-Guru-Bhakti Yoga, performed with all your parts surrendered to Me. It is not to do everything to your parts except surrender them to Me. It is not to indulge in your parts and watch them and manipulate them. It is to surrender to Me, to surrender your parts to Me. Every lapse teaches you something—do not do this, do the Yoga instead, do not lapse, do the Yoga of Communion with Me more and more profoundly.

[to the woman who spoke] What lapses in the Yoga were you noticing today? What did you do? What did you do bodily, emotionally, mentally, with your energy, with your breath? What was your particular way of lapsing today? Did you notice?

DEVOTEE: I was holding a tray for You, and as You would reach towards me for something on the tray, I would feel my navel contract. I felt my fearful character.

SRI DA AVABHASA: So you contracted, somehow?

DEVOTEE: At times. I noticed it, and I could feel and practice and again feel the Samadhi You describe. You have Given me the Gift to be able to stay in feeling-Communion with You and allow the contraction to become superficial.

SRI DA AVABHASA: This feeling-Communion, if it is true, is Yoga—Ishta-Guru-Bhakti Yoga. It submits all the parts of the human person directly into Communion with Me. Therefore, you focus yourself bodily, emotionally, mentally as attention, with the breath. You submit all these things to Me. You live them, or submit them to be lived, in Me. You are just focused in Me. There are things you did bodily, things you did emotionally, things you did mentally, things you did with your energy and your breath—these are the things to be noticed in your lapsing from the Yoga of devotion to Me, and do not do that anymore. That is self-understanding.

Self-understanding is not demonstrated to Me, and true hearing is not demonstrated to Me, by the words you say about it. What you say can be taken into account, perhaps, must necessarily be, and your words may be appropriate, but what you say is not the demonstration. The demonstration is that you engage the Yoga in all the circumstances of daily life—in service, in meditation, whatever your circumstances, however you live the "daily form" throughout every day and night.

Do you do the Yoga in all those circumstances, or do you lapse? If you lapse, you will talk about that. You tend to talk with others about the signs that are arising in your lapses from the Yoga of Communion with Me.

DEVOTEE: We make the mistake of talking about it from the body-based point of view.

SRI DA AVABHASA: You make the mistake of not noticing it and submitting to Me. Instead, you talk about it, and examine it further, then talk about it some more, work on it, try to figure it out, whereas it is just something to notice, something to observe.

Your response should be your response to Me. Simply submit to Me instead. Perhaps, in the process, you notice something you should do differently, something in your daily life or in your relationships, whatever it is. Then make an agreement not to do it anymore, and make it a matter of record. Confession is part of the process of this noticing. You notice something. Others may observe something about you. You agree, "I will do this differently, that differently." You do not agree to go on dramatizing and to talk about it again next week. No—you submit yourself more profoundly to persisting in the Yoga moment by moment. If there are details of living that obstruct your practice or put a limit on it, you make an agreement to not do that anymore. Your purpose is not to generate self-noticing, self-descriptions, self-analysis, to develop a dossier of descriptions about yourself. Your purpose is to intensify the Yoga of submission to Me—bodily, emotionally, mentally, with every breath. Your conversations with one another point to your lapses, but they are lapses from the Yoga of Communion with Me.

DEVOTEE: Beloved Gurudev, keeping a diary makes me sensitive to the bodily practice of releasing the self-contraction into Your Happiness again, and again, and again, and again.

SRI DA AVABHASA: You seem to be suggesting some self-applied technique, as if response to Me is something that you apply to yourself or try to do. Your response to Me is simply a characteristic of the fact that I am here. In Communion with Me, surrendering the self-contraction happens inherently, spontaneously. The Way of the Heart is Communion with Me, not working on yourself.

What do you do with your mind? Do not think-think-think. Give Me your attention. Keep your attention on Me. If you do that, the mind is quieted. To the extent it must be used at all, it becomes just useful, not endless blah-blah, like a constant reverie or dream that you cannot do anything about. Use the mind by giving Me your attention instead. Give Me your feeling-attention. Address Me bodily. Be related to Me bodily, in service, but as a dimension of attention itself, and make this submission, mentally, emotionally, and bodily, through the mechanism of the breath. Feel Me. Breathe Me. Give Me your attention. Be bodily always addressed to Me.

Why do you think, anyway? Because you are not giving Me your attention. Give Me your attention, feel Me, address Me bodily, breathe Me. There is no wandering in the mind—there is no room to wander in the mind! The mind wanders when attention wanders. Do not let attention wander. Keep attention with Me. This is the practice. There may be lapses, while you are growing. Nevertheless, this is the Admonition, and this is what you must do, more and more and more.

The only purpose of observing yourself is to notice the mechanism of the lapses—not to dwell on them or create all kinds of descriptions of them. It is just a noticing. Do not do what you notice, then. Give Me your attention instead. Attention wanders because of your stressful egoic "self-possession".

You think all the time, don't you?

DEVOTEE: I think a great deal.

SRI DA AVABHASA: You are thinking, thinking, thinking, thinking, thinking, thinking, thinking. It is not that thinking has no function in your moments of daily obligation. Thinking does have a function, but you do not do very much of such useful thinking. You do the wandering of attention, and, therefore, the mind just pours out its contents based on its conditioning. The mind is a bizarre display that makes you even more stressful and confused. If you have a purpose in thinking, if some obligation requires you to think, do so with clarity, with real attention, straightforwardly, figure out this or that, and then do this or that.

Now you see that the reason you are not aware of Reality is that you are not doing the Yoga. You are not submitting all your parts and functions to Reality. You are withdrawing them from Reality, and, therefore, you are left with only your self-imposed separation, trying to cope with it and seeking on its basis. Authentic existence is Yoga, or the submission of all the human parts to the Divine. The Means for the Divine Yoga is the Realizer—the One Who is to be Realized. You are mediocre because you are not doing the Yoga. Divorced from Reality, divorced from the Divine Self-Condition of all the conditions you are suffering, you are letting all your parts wander in egoic "self-possession".

You could be utterly purified and released of all conditions if you would do the Yoga of submitting to the Divine Reality. The process of Most Perfectly self-transcending God-Realization is as simple as that. Presently, however, you are divorced from Reality because of what you are doing, or, perhaps better said, because of what you are not doing. The thing that you are doing is preventing you from doing what is right.

The Way of the Heart is not about being a believer, or belonging to the club. The Way of the Heart, when it is full and right, is Yoga—Ishta-Guru-Bhakti Yoga. Just that, done with every aspect of the body-mind, and in every moment. There is no self-reference in it. It is just Guru-devotion. What do true devotees talk about, then? The Guru. They maintain their Contemplation by talking about the Guru instead of talking about themselves. Of course, there are things to do—fine. Do them in Contemplation of Me. Live rightly—fine. But not while remaining egoically "self-possessed" in the midst of action. Surrender to Me in the midst of your obligations. Surrender to Me, not as a conventional gesture but as the Yoga of Communion with Me in the midst of action, whatever the action is—service, puja, chanting, or meditation—which is most direct feeling-Contemplation of Me without any other obligations imposed upon body, emotion, mind, or breath.

The right occupation of apparently born beings is constant Divine Contemplation. By this you are Liberated—not by the action but by the Grace that, through your participation in the Divine Yoga, you allow to Fill you and Transform you and Liberate you. Your response to Grace must be there in the form of the Yoga, but the Yoga itself does not cure. The One you Contemplate cures. That I Am here should be sufficient Inspiration to My devotee for the practice of this Yoga.

Your purpose for being here is to do this Yoga. I should not have to do anything else than just Be here. Therefore, do the Yoga, and do not do with Me or apart from Me anything that desensitizes you to Me. Just do the Yoga and increase it through right "consideration". I Am here just to Do What I Am and What My Divine Blessing Is Inherently, and nothing else.

DEVOTEE: Sri Gurudev, thank You for Your Gift of Ishta-Guru-Seva. It gives me a way to extend Communion with You into my daily life, to Remember You and surrender to You.

SRI DA AVABHASA: If it were not so, then you could Contemplate Me only in meditation, when nobody is making demands on you physically, emotionally, mentally. No, the Yoga extends into every moment of every day.

Live rightly. Do not desensitize yourself—live rightly. But there are actions built into portions of every day, and you must do the Yoga there and then—all the time, then. I have shown you how to do this Yoga of self-surrendering devotional Contemplation of Me under all circumstances—with every function, in every relationship.

If you understand what the Yoga is, you know that it is also to be practiced in your intimate sexual relationship. Practice this Yoga in sexual occasions and in every other occasion. Submit body, emotion, mind, and breath in direct, self-surrendering feeling-Contemplation of Me, in your intimacy in general and also in moments of sexual activity, just as in any other circumstance of action or relatedness. The same Yogic obligation holds. If you fall back into the conditions themselves, the actions themselves, and the consolations, you are not doing the Yoga. Do the Yoga, and everything will be obvious to you about how to live your intimate relationship rightly, how to practice in the context of sexual activity rightly.

Ishta-Guru-Bhakti Yoga is the key to real life. If you are serious, you will do just that Yoga and nothing else.

ANOTHER DEVOTEE: Sri Gurudev, You have brought this simplicity to Me even more, to the point that I know there is no effort in turning to You.

SRI DA AVABHASA: You must do an action, but it cannot rightly be described as effort, because effort suggests the ego's working on itself. In your responsiveness to Me, in your devotion to Me that is awakened spontaneously, you must perform the action of self-surrender, but it is not an effort, because the response to Me is there, the devotion to Me is there, your impulse to Communion with Me is there. You cannot properly describe your responsibilities as an effort, therefore.

Yes, the Yoga itself is a simplicity to understand, but, more than that, if you do the Yoga your entire life becomes simplified. The more profoundly you enter into Communion with Me, the more profoundly your life will be simplified. The Way of the Heart is not about deliberate or strategic renunciation. Because of your Divine preoccupation with your Ishta-Guru, you not only forget yourself but you forget to do all kinds of things you did as a seeker. You stop being complicated. You become spontaneously simplified. You become a renunciate on that basis, then, and not strategically.

Even your conditioning does not make any difference. It only shows itself when you do not do the Yoga. Whenever you notice something arising, it is arising because you are not doing the Yoga of devotional Communion with Me. That is what there is to be noticed, not what is arising. What is there to do? Certainly not to mull over all the stuff. You just noticed this suffering, and you know why it is arising. Therefore, in that very moment, you devote yourself to Me, bodily, emotionally, mentally, with every breath. You simply reconfirm the Yoga with the noticing.

Such is self-observation in the Way of the Heart. It is not constantly watching yourself and communicating the effects of conditioning in the body-mind. There is nothing fruitful about such "self-watching", as I call it. Self-observation occurs naturally, in an ordinary manner, when you do the Yoga of Ishta-Guru-Bhakti. It is to notice that the effects of your conditioning arise when you lapse from the Yoga. Therefore, such true self-observation, or noticing, calls you to practice the Yoga in that moment.

Do Not Do That Anymore

December 6, 1993

DEVOTEE: Sri Gurudev, the moments when I am dull and lapsing have become so painful. Then I find I have to release even that pain or remorse, rather than allowing it to create more of a lapse.

SRI DA AVABHASA: And the question is?

DEVOTEE: The question is, am I concentrating too much in self-observation, or is the process as it should be and I am continually sensitizing myself to whatever arises?

SRI DA AVABHASA: The asana of My devotee is devotional self-surrender to Me, not self-observation. If you stand in the position of observing yourself, then you make self-observation the Way of the Heart and periodically, perhaps, you throw in some devotion to Me. As My devotee, your right asana is devotional self-surrender to Me, consistently applied. Do that practice, and self-observation occurs inevitably. Whenever there is a fall from the Yoga of submission, in any part or to any degree, something is observed and you feel beyond it. If you are always in the position of observing what is wrong, you will only observe more and more that is wrong.

You have told Me before that some of the things you do physically put the body out of balance and create symptoms in body, emotion, and mind. What does that suggest?

DEVOTEE: That I am not being responsible.

SRI DA AVABHASA: If you are doing things that bring about these symptoms, then what does that suggest to you?

DEVOTEE: It suggests a reluctance—it suggests that I am not surrendering.

SRI DA AVABHASA: You have not quite got it yet. You are supposed to be maintaining the asana of self-surrendering devotion in Communion with Me, yet you observe negative results from some physical things that you do. These results generate more limitations, which of course must then be surrendered. If you are doing some physical things that cause these problems to arise, what does that suggest to you?

DEVOTEE: That I should not do them.

SRI DA AVABHASA: Exactly!

DEVOTEE: Very simple.

SRI DA AVABHASA: Yes, it is. The whole point of observing that you are lapsing is to enter into self-surrendering Communion with Me. Then your immediate conclusion should be, "Do not do that anymore." If you cannot come to such an immediate conclusion, just what kind of intelligence are you using? You do not want to come to the conclusion "Do not do that anymore", because it is too difficult to not do that anymore. For this reason, you tend not to exercise intelligence. You try to deal with your symptoms instead.

You must be able to exercise practical intelligence. Notice what works, what does not work, what most fully serves the moment to moment practice of devotional surrender to Me, and then eliminate what does not work, modify your behavior. To be willing to exercise this practical intelligence and change what you do is part of the physical dimension of bodily self-surrender.

In general, you show the evidence of reluctance. You want to bargain with Me forever about practical self-discipline, as if it is not truly required, as if you can somehow live the religious life and also neglect this fundamental aspect of your practice. You cannot. When you fail to exercise practical intelligence and fail to change what you do, you perpetuate all kinds of limitations and problems and lapses and failures in practice. Therefore, you must be able to see just how all your physical habits and bodily activities limit your practice of devotion to Me. See it, and apply the appropriate discipline.

I have certainly described very thoroughly the complete range of such practical disciplines, but I have also indicated that the developing of the details must take into account all the factors that belong to you as an individual. Developing the details is part of the foundation practice of the Way of the Heart. The profundities of Spiritual life come in due course. The foundation—much of it, at least—establishes physical self-discipline, discipline of action, and discipline of your functional uses of the body. One of the reasons people take so long at the beginning of the Way of the Heart is that they do not want to exercise this practical intelligence, notice what works and what does not, and change their act.

There are all kinds of "doings". There is everything you do with food.

There is everything you do with sex and your attention to it. There is everything you do with daily relations. There is everything you do with service, work, responsibility, money, on and on. All these must become subject to right discipline. Establish right life through handling your life-business, and simplify your life appropriately. To do so is the fundamental practice at the beginning of the Way of the Heart. When you have taken care of those things and have established a bodily life-practice, then your practical life does not require much more "consideration". This seems to be a lesson that you find very difficult to learn. You like observing yourself, noticing things about yourself, noticing your symptoms, talking about your symptoms, but you are reluctant to do anything about your symptoms.

You tend to think of the religious life as an interior process of some kind, and you think you should not be required to pay much attention to the body or to deal with what you do functionally, relationally, and practically. This false view leads you into the "talking"-school disposition of watching, describing, and talking about it all but not doing anything about it. You talk. You make affirmations. You make your apologies. And then you make more affirmations. But you do not <u>do</u> anything about it. You just want to talk about your symptoms some more, as if there is an immense impediment in you to changing what you do. You are totally capable of changing what you do. Actually changing what you do is the part that is missing from your practice.

In general, I would say, the reluctance to exercise practical intelligence and make changes intentionally, hold yourself to it, be accountable for it, is a major fault. Instead of embracing the real life, the real practice, you maintain a disposition that is mediocre, amateurish, and relatively self-indulgent—and you realize all the results. At the practical level of the Way of the Heart, the process becomes your failing, lapsing, apologizing, and re-affirming—conventional religion, in other words, what is typical religion in the Western world, not really doing it but making your confession, or your apology, then being blessed and encouraged to do better, and affirming that you will. Then you go about basically doing the same thing some more.

What does such religion become? The repeated process of lapsing or failing, feeling some regret, confessing it, apologizing, and re-affirming the intention to live rightly but not actually doing so. Is that not typically what so-called religious people do? It is religious idealism that is basically social. It is not a God-Realizing process. It is the kind of religious life you have already learned in the world. And it is what you do around Me.

Because you are so casual about the karmic nature of your ordinary life, you do not understand or appreciate the damage you do by lapsing in your vows. You create offense to your Guru, or offense to the Divine. In addition, you even damage yourself. You make concrete vows that are assertions from the depth of yourself in your clarity, and then you fail to fulfill them, you lapse from them, you violate them. You are violating your own psyche and creating inevitable imbalances in yourself and damage to yourself that you do not take seriously but that make you double-minded, throw you out of balance, and make you complicated.

In the traditional setting, a person's word was taken very seriously. Nowadays, a person must sign a legal document before he or she can be taken seriously at all. In the past, however, one's word was enough, and the old saying "A man's word is his bond" was true. A person's word, male or female, should have the force of a vow. Your word is part of your integrity. Not just your social integrity but the integrity of the body-mind altogether, the integrity of the being, is to be measured by whether you are trustable, whether your word is true. One of the ways you grant integrity, or wholeness, to yourself is by doing whatever you must to fulfill your word.

You are weak in your vows. You feel you can forget them, deny them, lapse from them, relinquish them completely and even casually, or at least just apologize. You think of the Divine as some sort of Source that operates for your pleasure at all times, and you think that there are no laws, no real requirements, no obligations, no necessary responsibilities. You think you are just supposed to be on the receiving end, playing lovey-dovey. You do not appreciate the extent to which, in your egoic "self-possession" and double-mindedness, you have accumulated the patterns you are suffering now, nor do you appreciate the fact that you are perpetuating those patterns through your life-actions still and are not functioning in such a way that you bring wholeness to the being, purify it of its complications, bring true integrity to your life.

In your, generally, "Westernized" disposition, you have an orientation toward cleverness, even slyness. You do know that in your lack of integrity, in your false disposition, you realize all kinds of bad results. You suffer natural processes and all kinds of other processes in the body-mind. Yet instead of changing your action and devoting yourself to the Divine by going beyond yourself through surrender, you function cleverly. You try to figure out how all this is operating so that you can acquire an advantage over it without changing your action, figure out some way to play a trick of some kind to get yourself off the hook. False religion is one of those tricks, in fact. You do not change your action, and you do not live with integrity and true devotion.

You think of the Divine as some kind of indulgent Parent, here to be amused by your failures and to let you off the hook all the time. The world is full of billions of people who are trying that trick. If it worked, if it were true, why would people be suffering as they are? There are consequences for your actions, and not only social consequences but consequences in the person. Therefore, you must change your action, not for the sake of your own amusement or for the sake of getting what you want in some ordinary social sense but for the sake of God-Realization.

The "self" you are referring to is your suffering. You are coping with it. You are what you are suffering. You are the entire cause of it. You are what must be dealt with. You are what must be submitted. You are what must be changed.

Is there anything better than Communing with Me? Wouldn't you rather be doing that than whatever it is you are doing in your lapses? Then you must do whatever you must do to have it be so! Any impediment to Divine Communion that you notice, in your body-mind, in your life altogether, is an indication to you to discipline this, drop that, change that—and just that directly, because you would not have it be otherwise, you do not want to lapse into the self-contracted state and merely cope with it, you want to be entered into the sublime condition of true Communion with Me. If this is your point of view, Given to you by Grace and confirmed through your real experience, then it should inspire you to live rightly.

Understand, however, that surrendering to Me also requires you to change your actions. Yes, Ishta-Guru-Bhakti Yoga is the practice of self-surrender to Me moment by moment, but in your lapsing you notice all the wanderings of your body-mind, you notice this, that, and the other thing that are creating an impediment to Communion with Me. The Yoga is not to continue to do those things and surrender as they arise. You must change them intentionally. You must establish the base of right living and right practice that is the foundation of the Way of the Heart. For this reason, I have indicated that My devotees should not come into My physical Company here until they have established the foundation practice. Instead of coming here to My Great Hermitage Ashram on retreat relatively unadapted to the Way of the Heart, not focused, without a real history of Ishta-Guru-Bhakti, come on retreat when you have established the foundation of right life, handled your life-business, and established the fundamentals of practice. Then it is appropriate that you come into My Company.

The practice of Ishta-Guru-Bhakti Yoga requires that you deal with yourself responsibly, intentionally—but not effortfully, because you are practicing in the context of your devotional response to Me. Do not just wait for devotion to happen to you. Exercise yourself, rightly and intelligently. Notice what there is to notice that diminishes the Fullness of Communion with Me, change those things intentionally, and change them consistently. Your intention is definitely required. Therefore, do not presume that you are supposed to wait for positive changes to happen. Changing your life is your obligation, at the very beginning of the Way of the Heart, not later. Changing your life is the foundation of the Way of the Heart.

The Drama of the Total Body-Mind

December 10, 1993

SRI DA AVABHASA: Your mind is your reflection, the image in the pond. You are the one who is looking at the image. You are the one who is deluded. But you are the one who is posturing. You are the one who is believing in illusion. Therefore, merely to talk about yourself is not sufficient. You must actually look at what you are doing. Narcissus can describe the image in the pond forever. You must say to yourself, "Hey, Narcissus! Look at what you are doing! You are crouched over the pond there, staring at yourself in the water. Look at what you are doing!" Narcissus wants to describe the image in the pond. You must call his attention to what he is doing.

I have been asking you this question for twenty-two years. "What are you doing? What are you always doing?" This question is among My Great Questions to you, and this is what I am addressing—what you are doing, not what you are thinking, not your imagination and your idealism, but what you are doing. Find out. Understand yourself by observing your activity. Eventually, you will see it in its depth, at its root, but the process always begins with the observation of obvious action.

As I have told you again and again, your emotional-sexual life is a primary dimension of your existence that you must address in yourself and that you must allow others to address in you. Your feeling-surrender to Me will not become most profound unless you deal with the emotional-sexual limits in yourself.

Every one of you is involved in specific dramatizations that are totally obvious to Me. If you would examine yourself and one another according to My Instruction, those dramatizations would likewise be totally obvious to you. There is nothing metaphysical about them. They are very obvious and very ordinary.

A person's limitations and dramatizations are not in some hidden network of psychological soup. They are right there in what he or she does every day. Therefore, do not look at what a person says—look at what he or she does. What a person does points directly to the psychological roots of his or her dramatization. You think, however, that sitting around talking endless "case" will expose the psychological roots. The way to get at someone's fundamental dramatization is simply to observe what he or she does. The whole dramatization is obvious, even in the fractions of a person's behavior. The whole is present in every part. If you examine any fraction intensively, the entirety is revealed. It is all one thing—everything is one thing. Everything reveals the totality, if you get down to examining it.

What people think they are doing and what they are actually doing are usually two different things. Therefore, you must direct people to notice their actual behavior, and require them to address that. In the process of observing and disciplining habitual action, a person's emotional depth is revealed, and the sources of his or her behavior will become apparent.

The drama of the total body-mind must be observed—it is the most fundamental observation. The dramas of the various parts of the body-mind—the sexual dramas of the genitals, the power dramas of the solar plexus, the emotional dramas of the heart, and so on—are significant, but it is not enough to observe only them. Observe yourself in the context of all the sub-dramas, all the life-dramas. And you will see that all the different dramas are forms of the one drama that the total body-mind performs. That one drama is self-contraction. And you will not relinquish it until you understand that your entire life is suffering and you feel moved to go beyond suffering to Realize the Divine, or That Condition in Which all beings and all parts are arising.

The total body-mind is the one called "I". You can observe yourself in total if you observe what "I" is doing. Therefore, one of the fundamental questions I recommend for your pondering is, "What am 'I' always doing?" "I!" The "I" is only one action, and it comprises the entire body-mind. It is the action of the entire body-mind, not merely of any part or any combination of parts distinct from the whole. You can see this drama in all the parts if you observe them, but, even more, you can understand yourself most fundamentally, totally, if you observe the "I", the ego, that is the total body-mind.

This is the observation you must make ultimately. All the separate dramas are parts of this one dramatization that is the ego-"I". Most fundamental self-understanding is the observation and understanding of the ego-"I" itself, or the total body-mind. When you understand the self-contraction most fundamentally and become responsible for it, then you can surrender all the parts. You can surrender under all circumstances, in the midst of all the separate dramas.

The whole point of observing your tendencies is that you do not do them any more. There is always more and more to observe until you observe the whole, the fundamental drama, or action, that is behind them all. You can take responsibility for this, that, and the other thing along the way and apply discipline to these things, but doing so does not change anything fundamentally. There must be most fundamental self-understanding and, thereby, responsibility for everything. And all of this is to take place in the context of intensive moment to moment practice of heart-felt devotional surrender to Me and Communion with Me. Communion with Me is the context and circumstance in which all of this observing and understanding is to take place.

While observation of your dramas, particularly your emotional-sexual dramas, has its value, it is not enough. You are not going to surrender yourself simply because you notice that you habitually play out strategies and that the strategies have emotional-sexual components. Noticing these things about yourself is not in itself going to move you to surrender to Me. You must have a sense of your situation in God, or you will not surrender to Me. The purpose of surrender to Me is Most Perfectly self-transcending God-Realization, not merely character improvement. Your separation from God is the effect of what you are doing most fundamentally—not the sub-dramas that create your ordinary social life but the fundamental drama that separates you from the Divine.

Self-contraction in the form of emotional-sexual preoccupation is a principal means you use to avoid the Divine. Because you are preoccupied with this dimension of your life, it must be addressed very significantly. Yet truly it is secondary to the fundamental dramatization of your life, which is the self-contraction itself, and its effect, which is separation from God, or the Divine Self-Condition.

The Way of the Heart is the practice of Ishta-Guru-Bhakti Yoga. Self-observation and self-understanding are simply practical aspects of this Way of devotion to Me. The Way of the Heart is not just watching yourself and analyzing yourself. The Way of the Heart is not about preoccupation with separate self at all. The Way of the Heart is Ishta-Guru-Bhakti Yoga—devotion to Me, the continuous exercise of the counter-egoic effort, in the urge toward Most Perfectly self-transcending God-Realization through self-surrendering Communion with Me. That is the practice of the Way of the Heart. Self-observation, self-understanding, and self-discipline are all practical aspects of the Way, the means to improve upon your practice of devotion to Me. As My devotee, you are to be preoccupied with self-surrendering devotion to Me. All the rest supports your practice of devotion to Me and strengthens it.

What Is Your Conclusion About Reality?

December 12, 1993

SRI DA AVABHASA: You are wandering in your mind. In one minute you are one attitude or one presumption, and in the next minute another one—different days, different presumptions, different attitudes. You can be asked in one moment, "Is there a God? What is your presumption about this?" But your answer cannot be taken seriously. In the next moment you could have another opinion, and tomorrow a different point of view, another attitude.

What I want to clarify with you, what I want to "Consider" with you, is your conclusion about reality, your actual conclusion, your present-time presumption about reality, because your conclusion about reality is operative in your life. If your "considered" conclusion about reality is that there is the Divine, this conclusion will determine one way of life, a Godward Way of life, a God-Realizing Way of life. If your conclusion about reality does not include the Divine, if you think there is nothing Divine about it, if you have no firm conviction about the Reality of the Divine and the life that would lead you to God, then that operating presumption governs another way of life.

When I have asked such questions recently, a few people have said something about their experience of Me, their experience in My Company, and so on. I pointed out that your experience in My Company does not necessarily make any difference. If it does not lead you to the conclusion that there is the Divine, so that your life is transformed by it and governed differently, then your experience in My Company is just another presumption in your body of presumptions. Although your experience in My Company may seem to you profound, may seem to indicate the Reality of the Divine, even prove It, nevertheless, if you do not come to the conclusion that the Divine is Real, then your conclusion does not operate as proof. What is operative in your life is your presumption about reality, your conclusion about reality. That is what is determining your life, moment to moment.

You are always thinking, your mind is always wandering, just as you are always having experiences. You claim to be thinking, but if you are really thinking, really using the mind, then you would come to some intelligent conclusion about this matter. What you call "thinking" is just a train of thoughts determined by subjective and objective changes or intrusions. That is not thinking. That is mind-forms. Thinking is an activity of intelligence, exercised relative to everything arising, subjectively, objectively, altogether, exercised relative to your experience to the point of coming to conclusions about it. If you are just experiencing mind-forms that are changing from moment to moment and day to day, then no conclusion is registered, or only one conclusion is suggested: that you are bound to body and mind-forms and general perceptions of the physical world. This is the tacit conclusion when all you are doing is wandering in your mind.

The conclusion that the Divine is Real is the result of conversion, in fact, not the result of a mere intellectual process. If it is to be effective in your life, however, it must become a conviction in the mind, and in every function altogether, in your disposition altogether. To be governed by the presumption of the Divine means you have come to the conclusion about reality that it is arising in God and is to be surrendered in God. Life, then, is about God-Realization and not about conditions. Therefore, the important matter is this conversion, or your conclusion about reality.

What is reality? If your conclusion is that you are just possessed by the body-mind and the perception of a physical world, the conclusion governs one way of life. If your conclusion is that all these things arising are arising in God, that God is the Principle and the Reality to Which all conditions are owed, then that conclusion determines another Way of life. It is not enough for you to describe experiences in My Company. You need to "consider" this: What is your conclusion about reality? What is the governing presumption of your life?

You seem to be asking Me for some sort of trick or experience that will make you feel better in your egoically "self-possessed" state. That is not a God-Realizing life, not a Godwardly-oriented Way of life. It is an egoically "self-possessed" disposition, which expresses itself in that manner. I have asked you so many times here in these recent weeks, "Is God Real to you? What is God? What is your point of view?" In other words, "What is your conclusion about reality?" At most, as I said, some have suggested some experience of Me, some experiences in My Company, and so on, but experiences are not a conclusion about reality. They are just part of your egoically "self-possessed" disposition. Sometimes you have such experiences, sometimes you do not.

What point of view does govern your life? Your experiences here and there do not govern your life. They influence you in the moment. What is your point of view? What is your conclusion about reality? If you are My devotee, and you are coming to Me truly, you do not relate to Me merely as a man, ordinary or otherwise. If your conclusion about reality is that God is not So, God is not Real, or "Maybe there is God, maybe there is not, I doubt it, I don't know", then how are you related to Me as My devotee? What are you devoted to, exactly? You are relating to Me, doing some kind of surrendering to Me, or making devotional gestures to Me, as just another human being. For what end, then? To make yourself feel a little better at the moment? Are you hoping I will Give you some trick to make you feel better? Are you hoping I will make you feel better in the moment, amuse you, entertain you, relax you, give you some sort of experience? That is not Guru-devotion, that is not Ishta-Guru-Bhakti. How you relate to Me is determined by your conclusion about reality.

Is your mind just random thoughts? Or is there intelligence at the core of it that is convicted of the Divine Reality? The Hindu tradition includes schemes of descriptions of reality and the human being. The description of the sheaths is one such scheme. There is the mental sheath, and then there is the intellectual sheath. What is the difference between these? In the traditional books, the difference is not quite made clear. They sound like the same thing—manomayakosha, the mind-sheath, and vijnanamayakosha, the sheath of intellect. What is the difference between the two? It is just this. Vijnanamayakosha is the sheath of what may be called "intelligence", or "discrimination". There are various ways to describe it, but it is the force of intelligence that otherwise relates to and is at the root of mere thinking, random thoughts, mind-forms. If the mind is used with clarity, or, in other words, with intelligence, then there is a conviction about reality that relates to mind-forms and deals with them.

When you refer to "yourself", what "you" are you talking about? The intelligent persona? Or just the bucket, the flesh-body, in its wandering thoughts and emotional changes, occurring in conditional Nature? What "you" are you referring to? What is your point of view?

Sometimes you are just the body-based, feeling, thinking, emoting machine. Sometimes you relate to that machine with intelligence. Sometimes you go beyond even the exercise of intelligence into a more sublime disposition. In each case, you become a different "you", it seems. Each of these forms of identification is reflected as a different persona, a different disposition altogether, and you identify with every one of them, in its time. What is your firm conclusion about reality? Do you have one? Are you someone yet?

Or are you just many different appearances, like a multiple personality, depending on which sheath you identify with at the moment?

The apparent individual has no firmness, no stand, no point of view, is manifesting no conclusion or Realization, but is just a variable appearance, like a bush in the garden, changing with the seasons, a natural form that is going through changes. It is not a something, a someone, yet you refer to yourself all the time. You give the same name to each of these personae, each of these dispositions.

In other words, do you have a conclusion about reality? Are you intelligent? Do you manifest a conclusion about reality? Perhaps it depends on which day you are asked, or in which moment you are asked, or which one of your apparent forms you are identified with. You think you can get away without a conclusion about reality. You only sometimes elect to be intelligent. Therefore, you do not have a conclusion about reality—"you", because you are not always the intelligent "you". You are variously different kinds of "you's", different forms of the "I". Sometimes that one is intelligent and has a firm conclusion about reality, that the Divine Is, and that life is for God-Realization. Then there are other times when you relinquish the sheath of intelligence and identify with the wandering changes of the lower aspects of the personality—the physical or vital, the dimension of natural energy or emotional, and the lower psychic or mental, which is just a flow of changes of mind-forms, depending on what is going on inside and outside. Can that apparent one, who is identified with only the lower aspects of the body-mind, be My devotee?

That one is Godless, and, therefore, Guru-less. That one is not truly My devotee, although it can be associated in some sense with the practice of the Way of the Heart. It is not itself My devotee. The hearted "I", the intelligent "I", is brought to the front through all the many aspects of your life in My Company, but you must also exercise it. You cannot live truly or practice the Way of the Heart truly if you will not exercise the sheath of intelligence, that dimension of the apparent person that is intelligence, that examines all natural arising, understands it, comes to conclusions about it, and governs the life on that basis.

You seem to be electing to exercise only the lower sheaths, and you want to talk about them all the time. If you are "considering" life altogether, the Way of the Heart altogether, with Me, you have been Called to, and you are involved in, an intelligent exercise—not merely intellectual but intelligent—that makes use of the characteristics of the body-mind in the context of conditional Nature. This means that you must use the mind, use the capability of thought, not only functionally but relationally. You must use them with intelligence, exercise them with intelligence, and "consider" reality.

You cannot relinquish the sheath of intelligence and do anything but suffer and be egoically "self-possessed". When everything is there but the greater sheath and there is no real exercise of intelligence or anything deeper than that, you present yourself as this troubled body-mind, meaning the lower, natural, functional aspects of your appearance, which is constantly changing and suffering, reacting, desiring, seeking. There are all kinds of habit-patterns, conditioning, wants, inclinations, and tendencies, and you talk about all these, but not intelligently, not to the point of coming to firm conclusions and allowing yourself to be governed intelligently. I am always Calling you to do so, but you do not necessarily activate yourself in that manner. You are habituated to exercising yourself and being conditioned and identified with conditioning in the lower aspects of your appearance here. When Called to exercise yourself intelligently relative to your conditioning and to "consider" it, you tend to become rather silent, or you start babbling and rehearsing your insides, resorting to your conditioned subjectivity, as if that is all there is, as if intelligence has no functional capability, as if you have no greater experience, no greater disposition, no Revelation.

Another name for the sheath of intelligence is "buddhi". It is a part of almost every human being, although some are born in a very strange condition, with not much of this faculty. In general, however, all human beings have this capability, but it must be brought to the front. To practice Ishta-Guru-Bhakti Yoga, to live the Way of the Heart, to be My devotee, you must exercise this capability. You cannot practice the Way of the Heart rightly and truly on any other basis. If you are exercising this capability, then, through "consideration", you come to conclusions, and the conclusions you come to govern your life. Rather than your being governed by the lower functional manifestation with which you tend to identify, which is just conditioning and suffering, you are governed by this intelligence, this responsive intelligence, this heart-based intelligence.

You are not used to exercising yourself intelligently. To exercise yourself with intelligence is not a matter of habit. It must intentionally be done. The intentional exercise of intelligence makes you truly human, and in the earlier developmental stages of life, this exercise of intelligence should be more and more called upon, and in the third stage of life it should especially come to the point of maturity, it should become a real capability that you exercise consistently. If you have not come to that point yet, then you have not finished the business of the first three stages of life. You have not finished the adaptations, the growth, that the first three stages of life should involve. Instead, you have been involved in games of sensory response, wandering, arbitraries, reactivity.

You may have developed all kinds of conditioning in the body, in the general energy of the body, in the flow of mind-forms, but you did not adapt to the exercise of intelligence. It was not called upon strongly enough, it was not required of you, you were not obliged to found yourself in its exercise. Therefore, when you reached adult age—the age at which maturity in the first three stages of life is supposed to be established—your adaptation was not finished. You did not handle your business. You entered the presumed adult world with minimal intelligence, as just a conditioned personality, full of desires and wanderings, body-mind identification, and limitations and stress and seeking. There is hardly any intelligence in it. You may have gone to college, but you were not necessarily required to exercise this capability. You were not called to exercise real intelligence so that you came to conclusions about reality and became a man, male or female. Instead of that manliness, male or female, you are all kinds of changes in mind, and emotional reactivity, and bodily stress, bodily seeking, self-indulgence.

The exercise of intelligence, or coming to a conclusion about reality, is a fundamental part of wisdom. If you truly exercise intelligence, you come to a right conclusion about reality. Intelligence knows the conditions of ordinary conditional reality. It also knows and refers itself to the Unconditional, or Divine, Reality. This is why so much importance has been given to this what can be called "sheath" of intelligence, in the traditions of Yoga. It is an absolutely essential mechanism for the truly human life, for the religious life, therefore—absolutely essential. The mechanisms of egoity tend to be used as a way of divorcing the being from intelligence. In that case, you do not experience and know and come to a conclusion about conditional reality. Neither do you experience and know and come to a conclusion about the Divine Reality. You just wander in reactions and forms of conditioning in a kind of oblivion, a kind of soup of egoity, which you try to maintain as a kind of sensory state of good feeling and pleasure.

You are habituated to creating this state of pleasure in one way or another, through the various forms of self-indulgence. You use sex and sexual relationships and entertainments, even entertainments of mind, as ways to maintain a kind of soup of egoically "self-possessed" pleasure that is not interfered with by the reality of conditional existence or by the Divine Reality. It is not interfered with by anything. It is "Narcissus", hanging over the pond, consoled, dissociated from reality, both conditional and Unconditional. The soup of egoity is the state in which, by tendency, you live, from moment to moment. It is in general what human beings call "life". It is not intelligent. It does not know conditional existence for what it is. It does not know the Divine, and it does not submit to the Divine. It just sits by the pond, in the soup of egoic "self-possession", as if it were just a sensory immortal, a current of pleasure. As soon as God or the conditional reality intervenes, there is shock, and bewilderment, and not knowing what to do. This is the state you are in, in general, and this is the state to be transcended.

You will not transcend it, however, until you can break this habit, consistently. And among the things required to break it is the exercise of real intelligence, heart-intelligence. In that process, you must become Godward in your disposition. If you are exercising the capability of intelligence, you <u>are</u> coming to a conclusion, or have, in fact, come to a conclusion, about reality that accepts the nature of conditional Nature, but that also accepts and embraces the Divine, or That Which can be called by many other Names—and "the Divine" is a good one.

The Tacit Obviousness of God

December 13, 1993

SRI DA AVABHASA: What about God, then? What is your presumption about God? Where did all of this conditional reality come from? How does all of this happen to be? "Consider" it.

Is it possible to presume that there is no God and have it make sense? We have discussed the limitations of the conventional religious notion of God as the "Creator". Setting that discussion aside for the moment, however, isn't it worth "considering" the Mystery of the fact of all of this?

People who casually dismiss the Reality of God generally are dismissing ideas and being reactive. Yet how could all of this conditional existence be? If there is nothing but material existence and material processes, how could even that be? Such a proposition presumes, perhaps, that there must be some time or some place in which there is nothing. Yet if there is nothing, how could there be anything?

It is not merely logical, it is tacitly obvious, that some immense Power and Intelligence is required for all this to be. Whatever the connection between that Power and Intelligence and all particular events, isn't it tacitly obvious that there must be such an immense Power and Intelligence?

Well! That is God enough to begin with, and it is not a naive belief or conventional religious propaganda. The tacit acknowledgement that this conditional realm necessarily is arising in a great Power and Intelligence is enough God to begin with, isn't it? However That is ultimately to be described, and whatever It has to do with all of this conditionality altogether, and however It may be Realized, isn't it obviously, tacitly so?

This is not an intellectual acknowledgement. It is tacitly obvious that it is so. Yet as far as reality goes, all the materialists say there is nothing but matter, or material processes. They proclaim this because they cannot get out of the holes of the body. You are inside all the holes of your body, and you cannot get outside—not just the external holes, like your eyes and so on. There are other holes, too. There is a hole in the middle of your head. If you could get out of the hole in the middle of your head, you would see more of this universe, more of what is being manifested altogether. Your view of manifested existence, and the view of the materialists, is based on your being fastened behind your holes. Like the materialists, you have no greater experience.

Not everyone is locked behind their holes, however. Many people, not just Realizers, have all kinds of perceptions beyond the body, and there are the reports over thousands of years from such people, many of you among them, who have these experiences. Why should the reports be casually dismissed? There is a hole in the brain core, and when you go through it you go to someplace else, to many places else. The mechanics of it are obvious, and they can be directly perceived and directly experienced. Other planes, other worlds, other beings, other forms of manifestation subtler than this, are really existing in the conditional sense, just as this appearance is. Such a report is also worthy of being taken seriously, isn't it? Whatever your experience, there is also the vast experience of all beings altogether, and it is widely reported.

Even from more ordinary human beings who do not go outside the holes in the body there are countless reports that should not be dismissed, reports of forms of perception that are extraordinary but within the context of the body, forms of experiencing and perception, sometimes called "extrasensory perception", or "psychism", "premonition", "clairvoyance", "clairaudience". Not every single individual who makes such a report but the totality of this report is certainly to be taken seriously. Therefore, even conditional reality is a much bigger reality than people say when they are stuck behind their holes.

You need not think of God as the First Cause. In fact, it is part of the ego-game to think of God as the First Cause, or the Cause of everything. That Which is called "God" is That Great Power and Intelligence without Which there would not be anything. God need not be thought to be the Cause of anything. God is not to be blamed for all of this that you are involved in. God is That in Which everything is potential, certainly, but God is That within Which everything is arising. God is certainly that Power of Being, Which is Vast, Infinite, and Beyond comprehension, tacitly, obviously so.

How do you become Godless and non-religious if you exercise this simple intelligence? It is when you forget to do so that you become Godless. When you exercise intelligence, this tacit certainty, this intuition of God, is substantial. It is direct, directly experienced, completely obvious. You simply regard all of this in the disposition of your intuition, which leans you toward the Source. There is much more to find out, much more to Realize, but this disposition establishes you in the Godward disposition. Therefore, moment to moment you must not forget to exercise the disposition in which the Divine is tacitly, obviously so. You must not forget to do this. You forget to do it when you sink down to the inside of the holes, identified with the lesser body-mind. When you keep this intelligence alive, keep the heart alive, there is a tacit certainty of God, or the Ultimate Power of Being, the Ultimate Reality, the Ultimate Condition, the Truth, the Source.

One of you was saying that she is upset with God simply because she is here apparently identified with the body-mind. Why are you on this side of that hole in your head? God is not forcing you down inside there. <u>You</u> are. God is the Opportunity to go beyond it. God is not merely on the other side of this door in the head, however. More conditional reality is on the other side of that hole. God may be intuited there, "considered" there, and you may be moved Godwardly in those places as well, but they are not themselves God, any more than this conditional realm, in and of itself, is God. On the other hand, it is Only God. There is Only God. That within Which everything is arising is the Substance of everything arising. So here, so there.

Many think that the Way to God is by ascending, by going through the holes upward and further upward. That is not the Way to God. It can be part of a process in which God-Realization is entered into in due course, but movement through the holes, particularly through this central hole, is a means to enter into conditional reality more profoundly, a means to enter into spheres of conditional existence that have their own limitations, yes, but not the particular limitations associated with your experiencing on this side of the holes, interior to the holes, of this apparent body-mind. God is Beyond all conditions, Beyond all worlds, therefore Beyond all wandering through the brain-core.

Your egoically "self-possessed" bondage is the limit on God-Realization. It is also even a limit on experience in the most ordinary, or conditional, sense. You bind yourself by your own contraction, reactivity, seeking, egoic "self-possession".

There is another great hole in the body that is the ultimate, secret place. You must get on the other side of it. It is the hole in the right side of the heart. It is not a passage to other conditional realms. It is the passage Ultimately Beyond.

The cosmic domain is All-Conscious and absolutely "Bright". Yet you do not perceive it because you are on the inside of your holes, on the interior side of them. You are speaking, even now, from that position inside your holes there, interior to the body-mind, in other words. I am Speaking to you from Outside the holes and Directing My Self to you, even through this Vehicle, from Outside not only the holes in this apparent physical body but also all the holes in the universe.

I am Established, Always and Already, Eternally in That Position, and you are, for now, established in that other position. We have a common ground—this bodily appearance. Yet because of the position with which you are identifying, you may tend to think of Me and relate to Me as if I am just like you. You mistake the Vehicle I am using to Serve you to be same thing that you appear to be. This error is a limit on your devotion to Me, and, making that error, you speak as you have spoken in times past. You speak in terms of your experiencing inside your holes there, on the interior side. You address that, relate to it, experience it, identify it, and then say that it is Me. What you are really talking about is your own interior existence, your ego-based existence, your confined existence, which, yes, has some numinous or larger characteristics. By calling it Me, however, you are not coming to Me. You are simply meditating on yourself.

It is said in the traditions, therefore, never approach your Guru as merely a man. Do not make the error of presuming there is no difference between you and your Guru. Presume the difference. Do not become self-involved. Your relationship to the Guru is a <u>relationship</u>, not merely a "you" addressing your own interior and calling it your "Guru" but you going beyond yourself through submission to your Guru. The traditions admonish you, then, never, never to relate to your Guru merely as a man, but always relate to your Guru as the Divine, and always presume relationship to that one, not identity with that one. If there is identity at all, it is in the Great Matter of Realization Itself. Even then, there is a difference of function. The relationship exists in the domain of appearance even then. One never becomes equal to one's Guru. You are always surrendered to your Guru. Divine Realization is simply the Most Ultimate Sign of that submission.

All kinds of ideas are associated with religion in the various common institutions of religion, and those ideas seem to be about God. Nevertheless, they are about mankind and order among mankind—the order associated with civilized living, social life, political authority, structuring of society. The concern of conventional religious processes, therefore, is not God-Realization but social, political, and cultural order.

The Communications of God-Realizers are not about order. The Communications of God-Realizers of the various degrees are expressions of God-Realization, and a Call, therefore, for people to do likewise. That is another matter. That domain of religion transcends conventional, worldly religion of the common, institutionalized kind. It has to do, rather, with the true religious process that transcends all institutionalized religions. There is a kind of universality to true religion, whereas institutionalized religions of the, one might say, "worldly kind" are all about the differences among them. Such religions become identified with particular civilizations, particular politics, particular policies and social orders, and as soon as they come into association with one another they are in conflict. They notice the differences immediately, and they threaten one another and protect themselves. One could say that such religions are, to a greater or lesser degree, extensions of egoity. They are egoity magnified to include everyone—at least within the domain of the particular cultural order.

Therefore, ideas such as God the Creator—even the God of history or the God "doing everything"—are institutional ideas associated with worldly religion, not Communications from the "Point of View" of God-Realization. Such ideas about God appear within the dominant religion of a civilization or a particular social order that is more or less in charge, and everybody within that cultural sphere is supposed to adhere to its doctrine, either altogether or at least to the degree of functioning in a civilized manner within the social order. Even if such ideas about God are associated with the "God"-label, they are ordinary, human ideas.

What we are here to "consider" is the Real God That you may directly intuit, or get in touch with in your Divine Ignorance, and Realize through your devotion to Me and by My Grace. We are here to "consider" the real religious process. Your particular religious background by birth and childhood association or association since childhood is just part of the baggage of your egoity and your ordinary life. You must bring discriminative intelligence to all of that content, just as you must bring it to the ordinary, daily-life subjectivity of your human existence.

You tend to talk more about your ordinary, daily-life subjectivity and not so much about the larger baggage that is all about the same thing. All of you here, or most of you, or all of you in general, at some point, I gather, rebelled against the propagandized God-ideas and became non-religious, or complicated about religion, more or less Godless. You began seeking, hopefully for the Real God and not for another conventional, institutionalized form of God by which to make another kind of civilization merely. Yes, fine, a culture develops in My Company—it is inevitable. The "Consideration" in My Company, however, is about the Realization of the Real God and not merely about something that can be called "civilized" living, which is rather loveless and non-compassionate even though it talks the words.

Right life is associated with real religious life. It is not about platitudes, and aphorisms, and self-protected ideas that may be called "religious". It is about real love, real compassion, right life altogether, based on response to the Real God, authentic Grace, authentic Revelation. If you are living in My Company for real and rightly, then this is the process in which you are involved.

To authenticate your life in My Company, then, you must exercise yourself at heart and with discrimination. Use your greater faculties—the heart and intelligence—in response to Me, and change your life, individually but also collectively, as a community, as a gathering, of My devotees and in your relations with all beings, or all the rest of so-called civilization and its mayhem, and falseness, and Godlessness.

Last night I talked with you about your conclusions about reality, mainly your false, or Godless, conclusions. So far this evening we are talking about the tacit Obviousness of God. It is a wonder, then, that you could come to any other conclusion, or that you could now seriously propose any other conclusion.

If we converted the matter that is here as this man's body into the energy that is its equivalent, it would be vast and explode the place. If there is that much energy behind just the making of a man, imagine how much energy, then, is behind the totality of even just the physical universe! For the universe to exist requires an immense Force, an incomprehensible Force. That is good enough God to begin with, isn't it?

Yet that incomprehensible Force is not just shooting all over the place like a firecracker. Look at all these discrete forms and systems. You are misusing them, but That Force is obviously Intelligent. It is an immense Force of immense Intelligence. Isn't that good enough God to begin with?

DEVOTEE: It seems to suggest a Creator-God.

SRI DA AVABHASA: Not necessarily a Creator-God. The idea of the Creator-God suggests that God is responsible for everything that everybody does and everything that is happening.

DEVOTEE: There seems to be some truth in that idea, though, because without God none of this could be.

SRI DA AVABHASA: God is the Being-Force within Which all this is arising. You cannot hold God accountable for what you are doing, for how things are happening, for all your trouble. God is the Immense Resource, the Potential, for everything. Therefore, everything arises in God. You are yourself making the event according to your own conclusions, and fastening yourself to the limitations you choose. God is not responsible for that. God is the Way beyond that. God is That to Which you must turn, That Which you must Realize in order to be Liberated from your limitations, from your use of the collection of force—relatively small compared to the Totality—with which you are identified.

This tacit understanding, which is obvious if you think clearly, does not suggest a Creator-God. All kinds of things, and movements, and persons, and ideas can account for changes. God is that Force of Being, that

Immense Intelligence, that Incomprehensible Intelligence and Force That is the reason why anything can be at all, within Which everything is arising. Therefore, God is the Resort of all and the Ultimate Potential and Possibility of all. Such is the Nature of God, not this Creator-God notion, which, as I said, justifies a "civilized" way of life, or at least calls for it.

DEVOTEE: I know that in most of the exoteric religions the notion is, "How else could all of this be except for God, Who is immense Energy?"

SRI DA AVABHASA: There is some rightness in that notion, but the logic that is built upon it is made by a mind that is not God-Realized, in order to justify a "civilization", a "civilized" way of life, an order of belief, that contains many other factors.

You are only Godless when you fail to inspect reality directly and intelligently. When you are just egoically "self-possessed", wandering in your own limitations, your self-contraction, inside your holes, then you forget about your heart-understanding, and you start discounting it with your mind-forms.

Direct, tacit perception, awareness, acknowledgement, takes the form of what can rightly be called "faith"—a disposition of certainty in response to Me that can govern your life rightly, altogether newly. Such faith must appear in My Company. It is the conversion that establishes the Way of the Heart rightly and authenticates it. Without it, you are always returning to your suffered egoic disposition and approaching Me full of doubt, as if you had received nothing yet. You must <u>exercise</u> yourself in response to Me. Be intelligent and heart full. Allow the experience of My Company and the "consideration" of My Instruction to change your life.

People often say that "God is Love". When felt directly, the Divine Force, All-Pervasive, of Which everything is a modification, is All-Blissful, Free Force of Feeling—Love, therefore, Radiance without limitation. That does not mean that It is here to make utopia, however. It is here to Wake you up, here to Involve you. It is here to get your response, so that you will be governed by that response, come to conclusions about reality, and do the sadhana.

DEVOTEE: Not to be consoled.

SRI DA AVABHASA: Yes, being not merely "lovey-dovey"—you in your place, complacent and feeling consoled by this God-Love. You must respond, and you must be governed in your life intelligently by response. Never forget to respond to Me. Therefore, always be governed by the obligation to respond to Me, in every moment of every day, not just sometimes. This is your obligation. It is the Law. When you respond to Me, purifications occur, you advance in your practice of the Way of the

Heart, and you grasp something more of this Revelation of Mine. Then you move on by accepting the Law of that response, that Revelation, that conclusion. You grow more and more by your devotional response to Me. More is Revealed, but on the basis of your response in doing the sadhana you are Given, on the basis of the Yoga you will manifest in your sadhana. If you make light of this process, if you do not take it seriously, if you do not become serious, if you do not do the sadhana, then you use up much lifetime in the face of My Revelation without great change.

If you are really, seriously committed to not suffering, then you had better get on with Me! The thing you are choosing otherwise is inherently about suffering and will suffer. If you are finding some way to feel somewhat mediocre and to feel a little buzz of pleasure in the midst of it, without doing the sadhana all the time or most intensively, then you are just lying to yourself about your inevitable destiny. You are immunizing yourself. If you are really committed to not suffering, then you had better do this Yoga for real—no longer committed to the lower-based body-mind and its signs but committed to self-surrendering, self-forgetting, and Most Perfectly self-transcending God-Realization—and move on, therefore. The sign of someone who is really committed to not suffering is growth in the Way of the Heart. If you shuffle your feet in hesitation, you only commit yourself to that which inevitably suffers. Therefore, commit yourself to That Which is not suffering.

The "I" and the "It"

December 14, 1993

SRI DA AVABHASA: The exercise of the heart and of the faculty of intelligence authenticates the religious life. While you are still identifying with the lower aspects of the body-mind, you are bereft of the center, or the heart and intelligence. You are just the self-contracted self-identity, identified with the body, reactive emotions, random thoughts, attention wandering, breath out of balance. Yet, as My devotee, the Yoga of your practice is the devotion of body, emotion, mind, attention, the breath, and energy in Communion with Me. How can you do the Yoga of Ishta-Guru-Bhakti if you cannot operate as the heart and intelligence? The heart and intelligence do the Yoga. They bring the lower faculties of the body-mind under control, directing them into Divine Communion. If you cannot exercise those faculties, you cannot do the Yoga, and if you try to do the Yoga with only the lower faculties, you will not do the Yoga. You will wander in your attention. You will be egoically "self-possessed".

If your conclusion about reality is separateness unillumined, not aware of the Unity of existence, not aware of the Divine Condition of conditions, not surrendered to That, you will also not do the Yoga. You will not be governed by right understanding, or a right conclusion about reality. I have been asking the question "What is your conclusion about reality?" because your conclusion about reality governs your life. To come to a right conclusion, you must make use of all your faculties in response to reality, in response to What is Revealed, and also in response to what is just apparent.

You do not seem to be aware of the structure of the body-mind in its various parts. You appear to be exercising only some faculties, some aspects, of the body-mind, and the others are rather inert. You do not animate them. You may passively be aware of them somehow—there may be a heart-response in a moment of examination, perhaps, here and there—yet you do not exercise the more fundamental faculties.

You seem to think it is sufficient—and even necessary—to identify with the most rudimentary faculties: physical awareness, general energy in the body, the wanderings of emotion, mind-forms, the wanderings of attention, the movements of desire and breath. You consult these all the time, identify with them, and allow yourself to be governed by them. Your conclusion about Reality is based on your passive identification with these lower faculties.

I am Calling you to observe, understand, and notice that you are allowing senior faculties of the body-mind to be passive. Occasionally, there is the heart-response prior to the mechanisms of body and mind. Occasionally, you consent to be intelligent for a moment, to observe, to examine, to weigh things against one another, to measure their relative significance. Apart from such moments, which are relatively rare and generally engaged rather passively, you exercise the lesser faculties, the rather automatic ones, the grosser ones.

I have Called you to exercise, intentionally and directly, the central faculties of the human being, the ones that must govern the body-mind altogether. These are the faculties that must be brought to govern the lesser faculties and aspects of the body-mind. If you do not exercise them, however, if you do not responsibly embrace them and stand as them in relation to the body-mind and all of reality, then you just passively identify with and suffer the relative chaos of the lower body-mind. I Call you to be intelligent about your observation of conditional existence, to be intelligent in your response to Me and to My Word to you and to My Presence here.

You relinquish intelligence when you identify with the lower aspects of the body-mind. You relinquish the position of observing the body-mind and being responsible for it. On the one hand, you say, apparently intelligently, that your conclusion about reality is that it is a Unity. With the next breath, you tell Me about your separateness and tendencies. In one moment, you are presumably standing in the position of intelligence, observing your egoity and being responsible for it. In the next moment, you are not that at all anymore. You are ordinary mind, emotion, and body, just stuff floating around in the vast conditional process.

Not only do you identify with it, but you also give it a name. You call it "me" or "I". Intelligence does not do this. Intelligence refers to itself as "I", but it does not refer to phenomena as "I". The faculty of intelligence is in the position of observing the phenomena of the body-mind and its relations. The unintelligent persona calls ordinary mind, emotion, and body "I". It is not in a position to observe the body-mind and be responsible for it. It is in the position of being identified with the body-mind, and, therefore, it is unintelligent.

To exercise intelligence is to not identify with the lower faculties of the body-mind. How could anything be called "I", anyway, if existence is a Unity? If existence is a Unity, then every part of the body-mind is not separate, but it is one with all its likeness in the entire realm of cosmic Nature, just an immediate presentation of something that is universal.

Intelligence can analyze the body-mind and see that all of its components are universal components of the natural world. From the point of view of intelligence, everything is seen in terms of elementals. The immediate implication of the awareness that existence is a Unity is that everything is an aspect of a more subtle universal element. There is no "my" about it, no "me" about it. It is not even an "it" altogether. It is a local, temporary appearance within a greater field of elements.

At the senior, or central, level, you are awareness and intelligence. Awareness and intelligence are the central faculties of the person. Truly, when you are referring to "I", you are referring to that awareness and intelligence. Yet you confuse yourself with what you are observing, and, therefore, you relinquish the position of knowing the field and being responsible for it. You relinquish the position of awareness and intelligence in order to identify with mind-forms, emotion-forms, body-forms, elementals, thereby losing your responsibility, losing your awareness of the Unity of existence, and relinquishing your capability to discover the Source-Condition of intelligent awareness.

If existence is a Unity, the intelligent awareness is also a sign of something universal. It is a characteristic of the Whole. This Whole has many aspects, many elements, many dimensions, and the senior dimension is subjectivity.

When the apparent person disintegrates, every part returns to its universal field, the body to its various chemical and atomic elements, the emotional dimension, the energy dimension, the mind-forms, all return to their fields—intelligence likewise, and conscious awareness, then. The individual consciousness in its Absolute Place is What, then? The Divine Consciousness? Other elements? It returns to the universal, or Absolute, Consciousness That is What can be called "the Divine". It can be called by many names—"Ultimate Reality", "Truth," "God". So also in your case. The core dimension of your own person is intelligent awareness, likewise universally, and also Absolutely—because existence is a Unity. When you exercise your intelligence and come to this conclusion, the religious life follows, the life of commitment to existence in Divine Communion, wherein you are governed by the understanding that existence is a Unity. If you do not exercise your intelligence, you will not embrace the religious life, no matter how much you call yourself "religious".

Real religion requires the exercise of intelligent awareness.

When you are identified with the common life, you do not understand religion in its true sense. You identify with the lower facilities of the person, and you hardly exercise the greater and central faculties. To you, religion is about getting something to make you feel better, or something to perfect your lower-based self-condition. Therefore, you make false religion, which is not about God-Realization but about self-fulfillment. The common messages of religion are not about God-Realization. They are expressions of the hopes of ego-based individuals who want to feel good and escape the worst.

How will you live, now that you have been Given My Revelation to intelligence and the heart? What will you do now? Are you convicted by My Criticism or not? Have you come to a conclusion about reality based on this Revelation, or have you not? In the philosophical talk that is the *Bhagavad Gita*, Arjuna is the representation of True Man, exercising the heart and intelligence, functioning from the core position in response to Revelation. In your communication to Me, you are more like those whom Arjuna had to fight, distant relatives who were egoically "self-possessed", evil, destructive, and demonic, and who were destroying the Unity of existence.

It seems that I am not talking to Arjuna but to his relatives, the mlecchas, or barbarians. Even so, I am Calling you mlecchas to take up the fullness of life in My Company, to exercise the faculties that make you into mlecchas, Godless people, worldly beings, "Narcissus". Only by your responding to Me, by your willingness to exercise the essential faculties of the being, will you be relieved of your suffering, your ordinary destiny, and the destructiveness you are working on everyone.

You—you mlecchas—are the source of this dark time. You are making a culture and a world out of heresy, or Godlessness. You are making the dark time for all, and you are doing so rather casually, always generating more arguments for your egoically "self-possessed" and destructive habits of life. You always want to talk more and more about your lower-based egoity rather than responding in the heart and with intelligence, rather than exercising the central position of the being, the true "I" in the human person. The functional "I" is really awareness present as intelligence, observing and monitoring. You should be responsible for these things you are identifying with, but you will not exercise yourself responsibly and Godwardly until you are willing to use the faculties of your own person fully.

In the *Bhagavad Gita*, the God-Man Krishna says to Arjuna, "Remember Me and fight," meaning "Struggle with these, in effect—in a human individual—lower-based inclinations, or tendencies. Deal with, be responsible for, the peripheral aspects of the being." The heart must constantly be God-devoted, and the intelligence must be a reflection of the heart's devotion and must control mind, emotion, body, action. This is the necessary basis of the true religious life.

You must fulfill the Law. You must be committed to the Law absolutely and function on its basis, for real. The author who wrote the *Bhagavad Gita* knew that the main character must really respond. Therefore, at the end, Arjuna is not sulking and confused and egoically "self-possessed". He was at the beginning, but he is not so at the end. After a time of Revelation of the Word and Person of the Realizer, the Divine Person, the response is expected.

The entire lower body-mind is to be surrendered and conformed to intelligence and heart, and directed by them to the Divine Condition, to That Which is the very Source of intelligent awareness, Which is also like intelligent awareness but Which is Absolute, the Very Self, the Divine Self. On the basis of this heart-response made intelligent, you control the body-mind, you submit the lower body-mind—physical, emotional, mental—as the components of the Yoga that are to be controlled by the intelligent heart.

Arjuna was not very intelligent until Krishna dealt with him. Likewise, I am here for your response. You must become intelligent with your response to Me. You must come to conclusions about reality on the basis of intelligence, and control your body-mind, make it into Yoga, not merely keep it under control in the ordinary sense of good behavior but make it into Yoga, devote it, submit it, body, emotion, and mind, to Me, and Commune with Me through this submission.

DEVOTEE: As You said earlier, Sri Gurudev, what we call "I" is the lower aspect of the body-mind, which is really "it", not "I". "I" is the one who is aware of it.

SRI DA AVABHASA: You must notice this. To notice it does not require some psychic, visionary intrusion. It is obvious. You are awareness. Whatever that is ultimately, you are that. When you say "I", you are referring to awareness, but in the context of the body-mind. The "I" is the total body-mind, but the total body-mind governed from its core, which is awareness, intelligent about reality, controlling thought, emotion, and body, and, therefore, action. You are always this awareness. The "you" that thinks is this awareness.

That is all the Revelation that is required. It is just so. You are aware of the body-mind. Your central position in life is this awareness, which can exercise itself, must exercise itself, intelligently. It must examine things, see them as they are, take them into account, and come to right conclusions. This intelligent awareness, then, is addressing thoughts and emotions and body, and forming actions through these means. That is how you are built.

I am not talking about the Ultimate Nature of this awareness. I am simply describing your ordinary state. You are functioning as awareness, then intelligence, associated with mind, emotion, and body. This is how you are built. In the Hindu tradition, the structure is described in terms of sheaths, the more outer being the physical, then the dimensions of natural energy and the emotional aspects of the person, then mind-forms and the psychic life, then this intelligence that observes it and that should be the controller of it, and, deeper than that, the awareness itself. The body-mind is described from the periphery to the center as a collection of sheaths, with awareness at the center and body and its field of activities at the periphery. This is simply an educational model to help people understand just how they are functioning in ordinary terms. Understanding the principle, you must oblige yourself to function on its basis. The intelligent awareness must also be informed by Revelation.

You seem to think that you go to the Communion Hall as body, emotion, and mind, and that you are there to struggle with them. No, you go to the Communion Hall as intelligent awareness, to deal with the body, emotion, and mind. That is how to do meditation. That is how to do Yoga. You cannot eliminate intelligent awareness and do Yoga, because without intelligent awareness there is no one controlling the faculties of the body-mind, no one submitting them, no one surrendering them one-pointedly into Divine Communion.

You cannot just go to the Communion Hall and sit there as a mass of physical, emotional, and mental conditions and do Yoga. You may go there and relax a little bit, somehow, but it is not true Yoga.

I am simply talking about conscious awareness. Whatever that is Ultimately is to be Realized. Nevertheless, you are functioning as it right now. Are you not aware? Are you not conscious? Is this not the central fact of your presence here? Conscious awareness is essentially what you are. As such, you are aware of intelligence, mind-forms, emotions, body, action—your condition, the body-mind, the bodily person, the human person, is just this structure.

DEVOTEE: That awareness is not the mind. Is it the higher mind, the psychic mind?

SRI DA AVABHASA: It is awareness! Just that. Mind is observed by awareness. Thoughts arise to your awareness.

Picture a white cat. You are aware of it—isn't this clear? You are the one who is aware of it. You are not the white cat. You are aware of the white cat.

The central faculty you are exercising, the faculty of just being, is awareness. Next comes the thing you are aware of. You can be aware of a mental picture or thought or concept. You can be aware of an emotional state—anger, fear, sorrow, love. You can be aware of energy in the body.

You can be aware of the body, of physical states and physical shapes. You can be aware of the body's relations. You are aware at all times. You are functioning and present as the awareness of these things, and they arise in a hierarchical continuum, some closer to awareness and some more peripheral. Therefore, just awareness is what we are "considering" now.

I am Calling you to observe the simple, plain fact of just this obviousness. See that it is so. You need not do anything to yourself to make this plain fact so. You need not do Yoga or enter into some more profound esoteric state. It is just plain old so. It can be directly observed that this is so.

The central position is awareness. Everything else arises to it in a hierarchical progression, from subtle to gross, from intelligence to body. You are aware of the body. Right now the body could be in a pleasurable state or a terribly painful state, but its state does not make any difference. You are still aware of the body. The faculties of the person that are closer to this awareness are intelligence and mind, the more subjective, or internal, states. Peripheral to them are the grosser states, including the body itself and its gross relations. You are present here as this structure of personality, the central position of which is awareness and the peripheral position of which is the body.

If you are not established in the understanding that you are here as awareness and functioning as intelligence, you are just identified with the flesh body, its emotions and its energies and its thoughts. The body-mind goes through all kinds of changes, and it dies inevitably. Of course, it is an unsatisfactory condition and a source of suffering, if it is left to itself. Therefore, you become a seeker. Without exercising your greater faculties and finding their source, you simply want this suffered, peripheral personality to feel better.

Awareness is already continuing beyond the body-mind. No matter what happens to the body-mind while you live, you are still aware. The awareness itself never changes. It is aware of changes, but it never changes. It is just awareness, just consciousness. There are not different kinds of consciousness, different colors of it or different shapes of it. It is just consciousness. What it is ultimately is to be discovered—fine—but the fact of it, the reality of it, is constant. No matter what happens in the body-mind, you are still just aware of it and you are never changed. You yourself as awareness are never, in fact, affected by change. Awareness does not go through changes. It observes changes.

If you are unintelligent, then every time there is a change you identify with the change. "I am that change, then," you say. You think, you feel, when the body is suffering, "I am suffering," when reactive emotion arises, "I am angry, I am sorrowful, I am afraid." That which never changes is constantly presuming itself to be changed, to be a change. In this moment, it is painful—in the next moment, it feels good. You are always identifying this pure awareness with the changes that are peripheral to it. If you inspected this awareness, if you entered into it most profoundly, you would see clearly that it itself does not change, but it is just witnessing changes. Until it merely Witnesses them, however, it presumes itself to be the changes themselves.

All of this appearing is nothing but an apparent modification of the Inherent Radiance of Consciousness Itself. This is What is to be Realized Ultimately by entering into the matter, and when Given Grace to find out. Even before such Realization, however, even before then, the Great Matter can be examined right now, in this present situation. It begins with the examination of reality, experience, all of this arising in its totality, which you are able to observe, and also the structural nature of your own person.

I have a sense that you think it is good to do sadhana, so that eventually, after you do much sadhana, you will find out that God Exists. Sadhana is not done to find out that God Exists. Sadhana is done to Realize the Divine Self-Condition. The Reality of Truth, or the Divine, must be accepted at the beginning. You cannot do sadhana for real otherwise.

You are so used to conventional thinking about religion and the Divine that you imagine that the Divine Reality cannot be simply Obvious in your direct "consideration" in the moment. I am not talking about a theological God whose existence must be proven in the context of some discourse or tedious argument and is not obvious through direct "consideration", or whose existence is proven by some report. The Truth of existence is tacitly obvious to one who stands present from the heart and who is exercised intelligently as a whole person. The simple indicators, the simple words, of the Realizer authenticate themselves directly. It is just obviously so.

Intelligent awareness is responsibility.

If you do not want to suffer, then stop doing suffering. Do not just identify with it. Do not just go with the flow and still expect some great help or relief or magical destiny to occur. Suffering is something you are doing. What you call "suffering" is what you are doing. Yes, there are also mere conditions that are limited, changing, and passing, but your identification with all that is the suffering. It is your doing likewise that is the suffering.

Do otherwise. Function from the heart intelligently. Do the Yoga of Divine Communion, of Ishta-Guru-Bhakti. Thereby your own act that is suffering and your identification with and association with even what is passing is transcended.

Ishta-Guru-Bhakti Yoga is simply devotional submission to Me, Communion with Me, devotional submission of the faculties of the person.

Either you do that or you do not. What excuse do you use to not do it? You know what you do not do, but how do you justify not doing it in any moment when you do not simply submit the faculties of the body-mind? How do you justify it? How do you argue yourself out of it? You must find out.

You can simply be intelligently aware of whatever is arising in any moment, and you can do the Yoga. You are totally capable of doing this. Intelligent awareness itself is totally free to do it. There is no impediment.

Submission to the Source

December 15, 1993

SRI DA AVABHASA: By Grace, many changes occur in the process of Ishta-Guru-Bhakti Yoga. First, there is the purification of the lower vehicle of the personality—bodily purification, emotional purification, mental purification, proper balancing of the natural energies, and steadying of attention. Through this purifying, balancing, and enlivening process of the devotional Yoga, intelligent awareness, this apparent self, this individual "I", is released from attachment to the peripheral mechanism. In the earlier stages of the process, awareness is released from attachment to the grosser aspects of the peripheral mechanism. Then, as it advances in the course of the fourth stage of life, or perhaps enters even into the fifth stage of life, it is released from even the subtler aspects of the mechanism.

When all that work has been accomplished, the living being, which, at its root, is simply awareness, Realizes steadily that it is simply Witnessing whatever arises. It is no longer merely actively observing and dealing with what arises. Even more fundamentally, it Realizes that it is simply Standing in the Position of merely being the Witness of what is arising. This Realization occurs by Grace, and then the Perfect submission of awareness itself to the Realizer begins, wherein conscious awareness is submitted into the Very Person, the Very State, of Being Itself, of Consciousness Itself, Which is the Realizer.

In that ultimate process of submission, the knot in the right side of the heart—the knot of egoity, the primal knot that feels consciousness to be a separate "I"—falls, beyond the knot, into the Divine Realizer's Condition. If the process is truly Perfected, made Most Perfect, it becomes the seventh stage Awakening, by Grace, and there is no longer a presumed separate "I"-consciousness. It is lost, surrendered into the Divine Consciousness—no longer the separate "I", no longer the atman, but now the Divine Self-Condition, the Ultimate Person, Self-Existing and Self-Radiant, Who is simply Consciousness Itself, Absolute.

In that Realization Most Perfect, in the seventh stage of life, all appearances are tacitly, inherently obvious as nothing but transparent, or merely apparent, and un-necessary, and inherently non-binding modifications of the Self-Existing and Self-Radiant Divine Being. In that Awakening, then, all conditions, apparently personal or apparently in relationship, are Divinely Recognized, and the Self-Existing Self-Radiance of Divine Being is magnified in that Recognition, perpetually, even to the degree, Most Ultimately, of Divine Translation, or the Outshining of all conditions, or Perfect Awakeness to the Divine Self-Domain, the Domain that Is the Divine Person, Self-Existing and Self-Radiant Being Itself, Beyond all qualifications, all limitations.

At the beginning of the process of Spiritual development, human beings are like Arjuna at the beginning of the *Bhagavad Gita*—egoically "self-possessed", collapsed on themselves, in trouble, suffering, bewildered, functioning merely egoically, seeking, experiencing the results of functioning egoically, unable to act truly, seeming to be incapable of true intelligence. When the human being comes into contact with the true Realizer—when My devotee comes to Me—when that meeting occurs and the individual being responds and accepts the Instruction, examines it thoroughly and applies it, then the life changes. It begins to be transformed by Ishta-Guru-Bhakti Yoga, or the submission of all conditions in Divine Communion. It becomes purified, balanced, enlivened, clarified, and the human individual moves through and beyond the various developmental stages of life.

A fundamental part of that process is the Realizer's Transmission of Spiritual Blessing. At the beginning, however, there is simply the devotional response to the Realizer, the receiving of the Realizer's Instruction, the living on the basis of that Instruction, and the exercising of devotional Communion with the Realizer. Even in that process, the devotee may have some experience of the Realizer's Spiritual Presence in the form of certain effects. In due course, however, after a significant period of real practice of the Yoga of Ishta-Guru-Bhakti, when real purification, rebalancing, enlivening, and clarification have taken place and the individual is collected in devotion to the Realizer and has proven it to the degree that he or she is able to "Locate" the Spiritual Person of the Realizer, directly, then the sadhana is transformed, by virtue of the Realizer's Spiritual Transmission.

The Spiritual Transmission of the true Realizer is the Inherent Radiance of the Divine Being. It is also, otherwise, that Very Power of Which all conditions, even material conditions, are manifestations.

I have said that if you converted the body of this man here [indicating a man in the gathering] into equivalent energy, he would be an immense force. Imagine, therefore, the immense force of the totality of just the physical universe. That Force is the Divine Power, of Which everything is a manifestation, or a merely apparent modification. That Force is Inherent in the Divine Being. It is simply the Inherent Radiance of the Divine Being. In the play of the universe, it is the Energy, the Force, behind it all, the Shakti, the primal Force. The Realizer Transmits this Power to the devotee.

"Narcissus" must first be Called to look up, to respond to the Realizer, to receive Instruction, to see what he or she is doing and change his or her act. In due course, when the original sadhana is done, then the devotee becomes capable of receiving and doing Yoga with the Transmitted Power of the Realizer, Which is the same Power behind all conditional manifestation—the Inherent Radiance of the Divine Being. When the sadhana incorporates this Transmitted Power, the Divine Power does further work in the body-mind, even further purifying the physical vehicle and the lower life and purifying even the subtler and subtlest dimensions of the personality.

This great Power, this Shakti, this Transmitted Divine Blessing, even though It is the Power of Which everything is a manifestation or apparent modification, does not lead to conditions. When that Power is contacted through the Blessing of the Realizer, It leads to the Divine—not to conditions but to their Source. If the Realizer's Transmission is of the Most Perfect kind, so that the pure, true Hridaya-Shakti is Transmitted, then the Divine Spirit-Power leads to the Source-Position. The Witness-Position Awakens in due course, and the Power Drives to and through the right side of the heart, passes through that knot, and brings about the Most Perfect Awakening.

Is it clear, then, that, first, fundamental education in the Company of the Realizer is essential? You must respond to the Realizer with devotion. Your intelligence must become equipped to function rightly, lawfully, truly devotionally. Then you do the foundation work of sadhana, which is to submit the various parts of the body-mind devotionally to Communion with the Realizer, so that the entire life is transformed by the Yoga of devotion.

There is only One Power behind all manifestation. It is the Divine Power. It can be experienced in various forms. It can be experienced in Its concrete manifestations. All this is That. Yet all this is a gross modification of that Power. Among the Realizers of one or another degree Who Transmit the Divine Power, each One Transmits the Power according to his or her Realization, or stage of life. Even though only that One Power is Transmitted, It is Transmitted through the characteristics of the Realizer, and It leads, therefore, in the case of the devotees of that one, to the Realization that is characteristic of the Realizer.

The purpose of existence, and the law of existence, is submission to the Source. Ultimately, the process becomes simple establishment in the

Divine Self-Domain. This does not mean you should simply have a negative view of the conditions of this life. When your sadhana of Divine Communion is activated in the circumstance of this appearance here, there is no point in intellectually or otherwise feeling that this life has no use, no purpose, no significance. It is the setting of your practice of Divine Communion.

You are appearing in the grossest sphere of the Divine Source. However, you are not the grossest form of it. Many other types of living beings on Earth are functionally less developed than human beings, but they are likewise appearing in this grossest sphere. Rocks and apparently inanimate things are clearly in a grosser state than a human being—in general, anyway! You can even perceive depths of grossness that are darker than your general perception allows.

It can be said that Earth is the outer reach of the Cosmic Mandala, the periphery. There are many other planes, many other worlds—and not all of them are necessarily more fun than this one—some characteristics of which are of a subtler vibratory nature. Those planes and worlds may be said to be more highly developed than this, more benign, perhaps, or rightly exercised. In the course of the practice of true Divine Communion, you can, either through visionary visitation while alive in this world and plane or in the passage after death, enter into such subtler spheres of experience. Even there, however, the Law is the same. The Law of existence is to do the sadhana of Divine Communion, to be purified of limitations, and to move on. Most ultimately, there is Divine Translation into the Divine Self-Domain, not merely passage to the so-called "highest" subtle realm.

All cosmic, or conditional, realms are, in terms of the appearances within them, temporary. Therefore, they all exhibit limitations of one kind or another. In comparison to the limitations of this realm, those in the subtlest of spheres do not appear to be limitations. Yet each sphere has its limitations, and beings that are awake within those subtle spheres know the limitations, experience them, suffer them, and must move beyond them.

You are, right now, at the Source of all manifestation. The Source is now and ever Present, All-Pervading, and also Absolute. Yes, you come from that Source, but you are with that Source, now. The Place of Origin is not without. The Place of Origin is at the most Subjective Position—not merely within you, or interior to the body-mind, but in the Place Where you Stand, the Place of conscious awareness itself. You could explore the physical universe, and you would still never find the Source. To find the Source Itself, you must enter into the Inherently Perfectly Subjective Domain of the physical universe.

Traditionally, it is said that one cannot comprehend this Maya, or the cosmic play of appearances. It is not comprehensible in its objectivity.

You cannot get to the Source of it, unless you come into contact with the Originating Power and follow It to Its Source. The Divine Power brings you, Most Ultimately, to the Inherently Perfectly Subjective Domain—not to the infinitely out-there objective place but to the Inherently Perfectly Subjective Place.

The Way of the Heart can be made most direct and ultimately Most Perfect. The Way of the Heart is founded in truly most fundamental self-understanding—true hearing—which equips you to examine and do the Yoga so that you pass beyond the limitations of the developmental stages of life, beyond the tendencies, or forms of orientation, that would lead you into merely subtler domains within the Cosmic Mandala. Those who practice most intensively, most seriously, can, within this lifetime, enter into the sphere of the "Perfect Practice", not necessarily even requiring aspects of the progressive stages, in particular the ascending process in its intensively applied form. This does not mean that those who enter into the "Perfect Practice" will necessarily enter into the Divine Self-Domain through Divine Translation in this lifetime, but they are focused in a sadhana that, in its intention, and in its fundamental nature, can be purified of destiny. Even those who are significantly Realized in that "Perfect Practice" may, for various reasons, be reentered even into this sphere, after death, or perhaps into some subtler sphere, to do service there.

Here I am, Exemplifying that process.

The Joy of Godwardness

December 17, 1993

SRI DA AVABHASA: I have been discussing with you the structure of the human being, awareness being the central position from which everything is viewed by the human being. We were simply discussing just that structure. Yet instead of addressing the simple matter of the structure of the human being and how you work, you all fastened onto the characteristic of awareness, wanting to make much of it, wanting to somehow identify with it in some profound manner, and suggesting that because awareness is a simple characteristic of consciousness, you are already Realized somehow, or at least equipped for practice in the ultimate stages of life in the Way of the Heart. You interpreted the ordinary principle, the central position, in human beings, which is awareness, to suggest all these kinds of things. There was very little discussion of the ordinariness of awareness as a simple factor in daily life and practice. Even today, some of you are suggesting that you are glimpsing, perhaps, the State of Identification with the Divine Self-Consciousness.

There seems to be an urge in you to find some reason or another to bypass the necessity for sadhana, and to presume that somehow, always and already, you are equal to That Which is to be Realized Ultimately. Perhaps the way to address this error is to ask you to "consider" the difference between human awareness and the Divine Self-Consciousness.

DEVOTEE: Sri Gurudev, in the process of observing, understanding, and feeling beyond the self-contraction, there are intuitive glimpses of Self-Existing and Self-Radiant Feeling of Being Itself.

SRI DA AVABHASA: Intuitive glimpses? What does that mean? Is it like being a "peeping Narcissus"? You are looking at yourself and thinking it is God—not just an attractive boyfriend, or whatever?

Now your pond glimpses have gone this far, even! When you are actually looking at yourself, you do not think you are looking at just another who is attractive to you but you think you are looking at God!

Awareness is the simple, fundamental position of the human being, and everything else arises objective to it. When you exercise this awareness intelligently in relation to what arises, you are doing the sadhana, the Yoga. You want to talk about, "Oh, what does this mean, then? Is this the same as the Witness-Position?" You want to suggest some advance, or even Realization, in the simple process of ordinary, functional awareness, or some of the releases in beginner's practice. You want to suggest that exercising yourself as awareness in relation to what arises is somehow the equivalent of practice in the ultimate stages of life in the Way of the Heart, or even Most Ultimate Realization. You have been asking questions and making statements that suggest you are puzzled, or that you think somehow there is an equation to be made between functional human awareness and Divine Self-Realization.

How can you, as a beginner in the Way of the Heart, be sensitive to "radical" seventh stage Realization? You can sympathetically "consider" the Argument and the descriptions of the seventh stage Realization, but how does such "consideration" become seventh stage Realization? What does it have to do with it? You are poetically, or in whatever fashion, trying to make the equation. You want to presume somehow or other that you are already established in the Ultimate Condition. One of the games of the traditions, in fact, is to suggest that an equation is to be made between ordinary awareness and That Which is Absolute, even a logical equation. Having made that logical equation, then you affirm that it is so.

When you feel some energy in your body, you know—because I have told you—that it is a rather gross manifestation of the Energy of which everything is the modification. You want to think that the energy you are feeling is God, or God-Realization, even. Likewise, then, since your own awareness has the characteristic of consciousness, and since the Divine is Consciousness Itself, you want to feel or presume somehow that they are the same.

One of the functions of intelligence—the function, in fact, that is principally addressed in the traditions—is the function of discrimination, and, in particular, discrimination between the Real and the unreal, or, to put it another way, the Unconditional and the conditional, or the Divine and the human. Part of the function of intelligence, then, is to be able to make that distinction. The process of sadhana enables you to go beyond this apparent distinction, ultimately, but it is not merely a process of logic or conception.

I have pointed out to you that, yes, you are centrally functioning as awareness relative to whatever arises and everything else is objective to you, but you cannot find your awareness as an object. It is the central position of ordinary human living. Therefore, it is also the central position in which you do sadhana, not as detached awareness but as functional awareness, functioning through intelligence relative to what arises.

I also pointed out to you that another characteristic of this ordinary awareness is that it feels itself to be separate, individuated, personal. Just as you regard your body to be personal and a limitation and different from other bodies, so also this functional awareness feels itself to be different from other awarenesses, other consciousnesses, other beings. If that is so, how can it be equated with the Divine Self-Consciousness? The energy you feel in your body is a manifestation of the Ultimate Energy of Which everything is the modification. Yet to think that feeling bodily energy is the same as Realizing the Ultimate Energy is an illusion, an indiscriminate point of view. A non-discriminating point of view would make such an equation.

To use this man as an example again, if we just took his body and converted it into its equivalent energy, according to the formula $E=mc^2$, it would be a vast force. Since we have not done that in fact, he feels some five watts or so circulating through his body and those five watts are a modification of the Ultimate Energy. If the energy is so great when one body is converted into its equivalent energy, imagine what the entire display of the conditional cosmos would be if it were converted into its energy equivalent!

Just so, if your individuated conscious awareness were located and dissolved in that Very Consciousness Which is All and Only, there would be a like difference between your consciousness and That Consciousness Itself as there is between your felt energy and the All-Energy. Becoming sensitive to your own awareness, or to your own energy, is not the equivalent of God-Realization. To make an equation between your own energy and the Divine Shakti, or Inherent Self-Radiance, and between your own individuated consciousness and the Divine Consciousness is absurd.

You are toying with this idea, however. You want to be able to notice and identify with some principle that is your own, associated with your own existence, and feel or believe or presume that it is the Absolute. It is not the Absolute. It is just you, as a conditionally manifested, and very much conditioned, apparent personality.

When you observe any of the ordinary characteristics of the body-mind—a physical sensation, an emotional reaction—you are observing it, but also, at the same time, in some curious sense, you are identified with it. The Witness is not identified with what arises, not identified with any component of what arises. The observer, however, is. The functional, human observer does feel identified with what arises. You are suggesting you want to practice something about being aware that detaches you from what arises. You want now to suggest to yourself, emphasize the point of view somehow, that you are not identical to what arises. That is not what I have been talking about. That is what you have been talking about. You want to suggest some ultimate practice, whereas you are simply functioning, in one fashion or another, as the intelligent observer of what arises, and you are identified with what arises in that case.

The functional observer is awareness, and mind-forms, emotions, bodily sensations that arise are objects to it, but they are also itself, in some curious manner. You feel identified with these things that are arising. Therefore, this is the context of your practice, not identified with the observer, or awareness, and dissociated from or prior to conditions, but identified with conditions in the context of conditions. This is the matter we have been addressing here—this ordinary, human functioning, analyzed according to its various parts, from its central position to all of its periphery. Somehow or other, however, you want the discussion to turn to your being detached from conditions and being awareness apart. You are not awareness apart. You are functional awareness, awareness coincident with what arises, separate awareness, awareness that is identifying itself, or at least feeling itself to be in necessary association, with things arising. The awareness that you are functionally is not dissociated from conditions, is not apart from conditions, is not prior to conditions. It is functional awareness, separate awareness, ego-consciousness. It must submit, surrender, not presume itself to be something other than it is in order to avoid surrender.

You think you are the Divine. No. You are just you, "locally" (so-called) in your present appearance. You are not awareness apart from what arises. You are awareness coincident with what arises. Isn't this how you function from moment to moment? Your body, your reactions, your trouble, your difficulty, your suffering—your own awareness is chatting this, feeling troubled by these things arising, because they are not merely objective to you in the sense that you are totally dissociated from them. They are something you identify with. Your awareness is qualified by these things arising.

DEVOTEE: Yes, but I had assumed, Sri Gurudev, that the practice of awareness was to help release attachment to those things, identification with those things.

SRI DA AVABHASA: You must be able to clearly observe what is arising and intelligently relate to what is arising, in the midst of a life responsive to Me, a life of practice of Ishta-Guru-Bhakti Yoga and surrender of separate and separative self. Yes, you must relate to these objective matters that are arising—thoughts, emotional reactivity, bodily sensations, the relations of the body, the whole combination of all of that—yes, you must observe it, but not by detaching yourself from it or presuming that you have nothing to do with it. Such detachment is a conceptual effort founded in anxiety, founded in wishing you could somehow or other not be troubled by this arising.

You imagine, then, that by just identifying with awareness, as if it has nothing to do with objects, you will be free, whereas in fact you are not simply observing objects. You are a complex subjective-objective being, observing its own trouble and responding to Me. The practice I have Given you is not an exercise of detachment, or identifying with awareness and separating from objects. Rather, it is a matter of intelligently observing objects, and, in your response to Me, being intelligent in your dealing with them. You want to enforce some logical notion that because you are awareness and these things arise objectively, maybe that means you do not have anything to do with them, and, therefore, need not do anything about them, can even imagine yourself out of suffering them.

Narcissus imagines himself to be so distinct from the image in the pond that he thinks it is somebody else. He must wake up to the fact that it is himself. You must be similarly clear in the intelligent exercise of awareness. The game you are suggesting, however, is just another one of the illusions of egoity, just another presumption of separateness, or, in other words, a dramatization of the self-contraction itself. The separate awareness does not exist independent of conditions. Its very presumption of separateness is a sign of its identification with conditions. Therefore, in the context of feeling and being identified with conditions and troubled by them, you must do the sadhana, the Yoga, of the submission of all these factors of your life.

Why must you be responsible for what arises if, in your view, you are the detached awareness, prior to objects? If you are the detached awareness, then what does all this arising have to do with you? Somebody else must be doing it. That is what you want to presume—that it is not you, and, therefore, you are not doing it, and, therefore, you do not have to do anything about it. In other words, you are going about your daily life while thinking yourself to be just awareness and everything to be objective to it, and feeling you can, therefore, just relax from your association with everything.

This notion was giving you great relief, you said a few days ago—or "Narcissus" said. You have been playing a trick with this notion of awareness and wanting to make it your practice. At the same time, you have been Given the imperatives to practice otherwise, and you were doing that, too. But you were carrying on this alternative practice of your own invention, of being awareness and seeing everything as just an object to it, and, therefore, not awareness—and you are just awareness, and so you are able to relax your usual anxiety and double-bind relative to the difficulties that arise.

You are doing two practices, this one of your own invention and the other somehow generally associated with My Instruction. The one from which you said you were getting the experience of relief was the one of your own invention—of identifying with awareness, seeing everything as an object to it, and feeling relieved by that presumption.

DEVOTEE: So, Beloved, how do I intelligently or rightly use the understanding that this awareness is not the lower body-mind?

SRI DA AVABHASA: It is aware of the lower body-mind but also identified with it at the same time. Its central functioning position is awareness of what is arising. That does not mean it is not what is arising, or not in a disposition of identification with it. It is.

DEVOTEE: I am making the assumption that my practice is to observe these things that come up but not to give them attention, to surrender attention to You.

SRI DA AVABHASA: Through those things, submitting them to Me, since you are identified with them—but while having clarity about them, based on your response to Me and your receiving My Instruction, observing them really and intelligently. Then you are obliged to turn them into Yoga rather than simply to indulge in the display of what is arising.

You were suggesting an alternative practice, however, which is to identify with awareness as purely subjective, and to see that everything objective is not you and, therefore, you should relax even from your association with what arises. Because awareness feels individuated, feels separate, is troubled by what is arising, you want to play this trick of mind in order to immunize yourself, as if your awareness is Absolute, whereas it is not. It presumes itself to be separate, individual. It is so much identified with what arises that it is troubled by it and wants to somehow think itself out of it and feel detached. Detachment, then, is your solution. It is your habit, isn't it?

DEVOTEE: Yes, that is my tendency, Lord.

SRI DA AVABHASA: That is how you want to deal with life—detach yourself, get immune, avoid. It is called "avoiding relationship" in My language, "Narcissus". It can be exercised even by awareness itself, or by awareness associated with some coming to a presumed intelligent conclusion, thinking itself out, by your exercising yourself mentally, detaching yourself, being "solid", or, although you are emotionally alive, by cutting off emotion, not getting involved, staying away, not feeling, or, in bodily life, by being rather inert, rather dissociated, not given over to life bodily. Your method of egoity is detachment, dissociation, self-immunization.

You thought that I was talking about doing just that and, therefore, justifying just that to you as a form of practice. No, that is what I am criticizing, that is what I am Calling you to be aware of, that is what I am Calling you to relate to intelligently and become responsible for, that sadhana, truly done, so that the entire egoic vehicle is purified, balanced, enlivened, turned to Me utterly, fastened to Me, receiving My Grace, transformed in the process, so that the tacit Realization of the Witness-Position Awakens, all that sadhana done, all that Sign accomplished in the body-mind and evident there. It is not merely an intelligent conclusion but a Stand, made possible by Grace, in which you do not merely live detached but you exercise the Yoga of submission to That Which Is the Witness—not the witnessing, not the detachment, but That Which Is the Witness—and, by Grace, you are moved beyond the knot in the right side of the heart, the knot of the presumption of separate consciousness, and you enter into the Current of the Sphere of Being that is truly Divine, Beyond separate self. That is the "Perfect Practice".

That is not your practice at this time. You are not identified with the Witness-Position, so that you can enter into Its Domain. You are identified with your own separate awareness, your own separate presumptions of intelligence, your own mind, emotions, body, energies, natural circumstance, relations. You are trying to dissociate yourself from all that, so that you need not do the Yoga, need not make this sacrifice, this devotional submission, but you can just feel detached from it.

There is nothing detached about Ishta-Guru-Bhakti Yoga. It is profoundly related, profoundly submitted, profoundly attached, profoundly dealing with the contents of the individual body-mind, therefore submitting and going beyond this life-solution you have tended to try to make, going beyond detachment, whereas you are always trying to reaffirm it.

You must respond to Me, "consider" and live by My Instruction, and convert this body-mind into a Yoga of surrender to Me. That is your business—not detachment, not trying to find some trick of mind that suggests you need not do that work. You are puzzled because you want to try to do detachment instead of responding to Me and truly engaging this "consideration".

Basically, you do not want to practice Guru-devotion, and you do not want to practice self-discipline. You want to revolve in your own incident of self-pleasure, as much as you can indulge it, for as long as you can, and avoid your real situation of being subordinate to the Divine Person, requiring the Grace of the Realizer, and needing to live the life of practiced devotion in order to Realize, by Grace. You want to thrive on your own illusions of separateness. You want to practice "Narcissus" in My

Company, keep dwelling on the pond, and generate unintelligent conclusions about reality, conclusions without Revelation, and without real self-understanding, as well.

Your position, individuated in the midst of this portion of the universal sign, is subordinate to the Divine. And how did we begin this most recent series of discussions? By My asking you again, having already asked you many times before, What about God? What does God have to do with you? What do you understand about God? What is your conclusion about reality? Yet still there is not much talk from you about it, because what you are fastening onto as reality, what you are holding onto, is your own separate person and the illusions you generate to console yourself. From your point of view, God is in doubt, Ultimate Reality is in doubt—or, if not in doubt, somehow presumed to be <u>you</u>, even, you in your self-sufficiency, divorced from the Ultimate, wandering in your egoic "self-possession" and consolations. You want to make that sufficient and absolute. You want to tell yourself it is unnecessary to submit to the Divine, unnecessary to come to any conclusion about the reality of the Divine, the reality of Reality. You are struggling with the principal factors that sadhana requires—devotional self-submission and self-discipline, functioning as one subordinate to God, separate by its own act and requiring Grace.

There are many philosophical games in the Great Tradition, including the kind of false logic we have been discussing, in fact. Even the tradition of Advaita Vedanta is associated with this kind of thinking. You must understand that the tradition of Advaita Vedanta is not merely a philosophical or academic tradition. It is associated with a tradition of real practice, with real preliminaries even to listening to ultimate statements, or mahavakyas, like "Tat tvam Asi"—"You are That"—which seem like intelligent, logical exercises that any human being can undertake.

Not so. That philosophical language is associated with a tradition of great sadhana, and it is simply an attempt to make philosophical statements that correspond to Samadhi. These statements are to be made to those who are prepared for Samadhi, not merely egos identified with the ordinary life, who want to think greatly of themselves and immunize themselves. The statement "Thou art That" is a verbal expression that is associated with the great event of passing into Most Ultimate Samadhi.

Even simple communications about God, the popular notions about God, like God as the Creator of everything—it is just not true. The idea of the Creator-God is a popular religious idea that is used to enforce various kinds of beliefs associated with social religiosity. Beyond such social religiosity, however, the presumption that "God is Creator, God is making everything, God is doing everything" is like the statement "Tat tvam Asi"—

"Thou art That". Truly, it is a verbal expression of Samadhi. Only in the Samadhi of Divine Self-Realization can it be said that God is the Creator of everything, because only in that position is there Only One, and there are no others to create anything. Therefore, in the ecstatic disposition, the Most Ultimate Samadhi of Divine Self-Realization, it can be said, paradoxically, that God is Creating everything. But from the point of view of the ego, the separate consciousness identified with the body-mind and the natural world, it is not true. From that point of view, you are doing all kinds of things, and others are doing all kinds of things, all kinds of entities, powers, energies are all doing things, making things happen.

The right point of view, then, the right expression of the point of view of the beginner, previous to Most Ultimate Samadhi, previous to Divine Self-Realization, is that God is doing none of this. You are separate, separated from God. God must yet be Realized, you must submit yourself, you are subordinate to That One. You must become accountable for your own actions. You must change your act and not merely presume that God is making everything or doing everything.

In fact, the "Creator-God" notion is a bastardization of the ecstatic Communications of Realizers, and not a mode of belief appropriate for ordinary people. From the "Point of View" of Most Ultimate Realization, there is Only One. Therefore, paradoxically, the Divine is Making everything, but not from the point of view of being the separate person. From that point of view, all kinds of beings, including yourself, are making everything, changing everything, responsible for everything. The Divine is Prior to All and all and the One to be Realized, the One to be submitted to. Therefore, the common religious notion of God as the Creator is just as esoteric a communication as "Tat tvam Asi"—"Thou art That". Apart from Samadhi, apart from Realization, it is not true. Thou art not That, apart from Samadhi. When received by someone who is not in the Samadhi of Divine Self-Realization, when received by the ego, the statement "Thou art That" becomes a false idea, a heresy, and it is not true.

Many things are true from the "Point of View" of Most Ultimate Samadhi, or Divine Self-Realization, that are not at all true from the point of view of the ego. The Great Tradition is full of great statements, even communicated in philosophical terms and passed on to the most ordinary of people. In the context of popularized philosophy, those great statements are not true. They are true only from the "Point of View" of Most Ultimate Realization.

What is really true previous to Realization is what you must "consider", what you must understand in My Company, what must become the basis for real practice, right sadhana. In that same tradition of Advaita Vedanta, there is a very interesting summary statement, associated with Shankara, of devotion to the Divine. "From the point of view of the body, I am Your servant. From the point of view of the mind, I am a part of You, a fraction within You. From the point of view of the Self, truly, I am You."

Any statement of equation with the Divine is authentic only from the "Point of View" of Ultimate Realization. Yet, identified with the body, or, even more advanced, identified with the mind, subtly, as Yogis are, in the fourth and fifth stages of life—from the point of view of such identification, the great statements are not true, the statement "I am You", or, said another way, "Thou art That", is not true. Identified with the body, you are the servant of God, subordinate to the Divine. From the point of view of the mind, you are not the Divine. You are a part of the Great Unity, seeking Union with the Great Unity, or That Which is One. Therefore, previous to Ultimate Realization, the philosophy, the philosophical point of view, the presumption, must acknowledge the position you are in, acknowledge what you are identified with.

You are a servant, seeking Union, or doing the sadhana that can, by Grace, become absolute Identification with the Divine, Ultimately. You are not That. You are <u>you</u>, "Narcissus", egoically "self-possessed", independent. To call yourself "God" is obnoxious, the ultimate stupidity. Even the statement "God is the Creator", said from that point of view, is a false statement. Do you want to make God responsible for this mayhem for which you and all kinds of apparent entities and motions and powers are actually responsible? When there is no separate self, no separate principle, then you may say "God is the Creator"—but it is an ecstatic statement, you see, meaning there is Only One and you cannot find a separate thing in It.

Even the functional awareness, naturally active, is not one with the Divine. It presumes itself to be separate and in necessary conjunction with conditions arising. [to the woman who has been speaking] Therefore, it is not you, detached. It is the servant, and must live as such, accept its subordinate position, and surrender and live by Grace. Then you will not be so damned anxious!

DEVOTEE: Thank You, Beloved. I can see that I made the presumption that awareness is greater than it is.

SRI DA AVABHASA: It is! Just as the body is the Divine Shakti—but not as you are experiencing it and living it. Realize the Truth of that equation in Samadhi by doing real sadhana and equipping yourself to receive the Grace that will make it so.

God is the Self of all, the Energy of Which everything is a modification. Fine, yes, that is so, but it is not your Realization. You can submit to the One Who Is That by being the servant of That One, by surrendering yourself, by practicing the Yoga of devotion to That One. Presume That One Is That, not thou! That One.

Your tendency to be detached is not just some nice thing to confess. Another way of describing what you are doing is that it is sin—that which you are doing which separates you from the Divine, your refusal to surrender to the Divine, to accept the position of being a mere subordinate to the Great One. Rather than doing that, you want to make much of yourself. To reach the point of accepting your subordinate position, your life as a servant, submitted to the Great One, is the beginning of authentic life, true manliness, male or female. All you egalitarians here want to be independent monads, identical to the Absolute. No subordination, no surrender, no service. You are just here being palsy-walsy with God, saying you are the same.

Or you are having nothing to do with God. These days, people feel they must not even mention the words "God, Truth, Reality, the Ultimate". If you are educated, you are not supposed to mention God. You people are building an entire civilization on the denial of God, the denial of your role of service, your subordination to the Divine. Everybody is just oinking out their independent will and inclination to be consoled and self-glorified, worshipped even. The truth of the matter is that your appearing here, being self-conscious, is arising in Infinite Power and Force of Being. That is Consciousness Itself, not you.

Turn this man here bodily into the equivalent energy, and it is an immense force, a hydrogen bomb, that could blow up the whole place. Concentrated in him, however, it is a five-watt fool. Convert all of this mass that is appearing as the entire cosmos into its equivalent energy—That is Shakti, not your poor wattage and temporary prettiness! You are subordinate to That Shakti. The entire cosmos is subordinate to That. And you want to doubt Its existence? You want to doubt that there is such an immense Power? It is inherently obvious.

This should be your conclusion about reality. It is self-evident, if you would stop just gathering your attention around your self-consoling anxiety.

You are hardly willing to bend a leg and bow your head, whereas that is your function, that is your situation, to be always bowed and serving instead of spending your life talking about yourself and acting like an independent absolute, or imagining you are one. You are absolutely dependent on the One Who is the Source of this horror you have made. Being separated from God, you have every right to be anxious and fearful! You are making your own destiny instead of submitting to the One Who Is and being purified and having a better, or even Most Ultimate, destiny made by Grace. If you simply understood your position and functioned on that basis, everything would be clarified.

There at the pond you are all heroes, but you all are alive in the servants' quarters here. That is your real position. Yet you want to make much of yourselves, as if you are all kings. It is the kind of chat that goes on in the servants' quarters, in the bunkhouse at the end of the work day. Everybody is a hero, everybody is macho man, big woman, big deal, talking grandly about themselves, making grand gestures with their arms, making much of themselves in everybody's face, being a pain in the ass, everybody tougher than a nail, needing nothing, no one, insensitive, talking without feeling, just self-glorifying talk.

You feel afraid and anxious because you are not submitting yourself to the One on Whom you depend. You are just stuck with yourself. When you understand your situation, the position you are in, and act on that basis, Joy comes into your life, the Joy of Godwardness. And, yes, there is the "Perfect Practice", Ultimate Realization. Yes, there is. But not for you now. It is to be Realized, by Grace, by your doing the sadhana on the basis of your real situation, and being very real about it all the time.

Surrender the Faculties of the Body-Mind to Me

December 20, 1993

SRI DA AVABHASA: What is the limitation on your practice of Ishta-Guru-Bhakti Yoga?

DEVOTEE: When the difficult moments arise, I might not have the strength to practice.

SRI DA AVABHASA: Why is it difficult to give Me your attention? Does this require an effort?

DEVOTEE: I could explain it by saying I habitually hold on to the things that I am not willing to release, such as a difficulty in bringing bodily energy to service because I feel exhausted.

SRI DA AVABHASA: What does that have to do with devotional Communion with Me? You seem to be confusing functional matters with the Yoga of devotion to Me. You seem to be meditating on physical tiredness and a sense of failure. What does all that have to do with devotional Communion with Me? It is just you struggling with your functional life and becoming emotionally reactive about it. What does that have to do with the Yoga of Divine Communion? You seem to be saying that letting your attention wander and then struggling with yourself—"cutting through it"—is somehow Ishta-Guru-Bhakti Yoga.

DEVOTEE: Part of the Yoga, yes.

SRI DA AVABHASA: It is not! You seem to think that the Yoga is about self-attention, meditating on this or that arising in yourself and trying to deal with it. When content arises in body, emotion, or mind, you become involved in it, perhaps react to it, struggle to make it go away by doing something in opposition to it. While struggling with this content in yourself, you may sometimes make some sort of gesture toward Me. You Remember Me, you feel toward Me, or you do whatever you do in the midst of the struggle. In the meantime, however, fundamentally, you are giving all of your attention and mind, and, therefore, emotion and bodily energy also, to the contents of the body-mind-self, and making only a minimal gesture toward Me, which you call "Yoga".

The devotional Yoga of Ishta-Guru-Bhakti is not about struggling with the contents of the body-mind. The practice I have described to you is self-surrender and self-forgetting in devotion to Me.

You are making Rudi's error, and dramatizing the limit that I observed in Rudi's company. I tried to practice according to Rudi's instruction about practical life and the Yoga He proposed in the midst of life-struggles. He was always talking about surrender, surrender and opening, stretching oneself open, surrendering all the stresses that are arising, all the difficulties, achieving a state of surrender by struggling to relax and open and go beyond the sensations of stress and the difficulties.

Such effort is not true Yoga. It is the conditional self's struggling with its own content. The secret of the Way of the Heart, the secret of the Way that I have Given you, the secret of this Yoga of Ishta-Guru-Bhakti, is not to struggle with the content that is arising in the body-mind but to turn to Me.

If some content arises in the mind, then instead of trying to think your way through it, and struggle with it, and get emotional about it, and concentrate your entire life in it, you should direct the function of mind to Me. Do not try to release the content of the mind in order to get to Me. Surrender the function of mind itself to Me.

The root of mind is attention, not the stuff that is arising in the mind but attention. The epitome of the mind, the root of mind, the core of mind, the central function of mind, is attention. Therefore, when things arise in mind, instead of struggling with them, trying to get rid of them, trying to surrender them, trying to beef your way through them, you simply give Me your attention, or the core of your mind. You do not try to get rid of the content, or try to surrender the content to Me, or try to surrender the content in order to get to Me. You just surrender attention itself to Me. Give Me your attention.

No effort is required. You need not struggle with the mind-forms. In your surrender to Me, you disregard what is arising in mind. You surrender attention to Me, give Me your attention, and forget about mind. You do not try to make something happen in the mind, nor do you try to surrender the mind by surrendering its content. You surrender the <u>function</u> of mind by giving Me your attention.

When something arises emotionally, a reactive emotion of one kind or another, emotional concern, emotion in relation to anything conditional, instead of trying to open and relax and release the reactive emotion to get to Me or struggling with yourself for whatever reason, you direct the function of emotion to Me. The core of the function of emotion is simply feeling. You feel to Me. You give Me your feeling-attention, then. You direct attention, or the root of mind, and feeling, or the root of emotion, to Me.

Likewise, you conform the body to Me in the midst of whatever is arising physically. You direct yourself bodily to Me. Whatever functions you are performing in any moment of functional activity, you give Me your feeling-attention and you direct the body to serving Me, you direct it to be the servant instead of the object of your concern.

Instead of struggling with any of the contents of the body-mind, no matter what is arising in the moment, you direct its functions—not its contents but its functions—to Me, thereby collecting the whole body-mind as feeling-attention to Me.

This is the Yoga, or the moment to moment practice, and there are technical requirements for it. It is not the yielding of the functions of the body-mind to the idea that I am your Spiritual Master or your Ishta-Guru or your Heart-Master—there is nothing vague about this practice. You direct your feeling-attention to Me, to this bodily (human) Form. In fact, a fundamental part of the technical practice of this devotional Yoga is to recollect My bodily (human) Form. In the Communion Hall and in various other sacred places of the Way of the Heart, My Murti-Form is displayed for this purpose. On the mala you wear, you carry a photograph of Me so that you can glance at Me. You can recollect My bodily (human) Form in mind. You can practice Name-Invocation of Me. You can assist the practice of Ishta-Guru-Bhakti Yoga through self-Enquiry, or whatever the form of the "conscious process" you have chosen to engage.

Fundamentally, however, the Yoga is the directing of the body-mind to Me and not struggling with its contents and only trying to direct them to Me, or trying to get rid of them in an effort of surrender toward Me. Rather, yield the functions of the body-mind to Me at their root. Yield their leading characteristic.

Give Me your attention, give Me your feeling, give yourself over to Me, and disregard the contents. Do not keep checking back on them to see if they are changing! In your real practice of this Yoga, you forget them. You do not use them. You do not build upon them. You make them obsolete by not using them. In this manner, the Yoga purifies you by making the contents of the body-mind obsolete through non-use. The process is not an effort on your part to do something to the contents of the body-mind or to try not to use them. It is simply your turning to Me, turning your feeling-attention to Me, turning yourself altogether to Me, Contemplatively. That is the Yoga.

[to the man] What you have just described is quite the opposite. You have described a process of reading the contents of the body-mind and struggling with them, trying to do something with them, trying to force yourself to function, trying to force yourself to feel beyond a limitation of some kind, relax some limitation, let go of some limitation. However, you were not even successfully doing that. You were becoming emotionally reactive, because you were unable to do something about the content—your tiredness, or whatever the content might be in the moment—and then becoming mentally agitated, trying to think your way through the content, trying to think your way out of it.

That is not the Yoga. That is ordinary life. That is egoity. That is the self-contraction being dramatized, not made obsolete by Yoga but reinforced by non-Yoga. You simply intensify the problem by functioning in that fashion.

So—you are doing something like Rudi's work, trying to tear your guts out! That is one of the expressions He used to use. "Tear your guts out. Surrender! Open! Surrender it, relax it, and keep on ploughing through!" It is a very stressful, agitated intention, much like the ordinary technique of life that people ordinarily do and that Rudi magnified into a description that sounded like Yoga. Yet it is not effective in the sense that it truly goes beyond the limitations and enters into Divine Communion.

ANOTHER DEVOTEE: Sri Gurudev, this afternoon I started to feel the dilemma that usually arises for me, a form of doubt. I stayed in feeling-Contemplation of You in that moment . . .

SRI DA AVABHASA: If you had been in feeling-Contemplation of Me in the previous moment, you would not have had the thought that became the problem! The Yoga of the Way of the Heart is to Remember Me constantly, to do the Yoga constantly. Struggling with the body-mind is not the Yoga.

You must receive what you have been Given by Me. You must do the Yoga, because you have responded to Me. You are justifying your own habit and tendency and wanting to call it "devotion". There may be an aspect of your practice of the Way of the Heart that has something to do with Me—obviously you are giving Me some attention—but that does not mean you are doing this Yoga. Whatever your error, you must deal with it and not reinvent the Way of the Heart along the lines of your egoity.

The Way of the Heart is to be lived, for the sake of Most Perfectly self-transcending God-Realization, consistently and for real, with its appropriate technicalities engaged, artfully, moment by moment. The Way of the Heart is just that which I have Given you to practice, and not something else that is based on your own self-involvement. It is not enough to feel good about some preoccupation just because there is some reference to Me. That is not the Yoga, and it is not God-Realizing.

The Realizer Appears, you respond, you take His Instruction, you do the Yoga, you live the life with no bargaining, no reinventing of the Way of the Heart. If there is, then you are self-"guruing".

The Way of the Heart is not merely a matter of being with Me, being in association with Me, being around Me. It is the real practice, the real Yoga, of self-surrendering, self-forgetting, self-transcending Communion with Me, consistently done. This true Yoga is effective relative to egoity. This is the measure, then, of your life. It is the Yoga of Communion with Me if it is ego-transcending. If it is not, it is not!—no matter how much you enjoy being around Me.

Is reading the signs in the body-mind the Yoga I have Given you?

DEVOTEE: No, it is not.

SRI DA AVABHASA: You say that it is not, but when you are asked about your practice this is how you describe it. The Yoga is devotional Communion with Me, just that—directing all the faculties of the body-mind to Me instead of addressing or struggling with the contents that arise, by conditioning, in the body-mind. Of course, there is the natural observation here and there of signs of the body-mind in any activity. They are simply to be noticed and not dwelt upon. They are to be noticed and then confessed among others who can reflect to you something about your signs. Then use My Instruction, come to a conclusion about what discipline you should introduce into your living, and get on with it some more.

Why take your attention away from Me to be involved in the very thing that is your problem? The Yoga of the Divine Life has nothing to do with egoic "self-possession" and self-involvement. It is only and entirely about submitting yourself and all your functions to the Realizer, to the Divine Revealed. The Way of the Heart is founded on the devotional response to Me. The fundamental principle of the Way of the Heart is turning from separate self to Me—not in some vague, casual, little bit of emotional gesture. The whole body-mind follows. The whole body-mind is given over because of this devotional response to Me.

Think of Ramana Maharshi when He was seventeen years old. Suddenly He was totally possessed by fear of death when He was alone in His room. He examined all this and spontaneously awakened to the Freedom of the Self-Position. He did not then get up and say, "Well, I am not very old. I am just a kid, and I have not had much experience yet. Besides, one never knows what might come up tomorrow. I think I am just going to have to take this Realization with a grain of salt." No. From that moment, He based His life entirely on that principle of Realization.

My devotees are Called to do the same, to respond to Me and to base their lives on that response from then on, to base their lives on doing the Yoga of devotion to Me, and not merely sometimes or in some circumstances but all the time. I have Instructed you relative to every kind of circumstance, every kind of functional, relational, and practical position, every kind of arising. I have Taught you the right practice that applies to all circumstances. I do not think I have missed even a single one in My address to you. If I have, you can mention it and I will address it.

The fundamental matter is your devotion to Me—and your relinquishment of self-attention on that basis. No matter what is arising—in your life-circumstance, in the body, in emotion, in mind—no matter what, give Me your attention instead. It is just as simple as that—your whole attention. Instead of letting attention wander in the mind, put your attention on Me. Instead of letting attention wander into all your reactive emotions, give your attention to Me emotionally—in other words, relate to Me with feeling, give yourself to Me with feeling, feel Me, do more than just notice Me. No matter what is arising in your life, attend to Me. No matter what you are doing, do not do it for your own sake. Do it for Me. Assume the position of the servant for real, but do not do your service merely to do good works around Me. To do good works is fine, but the point of your service to Me is that you function in such a manner that you are always in Communion with Me, not self-focused but focused on Me—very specifically focused on Me.

The Yoga is to give your attention to Me in this bodily (human) Form. It is to recollect My bodily (human) Form. It is to find Me with your heart. You must turn to Me with your heart, not go down inside your heart and feel this, that, or the other thing. Yes, I <u>am</u> in your heart, but that Reality is to be Realized by you in the advanced stages of life in the Way of the Heart. Even practitioners in the advanced stages of life do not forget Me in My bodily Manifestation. The heart must find Me. The heart must be directed to Me. I am not inside, and no amount of focusing on the Unity of Existence is the same as meditating on Me.

There is only one way to practice this devotional Communion with Me, as a general practice. It is to recollect My bodily (human) Form, to give Me your feeling-attention. Use the form of the "conscious process" you have chosen—Name-Invocation of Me or self-Enquiry or any of the other forms I have Given for your level of practice. Whatever the technical form of your practice of the Way of the Heart, it is a matter of this turning of yourself to Me and forgetting yourself, not turning back on yourself to see if anything is changing, taking a quick look to see, "Did it change? Did it move? Am I healed? Do I feel comfortable? Am I relaxed? Give me another dose—do I feel any better yet? Okay, try it again. Is that ache gone? Am I not angry anymore?"

No. It is constant yielding to Me, constant attention to Me, not efforting relative to the contents but forgetting them, disregarding whether they are changing or not. They will inevitably change and pass in any case. Do not give these contents your attention. Give Me your attention, whole bodily, with feeling.

Then, by your not using the contents that are arising, they will fall away. This is how the things that are arising become obsolete. If you use them, if you direct attention to them in any way, they are reinforced. The only way whereby they are released is by your turning from them to Me. By your doing that consistently, the various egoic conditionings of the body-mind are purified, they fall away, they become weaker. There is always still more and more of that purifying process. It is not the point in any case. It is just a fact—which you can observe if you practice rightly in My Company—but it is not the point.

The point is that you enter into Divine Communion in every moment, that you are moved utterly beyond egoic "self-possession" and enjoy the destiny of Divine Self-Realization. That is the entire point, not life-improvement, which is strictly secondary. Of course, you want to bargain with Me, make a brief gesture to Me, and get the change right away. Ordinary praying religionists also want to spend a few minutes in prayer and then experience the changes. When you experience a moment of attention to God, right away you want to feel better, you want everything to be set right, you want all your karmas to be purified, you want utopia. Therefore, you are always checking yourself out in the midst of your so-called "practice" of devotion to Me, always re-remembering yourself, as if you do not know the purpose of the Way of the Heart and do not know Me.

The purpose of the Way of the Heart is to enter into My Sphere and leave yours!

If in the midst of life-events some emotional reaction comes up, instead of identifying with it, puzzling over it, getting involved in it, meditating on it, telling everybody else about it, and dramatizing it, you give Me your attention with feeling and disregard it. Instead of being hyperactive or wandering in your activities and doing all kinds of things at random on the basis of your ego-designs, you embrace the discipline of right life, always in Communion with Me. Whatever is not aligned to that discipline you just do not do anymore. You accept the discipline of relinquishing it or of transforming it if need be. One who responds to Me truly with devotion does just that, then. Based on that response to Me, that Communion with Me, you take My Instruction and you change your life.

ANOTHER DEVOTEE: Beloved Gurudev, today I became involved in my own content and complexity, to the point that I literally could not, it seemed in that moment, be released into that free space that You Grant so Gracefully.

SRI DA AVABHASA: You became self-meditative, in other words?

DEVOTEE: Yes. Yet even in the midst of it, I continued to feel into it, because I knew . . .

SRI DA AVABHASA: Into what?

DEVOTEE: Into what was arising.

SRI DA AVABHASA: Exactly. That is not Ishta-Guru-Bhakti Yoga. Instead of feeling into what is arising, you are supposed to give Me your whole attention, feeling to Me. Give Me your attention, make the body My servant, do not dwell on the contents arising, but always be entering into this attentive feeling-Communion with Me, forgetting yourself. That is the exercise to be done all day long, day and night, at all times. If you fail to do it, then you remember yourself again, become egoically "self-possessed" and self-involved again, and start doing another practice that you manufacture on your own, in your egoic "self-possession"—the practice of observing the contents.

The observation of contents will occur in any case, in various moments, but that observation must occur in the midst of moment to moment submission to Me, the practice of Communion with Me. Then if something is observed, fine, you take it into account. If it requires some change of life, some discipline, do it. Confess it to your friends. Be held accountable. It is just that simple.

The day that unfolds after you have gone to the Communion Hall in the early morning is not a vacation until nightfall when you go to the Communion Hall again. No. All the hours between the times when you go to the Communion Hall are the times of this same Yoga. You must do it persistently and artfully. Do not allow yourself the vacation of wandering into the content of the conditioned body-mind. The only thing it is going to show you is its conditioning, based on your egoic "self-possession" and denial of God. Your business is this Yoga, in the midst of your practice of it noticing this and that in order to apply a discipline of right life that is in conformity to Me, and in greater conformity to Me always.

Ishta-Guru-Bhakti is never a matter of meditating on those contents, never. Whenever you are doing that, you are self-"guruing", self-meditative, dissociated from Me, your attention collapsed on yourself, analyzing yourself, trying to figure your way out of it. Yet all the while, in all those moments, it was a simplicity: Give Me your attention with feeling. Surrender to Me. Serve Me. That is the Yoga to be engaged all the while, without lapses.

You think that self-understanding is about self-meditation and egoic "self-possession". No. It is about response to Me, about doing this Yoga, and, in appropriate moments, noticing that this or that requires further discipline or should just be forgotten in Communion with Me. In moments you dramatize in one way or another, and I address you and talk to you about it. But that is not the Yoga. If you get the point in that moment, good—the Yoga, the submission, giving Me your feeling-attention, is what you must do.

DEVOTEE: Forgetting separate self.

SRI DA AVABHASA: Yes. That is the whole point, not just to remember My aphorisms, the Words I said here and there. They can be recounted again the next time you read My Heart-Word. Fine, that is useful study. Study is another discipline I Give you. Even so, fundamentally your practice is <u>just this Yoga</u>, done all the while, persistently done, not struggling with egoic self but forgetting it, giving Me your attention and forgetting, not lapsing again and again, dropping your attention back on yourself to see if any change has happened yet. There should be no concern for it, because you are not here to perfect yourself. You are here to enter into My Sphere.

There are times to be confessed, to have yourself addressed, to agree to a discipline which is then written down and for which you are held accountable. Those times are specific here-and-there hours in which to do that. The rest of the time, do not talk about yourself. Talk about Me. Practice praise. Do not be occupied with one another's content. As a discipline, do what you must do about your tendency to do that for the sake of applying greater discipline. Do not give it much time.

DEVOTEE: Sri Gurudev, it seems that there are variations in the fullness of reception of You in the midst of practice of the Yoga.

SRI DA AVABHASA: In your practice of the basic Yoga, you are not here to receive Me. You are here to surrender to Me, not to check out your body-mind to see how much you are getting, to see how much of you is changed.

DEVOTEE: It seems that it is always just a matter of being carried by surrender to You.

SRI DA AVABHASA: It is not a matter of being carried by it. It is a matter of being entered into it.

DEVOTEE: In some moments more surrender seems to be required.

SRI DA AVABHASA: No. That is not true. The contents of the body-mind have nothing to do with the Yoga. Giving Me your feeling-attention is not an effort. It is not that sometimes there is something more to surrender than at other times. You are not trying to let go of the contents. You are just giving Me the functions of the body-mind. You are just turning to Me. It is just as easy in every moment. It does not make any difference what is arising in the body-mind, because the contents of the body-mind are not what you are there to deal with. You are there to give Me your attention, to feel Me, to forget yourself—not by making an effort to forget yourself but by directing the function of Remembrance to Me.

Give Me your feeling-attention, now and now and now and now. There is no effort in it. It is always the same. What is arising does not make any difference, because you do not have to do anything to what is arising. You just turn to Me, just that, without regard for what is arising but with total regard for Me.

You still want to tell Me something about yourself and about what you are struggling with. There is nothing to struggle with. Do you know what I mean by "nothing"? There is nothing to be struggled with. In this Ishta-Guru-Bhakti Yoga, there is nothing to be struggled with. There is simply the turning to Me. It is done easily, in every moment, because it does not require you to struggle with yourself to do it. You just forget about that which you would otherwise struggle with, and you give Me your feeling-attention. In that process, you forget yourself. You need not struggle to forget yourself. Just give Me your feeling-attention, just that. Remember My bodily (human) Form, Me right here. Invoke Me by My Name. Enquire a little bit, if that is what you do. You must give Me your feeling-attention, be absorbed in regard of Me. If you do that, you inherently forget yourself.

The beginning of the Way of the Heart, the foundation course, has to do with the devotional response to Me, self-forgetting, turning the functions of the body-mind to Me, Remembering Me, entering into the Bliss that is inherent in the Contemplation of Me, because all that is non-Bliss is forgotten, disregarded, not struggled with.

Devotion to Me is inherently Blissful. It must be done in every moment or else you remember yourself instead of Me. To remember yourself is not Bliss. It is stress and struggle. To Remember Me and, as an inevitable consequence, to forget yourself is Bliss. Therefore, at the beginning of the Way of the Heart, in the middle, and ultimately, the practice is the same devotional submission to Me, the Master, with all your parts, and the same Realizing of the Non-ordinary Reality.

Recently I received a poster that at first glance looks like a collection of wavy lines. If you stand directly in front of it and do not focus your eyes at a point (as you do when you are looking at an object—there is no object in the wavy lines in any case) and you surrender yourself perceptually, then, when the eyes are out of focus, the brain goes through a change. You can even feel the physical change in the brain. All of a sudden you see a three-dimensional image of forms—fishes, sharks, and whales—in a depth of space. Only when your perception of limits is out of focus, when you are unfocused, can you see it.

So it is with devotion to Me. When you abandon the focus on yourself in your address to Me, then you find Me. In that blissful Communion with Me, reality is obvious. You need not generate the intellect to describe it. There is no problem in it. Such is the basis of the Way of the Heart from the beginning.

To be out of focus on the separate self and given over to Me is a form of Samadhi that is Granted at the beginning to all of My devotees, or those who truly respond to Me and do this Yoga "out of focus", not focused on the egoic self. Even from the beginning, then, you enjoy the Samadhi of absorption in Me rather than in yourself. There is a tacit Revelation in that Samadhi that nourishes the heart. Therefore, you must always enter into that unfocused Communion with Me, not focused on separate self but given over to Me, wide, not confined. This is your practice. You must do it moment to moment, then.

ANOTHER DEVOTEE: Beloved Master, as I am more and more drawn into the Happiness of this surrender, I breathe You deeper, surrender my attention to You, conform my action in relationship to this Happiness.

SRI DA AVABHASA: In such devotional Communion with Me, you are not surrendering your thoughts to Me, and you are not surrendering your reactive emotions to Me, you are not trying to surrender your pain, discomfort, or this, that, or other thing bodily, or the circumstance you are combined with. You are forgetting all that, and you are just giving the function itself to Me—not the content of mind but attention, not the content of emotion but just feeling, not the content of the body but just the asana of being given over to Me, just surrendering the faculties to Me, turning them to Me.

Therefore, it is not a matter of struggling with the contents of the body-mind. Just give the faculties of the body-mind to Me, and, without your trying to surrender, in that process the contents will be surrendered. What I call "Rudi's error" was an effort relative to the contents. No. That is not devotion. True devotion, response to the Realizer, response to the Master, is just the intelligent disposition to grant the faculties to Me, to be turned to Me with feeling-attention. Everything else follows. If you could Realize this devotion itself, this devotion and faith, then the Way of the Heart would be very simple.

You must self-generate the practice of this Yoga. You must be in the disposition of response to Me wherein you simply and in every moment artfully do this Yoga. All the reminders of it are good—I have Given them to you for good reason. They support your practice. Therefore, practice in community and live the Way of the Heart among My devotees. Study My Heart-Word. Listen to My devotees tell My Leelas, and observe My Leelas as they are presently alive among you. All these things are supportive of your right and true practice of devotion to Me.

The core of your practice, however, is your response to Me, and, therefore, the responsible exercise of your devotion to Me is the core practice. Everything else is a support, just as "conductivity" is a support to the "conscious process", nonetheless necessary, useful, right. The core of "conductivity" is your consciously responding to Me and making your life out of your response to Me. Devotion to Me is the principle.

"Narcissus" is unillumined, uninformed, egoically "self-possessed", incapable. You must respond to Me, turn up from the pond, exercise yourself in devotion to Me. That is the Way of the Heart.

It is also the traditional way. Devotion to the Master is the secret of the entire Great Tradition of mankind. It has always been so. Devotion to the Master is the essential content of all the traditions, although they become diverted from it and become complicated and tend to accommodate the ego. There is also much of that in the Great Tradition. Nevertheless, devotion to the Master is the fundamental Truth, the Great Truth, the Great Secret, which you can see in the traditions everywhere variously displayed. To examine the traditions and see that it is so is a useful exercise. It is part of your study. To see the primacy of devotion to the Master proven in the traditions is just another useful sign to you, a useful intrusion upon you. Study of the Great Tradition is therefore a supportive exercise.

You will not find the Way of the Heart in the Great Tradition. As you "consider" My Heart-Word about the Great Tradition, you will find, if you examine it, that this essential Truth is there. It is the foundation of the entire Great Tradition of mankind. Nevertheless, most people forget this great principle, or do not take it all that seriously, or do not really know how to become involved in it. As a result, even in the traditional setting, people use books, metaphors, myths, and so forth, to somehow create a facsimile of the process of devotion to the Master. The process of Guru-devotion does not work in that manner. There must be direct Revelation, not the myth of the Realizer but the Realizer in Person, and the Way given by the Word That Emanates from That One Who is Samadhi Itself.

The Way that is suggested metaphorically and piecemeal, and that is here and there, to one degree or another, Manifested in the Great Tradition, is here Manifested whole in My own Person, and Given its full, right, non-mythological, true, real Basis. It should be a simple matter for all mankind, and for all beings altogether, to redress the wrongs of this now dark age. Such redress requires this conversion of all, one by one.

The Happiness That Transcends the World

December 23, 1993

One of the yearly celebrations in Free Daism is the Feast of the Da Love-Ananda Leela, also known as Danavira Mela (Sanskrit: "the Festival of the Hero of Giving"). As expressed in its two names, the feast is a celebration of the great Story, or Leela, of Heart-Master Da Love-Ananda's Heroic Giving to His devotees, which we celebrate by giving gifts to our Ishta-Guru and to each other. Danavira Mela is an entire period of the end of the year, beginning with the first Saturday in December and extending through January 1. In 1993, on December 23, the night before the gift-giving was to begin, Sri Da Avabhasa spoke to His devotees about the true meaning of this celebration in His Company.

SRI DA AVABHASA: Terrible weapons. Worldwide diseases. Ecological disaster. Political conflict. Competition the rule of the day. Deforestation, holes in the ozone layer, global warming, AIDS, stupidity, Godlessness, materialism—this is not the Golden Age! The principal movement of all the nations and groups in the world is to dissociate from one another. The population is growing. The practical requirements are being intensified.

Happy downtown America is over! Its likeness in the world will not happen. It was always in the cards. You are going to die, anyway. There is no reason to be surprised about death. It will occur in darkness, as far as the world goes.

You have the special Opportunity of My Company. Even though the times are as they are, and will continue to be so, you still have the great Opportunity. Therefore, we can celebrate the great Danavira Mela occasion as if we are in paradise together. The Heart is Paradise, regardless of the signs of the times. If you pay attention to the daily news, then you know the nature of the times, and there is no great solution for it. If people were serious about the devastation of the Earth, they would be investing themselves in cooperation and not making bad results. You must know, if you listen to the news at all, that such choices are not being made. Do not expect utopia to be announced on the daily news.

You do not notice the signs of the times. You are not noticing the shroud that is coming on the Earth because of your collective stupidity and Godlessness. The whole world is tuning into separateness and devastation. The general history to come is dark, and you should take the possibility seriously. Others in the past have lived in dark times, too. Just because the dark epoch is occurring on a bigger scale this time and appearing on TV does not mean that others have not lived through and suffered through and died in dark times.

You still have this Opportunity in My Company. Therefore, make much of it. In a sense, that Opportunity is epitomized by the Happiness of Danavira Mela. It is a Transcendental, a Divine, Happiness, a Heart-Happiness, to be made concrete in your relations with one another. And it is not just a periodic celebration. It is a disposition to be manifested all of your life. More and more, all My devotees must override the signs of the times and just respond to Me. Do not expect utopia to happen on Earth.

The times are dark. It will be so. Perhaps something better can be done—we will see. It requires that you also participate. In any case, the Way of the Heart is not about showing the signs of the times, or being reactive to them, or submitting to them in your person or in your worldly life. It is about responding to Me, living this holy life, transcending egoity, transcending the signs of the times, because the signs will get worse. Agreements have been made, which, perhaps, can somehow be rationalized to be positive in intent, but it is not so. The agreements made, hereafter to be manifested, will darken the entire Earth.

I am the Light That you must find, the Opportunity That is Continuous, and it is up to you to make much of it in your personal life and in your collective life with one another. The times in which you will be doing this are dark, by universal agreement. You will have more and more to overcome in your disposition of devotion to Me. Do not expect the world to congratulate you for it, or to give you permission to do it.

Who knows how long the Earth will be a survivable place for human beings? This is not the only world, in any case, and you were always going to die. Death is guaranteed, anyway. As the world takes on the color of death, you must more and more take on the color of the Heart.

Danavira Mela is a time for true rejoicing. So is every day, and all the time and years from now, for My devotees. We are not celebrating the conditions of the world on this Danavira Mela. We are celebrating your

Heart-Happiness in response to My Revelation to you. The world does not give you reasons to do this celebration in love—I do. Therefore, be grateful for it, and be serious about it, and do your part of right life. If you look to the world instead of to Me, you will have more and more reasons to be depressed and dark yourself, more and more reasons to be egoically "self-possessed".

You all here, My devotees, must take Me seriously, must take God seriously, must take the holy life seriously, in spite of the signs of the times. Give Me your attention, and you are Happy. This is the secret in every moment, then. This is how you will ride out the darkening time.

True life is about having nobody to blame. Respond, work it out, do it right, with no condemnation. Convert your life. Take the past, the present, and the future into account. Take Me into account, respond to Me, be converted in your life, and do differently from now on. Instead of blaming yourself, blaming others, blaming the past, blaming this, that, and the other thing, respond to Me and make right choices. Live the right life. Give energy to right life. Devote yourself to right life, the fundamental principle of which is heart-surrender to the Divine Realizer, to the Very Divine. As an expression of that surrender, associate with other beings as "self" rather than "not-self". Realize the boat you are in—in high seas and great storms and the potential for death—and do what is right. That is the secret of the celebration in which most of the world indulges at this time of year and that we must keep all year long.

People are going to lose their computers and their TV sets and their big money and their special occasion. Everyone, sooner or later, will be reduced to the purely human situation, and then they must choose God or not. The stupid materialism that presently rules the world will not last. Will not. Everyone will be ruined in the meantime, in any case. Only when everyone is ruined will people find out the Truth. That is how dark it must become.

The life of self-transcending practice in My Company is no ordeal at all. Don't you understand that the practice is to be joyous, loving Me, Remembering Me, forgetting all the rest? Yes, things must be dealt with, transcended, purified—fine—but meanwhile you are not identified with those things. When you are forgetting those things, absorbed in Me, the ordeal is just peripheral. Make a life out of Communion with Me! We did not get together tonight to be dark!

When Scrooge was converted, he discovered that the rest of the world stayed the way it was. He was you. You must also be converted. Stand at the center of the world, celebrating Me, celebrating your love for one another, made possible by your devotion to Me. Override the world. Do not be double-footed about fulfilling your obligation to Me—with one foot in the world and one foot in the Way of the Heart. Know for real what it takes, then. Not some oblivious notion about life—life is garbage, in general, as things are going. To celebrate this occasion with Me and with one another, you must be happier than the world. You must be at the center of the world, knowing the world as it is, and forget about it and live for love.

Do the life, and celebrate My Company all year long, and never submit to the world, never submit to separate self. Submit to Me, Commune with Me, and forget about the world. That is the life of Joy. And it is the Law that must be manifested in every moment of your life, for all the years you live. Understand, then, and do this, for real.

Danavira Mela will be a wonderful day that epitomizes all of our lives. Be like the converted Scrooge on that day, and right now. I just wanted to emphasize to you the reasons for Joy. Make your life out of Joy, and make this celebration out of it. And forget the world. And forget yourself. And love Me. Love one another. Be full of love. Be full of the Happiness That Transcends the world.

The Grace of Trust

January 7, 1994

SRI DA AVABHASA: Are there any selves? If selves are to exist, they must be something apart from everything else—if we can even use the words "everything" and "else".

As a convention of daily speech and action, you presume "I", the separate self, as if you know what it is and are totally familiar with it. You feel it is worth defending and worth continuing. I get the impression from you, however, that when you say "I" or "me" or "we" you have no idea what you are talking about. You are just using conventions of speech without any specificity, communicating ideas that are based not on the inspection of reality but on some vague tension you are suffering. The "I" you appear to be pointing to is not a fact, not a perception, not a defined anything. Yet all of your conversation is based on it.

When you say you are "feeling" this or that, you are making a self-reference. True feeling, feeling that is exercised Yogically, is beyond separate self. When you think of feeling, you think of separate self as its basis—you feeling. The feeling that is Ishta-Guru-Bhakti, however, is beyond separate self, and the "you" is lost.

Do you hear all the "I's" when you speak?

DEVOTEE: I would like to delete them.

SRI DA AVABHASA: But you do not, and you cannot. When you say you are feeling, you are speaking about feeling in the context of "I", or "I"-ness.

DEVOTEE: How can I—no, how can this be changed?

SRI DA AVABHASA: It is called "the Way of the Heart"! I call it many things—"Ishta-Guru-Bhakti Yoga", also, and so on.

Ishta-Guru-Bhakti Yoga is a process, but you must understand that in that process limitations are still operative and you must be able to notice them. You develop the capability to notice them by Communing with Me.

DEVOTEE: It is painful.

SRI DA AVABHASA: Yes. It is tapas. Good, good, good! Uncomfortable, uncomfortable, very uncomfortable. Not ordinary, not fun all the time. Sometimes it feels good, and sometimes it does not feel so good, because this "I"-construct is there all the time and you must struggle with it always by right practice. You are profoundly identified with this limitation out of which you have made the conventions of daily life and which you also superimpose even on non-ordinary, or extraordinary, phenomenal experiences, until it is loose absolutely in the Divine Samadhi and there is none of it—but only in that case. Until then, the tapas must be endured, and the gesture must be made again.

In the advances through the stages of life, there are extraordinary or non-ordinary experiences, yet always you must be humbled by observing once again the limit that you are remembering and holding onto. Do the tapas of this Yoga of devotion, self-submission, self-forgetting. I think I have told you. The Yoga of Ishta-Guru-Bhakti is Graceful in any instant, but on the other hand it is a process, and you must be able and willing to acknowledge and go beyond the limitations, even in advancement, even in the midst of or after non-ordinary or extraordinary events and experiences.

You are part of a process beyond your own impulses and thoughts, but you do not think it is so. Perhaps every now and then you notice something odd about the conjunctions, and you say, "Hmm—maybe there is something more!" But you do not consistently and really and altogether act in the domain that is beyond your local body-mind. You do not see the connections. You do not presume the process. Consequently, you are very much studied and difficult and concerned about your own self-position, and you forget or doubt the greater process. You do not notice the Unity, until you can stop noticing yourself and feel and notice the total context of your existence, and observe it and see how it works.

Many years ago I gave My Self up to just this noticing, during the time when I lived on the beach, when the psycho-physical nature of conditional existence was directly observed by My just noticing all of it without presumptions, without preconceptions, and by My observing the discipline of the exact noticing of everything without presuming anything.

You, however, observe with presumptions, and, therefore, you do not notice the context in which everything is actually happening. You are basically just fastened to your own apparent unit, as if it is something separate from a greater Unity or Process, and every now and then you may get a little taste of something more, just a little taste.

You must be doing something other than <u>it</u>, if <u>it</u> is to be noticed. This is the principle of Ishta-Guru-Bhakti—forgetting separate self in Communion with Me. In that Communion, observations are made that are revealing. Therefore, yes, it is a matter of leaving conditional existence alone, but not by just being in it in the usual sense and saying that you are leaving it alone. You must be doing something else, something unique, practicing counter-egoic activity, doing what is beyond self-concern and casual observation.

When feeling is allowed to become self-surrender and self-forgetting, it moves into a different dimension of participation than feeling that is generated, for whatever reason, from the egoic self-position. In their ordinary disposition and circumstance of daily life, people feel to one degree or another, and in one fashion or another, and they describe these feelings all the time. Most of the time they describe reactive emotions, and sometimes not so reactive emotions, which they call "love". The feeling of love toward someone is not necessarily free of egoic "self-possession". If egoic "self-possession" is the position in which such love is felt and generated, it is still egoically based. The true exercise of feeling is responsive, not merely a self-act. When feeling becomes surrender and forgetting of separate self, it is another matter. The word "feeling" itself does not indicate which one of the two it is.

A basic characteristic you here, as a human person, are exhibiting and talking about and dramatizing from day to day is a disposition of mistrust. You do not trust conditional reality or the Divine Reality. Trust of reality altogether is another way of defining the word "faith". You tend to think, according to convention, that faith is a matter of believing something that you are called to believe or that is recommended for your belief. Faith is really a heart-disposition of trust in the context of reality. You tend to describe yourself as someone who does not really trust very much. You are alienated, you feel psychologically mistrustful, and, therefore, you invent all kinds of games for your own sake, to make you feel better, to make you survive, or to enable you to conquer or enjoy victory over what you do not trust—which is reality. You do not trust reality. You are egoically "self-possessed" and mortal, and you know that all kinds of limitations exist within you and in relationship to others and to the natural world, even to existence altogether, and this knowledge registers in you as a feeling of mistrust.

The open heart is inherently characterized by faith, not belief in this or that. Faith is not a thing in mind. It is a disposition, a feeling of trust. That feeling of trust is the root of sanity. By comparison, you are relatively insane, because there is a fundamental disposition of mistrust. The body is going to die, people can leave you, people can abuse you, you can suffer, you can become diseased—"I, I, I, me, me, me". These are all the signals of mistrust, as if you had observed reality so thoroughly that you know mistrust is an appropriate disposition. But you do not. You are just localized in your self-contraction, and you make a philosophy out of it, and you talk about reality as if you know reality. Yet all you are doing is dramatizing a fundamental psychological disposition of mistrust, which governs your life.

Another way of describing egoity is that it is a fundamental feeling of alienation and mistrust, whereas the core of the religious life, truly animated, truly lived and found, is the heart-disposition of trust. Trust is another way of describing true feeling, then, self-surrendered, self-forgetting. True feeling is a fundamental sense of trust, and that is faith. Faith is not the feeling that you can escape death, or that the body need not suffer, or that nothing bad will happen in life—those things happen anyway, one way or another. Even when such things do happen, the truly religiously awakened person enjoys the feeling of trust, and trust is at the root, or the core. It is not the superficial gesture of mind, not "I read this, therefore I believe that." It is a core disposition of trust, well-being, integrity.

The root of trust is no-self, the separate self surrendered and forgotten in the embracing of reality altogether. Even though you cannot comprehend reality with your mind, you embrace it in the disposition of self-giving, which shows itself in the human being as a sign of true sanity, well-being, in the midst of all the mortal display that bodily manifested beings suffer.

DEVOTEE: Sri Gurudev, in Your Life You have Embraced it all. You have that disposition of trust, and Your Divine Play is spontaneous. I feel that if I were not in the position of separate self, conditional reality would be chaos.

SRI DA AVABHASA: I am sane, because I am "Crazy" . . .

DEVOTEE: You are Free!

SRI DA AVABHASA: . . . not in the sense that I am insane. Yet this Body, this Appearance here, is subject to the same changes you all suffer.

DEVOTEE: You are without recoil from the threat of life.

SRI DA AVABHASA: Yes! I am looking for a sign of your sanity, faith in that sense, not just belief in doctrines and reports, although they may inform you to one degree or another. Faith is a deep matter, a profound matter at the core of the being in the heart. Profound trust Awakens in the heart of one who responds to the Realizer and the Blessing of the Realizer, and this heart-Awakening is the source of sanity. Then you do not talk anymore in your usual rehearsal of your disturbances, your fears, your strategies, your scientific materialism, "because I was brought up that way". No.

There is a Core, a Well, a Refreshment Where you live, Where you arise—a Refreshed, Cool Water, a Sweetness, That cannot be denied and That makes you sane. When it Radiates throughout the entire body-mind, you do not play at being disturbed anymore, not by effort but because you have drunk from that Well and It guarantees you sanity—because of trust, basically. Trust is the source of true love, not the egoically "self-possessed" motivation to be satisfied in this or that relation, not the effort of interest and the search for satisfaction—no. At the root, previous to everything, previous to all actions, previous to all strategies and results, there is a fundamental trust, or, in other words, a "Hole in the universe" that cannot be overcome. It is the foundation sign of a religious life truly lived, and it is not based on beliefs or mind-forms. It is not based on being consoled in daily life.

It is a fundamental fearlessness, a trustfulness. Its cause, that which Awakens it, is Guru-devotion, response to the One Who is Free, Who is True. Observed, known, received, it authenticates itself directly, and there is no doubt about it! It cannot be explained altogether, but there is just no doubt about it. It grants you the Grace of trust. It purifies you at the heart, it radiates through all the body-mind, it relieves you of the stress of egoic "self-possession", and it allows you to give yourself more. If you did not trust, you would not give yourself more—you would not surrender, you would not forget yourself. Trust is at the origin of your response to Me, and it makes you sane!

You can respond to Me and be given over to Me and trust Me absolutely. Trust is the basis of Ishta-Guru-Bhakti Yoga. Such trust is not manufactured by My saying things to you and telling you to believe this, that, and the other thing. No. Just Me, here! All the Instructions in the books I have Given you are <u>My</u> Communications to you. <u>I</u> am the Revelation, and you must respond to Me. The devotional relationship to Me is the root of this Way, and it is not a matter of words. It is a tacit and very direct matter, if you allow yourself to feel Me.

You must feel Me so deep that, instead of complication and crazy-as-a-bed-bug stuff, at the core is a fundamental openness, a feeling of trust that lets you go more, lets you do more, lets you go further, lets you grow.

The paradox of this trust, this faith, in its Ultimate Realization, as You see in My Demonstration, is that it is not divorced from the phenomenal signs. It is just free of them, and it is the principle whereby even phenomenal signs can be transformed, to the degree they can be. In any case, in due course, the phenomenal realm will vanish.

The core of religion is trust, heart-trust, not intellectual comprehension of the conditional reality and the Divine Reality. The Divine is just there before you, just there Given, just there Revealed. Only the heart, only the core, can respond most directly, and it becomes cured. The Words I Utter, My Instructions, yes, they Serve, but just Me—you become sane by virtue of the fact that I am here. The core, the root, of that sanity is the Awakening of this feeling of trust that melts the bosom, or the core of the feeling of existence. Then carry on with the Yoga, and many things are Revealed and experienced, yes, good, but you must be sane to Realize God.

Therefore, the first step in the religious life is to become sane, by making the response that is traditionally and conventionally called "faith". It is not generated by belief in doctrines. It Awakens directly in the face of the Realizer, Who is the fundamental Instrument and Means. The devotional response to the Realizer makes you sane right on the spot, in the heart, and, yes, it must radiate throughout the body-mind. Therefore, you do the Yoga, embrace My Instruction, do the discipline, because you are, at the root, sane already. You have been cured.

Conversion is the curing of the heart, not just a change of mind stimulated in a moment of sing-song doctrine. Conversion is faith, trust, fundamental integrity established at the root, and you go on from there. That trust, that sublimity, that integrity at the root, is the foundation of Ishta-Guru-Bhakti Yoga. Everything else, the entire Way of the Heart, is built on the response of trust in the Divine Person, just Me. Just Me. I Am That.

The root of the Way of the Heart is Ishta-Guru-Bhakti, the devotional heart-response to Me. Do not hide it, then. Do not try to get Me to talk you into Realizing it. Give Me your attention here. See what is before your eyes. Just that! Then do so in every moment of your life, instead of falling back on your crush of egoic "self-possession" and dis-ease and self-concern. Give Me your attention, feel the well-being of our relationship, and that is the foundation of this practice—not just later, but even at the beginning.

DEVOTEE: Sri Gurudev, in my faith and trust in You, I have come to understand that there is no arbitrariness in what You Give me as sadhana. It is determined by You, the Realizer, so that I have the capability to accept it and surrender to You as the Divine Person.

SRI DA AVABHASA: You must allow Me to be "Crazy", rather than fixing Me in a mold and making Me into the local pastor, confining Me to some sequence of words or some catechism about how it is. You must allow Me to Function just As I Am. Let Me act spontaneously. Let Me be totally silent, if that is what I prefer to do. I have Given you enough Words—I think I have. There is not much more to be said.

DEVOTEE: Beloved, You are so remarkable in Your Sign. The first time I saw You, I felt completely exposed. Everything about me was just seen by You, visible. [SRI DA AVABHASA: Yes.] Yet there was a tacit communication that it was all right.

SRI DA AVABHASA: As long as you forget your separate and separative self. But you do not forget it by trying to forget it. You forget it by Remembering Me, by giving Me your body, your breath, your feeling, your mind as attention, all of it. Just give it to Me and forget it. By forgetting it, surrender it. By giving Me your attention, forget and surrender it. Efforting to forget and surrender it is not the Way of the Heart. By your response to Me, by giving yourself body, mind, attention, feeling, breath, Remembering Me in that sense, Communing with Me in that sense, you surrender and forget separate self.

Are You an "I"?

January 8, 1994

DEVOTEE: Beloved Sri Gurudev, when I observe cosmic reality, I see that things in daily life arise, and change, and die.

SRI DA AVABHASA: "Things"?

DEVOTEE: Simple things, such as flowers, animals, things that I have observed in my life.

SRI DA AVABHASA: You are already using words—"flowers", "animals"—as if you mean something very specific that you have totally accounted for.

DEVOTEE: But I have not. You have made that clear.

SRI DA AVABHASA: You also attribute qualities to these "things", the quality of change, for example, while you have yet to observe even the so-called things themselves. Already your words are full of presumptions and lacking the exactness of observation and knowledge.

DEVOTEE: You have addressed us many times about our referring to ourselves as "I". I have been observing . . .

SRI DA AVABHASA: To say "I" is like saying "flower". You are suggesting that "I" is a something very specific that you have thoroughly investigated and that you know. Is it actually so?

DEVOTEE: Well, Beloved, I have been observing it far more than ever before. I have seen that when I refer to "I", many of the things that I . . .

SRI DA AVABHASA: How do you know it is an "I" yet?

DEVOTEE: That is precisely it. I refer to "I" as just about everything. When I am feeling anger, experiencing states of body, feeling emotionally upset, feeling anxiety, I always call the feeling "I" when I am talking about it with someone else. I say, "I am anxious," "I am this and that".

SRI DA AVABHASA: Yes, it is a convention of daily speech. Is there such a thing as "I"?

DEVOTEE: I am beginning to see that there is no such thing. It is something that is passing constantly, not something that is steady.

SRI DA AVABHASA: Is it an "it"?

DEVOTEE: I do not know.

SRI DA AVABHASA: Is it a specific?

DEVOTEE: It is not a specific.

SRI DA AVABHASA: Is it an "anything" separate from anything else? Where does it begin? Where does it end?

DEVOTEE: It does not.

SRI DA AVABHASA: Are you sure?

DEVOTEE: It does not seem to, from what I have seen. It just . . .

SRI DA AVABHASA: "It"? What "it"?

DEVOTEE: It is no "it".

SRI DA AVABHASA: Who knows?

DEVOTEE: I do not.

SRI DA AVABHASA: You are suggesting that you do. You are suggesting that there is this "it", and it is something specific, and everything else is a thing, else, something, it, specific. Your mind is based on this game of presumption, but is there an actual experience that corresponds to the presumptions of your mind? Do you have an experience of an actual, specifically defined "I", or a flower, a plant, a tree, an anything?

DEVOTEE: No.

SRI DA AVABHASA: Do you have an actual experience of anything separate and specific? Your language is filled with specifics, suggesting, therefore, that reality is all these specifics, the "I", and every "thing" else—every thing is very specific, and all things are separate from one another. Your words suggest a particular reality. Have you actually experienced a reality that corresponds to your words?

DEVOTEE: I am not sure that I understand what You are asking.

SRI DA AVABHASA: Where do you begin?

DEVOTEE: I do not know.

SRI DA AVABHASA: Then how can you name it? How does it get to be an "it"?

DEVOTEE: I have a false presumption that it is an "it".

SRI DA AVABHASA: What is this "I"?

DEVOTEE: It is what I identify as all these things . . .

SRI DA AVABHASA: You already said "I".

DEVOTEE: It is very difficult not to, Lord.

SRI DA AVABHASA: It is a habit of speech, a game of concepts, or presumptions, by which you are presuming to define your own existence. You do not seem to have an actual experience that corresponds to it, however. Where do you begin? Where do you end, and where does everything else begin? What do you mean when you say "I"? What are you referring to? Are you just talking nonsense all the time?

DEVOTEE: Yes, it appears I am.

SRI DA AVABHASA: Well—"consider" it. "Consider" it.

You are all always—not in every moment of your life but rather constantly—talking to one another and talking to yourself in your interior thinking. In some sense, it seems that you base your entire existence on this flow of words of internal and of apparently relational, or external, conversation. Generally, when you refer to reality, you are referring to the flow of words, of concepts, of presumptions, and not really to anything else—not to a something that actually exists. When you say "I", or "flower", or "tree", or someone's name, you are not referring to an actuality that you are experiencing and that is specifically defined. You are referring to a concept of reality, a convention about reality. If you set aside the process of mind, with all its constructs and all its presumptions, what is reality? What is the actual experience?

DEVOTEE: Beloved, many times, particularly following periods of meditation, when I will come out of the Communion Hall, my body . . .

SRI DA AVABHASA: You. You just said "I", as if you know what exactly you are referring to. And then you said "my body". Let's address that one instead of "I". What about "the body"? Is it a something, separate, independent?

DEVOTEE: No.

SRI DA AVABHASA: You are existing in a vast, gaseous, fluid that is rather invisible. You are very much like a fish in water. In bodily terms, you are moving about in a fluid. Yet this fluid is not just stuff that is objective to you. The body is profoundly combined with it. Where does the body end and the fluid appear? Where is the difference?

DEVOTEE: There isn't any. I felt this last night, Lord. A candle was lighted in my room, and I felt that the light that was emanating from the candle was part of this body, coming into this body, and the breath that I would take would then come out. It was a very strong sense of non-separation.

SRI DA AVABHASA: The body exists in a sea of gas. It also exists in a sea of energy. It exists in a sea of elements of all kinds. Although you can refer to your mind, it is not just a something. It is part of a multi-planed sphere of forces—chemical, biochemical, molecular, energic—that proceed in a vast, unlimited sphere. There is no separate breath. Breath occurs within this sea of gas. There is no separate energy. There is one energy, which is conducted, somehow or other, in some sort of who-knows-whatsy and which is not separate from it.

So where is "the body"? Where does it begin? What makes it a "the" anyway? Examine it, alive, and then "consider" the complexity of so-called "it". All its parts function in patterns in relationship to one another, in opposition to one another, independent of one another. The so-called body is full of organisms. How does it get to be an "I"? It is just a conjunction of forces, and they conjoin in different ways—out here, over here, over here. Where is the "I"? Where is "the body"? Where are all the separate things you are presuming in your habits of mind? Is there a reality that corresponds to the reality in the mind—so called "the"—that you think and say? Does that mind-reality otherwise exist? Does the world your speech presumes exist? Or is it just a mental construct, a presumption—divorced, in fact, from reality?

DEVOTEE: Beloved, it seems it does exist. I have always presumed when I have spoken, and when I first began to speak with You now, that it is separate.

SRI DA AVABHASA: What is?

DEVOTEE: The world as You just referred to, the world as separate . . .

SRI DA AVABHASA: It does not correspond to your mental presumptions though, apparently.

DEVOTEE: No.

SRI DA AVABHASA: The world that you presume in the forms of your thinking does not exist apart from your thinking. When you speak, you think you are referring to the world. You do not think you are just talking about your talk. You presume you are talking about a larger reality. In fact, however, it seems that you are not talking about a larger reality. You just presume you are. The larger reality is utterly unlike what you think.

DEVOTEE: This false presumption is made in mind. Does mind begin with these separate ideas and concepts?

SRI DA AVABHASA: Where does it all come from? It does not come from the world, or from reality. Where does it come from? Since you do not have the ability to live in the world as it actually is, do you oblige yourself to invent another one?

DEVOTEE: Lord, is mind something that is inherent in the structure of the body? Is this presumption carried over from lifetime to lifetime?

SRI DA AVABHASA: Examine it. [to everyone] Does this make sense to the rest of you? "Consider", then, the reality that your thoughts presume. Does that reality exist apart from your thoughts?

ANOTHER DEVOTEE: Sri Gurudev, You have made it clear that except in the fullness of our surrender to You there is no reliable position from which to observe reality. Today, as I moved into daily service and responsibilities, I felt my presumptions about what it is I am doing.

SRI DA AVABHASA: You just said "my", and "what 'I' am doing", which are already constructs based on the logic of mind.

DEVOTEE: It seems there is either this place of surrender, or there is the presumption.

SRI DA AVABHASA: What is the <u>real</u> state of individual consciousness, or individual being, then? It appears that you are all involved in an illusion, not in the sense that all this apparent solidity is being imagined—although that proposition could be "considered" further—but in the sense that you are living in a pool of thoughts and you are identified with a pattern of thinking that does not correspond to reality. Reality is not constructed in the manner that your thoughts suggest. Because you are identified with that mind, or that pattern of presumption, you are living in unreality, or in an unreal, or illusory, state of conscious awareness. It is the common un-reality that human beings presume in general. Human beings imagine that to live in this un-reality is all right. They think that this unreality should be the basis for life and for all judgment about everything altogether, including, then, the cosmos and the Divine—everything. Everything is supposed to be examined from the point of view of this collection of presumptions, this false logic about reality.

Therefore, if you are identified with this false mind, how could you possibly understand, or even experience, cosmic reality or the Very

Divine? How can life be lived rightly if it is based on such a false mind? How can it discover Truth? How can it Realize Truth? How can it even experience authentically?

It would seem, then, that the real state of conscious awareness, the real state of individual being, is utterly free of this construct of mind with which you are identified and by which you habitually live, or exist. The only real state of conscious awareness, then, is true to reality, utterly one with reality, whereas the state in which you are living and thinking is utterly dissociated from true reality, actual reality—conditional reality and Ultimate Reality. The only true consciousness, then, is Divine Consciousness Itself. To describe Consciousness Itself in another way, it is Samadhi, rather than ordinary, or conventional, conscious awareness.

In the state of conscious awareness that is free of the mind, or false constructs, reality is inherently obvious. In the state of mind in which you live, however, in this construct of presumptions in which you live, reality is totally not obvious. You are fundamentally divorced from it and alienated from it. You do not even experience it. You have all kinds of questions, of course, because you are suffering in the midst of this body of presumptions that contain fundamental, inherent errors. As a result, you suffer, and you feel profoundly limited. You deeply feel that something is basically wrong, but you are trying to think your way out of your suffering. To solve the "problem", you are trying to exercise the very "thing" that you are suffering. Obviously, to solve, so to speak, the so-called problem, you must identify it and deal with it directly.

ANOTHER DEVOTEE: Beloved, it seems that what You are talking about is the point of view we identify with.

SRI DA AVABHASA: You are already using the conventions of "'the' point of view", "'we' identify with". Of course, we will use conventions of speech, as we always do in these conversations, but we must also address them. Every word you say, every sentence you speak, is based on false logic.

You are earnestly asking Me a question, hoping I will earnestly respond and answer it and thus solve your problem. Without your greater understanding, the conversation between us is basically just a play of mind, an exchange of language, a play on the language.

DEVOTEE: It could be just that, but in my surrender to You there is a hole in that point of view.

SRI DA AVABHASA: Yes, there is—if you understand what such surrender truly means, what it is truly all about, what kind of action it is, altogether, what kind of response is at its base. You could say the words, "surrender to You", or "Guru-devotion", and what you say could be false, or certainly inadequate, if you do not thoroughly understand and if you do not have the capability for doing what is truly intended by the words.

The real practice of Ishta-Guru-Bhakti Yoga goes beyond the presumptions of mind, or the logic of egoity. If it does not, it is not real surrender, not real Ishta-Guru-Bhakti. I suggest that instead of talking about the words, talking about the mind, talking about you, we talk about the cosmic reality, and, by examining it, see if what I am suggesting is so. I suggest that we find out, by examining cosmic reality, whether your patterns of thought have anything to do with it.

DEVOTEE: It seems completely obvious, if we have been practicing Ishta-Guru-Bhakti.

SRI DA AVABHASA: But you are still talking. What about cosmic reality? What about reality apart from your thoughts? If you speak, we must relate what you are saying to reality, to see if there is a correspondence.

Therefore, say a sentence. Any sentence will do, because the whole language is based on the same presumption. Every piece of it, therefore, is a reflection of all the rest. It is all based on the same logic.

DEVOTEE: Reality must be beyond words.

SRI DA AVABHASA: It must? What kind of utterance is this? How do you know? In principle, the words could exactly correspond to reality. That is what we should be examining. You want to make some primal utterance to the effect that in principle words do not have anything to do with reality. Maybe they do. That is what we want to find out. If they do not, you must really find out that they do not, you must observe reality to the point of a profound conviction that it is so, not just use your mind to agree with Me but really examine reality over against your thoughts to see if there is a correspondence. If there is not, perhaps it will blow your mind.

DEVOTEE: It seems that speech is made on the basis of conventional agreements between individuals who presume themselves to be separate, and who therefore do not know anything about Divine Reality.

SRI DA AVABHASA: Any reality. Let us just talk about the reality here, anything we can address about cosmic reality here, in the sphere of all this here, and what may be perceived or addressed from here, without talking about elsewhere, or memories, and so on.

ANOTHER DEVOTEE: In Your Company, we are surrendering mind, or attention, to You, and in the midst of that surrender . . .

SRI DA AVABHASA: Are you?

DEVOTEE: Yes.

SRI DA AVABHASA: In what sense?

DEVOTEE: Surrendering mind, attention, feeling, emotion to You.

SRI DA AVABHASA: Yes, and what do you mean by "You"?

DEVOTEE: Your bodily (human) Form—just Your bodily (human) Form.

SRI DA AVABHASA: Just that?

DEVOTEE: When I surrender mind, emotion, body, to Your bodily (human) Form, the whole sensation of "me" loosens up and there is a feeling of What is Beyond that.

SRI DA AVABHASA: It is a gesture of relinquishing self-attention? [DEVOTEE: Yes.] What is the "You"? You just said "You" in My direction, here.

DEVOTEE: The Very Divine.

SRI DA AVABHASA: What does that mean? What do you know about the Very Divine that you can refer to It in speech as a "the", and a "Very", and a "Divine"?

DEVOTEE: It is the interconnectedness in which everything arises.

SRI DA AVABHASA: The connectedness?

DEVOTEE: The fluid, the fluid.

SRI DA AVABHASA: You see? When you start talking about it, and we really examine the speech and not just allow it to be a flow of conventional communications, it sounds absurd and presumptuous. That should suggest to you that Ishta-Guru-Bhakti Yoga takes place beyond the patterns of speech. It is based on an acknowledgement, an intuition, a feeling contact that is not comprehended in your language, nor is it comprehended in your mind. If you try to make a mental description of it or describe it in speech—say some words about it, write some books about it—you immediately translate the intuition and the feeling into the realm of mind and conventional presumption. What you say about it may sound logical, or inspiring, or convincing, but it does not correspond to the reality of Ishta-Guru-Bhakti Yoga. You find yourself talking about so-called "things" of which you have no experience, in terms of your language at any rate.

DEVOTEE: Beloved, there is a difference between Your language and ours. When You speak, Your language facilitates this understanding.

SRI DA AVABHASA: Yes, fine. But the reality of Ishta-Guru-Bhakti Yoga is beyond the mind. Otherwise, what would be the point of surrendering to this bodily (human) Form? You might just as well surrender to the body of that man over there or My parrot's body or a tree. The principle is not to surrender to some arbitrary bodily (human) form. No. It is to surrender to a unique Revelation, so that a unique process is generated. Ishta-Guru-Bhakti it is not based on the logic of mind, or conventional speech, or conventional existence in human form. It is another matter altogether. Therefore, you do not surrender to any bodily (human) form, or any apparent thing, or your, so to speak, body. No. You surrender to That Which Reveals Itself to Be True and Which Attracts you as such. You surrender to the Realizer as Realizer, not as an ordinary man, and not merely as a body like any other body. In effect, in reality, you are surrendering into the Divine Consciousness Itself. You are surrendering into Samadhi.

DEVOTEE: Sri Gurudev, in the surrender, it is clear that words or language cannot contain You, because language is just concepts.

SRI DA AVABHASA: Yet you do speak about Me. It seems, in fact, that you are even obliged to do so to make sense to one another.

DEVOTEE: Any presumption limits the surrender.

SRI DA AVABHASA: The surrender is self-forgetting. Therefore, it is not about the mind. It leaves mind behind, or lets it go.

In any case, what about the cosmic reality? Is anybody going to address even this specimen, here perceived?

ANOTHER DEVOTEE: Yes, Lord. The "consideration" tonight makes it obvious that . . .

SRI DA AVABHASA: Now you are making a pronouncement. What about the cosmic reality?

DEVOTEE: It is not at all as perceived.

SRI DA AVABHASA: Now you are making a judgment about it. What about "it", so-called.

DEVOTEE: Cosmic reality . . .

SRI DA AVABHASA: Nope, nope, nope. Now you are abstracting it.

DEVOTEE: Beloved, this Condition . . .

SRI DA AVABHASA: Which?

DEVOTEE: The Very Condition That is All-Pervading.

SRI DA AVABHASA: Come on—are you going to talk straight? Do you eat with metaphysical forks? Is there anything to say here?

ANOTHER DEVOTEE: The one thing about cosmic reality that appears to me to be safe to say is . . .

SRI DA AVABHASA: We will see! We will see!

DEVOTEE: . . . we exist.

SRI DA AVABHASA: We?

DEVOTEE: There is existence, awareness. I sit here, and I am aware that I am. I do not know what I am, necessarily, or anything else, but I know that I am.

SRI DA AVABHASA: You are still calling it an "I".

DEVOTEE: That is right.

SRI DA AVABHASA: And that suggests it is defined, somehow.

DEVOTEE: That is right. It is limited, because I am speaking about . . .

SRI DA AVABHASA: Is it?

DEVOTEE: But there is . . .

SRI DA AVABHASA: Is it?

DEVOTEE: . . . a sense of existence itself . . .

SRI DA AVABHASA: Is it?

DEVOTEE: Well, that stops me!

SRI DA AVABHASA: Because of the habits of speech, you presume that "I" is limited. But, in your experience is it limited?

You cannot trust the mere "it" of your perceptions, not in and of themselves. Perhaps you can trust them in some sense, in the sense that they enable you to function day by day, but you cannot trust them in the sense that the phenomenal world you perceive will preserve your existence and make you happy and provide a pleasurable domain of life. Even to survive one more hour requires some necessary struggle.

DEVOTEE: I know that if I step in front of a truck I am going to die immediately, probably.

SRI DA AVABHASA: You do not even have to do that. You can avoid stepping in front of trucks.

DEVOTEE: Absolutely.

SRI DA AVABHASA: There are all kinds of other things upon which your life depends with which you must participate and even struggle, perhaps, moment by moment.

DEVOTEE: What I was referring to, though, are the rules we can learn . . .

SRI DA AVABHASA: "We"? Now you are talking about conventional existence again, the drama you are already involved in—which, it appears, you have agreed is unsatisfactory, .not Ultimate, not Inherently Happy, in its context of changes.

DEVOTEE: I sit here, and I am aware. I know I am alive.

SRI DA AVABHASA: "I". What do you mean?

DEVOTEE: I understand from Your Teaching that there is a contraction in it.

SRI DA AVABHASA: Yes, but this is the word game. Let's not play the word game.

DEVOTEE: There is consciousness associated with this body-mind.

SRI DA AVABHASA: "This"? What body-mind? You are suggesting it is a "something" that you experience as very specific, identifiable, and separate from everything else. Is it really so?

DEVOTEE: No, I think it has to do with my self-concern. I think that is exactly what it is.

SRI DA AVABHASA: There you are again, referring to yourself, as if "I" means something very specific, discrete, separate, something that you have observed and that you wholly know. Therefore, you use a word that corresponds to it. There is not anything corresponding to the word. There is nothing in the likeness of your words. Those words are a totally different construct of reality than the one you experience. Nevertheless, you cannot experience reality directly, because you are identified with this pattern of words, this pattern of presumptions and thoughts that construct reality in a particular fashion, just as the body—if I can speak conventionally—in the room—again speaking conventionally—because of its point of view, in space and so forth, constructs perception in a particular fashion, whereas every other apparent body, at some other where in the room, constructs perception differently.

Just so, the mind itself is a construct not only that is different from reality, as you would realize if you could experience reality directly, but that prevents you from experiencing reality. As soon as you—we are using the conventions of speech now—look to perceive or examine anything, the pattern of thought and presumption intervenes and says, "This is what it is," whereas it is not. If the pattern of presumptions were loosed, not activated, then what is reality?

DEVOTEE: The feeling of existence, itself, it seems to me, is the fundamental quality.

SRI DA AVABHASA: It is patterned by this construct of mind, so that when you say you feel you exist—"I am aware. Therefore, I exist"—at the same time, as you have just indicated, you feel "I" is limited, you feel that it is identified with the body-mind in some sense, threatened by the happenings in the body-mind, that it could possibly come to an end, on and on and on. The pattern of thinking, of thoughts, of presumptions, determines that point of view. If you examine the reality itself that you are making words about and patterning in your mind according to certain logic, what is it? What is the nature of cosmic existence apart from the logic of mind, which defines reality in a particular fashion and fastens it around the "I" presumption?

DEVOTEE: Is it describable, then?

SRI DA AVABHASA: It is there to be examined.

DEVOTEE: It does not seem possible to describe it. We refer to the "I", so our perception of reality is constricted again. Reality is not describable.

SRI DA AVABHASA: Even if it is not describable, it is important to go beyond the descriptions with which you have already identified. Having done so, perhaps you can find a way to use language that is at least a reasonable expression of what you have realized to be true.

Let us try to deal with this one matter: Point out to Me any single thing.

DEVOTEE: Michael.

SRI DA AVABHASA: That is a single thing?

DEVOTEE: Oh, no! There is no single thing. There is no possible single thing.

SRI DA AVABHASA: No no no—do not make judgments here, as you do all day long every time you say a sentence. So, examine a single thing.

DEVOTEE: The fan.

SRI DA AVABHASA: That is a thing? We say "fan" in English. It is described as an "it" that is "fan". What makes it an "it"? Is there any "itness" about it that makes it totally separate from anything else whatsoever?

DEVOTEE: It appears to be something substantial.

SRI DA AVABHASA: It appears so because of your habit of thinking. If you examine <u>it</u>, does it still keep on being an "it"? Or is it indistinguishably involved in a larger process from which it cannot be separate?

DEVOTEE: Its function is unique.

SRI DA AVABHASA: According to any pattern of thinking and presumption, perhaps, but does it have any "itness" about it if you examine it thoroughly in all its details? Where does it begin? Where does it end? What does it not have anything to do with?

DEVOTEE: Sri Gurudev, it seems that a feeling is associated with anything to which we give our attention, like that [indicating the "fan"] over there.

SRI DA AVABHASA: The feeling is based on a construct of mind that is already presumed. Examine the so-called thing itself. How does it become an "it"? Or is "it" just a presumption?

DEVOTEE: Sri Gurudev, to engage this exercise, I must drop the mind that I am always using.

SRI DA AVABHASA: Yes. You must examine the "fan". Just as if you are going to surrender to Me, you must forget yourself. So, forget yourself, and let's talk about this "fan" here. It has many parts, doesn't it? If it has many parts, how does it get to be an "it"? That disk in the middle of the round part is an "it", in some sense, isn't it? If it is an "it", and then the wire cage around it is an "it", how does the whole thing get to be an "it"?

"It" is a word for it, but what about this so-called object here? [again indicating the "fan"] It has many visible parts. There is a wire hanging from it that goes somewhere. It has what we call "a motor" inside it, and electricity—where does the electricity come from? Where does all the energy come from? And look at each of these parts—each one appears to be made out of different materials. Some are plastic, others are metal. The parts are all made out of particular elements that are nevertheless difficult to distinguish. Apart from certain masses of charge, they are variations on the same thing.

Before we get to the molecular level, however, look at just the elemental level, the chemical level. How is this thing distinguishable from the elements of which it is apparently made? It will go back to those elements, it will go back to those molecular forces, it will go back to those atomic forces. Right now it is made of those.

Because of a certain habit and construct of mind and body, you are seeing basically just the physical apparent something sitting there. You are not seeing its atoms, unless you are enjoying a unique kind of visualization. You see just its solidity. You do not take its depth into account. Yet it is made of that depth right now. Just as, apart from your point of view, the room is what it is altogether, so also this so-called "fan" here, which is many parts and not just an "it", is made up of many elementals—chemical elementals and then molecular and atomic elementals.

The "fan" is just energy. It is just light. It is absolutely one with the mass of those elementals. It cannot be distinguished from them. In actuality, that is so. As a visual construct, an object over against the body with which you feel identified, it is one thing, according to your presumptions, but when you examine the so-called "thing" itself, it is not a "thing" anymore. It is not distinguishable from the mass of fields of appearance, or energy, force. It is energy, and, therefore, it is not an "it" at all. It is utterly ambiguous and indefinable.

DEVOTEE: Another thing that gives it "itness" is the fact that when I look at this "fan" tomorrow it will be the same thing.

SRI DA AVABHASA: Not altogether. It is the kind of so-called "thing" that goes through changes more slowly than some other kinds of things. Tomorrow it will have already gone through some changes, and so will so-called "you".

You tend to think in terms of "itnesses" because of a certain habit of mind and because of your identification with the body. When you examine all these "itnesses" directly, they do not turn out to be "its" or "things" or separate "anythings". They are not distinguishable from an indefinable field. They are, therefore, themselves, not definable. Yet you do define them. You make presumptions about them. You call them "its", just as you call yourself "I". If you examine the reality that your language presumes to be specific and full of separatenesses, the reality itself does not show itself to be of the same nature.

The cosmic domain is of a different nature than the reality your mind presumes.

What other object?

DEVOTEE: Beloved Gurudev, another way of disproving its "itness" is that if the world were to explode in the next moment, that "fan" would explode with it and would no longer exist.

SRI DA AVABHASA: It would exist just as much as it does now, and in exactly the same sense that it exists now. It would not be changed in the slightest relative to its actual condition at this moment, but its appearance from your point of view would change—presuming your point of view continued. Just as the room, seen from absolutely all points of view, does not look at all like you perceive it now, so also this "fan" is not at all what you perceive it to be. It is not an "it". If it is not an "it", are you an "I"? The same thing is the case with so-called "John" [the man who just spoke]. Like all of you, he is constantly calling himself "I"—he refers to "I", he refers to "me", as if that is a specific something, as if he is seeing the whole elephant and knows exactly what he means by "I". [to the man]

Do you? Even the body, like the "fan", is one with the universal field and the sub-fields within that universal field. In other words, it is one with the universal field of energy, or light, and the sub-fields within it—atomic, molecular, chemical, and so on.

Like the "fan", the body has many parts. Each of those parts can be called an "it". Many of the parts of the body operate apparently independently, even contrary to the benefit of other parts of the body. The body does not seem to be just "one thing" then. It is full of contraries, separate parts, separate elements. It contains organisms that can be removed. You could take a sample of blood and look under a microscope at everything moving around in there. Yet you are calling them "I"! They also, presumably, in some sense think of themselves as "I"!

The body is a kind of campground, or a mad community, and yet you call it "I", as if it is just one thing, as if it is specific and separate and isolated from all other things, separate from any kind of field beyond itself. In actuality, however, if you examine it, it is not so.

DEVOTEE: The body is completely dependent on everything that is occurring simultaneously.

SRI DA AVABHASA: And one with it all.

DEVOTEE: Whatever the configuration is in that moment. As You said, if the world explodes, the "fan" also explodes, and its appearance changes but not its essence.

SRI DA AVABHASA: Its condition does not really change. So, if you die, the condition that is actually so, actually true, of so-called you in this moment will be the same then as it is now, because it is identified with the universal reality, as you are, in reality. The death of the body does not change anything of that. In another context than death, however, the dimensions of the discrete personality may also disintegrate. In Ultimate Samadhi, in Divine Self-Realization, it all disintegrates, and there is nothing but the One Condition, or Reality, that always was the case.

Nothing is ever destroyed. Appearances pass through forms of transformation, but the Ultimate Condition, Which was the case for them to begin with, Persists. Parts pass into elements, are transformed again, made into new apparent forms, but the Ultimate Field in Which the elements and forms are arising Persists all the while. When all of the planes of appearance disintegrate, just That One Ultimate Field remains. It is the Divine Condition, the Ultimate Condition.

DEVOTEE: There is one word that might describe it to an extent—it is just Energy, simply Energy. But it also seems to be connected to Intelligence. I was thinking of Your question to us, "What is cosmic reality?"

SRI DA AVABHASA: The "answer" is what there is to discover, by going beyond the various planes of appearance—from the grosser planes into the subtle, or from the chemical-elemental to the atomic. It is a transition of identity. What is the greater field, or domain, in which the atomic exists? What is the greater field or domain in which light exists? By going through the process of disintegration, or the return of parts to their elements and the disintegration of the planes themselves, Most Ultimately there is the Realization of That Condition in Which it is all arising.

This is another way of describing Divine Self-Realization, then—to participate in that sacrifice whereby all the parts disintegrate into their planes, or fields, and the planes, or fields, themselves are passed beyond or disintegrated in the ones in which they arise and which are senior to them. Then those greater planes are passed through and disintegrated, until just That One Condition Stands of Which they are all only modifications.

Find out! Find out! You just want to sit there being you, as you usually are, and ask all your questions and not go through any changes in order to find out. I could tell you—I have told you—but My telling you is not the same as Realization in your case. You must go through the sacrifice to find out these things in real detail, and actually.

DEVOTEE: Beloved, it seems that if the presumption is not made that the individual self is separate, the presumption of separateness can be released relative to every apparently separate thing.

SRI DA AVABHASA: Yes. I call it "Divine Recognition", the unique capability, or Siddhi, of the seventh stage of life.

DEVOTEE: Sri Gurudev, You are completely released of that presumption, and Your Freedom becomes, somehow, possible for us. The fact that You are Incarnated, apparently conditionally, yet totally Free of the presumption of separateness, is Awakening the same Freedom in apparently separate beings in this realm.

SRI DA AVABHASA: Yes. I have Entered into this cosmic domain, utterly, down to the cells, and I have Realized Divine Samadhi in this apparent circumstance. Therefore, the Siddhi of My Realization is projected universally, and It may be Realized hereafter by anyone who does the sadhana of Ishta-Guru-Bhakti Yoga in relation to Me. My Siddhi is effective for the sake of this Realization. It is the Means. It will always be the Means, even after the passing of this physical body.

DEVOTEE: When Your Siddhi is Transmitted, It even releases the sense of this individual being.

SRI DA AVABHASA: Yes, it does—if you enter into My Divine Samadhi through devotional Communion with Me.

Leonardo's Molecules and the Original Ralph

March 13, 1994

DEVOTEE: Sri Gurudev, I have read that with every breath we are breathing something like 125 molecules of air that Leonardo da Vinci breathed. He lived a long time ago, and the air he breathed has circulated through the biosphere.

SRI DA AVABHASA: There must be something like 125 molecules of the air everybody else breathed who lived in his time, too. You may be breathing some genius, but you are also breathing many, many fools. Most of the people in the time of Leonardo were fools, so you are mainly breathing fool from that time and a little bit of genius, which is not going to do you very much good over against all the fool you are breathing.

DEVOTEE: That is right. But, Sri Gurudev, each of the molecules that You Yourself have breathed does not simply go into the lungs and come out unchanged. The molecules You breathe are actually combined with Your Being. You draw them in, and You Associate with them intimately in Your bodily (human) Form.

SRI DA AVABHASA: Yes. Leonardo's molecules and the molecules of everybody else, all of you, even anything in My physical Sphere here, all the stars, every particle of the universe.

Think how many beyond 125 particles we are all breathing here of everything that existed <u>before</u> Leonardo da Vinci.

DEVOTEE: Dinosaurs and all that.

SRI DA AVABHASA: Everything, from billions of years ago, back to the 20 billion where it all supposedly, according to current theory, began. The big bang was not just a blast in space. It was a blast that <u>made</u> space. Before the big bang there was no space. It is not that the big bang occurred in space. Without the big bang, there is no space. So where did the so-called "big bang" occur?

You imagine that by thinking about the big bang and all kinds of other theories you understand something. Truly, you do not understand anything. You just become familiar with the "Everything" by inventing concepts that separate you from the "Everything", and you become rather self-satisfied with your cosmology and your "understanding", so-called, of reality. It is just your own mind again. The only big bang you know about is in your own concepts, got from a little bit of reading. You might as well call it "the Ralph" and say nothing else about it. "There is the original and originating Ralph, and there is nothing to say about it—poetically, scientifically—by way of explanation, by way of concept. No. It is just a Ralph, and there is no way to understand it."

Ultimately, there is not the slightest bit of difference between the most sophisticated explanations of scientific cosmology and the Adam-and-Eve story in Genesis, in the *Old Testament.* They are both mental exercises whereby human beings try to get control over something over which they have no control whatsoever. And since you cannot oink up real big and knock the universe flat, you become involved in a great deal of thinking about it—and there you get tough. "Hah! We've got the big bang, and we are in control!" You cannot beat the universe, but you think about conquering it. And when you come up with a concept like the "big bang", all of a sudden you are in charge and everything is obvious and you are in control. Since you cannot control the universe physically, you do it conceptually.

The big bang is just another myth. Ultimately, it has no more importance than Adam and Eve in the Garden. It is about the same thing. It is just a way of feeling comfortable with something about which you should not feel any comfort whatsoever. It is just a form of stupid familiarity.

It is just a Ralph. All of this is Ralph, and that is it. It is just a Ralphing. You are being Ralphed. You are Ralph. You do Ralph. You believe in Ralph. You hate Ralph and resist Ralph. You are troubled about Ralph. You fear Ralph. And you are going to die from Ralph sooner or later. You breathe Ralph. You think Ralph. You are in charge of Ralph. Ralph is in charge of you.

It is all nonsense, you see?

Real life, true existence, all comes down to a non-conceptual Reality, the Reality of Non-Separateness. You have no ultimate explanation for It and no way to differentiate yourself from It or get in control of It. You just must give yourself up to the "Ralph", the Unknown and Unknowable, That Which is Beyond yourself. You cannot Realize the Real until you stop being yourself, stop separating yourself, and stop suffering the illusions of separateness.

When there is no separation, no gesture, effort, or result of self-contraction, then the "Ralph", or God, Truth, Reality, is Inherently Obvious.

Throw Yourself into the Fire

January 15, 1994

1.

SRI DA AVABHASA: I saw a video recently about a man who was held hostage in a foreign country for five years. Although he was moved from place to place during the years of his imprisonment, generally he was trapped in a dark room that was a little wider than a cot. He was given one small meal every morning, and once a day he was allowed to go to the latrine.

He said that at first, because he is of a religious disposition, he prayed to be released. He expected, and asked, and prayed that his imprisonment would end. He felt confined, and he thought only about escaping his situation.

Then, he said, he stopped praying in those terms. He accepted his confinement and stopped thinking about being released. He realized that his struggle was basically fruitless. There was nothing he could do about his situation, which just continued to be. He began examining the situation just as it was. It was his situation. He was living in that place. Imprisonment was his life.

Only with that acceptance did he come to terms with his fears and reactions and his suffering in confinement, and he began to realize a process of growth. He learned many lessons over those five terrible years, but he came away from the ordeal feeling that he had received an advantage. It was not that he liked being in prison—certainly not—but he felt he had understood something and that he had overcome something in himself.

Fear, for instance. He felt very frightened—for obvious reasons, since he was not only confined but under threat, he could neither deal with his circumstance nor escape it, and he was physically abused. Yet once he had accepted his situation and was no longer struggling against it, he had a great deal of time to examine his fear. Over time, he said, fear became more and more just this little something that he was doing. He made a gesture like this [Sri Gurudev holds up His thumb and index finger about two inches apart] to indicate just that small something he was doing. Eventually the fear vanished.

This man was suggesting that there are advantages to a situation of confinement. Many people in the past have chosen just such a circumstance of renunciation. When you accept a situation of discipline, even of confinement or isolation, when there is no more seeking, in other words, no more struggling to escape your situation, and you are able just to deal with the event that you are, in the context of reality—and your situation need not be so extreme as this man's—only when you are no longer seeking to escape the confinement, the pressure, the suffering, the limitation, the mortality of existence, and you can just deal directly with your own mechanism of reaction, only then is there a breakthrough beyond the common and petty limitations you are suffering psychologically and Spiritually.

Some traditions suggest that only most extreme self-discipline in isolation produces this result. In some cases it may be true. Something like traditional renunciation is certainly necessary. You must somehow or other bring a halt to the mode of seeking, of being confused, self-indulgent, peripheral, superficial. You must by choice, or by circumstance, be confined to just the examination of what is, without struggling to get out of it. Then, and only then, do you go through the crisis of breaking out of your limitations.

Now, this man did not come out of confinement Enlightened, but he did come out of it with some real self-understanding and a sense that he had overcome something fundamental in himself, something fundamental about his suffering.

The ordinary person, on the other hand, with all the gamings of an ordinary life and a history of adaptation to it, refuses confinement of any kind. Likewise, you, in your ordinariness, want to be "free", to use the common language—meaning that you want to be able to act without obligation or intrusion. Perhaps, having assumed the life of self-discipline for the first time for real, as My devotee, you are like someone in confinement who is still wanting to escape—you are still playing games with the practice I have Given you, still being casual in your adaptation to the Way of the Heart, still being superficial in your devotion to Me, still letting your mind wander instead of practicing Ishta-Guru-Bhakti moment to moment.

You must become profoundly serious in your practice of the Way of the Heart. Embrace the discipline you have been Given, so that you can endure the crisis of true hearing and then of what is beyond it. At some point, when you truly embrace the Way of the Heart and stop struggling to get out of it, stop being superficial and ambiguous, and stop giving yourself back doors through which to escape, there is a turnabout, and you focus on the event in which you are, apparently, suffering. Essentially, it is not an environmental event, or an event in your relationships as you usually understand or perceive them. It is an event of your own activity. It is the act of self-contraction. It is not merely a generalized bewilderment. It is something you directly perceive, something you concretely, one-pointedly, understand thoroughly, and you grasp the principle that will enable you to grow further.

All of the religious life, then, in summary, at its foundation, is just such a discipline, a kind of confinement, or a relinquishment of the arbitrariness, casualness, superficiality, wandering, and seeking of your usual act of attention, to such a degree that you become focused, calmed, and able to deal directly with the suffering that prevents Divine Self-Realization. Therefore, even our discussions about what is basically the social dimension of your life within the community of My devotees is a process of making the details of your practice much more concrete—fully concrete, one hopes—so that you no longer have any back doors, or arbitraries and double-mindedness, but always, instead, in every circumstance, in every moment, you are involved in this focus of Ishta-Guru-Bhakti Yoga, so firmly established in it, so profoundly involved in it, that the real crisis of the religious life can occur.

Until then, you are still playing games with your practice of the Way of the Heart, still only talking about instead of actually practicing Ishta-Guru-Bhakti Yoga. Until you truly embrace the discipline of the Way of the Heart, you are avoiding the transformative crisis, dabbling, being a dilettante about religion. You need not submit to the starkest confinement, like the man in the prison, in a cell, unable to move, without physical liberty. Still, whatever your circumstance of right life in My Company, it must effectively be something like such confinement, so that you are not indulging the waywardness, the seeking, the egoic "self-possession", of egoity but instead you are remaining focused and self-submitted, self-forgetting, enduring whatever is arising but not meditating on it and always submitting beyond it.

To create a real foundation for the religious life of the Way of the Heart in particular, you must become so focused. This means that you must handle your life-business, which, in summary, is to create the circle of practice without any openings, or back doors, or room for seeking and egoic dramatization. The process that is the Way of the Heart truly works when you stop making room for your egoity and stop letting yourself off the hook of practice. Until then, there can be some improvements, something positive can even be said about your practice, but the crises that are the necessities of the religious life do not truly occur and become permanently the basis of your life until you draw that circle and stop struggling within it.

Of course, I have always lived within the circle of such confinement. The jobs I had, for instance, during the time of My own Sadhana, were all temporary jobs, door-to-door sales jobs or the equivalent. I have never really done any other kind of work. Doing ordinary work as an ordinary matter of survival was the same kind of thing I did otherwise—living within that circle, always addressing that same thing, constantly focused, never distracted.

Keep your attention on the obligation and on the One Who Obliges you, not on separate self. Why do you think that in many traditional cultures the first instruction, the first lesson, the first reminder, is always that you are mortal, that you are going to die? Why do I keep Calling you to acknowledge this reality? Because mortality is the circle in which you grow and overcome. Transcendence of separate self is the process. And the Realization is That Which is Beyond the circle, That within Which even the circle is appearing.

If you are anxious about death, you are like the man in his fear, trapped in prison—wanting to escape, not dealing with the mortality, the reality, the confinement, the circle, just anxious, afraid, wanting to get out. However, it is not enough for the practice of true religion just to relax some of your anxiety. Participate in this death of a kind, by accepting the circle, the confinement, and all the discipline in My Company associated with it. Confined in My Company, every moment of attention given to Me, self-surrendering and self-forgetting, accept this circle of life rather than trying to escape it. Do not let yourself escape it. Endure the process of listening, hearing, and beyond.

Death is not just something that is going to happen eventually and you agree that there is nothing you can do about it and so you can relax a little. You must participate in death. Death is the meaning of conditional existence, the very act of it, the principal ceremony, not just at the end of physical life but all the time you live. Therefore, conditional existence is a great sacrifice, and you must become a participant in it. Accept this obligation of sacrifice and allow your confinement to it through self-discipline, through true Yoga, through obliging your egoic "self-possession" to melt, so that you become a participant in this great sacrifice, so that you become sensitized to the Divine Being, Truth, and Reality in Which all is arising, and go Beyond the realm of cosmic appearances.

2.

SRI DA AVABHASA: Death is the process of conditional existence. Death is not going to happen to you. Death is your business. Death is the Way of Liberation. I do not mean death in the sense of destroying the body or committing suicide but in the sense of the process of self-surrender, self-forgetting, self-yielding.

All these bodies are just puja articles. The elements you throw into the Puja Fire are representations of your own body and all the bodies of humanity, of all elemental forms, all forms, everything conditional. The Fire Puja is an expression of the Way of the Heart—sacrifice, death, relinquishment of separate self. The circle of mortality and limitation that surrounds the Puja Fire is the context of sadhana. You are staying focused on the fire at the center of the circle, not trying to escape the Fire but continuing to throw into the Fire the elements of the body, life-energy, the breath, feeling, mind, thoughts, attention, experiences, throwing it all into the center and never digressing, never letting the fire go out, never pulling aside any stone that rings the circle to let yourself out, never forgetting the Fire.

The Divine Way is a great Sacrifice in which all things conditional are participating, inherently. Yet you can forget this reality. You can be persuaded otherwise. You can be deluded. Therefore, the Revelation is Given to you, so that you remain focused, pull all the stones in, keep the circle, maintain the discipline, do the sacrifice that is your business. Only sacrifice—not seeking, egoic "self-possession", self-meditation, complaining—is Ishta-Guru-Bhakti Yoga, the Way of Realization.

Do you like complaining? Sit in a three-feet by five-feet room in a prison for five years and see what happens to your complaints! You are just being petty because you think that you have options and that you can work everyone over and avoid your obligations. Be made serious, and then you will do what is right.

Collectively My devotees are a circle. What are you doing every day? Self-surrendered and self-forgetting, you are staying within the circle, tending the Fire, keeping your attention with Me. You have all kinds of relatively ordinary obligations, yes, but, as My devotee, what is your life about? It is puja, the Puja of Divine Self-Realization. Therefore, stay concentrated, and do the puja constantly. Never digress. Effectively then, never complain. Complaint is trying to escape out the side, out of the circle, out the door, out of this confinement, which is just a crush that generates the heat of concentration, the necessary heat of seriousness that makes self-overcoming, that makes Divine Communion, that allows room for Grace, that allows for Realization.

Handling your business is just doing the puja, continuing to throw the elements into the Fire, keeping everything in order, keeping everything concentrated. Do not be a fool. Do not digress. Every moment is Ishta-Guru-Bhakti Yoga, the body, the feeling, the emotion, the mind, therefore attention, every breath, all energy, constantly concentrated in Me. I am the Fire and the One to Whom you submit, the Realizer and the Realization. It is always this process, whatever the function in which you are involved, whatever the circumstance. It is always the same puja.

This is how you must understand your practice of the Way of the Heart. It is a simplicity. It is always the same thing in different apparent forms, always the same, just as simple as tending the Fire with great seriousness, not as an external observance but as a great process.

By handling your business, you make the circle of stones, put the wood in, light the Fire, create the circumstance of the puja, that is all, and then you do the puja. There is only one thing to do, to throw the various elements—your various obligations—into the Fire to serve this Great Puja. That is all you are doing. That is all My devotees are doing forever. That is it.

DEVOTEE: And Sri Gurudev, Your Shout is the expression of Your Compassion. You do not allow us to falter in our attention.

SRI DA AVABHASA: Why should I be amused by your digression from That Which Serves you ultimately? You must stay concentrated. The puja must be continued. There must be no digression, because it is the sacrifice that benefits beings and that is the purpose of life.

There must be no complaints, no competition, no abusiveness. Maintain the order that allows all aspects of the puja to be done, and just get on with it. What need is there to talk about separate self, then? Separate self is supposed to be thrown into the Fire! Do not talk about it, do not meditate on it. Throw it in there! Note a thing or two about it, discuss it in your group, get a discipline, and get on with it. That is it. That is as much talk about separate self as is useful. Keep the Puja Fire burning. Allow the work to continue. Never interfere with it. Never threaten it. Always guarantee it by your every act, every day of your life. This is the disposition that I expect of all My devotees.

Stop interfering with the Fire Sacrifice, stop undermining it, stop complaining, stop talking "case", stop coming and going, stop all that essential idiocy of egoic dramatization. It is not the Way of the Heart. Understand the serious situation in which you exist, and in which everyone exists. Throw yourself into the Fire! If you are merely cast into it, you only suffer it. The only way not to merely suffer in the sacrifice is to participate in it, to volunteer to be conformed to the Law. I am here to tell you, to show you, to Demonstrate to you, that you need have no fear about participating in the sacrifice. It leads to Realization Ultimately. There is Only God. The ways of the common world are false.

Rightly lived, life is a ritual of sacrifice. There is an order to it. There are obligations in it. There are specific things you must constantly be doing. Life can be rightly understood and made simple and direct. It should be. Life must be so, or it is just chaos, madness, going to death, just fear and seeking.

Those who are only anxious about death, those who fear death, are looking forward to being dead. Those who participate in death as the Law, as the life of sacrifice, are looking forward to what is beyond death. They enjoy a totally different orientation, a totally different disposition, in life. Death is simply a process, a means. Such should be your understanding and your disposition in life, rather than standing back from the Fire, anxious and afraid. Participate in it. Embrace death, not for the sake of being dead but because it is the Law, because it is the process of existence. Such participation becomes the Realization of deathlessness, of That Which is Beyond limitation, Beyond separate self, Beyond these conditions.

Many more conditions, planes, and possibilities exist, into which you could enter, even now, but none of them are the Divine Self-Domain, either. They are simply, all of them, places in which to continue participation in this sacrifice until everything is thrown in, everything is burned, everything is gone beyond in Divine Translation. Divine Translation is not something you can aspire to idealistically. Its Realization does not occur apart from Utter Sacrifice, Absolute, everything thrown in, nothing withheld.

Therefore, do not expect Divine Translation to just happen to you. Divine Translation does not happen to you. It is the Ultimate Realization of the sacrifice in which you are Called to participate. You cannot go from your disposition [Sri Gurudev snaps His fingers] to Divine Translation. No—you must make the sacrifice. You must join in the puja. You must do it utterly. Divine Translation is not something that happens automatically to you after death. While you live here, all the moments of conditional existence are present in your own manifestation. Do this puja most profoundly. Do it constantly. How much is left over after death depends on what you did not throw into the Fire while you lived. If Divine Translation is to be your Realization, then live the Puja of the Way of the Heart. Throw it all in, if you would be Translated into the Divine Self Domain, and hold nothing back. Do not expect it to happen to you just because you are a member of the club, or because you did some sadhana. Divine Translation is not merely a casual possibility among all other possibilities after death. It is the Ultimate, Utter, Absolute, Divine fulfillment of the Law. It is not Divine Translation otherwise.

How much you throw into the Fire while you live determines whether you Realize Divine Translation or pass into other possibilities. Into what realm of possibilities? How much closer to the core of the Cosmic Mandala? Again, how much did you throw into the Fire, for real, not merely as a ritual representation of the sacrifice but doing it, being it, without withholding, utterly self-submitted, utterly self-forgotten, more and more profoundly, every day of your life. This is the work of My devotee. This is true life.

The life-disciplines of the body—disciplines of dress, money, food, sex, all those disciplines—create the sacred space, place you into the sacred environment, of the puja and make your ordinary life non-ordinary, or sacred. Therefore, be serious about it. Address it as such. Honor it as such. Respect it as such. Do it without complaining and with more giving, more surrender. All the heat that arises is the Fire. It is the heat that burns. The heat purifies. The heat straightens. The heat balances. The heat Awakens.

There are no guarantees of your continuation even for one more moment. While your existence continues, however, there is the Law, there is rightness to do. Still, nothing can be taken for granted. There is always more to do under the same circumstance, the same pressure of the circle, the same mortality, with the same surrender, the same intensity, the same seriousness. The struggle that is the puja must continue. Be right, and even if time would vanish ten seconds from now, sacrifice is still the Law, for all of you, in every moment of life.

Grasp this seriousness, and do not just be a middle-class fool expecting to live forever, forgetting death, forgetting the circle, forgetting the puja, forgetting God, forgetting self-discipline, forgetting surrender, watching TV, being a damn fool—no! To do so is insanity. It is hell, and it makes more and more of it.

Be grateful for the circle, the Law, the heart-feeling that stays in you always, because you do not forget the situation you are in and what you are here to do. No relationships can be taken for granted. Nothing can be taken for granted. Everything must be surrendered constantly.

Be dyed in My Color. Be Pervaded by It in every inch and every function, until your whole body, even your flesh, is orange—signifying renunciation, self-surrender, self-forgetting.

Continue this devotion to Me at the Fire. Always. Always dying. Always giving up. Always forgetting. Always surrendering. Always throwing in more elements, more pieces. Every moment of self-observation is just "Oh, I will put that in the cup, and I will throw it in," not talking your "case" and meditating on yourself but accepting the discipline of throwing everything into the fire, having no time to digress, no time to be involved in your "case", no time to take anything for granted. What if some lunatic throws a bomb and blows the whole world to smithereens tonight? It could happen! All kinds of other craziness does. You should be there at the Fire, throwing in everything to cancel the effectiveness of the dark sign, to exist in Light, and to pass Beyond all limitations. To do that is your business.

For your sake, I have lived the ordinary life that everyone lives, and always as a Renunciate, always as the Fire. Therefore, conditional existence, bodily existence, has never contaminated Me, because I am the Fire and I always Do the Fire. Because of this, I have been able to Submit to you, make example to you, reflect you to yourselves.

I am not doing "Me". I am reflecting you to yourself, and I keep the Fire going all the while.

God Is Guru

January 15 and 18, 1994

SRI DA AVABHASA: The various religious traditions tend to concentrate on one or perhaps a few views of the Divine, and the Divine can be described in all of those terms. Thus, God has been Revealed through various religious communications as Creator, as Ultimate Source, as a kind of abstract Condition beyond any human conception, and so on and on and on. Yet what is the fundamental Revelation?

The principal Revelation is the Revelation you have been Given by Me, the Revelation that includes all other Revelations: God is Guru, and the Way of Divine Liberation is submission to God as Guru. This is the senior understanding of God, and practice on its basis is the senior practice of religion that encompasses all other practices. All other presumptions about the Divine Revelation lead to variations, or limitations, on the Divine Way, according to the various stages of life.

Until there is the Inherently Perfect Divine Revelation, all Revelations are partial. "God is Ultimate Principle", "God is Source", "God is Creator"—although all those descriptions, if rightly understood, are true, the fundamental description of God is that God is Guru, God is Master, God is the Revealer and the Revelation. And the Way is the relationship to That One, through self-surrender and self-forgetting, whereby everything is Given by Grace in the process of ego-dissolution.

Therefore, there is nothing else to do but self-surrender, self-forgetting, devotional Communion with Me, the Guru, not just in that moment when you are present in My physical Company but always and forever, even after the Lifetime of This physical Body. Always. Always be My devotee, practicing the Divine Way of the Heart. As My devotee, you can always practice devotion to Me fully, without limitation, when you are not in My physical Company.

I am not Calling you just to understand that I am God, Who can also be described as something other than Guru. I am Calling you to understand My Revelation as the Revelation of What God Is—Guru. God is Guru, not just Creator, Sustainer, Destroyer, Ultimate Principle—yes, all of that also, fine—but What God truly Is, is Guru, Master, Realizer, Revealer, the Revelation Itself, the Means, the One to be Realized.

That Revelation must Be. And It must Be in your likeness, participating in life as you do—but God, Accounting for all, Blessing all, Establishing the Divine Siddhis in the context of everything possible, in the context of everything that is.

This is the Great Matter.

◆ ◆ ◆

SRI DA AVABHASA: People who are moved to practice religion and who are also without Realization talk about God. Even people who are not religious talk about God—they speak negatively about God or they deny God. In spite of the fact that the world has been served by Realizers since ancient times, people still talk about God in merely philosophical, even conjectural, terms. "God is the Creator." "God is the Divine Self." "God is the Absolute." How is a person supposed to relate to God according to those definitions?

If you relate to God as Creator, you think that God created you and all of this appearance, and you expect God to continue to make it perfect. You ask God for boons, and you blame God when your expectations and wants are not fulfilled. The approach to God as Creator, not from the "Point of View" of Divine Self-Realization but from the point of the ego, or the limited, human person, does not make true religion. It makes an ego-based religion of relating to God on the basis of egoic expectations. Such religion makes God the slave of egos, and, ultimately, such religion tends to justify merely social religiosity and utopian expectations.

Therefore, only in Most Ultimate Samadhi, or Divine Self-Realization, can it be said that God is Creator, because the Realization of that Samadhi is that there is Only One. Previous to Divine Self-Realization, one understands that all kinds of causes are manifested in the conditional universe, and these causes make everything happen. Therefore, one cannot say that God is the Cause or that God is to blame. When there is the Realization that there is Only One, then, paradoxically, it can be said that God is Creator, the Maker of all of this, and the Source of all this.

Some without Realization think about God as the Absolute, or the Divine Self. What are they relating to? How do they do sadhana? Such statements as "God is the Absolute" and "God is the Divine Self" are the Confessions of Realization, Descriptions of God by those in a state of one or another degree of Realization. What is the proper relationship to the

Divine, or the Ultimate Reality, the Ultimate Person, of someone who is not the Realizer, someone who is the ordinary person, the religious person, the Spiritual practitioner—you? You are not Realizing God, and the notion that God is That Which you have not yet Realized turns your practice of religion and Spirituality into the practices and limited presumptions of non-Realization.

What, therefore, is the Nature of the God to Whom all can relate, the God Who can be Realized, embraced, associated with, Communed with, presently, by all, even in all the stages of Realization?

It is God as Guru, God as the Realizer and the Revelation of God—Present through all kinds of paradoxical Services that Instruct, that Awaken, that Move, that Draw you into right practice of life on the basis of right understanding of the Divine.

The God of all, the God that is the basis of right religious and Spiritual practice, is God as Guru, God as Master, God as the Realizer, the Revealer, and the Revelation, That Which is to be Realized, the One to Whom you surrender in your right disposition, with right understanding. That One does not congratulate the ego but Draws the ego beyond itself and Vanishes it in Communion. This mastery of the separate self is the true God-Sign, the true God-Description, the true God-Force—the relationship to Which is right life. The Ultimate and True and Right Revelation of God is God as Guru, Master, Realizer, Revealer, Revelation, the One to Whom you surrender, the One to be Realized.

The Sign of Real God has been Given in its various forms through Realizers of one degree or another throughout history. A tradition of Guru-devotion exists, then, and those who have been Served by the Realizer make a great voice about it, because the Realizer is the Divine Revelation That Grants life its rightness, and That makes sense out of conditional existence, rather than nonsense, absurdity, obsession, mere seeking, and suffering.

Right attachment to God is attachment to God as Guru, Master, Realizer, Revealer, the Very Revelation Itself. This devotion is the context and source of true sadhana. All the other ways of describing God, or the Divine, or the Ultimate Condition in Reality to be Realized, are also true in one or another context and from the point of view of one or another Samadhi. They are only partial descriptions, however, that contribute to the larger description of the Divine Person.

The fundamental description of God is that God is Guru.

The Nameless, Mindless, Thoughtless, Presumptionless, Knowledgeless Feeling-Current of Existence

January 18, 1994

DEVOTEE: Sri Gurudev, You mentioned that without mind everything that we apparently perceive would not be as we perceive it.

SRI DA AVABHASA: Not only without mind but without the particular body-mind you are apparently associated with, if I can use the word "you" in the conventional sense. Science points to evidence that there are different ways of perceiving, so to speak, this world. Human beings have a generally characteristic way of perceiving the world, and rhinoceroses another one, and so on and on. Perceptions are determined not only by presumptions in mind. Where do perceptions come from, anyway? From this mechanism that is arising and with which you identify. The body-mind governs the perceptions—and the presumptions.

You think that as a human being you are in an extraordinary position to know reality, only because you are identified with a blob of meat, housed in a skull, that is using energy in a particular way and that says to itself, "That is reality." That is reality? At most, it is an angle on it, a convention of it, a presumption about it. The rhinoceros, the dung beetle, the human, the chameleon, the house fly—all have a different angle on it, a different presumption, based on the mechanism with which they identify. Yet it is the same reality all the while. And what is it?

You all are in this so-called "room", so-called "you all", seeing the room from a particular point of view, wrapped up in a particular mechanism that perceives energy in a certain way. Therefore, you say, "room", "you", "I", "It looks as it does, and I do what I do", and that is your summary of the universe. You are not even seeing the room! You cannot, unless you transcend the mechanism of perception. Such transcendence is Samadhi. Apart from Samadhi, though, you are identified with a particular mechanism that makes a certain appearance of reality seem to be so, and then acts on that basis.

If you want to "consider" reality, that is another matter. If you just want to talk in exchanges with others about what you perceive and play games with one another about what you perceive, fine, but while doing that you are living in a science-fiction novel of absurd presumptions based on psycho-physical structures that actually blind you to reality, lock you into a point of view in space or in time, and show energy to you, God to you, reality to you, in a particular fashion. Stuck with that, you know nothing about Reality, God, Truth, even the room. Nothing!

The room just is, but you are here locked up in that skull of meat, and you have an angle on it, and you are struggling to survive as it, and you think you are prepared to be a great philosopher! What are scientists doing, anyway? They are pretending to be philosophers, but all they are doing is yanking perceptions out of their eyeballs through that particular brain, talking about how things seem, and trying to get an advantage over what they perceive. They are the local priests of this time and place.

What about Reality Itself? To Realize Reality Itself, you must go beyond the mechanisms of your presumptions, even the mechanism of perception. In the meantime, you cannot even see the room as it is, and you cannot inspect Existence Itself, Being Itself, because you do not even know what a single thing is! That is your real situation, you see, not all the blah-blah on TV and all your games of seeking and mental gymnastics and pretending to one another that you know reality. You know nothing about reality. You are playing a game of presumptions with a language that inhabits you and that automatically gives signals and pictures and ideas that are not reality but only a play of appearance, like a computer program, or the videos you take in and out of the video deck.

"I want to watch that movie. I don't like that one"—you take out one video and try another one. Yet in life you have only one program. How do you get it out of the deck? How do you find out what reality is? In the meantime, you are only commenting on your perception and your presumptions and playing on them. You have been doing it for thousands of years, creating all of human history, its philosophies, its presumptions, its wars, its struggle, its seeking, its devastation, its incredible suffering—everybody destroying one another and playing games. It is a mummery, a mock show, not reality but a play based on presumptions.

You do not even know what the room looks like as it is, and you do not know what anything is. That is really your situation, and the disposition of that Divine Ignorance is shown, experienced, realized, in Divine Communion, in every moment of Ishta-Guru-Bhakti. In Ishta-Guru-Bhakti, the presumptions about reality are not taken seriously. They are surrendered and forgotten, and you exist in that Nameless Disposition in which you do not know what anything is, in which your perceptions, which are made by the mechanism itself, are not the measure of reality. There is nothing but an Incomprehensible Feeling, and no presumptions are of ultimate importance.

That is God-Communion. It washes you, because all the presumptions are not being used. They are made obsolete. In the disposition of Reality, you are without presumptions, self-forgotten, the mechanism not taken into account as a source of knowledge about reality.

There is no knowledge of reality. There is only the Divine Ignorance of it, and the Divine Ignorance of it is the Realization of reality. As you persist in Divine Ignorance, things become washed more and more and more, fields are opened up, there are transitions during life, after death, on and on and on, in the Samadhis that are possible by My Grace. The lock of the presumptions of nonsense is vanished, and there is not merely a Feeling without comprehension but there is absolute Certainty, direct, absolute Realization. Such Realization is uncommon conscious awareness. It is uncommon existence. It is profound. It authenticates itself. There is no doubt about it when it occurs. It is all the Reality there Is, and, truly, nothing can be said about it.

On the other hand, aware of your common presumptions and conventions, in that Realization you can say something that is not one with them—paradoxical things, suggestive and inspiring things, can be said.

What should you Avabhasan Daists tell people when they ask you about your life and practice? When they ask you about reality? There are many things you can say, but something fundamental you can say is, "Really, all there is, is a Thoughtless, Mindless, Knowledgeless Feeling of Being. That is about it. And I am going to get on with That."

You go on to confess that you only Realize this Feeling of Being by Grace of My Presence here, My Instruction of you, My "Consideration" with you, My discriminative examination of everything you say and do. You have discovered that the means to be established in that simple Reality is self-surrendering and self-forgetting Communion with Me. By this means, many changes are occurring, and you are very grateful for that. You are getting on with it. That is the whole of religion. It is self-authenticating, obviously true, and you are serious about it. Everything else is knowledge, everything else is presumption, everything else is human stupidity, not Divine Ignorance, and you are not interested in being like cattle and flowing with the winds of doctrine. Confess this when people ask you about your practice.

You do not even know what the room looks like, and you do not even know what a single thing is. What more is there to say in commentary about TV doctrines and the rest of it? It is all a mummery, a science-fiction paradox, just a popularization of scientific ideas, perhaps amusing but not the words of a Master. What do science fiction writers write about? They write in different ways about the fact that the whole universe is scientific. Whenever beings are encountered on some other world or plane or planet, they are all into big science, like Earthlings, getting into their variously designed rocket ships and blasting one another, as in the popular fantasies. It is nonsense.

Nevertheless, it is the same kind of thing you are doing, sitting here in this room that you cannot see, not even knowing what a single thing is, thinking all the thoughts you are thinking right now. That is also absurd. The only reality you associate with for real is that Nameless, Mindless, Thoughtless, Presumptionless, Knowledgeless Feeling-Current of Existence Itself. It is the foundation of religion. That is What is to be gotten with and gone on with. All Realization is in That. All the rest is popular amusement—suffering, in other words, a science-fiction novel in which you really die, and in which you are really ignorant and subject to paradoxes you do not understand.

Aside from the more painful circumstances, which do come to all at one time or another, sooner or later and then finally—those worst, or nearly worst, of events aside—still, in every moment you are just like someone with an incapacitating physical pain. You are obsessed with the pain, which is forcing your attention, forcing the concentration of body, feeling, emotion, mind, attention, every breath, to be confined to a limited and conditional event. Every moment is like that, not just the worst moments, the most painful ones. Every moment is exactly this.

Therefore, I Call you to give your attention to Me. This is the Gift, this is the Realization, moment by moment, day by day, in the midst of all of these arising appearances that concentrate you otherwise. Every moment is different, but always you are tending to be concentrated—bodily, emotionally, mentally, with every breath—in limitations. Ishta-Guru-Bhakti Yoga, the Way of the Heart in My Company, is always, whatever is arising in any moment, to be self-surrendered and self-forgotten in Communion with Me, always to be entering into That Which is Reality Itself, through Communion with Me and forgetting the rest.

All the events of your life are inherent in the fault you have already presumed. They are not the Way of Divine Self-Realization, and they are not Reality Itself. In every moment, then, your obligation is Ishta-Guru-

Bhakti Yoga, this self-surrender directly to Me, in Communion with Me, forgetting yourself, not making much of the apparent events but forgetting them and giving Me your body, your emotion, your feeling, your attention, your mind, with every breath—moment by moment by moment. Be preoccupied with Me and forget the rest, not by intending to forget them but by being preoccupied with Me. Do not look back.

Through this practice you grow. This practice is the true religious life, not popular doctrines like the medieval principles of faith in transubstantiation but the direct simplicity in reality. In that practice, everything is washed, everything is overcome, and the whole process occurs by Grace. Give yourself up to it utterly, and then you will be an ecstatic like the people you read about in books.

So—[to the man who began the conversation] here you are, just another science-fiction character, wanting to go off into the galaxy with his "I, I, I, I, I". But let us try to deal with the question. What is the question? Hmm?

DEVOTEE: Beloved, I was wondering before where all this presumption came from, and why it is.

SRI DA AVABHASA: See how much you have covered already—"all this presumption and why it is". Now we get the question.

DEVOTEE: You have made absolutely apparent in this conversation, Beloved, that even when I try to figure this out and concentrate on it, all I am doing is reaffirming the presumed "I" and the presumption of "I".

SRI DA AVABHASA: The reason you like hearing stories about saints and ecstatics is that they are people who do not do what people usually do. You would like to be someone who is doing what people do not ordinarily do. You would like to be in that ecstatic position, "crazy" like them in your own manner. Fine! So do it! You have been given the means. We have had our "consideration". Be an ecstatic, then. That is My Recommendation.

By the Yoga of Ishta-Guru-Bhakti, stay in the Simplicity that is Reality Itself, Which is just this Current of the Feeling of Existence Itself. Everything else is—where is it? All I see is Who I Am. And It Is One, and there is no differentiation in It. I have no doubt about It. It is just So. It is not a product of thought. My Recognition is Inherent, Instant, never changed, never limited, never undone, never threatened. Is it so of you?

I always thought, from birth, that it was the same for everybody. I thought everybody was like this. But I observed them, I questioned them, I experienced them, and I found out it is not so. The Obvious is not Obvious to everyone. More and more moved in My combinations with them, I became more and more like them, like you, to the point where I forgot My Self. But, still, My Self was there and came through and made My Sadhana of Re-Realizing My Self.

That is My Realization. What about yours? There is no excuse for a petty, un-Enlightened life, it seems to Me, when there is so much Only Reality here. Therefore, why are you making so much of ordinary life? Why not abandon yourself to Reality? It has always seemed utterly even reasonable to Me to do that. It has always been remarkable to Me that you do not choose it, and you always have another argument for not doing so. It is amazing to Me.

By the way, I am not causing you to refuse to do this, so do not say I am the Cause of your reluctance. It cannot even be said that you are the "cause" of it, because you do not know who you are. You do not even know what a single thing is. You cannot even see the room as it is. This has always been self-evidently crazy to Me. You all have another opinion, apparently, and out of that comes your question—so what is it?

You Cannot Think and Talk at the Same Time

March 13, 1994

SRI DA AVABHASA: It is interesting that you cannot think and talk at the same time. Perhaps it has never occurred to you that this is so. Examine it: You cannot think and talk at the same time. In order to talk, you must stop thinking. When you are talking, you are not thinking. Sometimes you think, and then you talk. You figure out what you are going to say, and then you say it. But when you talk, you do not think. You cannot think and talk. You cannot do two things with the same faculty at the same time. You cannot think and talk at the same time. You cannot. Try it. When you start talking, all of a sudden you are not thinking.

Well, then! Who is talking? What is talking? Not the thinker. Then where is the talking coming from?

There is an analogy to this. When some people drink, they drink to the point that they become unconscious, or certainly the next day they do not remember what they were doing. Perhaps you have had this experience. You were told by others that you were talking all the time, doing this and that all the time, yet you have no memory of it. In such a situation, you are not a participant in the usual sense. Who was talking? Who entertained everybody while you were not there? You got to do all kinds of ego-time, and you were not even present. Who actually did it?

Another analogy is the beat of the heart while you sleep. Even while you are awake, you do not beat the heart. There is not a thing you can do about the heartbeat. Of course, you can react or do various other things that might affect your heartbeat, but, in general, you cannot directly beat the heart.

Even so, you identify with thinking as if you are doing it. You identify with talking as if you are doing it. Each of these functions is just like the heartbeat. It is a happening. It can go on without you—and does. While it is happening, if you have attention for it, anyway, you presume that it is you. When you speak, you presume that you as the thinker are speaking. Yet you cannot think and speak at the same time. When you speak, you stop thinking. How do you get to do it, then? If you cannot think while you are speaking, then what are you speaking about? How can you even manage it? I guess it is something like moving the sludge through your intestines. You do not have anything to do with that, either, but it still happens.

It is the same with talk. You thinkity-thinkity-thinkity-thinkity-think. At some point a little sphincter in your head gets an urge, and you go, "YAMMER-YAMMER-YAMMER-YAMMER-YAMMER!"

Talking and thinking cannot be done at the same time. You cannot chew gum and whistle "Dixie" at the same time—or however the popular proverb says it.

In the esoteric Spiritual traditions, the psyche is the principle of evolutionary development. In the Way of the Heart, however, the psyche is just another groin, another intestine, another bit of business to be purified, to be eliminated. Thinking and speaking are the same as defecating, farting, urinating, burping. There is no hierarchy of importance, as if it is better to talk than to fart, or better to think than to eliminate. No. They are all the same. All the same. I am not being exaggerated!

DEVOTEE: I have noticed that . . .

SRI DA AVABHASA: You are not thinking now, are you?

DEVOTEE: No. Talking.

SRI DA AVABHASA: What does talking have to do with thinking, then? Thinking is something you do when you do not talk. Thinking has its right function, and it is in fact essential that you engage the thought process with real intelligence and discrimination, as I Call you to do. But you just occupy yourself with random, useless thoughts whenever you are not talking or engaging in some other activity that interrupts your stream of thinking. That is not real thinking. It is a leftover, a backfire.

Exercise thinking as an intelligent act, whenever it is required. Altogether, it is better not to be preoccupied with endless talking and thinking, better to be silent in mind and in speech. In order to be silent, however, you cannot struggle with mind and speech. You must practice Ishta-Guru-Bhakti Yoga, you see, and surrender yourself with all the faculties of the body-mind into Communion with Me, forgetting yourself.

It is better to be quieted altogether. Altogether. You cannot do that by <u>trying</u> to be quiet, or by self-"guruing". Just surrender to Me and forget yourself. Forgetting yourself is the best thing to do, fundamentally the only thing to do.

When something arises, address it with Ishta-Guru-Bhakti Yoga. If thinking is necessary in the context of your service, fine—give whatever it is a moment or two, figure it out, and go on about your business. If it is just a practical matter, then a thought here, a gesture there, handling your business—fine.

You can Invoke Me by My Name constantly. Or you can ponder My Great Questions constantly, or Enquire constantly in the form "Avoiding relationship?" Then you surrender to Me and transcend thinking. You surrender and forget yourself altogether. You not only do not indulge in these separative activities by way of identification with the body-mind, but you enter into Communion with Me. And you feel more and more profoundly what that Communion is. This Wonder Beyond objectivity would be your interest, then.

Nothing, no thing, nothing but Sublimity—Beyond self-remembrance, Beyond self-contraction, Beyond identification with the body-mind, without objects—an incomprehensible Wonder. My devotees enter into this Disposition even at the beginning. They notice It more and more, and they notice Its profundity more and more. They are interested in It more and more.

To Realize this Divine Wonder is all My devotees want to do.

The Basic Principle

January 26, 1994

SRI DA AVABHASA: When adaptations arise, and quite commonly they do, rather mechanically, people generally, in the next moment, because they are stuck with some adaptation, tend to try to do something about it. They try to manipulate the event and make the subjective aspects of it stop. They try to do something to get out of the suffering of it by working on the thing itself. Another tendency is just to go with the program, and then to try to do something about it only when it begins to be suffered. In both cases, the addiction is reinforced. As long as you are focusing attention in the difficulty, you are reinforcing it. The only way to make the thing you are suffering obsolete is to not use it.

The principle of the Way of the Heart is to not use the signs of addiction, the signs of the ego. The Way of the Heart is not a struggle with the ego or even an effort to avoid it. The Way of the Heart is not in the slightest about using or becoming involved in the ego's program. It is not even a matter of wanting the ego to disappear. Right practice has nothing to do with any of those devices. Instead of placing attention in all of that, on the basis of some fundamental self-understanding and your direct response to Me you give Me your attention, your feeling, your body, with every breath. You enter into feeling-Contemplation of Me, and not as a strategy to somehow get rid of the difficulty. Whatever happens to the apparent problem, you simply enter into feeling-Contemplation of Me. This is the principle of practice in the Way of the Heart, rather than ego-based efforts that try to deal with the separate self.

DEVOTEE: It seems it is more a matter of trying to find these areas that arise in each of us. I can see them in myself and in others, too. We can help each other to acknowledge them and make them forms of Remembrance.

SRI DA AVABHASA: Not forms of Remembrance but just the Remembrance instead. Not somehow animating the difficulty itself in a devotional manner but just practicing the Yoga of devotion to Me, giving Me your attention.

Attention is the fundamental principle of the mind. Therefore, instead of wandering around in thoughts, give Me the faculty of mind, which is attention itself. Give Me the faculty of emotion, which is feeling itself, not the various categories of emotion but feeling itself. Give Me the body altogether, through full feeling-intention enacted through service. All of these are connected by the breath, so all of this is breathed, also. The gesture of surrender is done via the breath. Attention, feeling, and the body are breathed in Communion with Me, given over to breathe Me. This is the Yoga in every moment, and not any device or strategy of any kind toward the programs of egoity.

The usual device of the ego, and, therefore, of ordinary people, no matter what arises, is to become involved in what arises, either by indulging in it or by trying to manipulate it somehow—thinking about it, trying to figure it out, working on it on its own terms. That is not the Way of the Heart. That is not the Yoga I have Given to you. I have spent much of the last twenty-two years in Helping you to get this point, because you have tended to make a culture out of dealing with separate self, meditating on separate self, struggling with separate self, talking about separate self, dramatizing separate self.

As I have told you, the Way of the Heart is about self-understanding, yes, but self-understanding as an aspect of self-transcendence. You have tended to take this to mean that the process of the Way of the Heart is about struggling with separate self—thinking about it and talking about it interminably. It is not. The principle of the Way of the Heart is Ishta-Guru-Bhakti Yoga. In your practice of that, of course the separate self is observed and disciplines are assumed relative to it, as part of the response to Me, Communion with Me, wherein separate self is surrendered and forgotten.

Self-surrender in the Way of the Heart is not a strategy to do something to the separate self. It is to use the fundamental faculties of the body-mind that would otherwise be preoccupied with separate self and its programs. It is to take those faculties and give them to Me in every moment. That is self-forgetting. That is true surrender. Trying to use the separate self to surrender is an effort to struggle with the separate self. The fundamental faculties of the body-mind are not bound to the egoic program in the moment. The mind may be thinking, thinking, thinking, full of the program, but attention can be given to Me. Attention has no quality. There may be all the reactive emotions, but feeling itself is not modified. It can be given to Me. The condition of the body at the moment may be disease and disturbance, but the body itself, just that, can be rendered to Me. The cycle of the breath may be modified by forms of mind, reactive emotion, and bodily states, but the breath itself is not modified. It can be rendered to Me, given to Me.

Therefore, the Yoga of Ishta-Guru-Bhakti is to devote to Me, in every moment, these fundamental faculties of the body-mind, which would otherwise be preoccupied with separate self. The Yoga of Ishta-Guru-Bhakti does not use the separate self in any sense. It makes the separate self obsolete by not using it, and, in due course, the separate self vanishes. Yet you do not do the Yoga so that you can keep checking on the separate self: "Has it changed yet? Do I feel better yet?" No. It is forgotten. And, in the forgetting, in Communion with Me, you make room for My Blessing to do Its Work, and you let the thing become obsolete by non-use. The fundamental principle of the Yoga is to let the programs of the ego become obsolete by not using them, by not using any of the energy of them, not granting attention to them, not struggling with them, only practicing the Yoga of Communion with Me by using the faculties of the body-mind that would otherwise be devoted to separate self.

This is the basic principle I have Struggled all these twenty-two years to Help everyone to understand, by breaking you out of your egoic point of view whereby you even transform the Way of the Heart into a version of egoity.

This is the critical understanding at the foundation of the Way of the Heart. It is what My devotees must realize, by their adaptation to the process of listening to Me that is at the beginning of the Way of the Heart.

A Single Spontaneous Gesture

January 27, 1994

SRI DA AVABHASA: The four faculties of the body-mind account for all of your functions. If any one or a combination of them is not surrendered to Me, not brought into Communion with Me, they revert to the domain of egoity, the games of egoity, and, therefore, the content of egoity. If you submit these four functions that are at the root of all aspects of human existence, then the ego-game is canceled, it is forgotten, it is not indulged in, it is not reinforced. Therefore, remember that these are the four functions whereby you surrender the body-mind to Me. They cover everything.

To surrender attention without surrendering feeling, without surrendering the body, and without coordinating these with the breath is not enough. It is the same with any other faculty.

It is equally easy to surrender all four of the functions, because in and of themselves they have no content. Attention has no content, feeling has no content in itself, the body has no content—just it is surrendered. The breath may be modified, but if just it is brought into Communion with Me it has no content. It is equally easy to grant Me all of these. There is no special difficulty with any of them. The Yoga is simply a matter of your doing it, and there is no struggle, unless you are appealing to the content of the separate self. The faculty is always available. You can either turn it to the content, or you can turn it to Me. There is no struggle in turning any of these faculties to Me. It is just a matter of what you will turn the faculties to. It is easy to turn any one of them to Me, because you need not first deal with content. The faculty is senior to the content.

Therefore, there are no moments when surrender is more difficult than others, unless you are devoted to the content of separate self. If you are just Remembering Me, if surrendering yourself to Me is your disposition and intention, then surrender to Me is easy. The Yoga is just a matter of doing the surrender. There is no in-between to deal with. The faculty is pure.

When you are sensitive to the Yoga, surrender of the four faculties is a single gesture, rather than "Okay, now I am giving my feeling, now I am giving my body, now I am breathing". Surrender of the faculties is a spontaneous, simple gesture that covers all, once you have adapted to it.

DEVOTEE: By tendency, I am less a feeling person. It seems easier for me to give You my attention than to give You my feeling as a first gesture.

SRI DA AVABHASA: If you are attracted to Me, there is no "my" about it. You are still on the conditional side of this process. The virtue of the Yoga, what makes it possible, is not your struggle with separate self to grant Me these gifts. My Attraction, My Attractiveness—I My Self am the Virtue of this Yoga. If you just turn to Me—and perhaps you do turn with attention or one of the other faculties first—everything else will follow. When you find Me Attractive to you, it is easy to grant all of this to Me. If you are just involved with yourself and trying to turn, making surrender into a struggle, what you are doing has nothing to do with Me.

DEVOTEE: I understand. When there is the devotional acknowledgement of You in the moment of attraction to You, there is no struggle at all.

SRI DA AVABHASA: Yes, when you stay with Me for real, when you give Me yourself for real now, when you do not fall back into all your egoity, surrender is easy to do constantly. You would not do otherwise. You would not have it be otherwise. If you indulge in a lapse, it seems that there is more you must struggle with first before you can surrender. The more you lapse, the more difficult it is. The more vacations you take, the more surrender to Me seems like a struggle. The more you forget Me, the harder it is to Remember Me. If you understand this, you will not take casual vacations from Ishta-Guru-Bhakti Yoga, because you know how difficult it is afterwards. Accomplish the Yoga persistently, and you will see how easy it is to persist in the next moment. But indulge in the lapses, and you will have all kinds of questions and you will suggest to Me that surrender is complicated.

Sometimes it is necessary to just go on retreat. When the Yoga becomes difficult, go on retreat. You have the opportunity for retreat every week, on Da Guruvara. At other times, take a few days, take a week or two. Do what you must to stay in the right disposition of surrender to Me, not in the disposition made by the lapses.

The Devotional Yoga of the Breath

February 4, 1994

SRI DA AVABHASA: My Admonition that you Commune with Me with every breath, or Remember Me with every breath, or Invoke Me with every breath, does not mean that you technically engage every inhalation and exhalation. It is an Admonition you must fulfill artfully, in such a way that even though you are not engaging every breath as a technical practice, nevertheless every breath effectively is Communion with Me. The practice is done artfully, and, therefore, rather randomly.

The general practice I have Given you is not about observing breaths, counting breaths, noticing breaths in any technical fashion. It is about entering into relationship with Me via the breath, Communing with Me via the breath. The breath is not the subject of your practice. I Am! All the faculties of the body-mind must be devoted to Me, and, since breath is a primary faculty, you must exercise yourself in relation to Me via the breath. The practice is not to get very curious about the breaths themselves, or finicky about breathing. It is to devote yourself to Me completely and to use the leading faculties of the body-mind as a principal mechanism for it. It is a devotional practice, then, not merely a functional one.

Fundamentally, the practice of Ishta-Guru-Bhakti I have Given you is a moment to moment practice. Its use is not limited to meditation. It is simply, in effect, to Invoke Me. In terms of the breath, it is to practice reception and release directly in relation to Me—receiving Me, releasing yourself, releasing all content. It is a random noticing and engaging of the breath. If the practice is done rightly, artfully, at random, then effectively every breath becomes feeling-Communion with Me, the process of receiving Me, releasing yourself into Communion with Me, giving Me your attention, giving Me all feeling, directing the body toward Me, and thereby Invoking Me. By observing these mechanisms, bring them to Me.

There is a process of adaptation to doing this, not only in meditation but in daily life, under all circumstances. As you adapt to this artful practice of real and concrete devotion to Me, in due course it becomes rather simple, even automatic—but not mechanical. It just begins to flow, it just begins to happen, and all of its aspects fall into place very simply.

Components of the practice of "conductivity" are also associated with the breath, and I have described these in *The Dawn Horse Testament*. Yes, you must adapt to the practice of "conductivity" technically. You must remember to do so. You must intentionally introduce its various parts artfully. As your adaptation develops, however, "conductivity" becomes more and more simple and straightforward—all the parts come together. It does not require so much mental noticing anymore. It is very simple and spontaneous, yet it accounts for everything.

The breath is the link between all of the primary faculties of the body-mind. It is a physical act. Therefore, it is associated with the body. It is a feeling matter. Therefore, it is associated with emotion. It requires attention. Therefore, it requires the leading faculty of mind. The practice is not to direct body, emotion, and attention to the breath, however. It is to direct all those, and the breath, toward Me. It is a matter of participating in Me, entering fully into relationship to Me, concretely, with all the faculties yielded.

First there is your response to Me, but then you must learn this artful, and in some ways technical, practice, by progressive adaptation. Just that adaptation is part of the beginner's practice of the Way of the Heart. You must consistently apply yourself, and you must study My Instruction.

The Foundation Practice

February 4, 1994

SRI DA AVABHASA: In the beginning of your practice of the Way of the Heart, you are relating to My bodily (human) Form. By feeling and Contemplating My bodily (human) Form, you Commune with Me As I Am altogether, but the specific and experiential context of your practice is the Murti of My bodily (human) Form.

In the Spiritual stages of life in the Way of the Heart, before the "Perfect Practice", devotion to Me in My bodily (human) Form continues, but now with the addition of the larger Murti of My Spiritual (and Always Blessing) Presence. In the advanced, or Spiritually-activated, stages of life in the Way of the Heart, it is proper to speak of My Guru-Shakti.

Then, in the "Perfect Practice", or the ultimate stages of life in the Way of the Heart, in addition to the Murti of My bodily (human) Form, and the Murti of My Spiritual Presence, you relate to Me as "Atma-Murti", that Form of Me that is My Very (and Inherently Perfect) State.

In this manner, the process of the Way of the Heart progressively develops responsible Communion with Me in My various Murti-Forms.

It is not that in the ultimate stages of life in the Way of the Heart you are only dealing with Me as "Atma-Murti", or the Murti of the Inherently Spiritual and Transcendental Divine Self. No. In the ultimate stages, you are dealing with all My Forms—My bodily (human) Form, My Spiritual (and Always Blessing) Presence, and My Very (and Inherently Perfect) State. At the beginning, you are dealing, simply, with My bodily (human) Form as the Revelation in the context of your Communion with Me. It is not that you move on to My Spiritual Form in the advanced stages of life in the Way of the Heart. To your Communion with Me in this bodily (human) Form, you add Communion with Me in My Spirit-Form. In the ultimate stages of life in the Way of the Heart you add "Atma-Murti", My Ultimate Form, in the context of the others. So it is complete.

The foundation for your Spiritual practice in My Company is your devotion to This Murti Sitting here before you, This Revelation-Form. It is by your beginner's devotional practice in relation to Me in This Form that you become capable of Communing with Me in My other Forms. There is no real Spiritual practice in My Company until you have established the foundation devotion to Me in My bodily (human) Form. Devotion to My bodily (human) Form is the context of your moment to moment practice of Remembrance of Me, Communion with Me, Invocation of Me—not by relating to some abstraction of Me but by holding to This Form, returning to This Form constantly, by directing the concrete faculties of your own bodily (human) form to Me.

When that work is done, when that foundation is established, then you can function in Spiritual terms, in the subtler context of your existence. However, the work in the grossest context of the body-mind must be established first. It cannot be bypassed.

When you are devoted to My bodily (human) Form, when you have gone through the real ordeal, process, and purification that occurs in the context of the foundation devotion, then the body-mind is prepared to find Me—I My Self—Spiritually.

Even beginners can have some experience of My Spiritual Presence through its effects. The fact that you do does not mean you are equipped yet to do the Spiritual sadhana. You must do the sadhana that deals with the gross context of your existence, and the gross context of your egoity, therefore. Nonetheless, it is right to understand that the beginner's practice is preliminary. It is not supposed to occupy your entire lifetime. If you choose to have it so, that is your choice, but it is not necessary. You are Called to really do the foundation practice of the Way of the Heart, but also to mature in a finite period of time. It will not be just a few weeks, but, in general, it need not take your entire life. In general, all My devotees should be capable of the Spiritual sadhana in this lifetime.

Nonetheless, the beginning of the Way of the Heart is a real ordeal, and its realization is not a matter of words, merely. It must really be done.

DEVOTEE: Beloved Gurudev, I feel the effectiveness of this Yoga, but there is a great difference between the beginner's adaptation to it and the disposition wherein feeling-Contemplation is brought to all circumstances of daily life. How does one come to that point?

SRI DA AVABHASA: By doing it more and more. It becomes complete by practice, in other words, not by some trick of learning how to make it so. You must intentionally do this practice under all circumstances until it is fully and truly practiced under all circumstances.

How Magical! How Profound!

February 4, 1994

SRI DA AVABHASA: Only God is Worthy. Therefore, every moment should be devoted to the One Who Is.

There is nothing but this Self-Existing and Self-Radiant Consciousness Itself, Divine Being Itself—nothing. That is all there is. Truly, there is Only One—Absolute, All Love-Bliss. That is the Condition to be Realized. That is Who I Am. When you respond to Me, your life takes that God-Realizing course.

Allow the process to become great. Devote your life to Me utterly. Fulfill your obligations in the body, all the while submitted to Me. This is the Way of My devotee, always vocalizing praise of Me, devotion to Me, every moment of your life transformed by this great impulse toward Me. This is what you must do around Me.

Give Me everything, and forget it all. Your daily life carries obligation—fine. Your puja is to devote yourself to Me and forget about yourself. Having had your glimpse of Me, now you must make a life out of it.

In the few photographs of Baba Muktananda with His Guru, Swami Nityananda, Baba Muktananda is sitting at Swami Nityananda's Feet with His hands folded. His hairs are practically falling out! In the presence of His Master, He was so full of love that it seemed His whole body would disintegrate. He observed certain manners, fine, but there was just this devotion, this love, this overwhelming love for His Master, the Bliss of it. He hardly can contain himself, yet manners require that He do so. Once He had met His Master, He was obsessed with His Master, His heart wrenched by His devotion, so full and so profound that He could not think about anything else, could not think about anything else. "What do I think about but my Master?" So He was.

What a Master My Baba Muktananda was! What a Master! What a devotee! That is the way you should live with Me!

You need not read about devotion in the traditional books. Here I Am! As My devotee, therefore, your right sign is total conversion of your life, total conversion of the heart, by your obsession with the Master. When you see That One with clear eyes, how can you help yourself! What else is there to do? Such devotion does not prevent you from functioning and handling your life-business, nothing of the kind. All the while Remembering your Master, all the while obsessed, all the while governed by that Person, all the while thinking of the Master, all the while, in every moment—this is what it is to be My devotee. It is the same sign given by great devotees in the past, this feeling-Remembrance, this total concentration in the Realizer, the One Who Is, even there bodily, before you.

This is real life. Wonderful! What a Joy! What Beauty there is to it! How Magical! How Profound! You, your heart opened, thrown on the floor, your head at the Master's Feet, always remembering your Master—that is real life, not the garbage you have lived so far and that you are bargaining to keep! What else is there to think about? The thoughts that start rolling are nonsense! "All I am interested in is my Master." That is the confession of My devotee. There is nothing else to be interested in. Such devotion changes your life, occupies your life, makes you entirely different. The Master is all there is, all there is to live for, you constantly fastened on His Feet, His Body, His facial expressions, everything about Him. This is devotion—with no reluctance, no mere mannerliness or outer observances.

Real life is obsession with the Guru—total obsession with the Guru, total obsession with the Master—it changes your life and makes you a fool of a kind. Still you do all your daily business—fine. It is no big deal, not a distraction, just Yoga—all the while Remembering Me.

Become sublime by your absorption in Me, but every day, in every moment. The only reason you are serving away from My physical Company is because it is My Admonition to You. You would rather be in the room with Me. Therefore, Remember My Face, cling to Me always. Be obsessed with Me. Do not be afraid to be obsessed with Me. <u>Be</u> obsessed! That is devotion, you almost incapable of another thought or the movement of attention to anything else. "Here I am, doing this service because the Master has told me to do it"—all the while Remembering your Master—"How could I think of anything else? There is nothing so Beautiful, nothing so Wonderful, nothing else to Realize. Everything else is suffering."

Real life is obsession with That Which is Beyond life, That Which is, miraculously, somehow Shown in life but Which moves you beyond it.

Such real and right life makes you a renunciate. It makes you a true devotee first. It makes you forget everything. Instead of cutting anything off in your life, you just forget about all of it. Everything normalizes. Everything falls into its proper order. You do things that are right, and you do them Yogically, in devotion to Me.

I Am just the Divine One, just the Living One, Showing Itself here. I Am just this Shakti, this Form, this Divine Sign. Be obsessed! Be governed by this Vision. That, and nothing else, is devotion to Me. No reluctance, no mere mannerliness—no. All the time be distorted by this devotion to the Master. Like My Baba Muktananda, who just maintained His devotion and understood further, no matter what was arising. He went through the ordeal of being purified, by maintaining the fixity of His devotion to His Master. His whole life was made of that devotion. His virtue was the Blessing of His Master—and He so confessed, over, and over, and over again. He became Great because of His devotion to His Master, His fixity on His Master. He could not think otherwise. He could only think how Wonderful His Master was, how Beautiful. He could not think of anything else!

You become Great through absolute adoration of the One Who is Great. If I thought there was anything in Me that is not worthy of your adoration, I would tell you! I do not lie. I have been through the entire affair of the Sadhana of Perfectly self-transcending God-Realization.

Therefore, you must become "crazy" with devotion to Me, "crazy" with the adoration of Me. This is what My Baba did, My Baba Muktananda. My Nityananda was My Baba, too, and My Rudi Baba. I am a "Baba", too, but all the things are left behind by Me. There are no limits in Me. I am this Very Force, the One you call "Guru", the One you call "Shakti", the One you call "the Goddess", the One you call "God". Just That. No limitations. The Perfect Vehicle for your adoration, for your Salvation, for your Liberation. Become full of your adoration of Me, your submission to Me. I will not harm you. Will not. Would not. Cannot. Magnify your adoration of Me, your devotion to Me.

This One is Naked and Free of limitations. No greater Sign has ever been Given. How can you not take up the Way of the Heart in My Company? How can you not adore Me? How can you not practice this devotion to Me? How can your life not be changed? How can your behavior not be changed? Are you going to remember only yourself? Sulk? Be displeased, react, bargain?

God-Realization is about obsession with the Master, adoration of the Realizer, always this devotion, always expressed. That is the Great Secret. It is the one Principle ever communicated in the Great Tradition of mankind. All the rest is secondary.

Just be My devotee, always serving Me, knowing Who I Am, like Baba Muktananda sitting there trying to contain Himself. Yes. There is a certain kind of containment in your adoration, because you live, but the heart is bursting. The feeling of the Master is the Ultimate Controller. It Controls every moment of your life. You cannot think about anything else.

That is how you become a renunciate, not by cutting things off but by this obsession, this adoration, this love, this devotion. Then you forget about everything. What do you care about your arrangements, or how your karmas are going to work out, or whether you are going to die of cancer, or whether you have a good boyfriend or girlfriend! For the true devotee, the only purpose of life is the adoration of the God-Form to the point of utter conformity. Such adoration changes your entire life, and it makes you a renunciate. All the renunciation you require will be manifested spontaneously, if you enter into devotion to Me obsessively and completely.

A true devotee never wants to be anywhere but at the Master's Feet, looking into His Face, looking at His Body, never wanting to be anywhere else—and never going anywhere else, then! Even if the Master says, "Leave the room, go do this, that, and the other thing," still the true devotee is there glancing at the Master. There is no other object of interest.

As such a devotee, everything you do, apparently otherwise, is just fulfilling the Master's Instruction for the sake of your sadhana, for the sake of your Realization. Your service is not a forgetting of the Master. You would rather not do it, you would rather not go to the intimate room, you would rather not go to lunch—you would rather not, except that the Master says to do it, so you do it without distraction, continuing to be obsessed, continuing your adoration. All you want to do is lay your body down in front of your Master and luxuriate there, become an odalisque in the face of your Great Friend, the One Who Is. To function at all is a great ordeal of being obedient to your Master, because you would rather do nothing, you would rather just be there.

The Master Admonishes you, "Do this practice, fulfill this obligation, handle this business." And so you do, but in that obsession, in that adoration, just fulfilling your Master's Admonition but never forgetting Him, never given up to the function of separate self, to the world itself, to your programs of egoic "self-possession". If you were My true devotee and this were your disposition, there would be <u>nothing</u> to listening, <u>nothing</u> to hearing. It would be nothing. It would happen quickly.

Oh, yes! What is there more to do when there is this obsession with your Master's own Form? Everything is cut through quickly, cut through directly. All there is, is the Love-Bliss of your adoration, your devotion, that feeling, the heart wide open, a hole in your head, holes all over your heart, holes all over your body, no karmas to take into account, no destiny you would have happen to your body. Your only object is your Master. And that devotional obsession is the religious life.

You must become Mad with this devotion. Everything is purified by it. It is the one Great Principle of existence. All I am doing in this conversation with you tonight is Giving you permission to do so. You will do what you will.

The Heat of Reality

February 10, 1994

SRI DA AVABHASA: Devotion to Me is the Way of the Heart. In the context of the various forms of self-discipline, you observe the limit on your devotion to Me, and you assume various disciplines that further sensitize you to Me. You practice Ishta-Guru-Bhakti Yoga intentionally, more and more in every moment, bodily, with feeling, with attention, with every breath. More and more the reality of the self-base is exposed. You are concentrated in the dilemma of it, in some sense, until it breaks. There are no vacations from the Yoga, just the practice of self-surrendering and self-forgetting Communion with Me—and this knot in the same moment, self-surrendering devotion and the knot, too. In that tapas, hearing awakens. If you avoid the tapas, avoid the concentration and the heat, then you will not allow hearing to occur.

You have My Life as a Sign to you of just this sadhana. What did I do all the while at Columbia College? I was not getting an education so that I could have a profession. I was investing My Self in this Profundity, without satisfaction, utterly dissatisfied, in every moment concentrated in it, working in it. On the beach in California, I was not watching the sunsets, seeing the sea roll in, feeling bodily whole, all My meridians balanced. No. Everything was observed, inside and outside, and written down. I stayed in the concentration, in the sweat of it, the heat of it, the dilemma of it, the disturbance of it, the un-Happiness of it, working constantly, moment by moment by moment. That is how it broke.

I did not take any vacations. I was doing all kinds of ordinary things, but I always maintained this concentration. Always a fundamental dissatisfaction, and I was not really distracted. "It is just a thing, just a 'that', a sensation, a thought, an object. Just that, just that, just that, just that." Always swollen with this disturbance. No vacations. Incapable of a vacation from it, actually.

Look at all the smiling Westerners doing Yoga. They are trying to feel good. You all do the same thing in your own fashion, whereas to remain in the dilemma, the heat, the dissatisfaction, the sadhana, is not an amusement. It is an ordeal. To stay in the ordeal is sadhana. To step out of it is the avoidance of sadhana, the dramatization of egoity, or self-contraction. You show your impulse, then, by your vacations. If you are to be taken seriously by Me, I must observe that you stay in the heat, stay in the dissatisfaction. Not just all the time trying to manufacture an ideal life, a comfortable life, utopian existence—blankets, sheets, baskets, good meals, acupuncture treatments to keep your meridians flowing—no. Such comfort is strictly peripheral, mostly nonsense, even. To be doing sadhana in My Company is to be in the ordeal of it, the dissatisfaction of it, yet not a reactive character. The person in the ordeal of real sadhana is a truly benign character, not playing the ordinary games of life to keep the separate self happy, as if it could be, as if its happiness is the point—no—staying in the dilemma of it, the dissatisfaction of it.

In every moment, then, you are not flying off bodily or in your feeling or in your attention or in your breath to this, that, and the other thing, but you are concentrated in Me—that is the discipline. And in every moment in which you engage that practice of Ishta-Guru-Bhakti Yoga, the difference, the alternative effort, the conditioning, the ego-game, will show itself. It will resist. That is what makes Ishta-Guru-Bhakti Yoga an ordeal. Ishta-Guru-Bhakti Yoga is not pleasantness. It is intending to do it and really doing it, exercising yourself as it, feeling the difference, the resistance, and suffering it. Suffering it makes the heat, and that is how the thing breaks.

But you want to avoid tapas. You want relative comfort. You want life to turn out to be good, the separate self to turn out to be Happy. You do not want to be in the dilemma, the stress, the heat, the discomfort, the ordeal of real sadhana. Yes, you like the idea of the things that would result if you did sadhana. You like talking about that, thinking about that—seventh stage Realization, Samadhi—but you do not want to do what it requires, which is to stay in the heat of the ordeal all the time. Adding more and more disciplines to your life is not about correcting your behavior and becoming a more ideal person. It grants more heat, more concentration—to really feel what you are about so that it becomes obvious, to be sensitized to what you are about to the point of understanding yourself most fundamentally, that you <u>are</u> self-contraction, and THAT IS IT! That is <u>all</u> there is to it! That is it—all!

That understood, no more efforts are made in that direction. You are all the while Enquiring or Invoking Me, meditating on Me.

What does it take for your Communion with Me to be Only Love-

Blissful—Only, Absolutely? What does it take to be Only, Absolutely Love-Blissful? You are practicing Ishta-Guru-Bhakti Yoga, and there is Joy and Happiness in it, a dimension of bliss to it, certainly, but also there is just the separate self as the foundation of it. It is not Absolute Love-Bliss, All Love-Bliss. It is not Samadhi yet. The self-contraction is the reason why. That is what must be understood and broken. Then Ishta-Guru-Bhakti Yoga becomes Samadhi. Then it becomes Love-Blissful Communion, without separate self. But until this knot is most fundamentally understood, so that you can, as a matter of responsibility, go beyond it, in any moment—until then, the component of self-contraction is always present, in every moment of Ishta-Guru-Bhakti Yoga, in every moment of Ishta-Guru-Seva, in every moment of life, therefore.

And that disturbance, that dissatisfaction, is something you <u>should</u> be sensitive to and not discount, claiming, "I am just all-blissful with my Master." This attitude suggests that somehow, without the transcendence of separate self, Ishta-Guru-Bhakti Yoga is a sufficient way of life, whereas it is sadhana and it becomes sufficient only in the case of Divine Self-Realization. Until then, the dilemma persists. The disturbance that is your own individual self persists. Rather than taking vacations from feeling the disturbance, allow yourself to be sensitive to it in the continuous practice of devotion to Me. Stay in the heat of it, until you are so swollen with the heat of it, so feverish with it, so most profoundly disturbed with it, that suddenly it becomes obvious, completely clear, totally obvious. It is your own action, and you could do otherwise. Totally obvious.

You will not come to that point of awakening if you avoid the discomfort of sadhana. Some of you have been describing how you avoid the discomfort. There is even a basic attitude in you that you should avoid discomfort and that even the circumstance of your sadhana should be essentially comfortable. Certainly you are wanting it and trying to engineer it. Actually, the context of true sadhana is discomfort. It is just so. By your own confession, you are still rehearsing the efforts to get comfortable, as if being comfortable is about something, whereas reality is discomfort. It is just so. Rather than complaining or trying to make another arrangement, this is what you must grasp, and you must also remain in the discomfort until you grasp it.

Do not take any nonsense from the body-mind. Do not play games. Understand what the body-mind is all about. It is just ego-strategies, trying to find a way to avoid being uncomfortable. The basic premise of your life is that you do not want to be uncomfortable. You are struggling, complaining, getting hysterical, abusing others, accumulating things, having meals—always trying to avoid being uncomfortable. Whereas uncomfortable is <u>it</u>! Uncomfortable is reality, even when there are circumstances of apparent comfort. It is always uncomfortable and you cannot escape the discomfort. But you are trying to escape it. That is why you complain. That is why you get hysterical. You are involved in an effort to escape it, whereas real sadhana, really, seriously done, accepts the discomfort, endures it, understands it ultimately, knows it cannot escape.

Me on the beach—instead of avoiding the discomfort, just noticing this, that, that, that, that. No efforts. No seeking. No trying to modify it. Just notice *it*. Stay noticing the discomfort. Do not complain about it. It is *you*. But it is not you just because of the circumstances of the moment. It is just plain old you. You *are* discomfort. You *are* dis-ease. Zero in on that to the point of awakening the most profound self-understanding that is true sadhana, to the point of true hearing.

Your seeking is an acknowledgement of the fact that right now you do not feel good, and you *do* something so that in the next right-now you will feel good. When you get to the next right-now, you still do not feel good. Some peripheral aspect of your experiencing probably feels good here tonight, but *really*, *fully* be aware right now. You *do* *not* feel good. Even when you are having sex, you do not feel good. Peripherally, in some sense, sex may feel good, but not fundamentally. You *never* fundamentally feel good. You *always* fundamentally feel bad. When you realize you cannot escape feeling bad, that is when you are getting on toward true hearing. The not feeling good is not merely a fact of conditional Nature. It is your own action. You are experiencing the knot of your own disposition, and it is, in some literal sense, a knot. It is a contraction that distorts the force of existence. It tightens around it. It smothers it. It distorts it. It makes it into pain. It makes it into separateness.

You have tried all your searches. You have indulged in your various searches. You are old enough to have done all the basics of seeking. But did you really observe yourself in all those moments? Ramakrishna got the notion that He wanted to smoke what He called a "hookey-pookey pipe", a hookah, with some intoxicating local smoke in it. It was on His mind. The thought occurred, fine, but then it occurred again. And then the next day. Finally, He was obsessively thinking about smoking a hookey-pookey pipe. He told one of His devotees, "Go bring me the stupid hookey-pookey pipe." [Sri Gurudev pretends to hold the stem of a hookah to His lips and makes sucking sounds.] Then, it is reported, He said, "See, mind? This is called 'smoking a hookey-pookey pipe'." He was doing what He was obsessed with doing, and He realized there was no pleasure in it. He was not Happy. He observed the effects in the body and what it might do to the various aspects of the conditional personality, but there was no fundamental Happiness in it.

You go to your pleasure, your distraction, and do not notice that there is no fundamental pleasure in it. You imagine that you are being satisfied, even though you are not. And then you do it some more, never noticing that all of your doings are based on the fact of your dissatisfaction. None of your fulfillments is satisfied. You are always dissatisfied. You can be distracted by the pleasure, feel relatively relieved, but that is not Happiness. Where is the Happiness, the Unconcerned Fullness of Absolute Freedom? It is never there, but That is what you want, and you are trying to Realize It as the self-contraction, the separate self, the ego identified with this, that, and the other thing. There never *is* any Happiness, *never*! This is what there is to be observed. This is what true hearing is about—realizing that you are *never* *Happy*. You are *always* self-contraction, *always*, no matter what you do, no matter what the circumstance, no matter what the relation, no matter what the event, the function, the experience. You are *never* Happy, never satisfied.

Look at mankind in general. In times of war, emergency, special difficulties, all of a sudden people have great relational energy and functional energy. They do not care for their own comfort. They are relieved of all of their usual ego-games, and they come together. But when there is no emergency, everybody is in competition and pursuing the usual egoic purposes.

Sadhana, then, if you view it in its traditional form, is about everybody's functioning, individually—and, therefore, also collectively—as if they are in an emergency situation where the usual games of egoity do not come into play, because there is a greater demand that everybody is responding to. That is what makes sadhana. That is what makes the Way of the Heart sadhana, existing in that emergency situation rather than in the comfortable we-are-trying-to-make-an-ideal-community game and looking out for this, that, or the other detail of your own pleasure and arrangement or conditioning.

Those who are doing real sadhana in the traditional manner are always avoiding the vacations, eliminating the vacations and the ordinary comforts. They typically simplify their lives to the extreme and eliminate the games they would play in the ordinary world, just to keep themselves in the heat all the time. They do it voluntarily, even though outwardly their situation may be relatively ordinary and so-called normal.

You know you are mortal, but until you hear the exact date of your death, you are going to keep indulging yourself. In an emergency situation, you would forget about your indulgence completely, instantly—a personal emergency, for instance, like being told that you have a terrible disease and you are going to die in ten months. There are also collective emergencies—a great storm, a war. All of a sudden, everybody is in the heat of reality, distracted beyond themselves, with great free energy and attention. But in the conventional situation, people have very little free energy and attention.

Those who have done sadhana understand this mechanism, and they personally, and, therefore, collectively, with all who have the same point of view, maintain the emergency as a fact of life, as the very circumstance of life—always in the wartime, always in the emergency, always in the great flood, the great catastrophe, death the next moment. Always. Effectively, that is what sadhana is about.

Sadhana is not just an individual matter. It is a collective matter. Everybody is going to die. Everything is going to come to an end. Everything is always threatened. Always. This is no place to have fun. It is a total threat, an instant ending. Right now. You do not tend to think that way. You want to be relaxed and comfortable, use Ishta-Guru-Bhakti Yoga as a consolation. In that manner, you use Me as a conventional or even social other. You just do a little bit of sadhana, enough to make you feel good, consoled, hopeful, and you generally use the practice of devotion to Me as just another way of being relaxed and self-indulgent, reinforcing your impulses to enjoy a pleasurable, middle-class life rather than enduring the emergency situation of profundity.

The separate self <u>is</u> only pain and dissatisfaction, and What must be Realized <u>is</u> a matter of emergency. You are in the same boat with everyone else, and your life should be devoted to confronting your real situation. You are always in the circumstance of the great catastrophe, even though outwardly things may look apparently orderly. A simplified life is appropriate and it is within your capability to have it be so, but nevertheless you are always in that emergency. Therefore, indulgence in separate self is not called for. In emergency, it is not even in your disposition.

Ishta-Guru-Bhakti Yoga is about Realizing Me. Knowing that, and if you had your choice, you would not be in your position for even one more moment, because it is un-Happy, it is mortal, it is threatened, it is disturbed. If you had your choice right now, you would not be in your situation. But, apparently not having the ability to be in a totally different situation, you just look for some changes that are more congenial, comfortable, consoling, distracting. This is how you avoid God. This is why there is so little God-talk from you. You are just self-involved.

The self-contraction is not <u>objective</u> to you. It is your own position. It is your own action. And that is what the discovery in hearing is all about. But now you are experiencing all kinds of effects, un-Happiness, displeasure, as if they are coming on you objectively for one or another reason. No sheets, no blankets, no baskets. If you could just get those things, then you would be Happy. No. That is not it. You are subject to <u>fear</u>. Not only death, but fear. Why would you want to be subject to fear? There is no Happiness as long as you are subject to fear. Perhaps the right definition of Happiness is that there is not only no fear in it but also no possibility of it. None! That is Happiness.

Instead of living the life that is required if you are to be totally Liberated from fear, you prefer to do this or that cleverly, by various devices, to feel somewhat consoled or distracted from fear. That is the ordinary game, but it has nothing to do with Most Perfectly self-transcending God-Realization, nothing to do with hearing, nothing to do with ego-transcendence. Your habits of life, all based on the self-contraction, are about seeking relative relief, whereas sadhana is not about seeking relative relief from this discomfort but about enduring the discomfort, practicing beyond it, until you understand that it is your own action and awaken to the capability of transcending it.

The Godly Struggle

February 11, 1994

SRI DA AVABHASA: Doing Ishta-Guru-Bhakti Yoga does not make you comfortable. There can be no laziness in it. Indulging the body, indulging emotion, indulging attention, mind, even breath, in all of the objects and preoccupations of egoity is comfortable, in some sense. The events of life can become uncomfortable, but you can enjoy relatively more comfort by indulging yourself than by practicing Ishta-Guru-Bhakti Yoga. You can be very much relaxed into yourself and think that you are trying to feel Me, for example, but it is not by relaxing into yourself and trying to feel Me that you do Ishta-Guru-Bhakti Yoga. It is by giving yourself. It is by very forcefully taking your attention, your feeling, your breath, your body away from the preoccupations in which they might be indulging by tendency, and giving them to Me, fixing them on Me. To do this in every moment, you must be constantly taking these faculties of the body-mind away from where they would be going otherwise and surrendering them to Me.

This is a very different kind of practice than the more comfortable, more passive, more falling-into-yourself-and-relaxing attitude, which is the result of the ego's wanting to be consoled by Me rather than surrendered to Me. Such a childish, "Narcissistic" attitude is the attitude of conventional religiosity. It is a sign of the presumption that God is a sort of slave, if you like, there to do your bidding, there to do you some good, make you feel good, give you the things you want. It is not the counter-egoic effort of Ishta-Guru-Bhakti.

The counter-egoic action that is Ishta-Guru-Bhakti Yoga is very direct, very profound—and very intense. It is not comfortable. It requires you to steal these faculties of the body-mind away from their common objects, away from their course of comfort, their egoic "self-possession", their wanting to just feel good somehow, and give them over to Me instead.

DEVOTEE: Sri Gurudev, I am grateful for the discipline You have Given me to bring great energy to life and accomplish many things, so that I do not fall back on myself.

SRI DA AVABHASA: Yes, that is good counter-egoic practice, a good environment in which to practice Ishta-Guru-Bhakti Yoga. It is not itself Ishta-Guru-Bhakti Yoga, however.

DEVOTEE: I do it because I want my life of Communion with You to be deeper and fuller.

SRI DA AVABHASA: The Deep is not in you. The Deep is in Me. Ishta-Guru-Bhakti is not going deep into yourself. It is going deep into Me! It is not inside here [hunching His shoulders and gesturing with both hands toward His chest] It is here, to Me [holding both hands up and open in the gesture of surrender]. It is not self-concern—it is the relinquishment of self-concern.

You have not yet come to the point of observing, most fundamentally understanding, and, therefore, becoming responsible for the self-contraction. You are expecting to do something as the separate self that becomes full Communion with Me. You are regretful that most of the time, perhaps, you feel not fully surrendered, not fully self-forgetting. What is there to regret about it? That is the way it is. You want to use some trick to escape the self-contraction and feel comfortable instead.

Now that you are sensitized to the self-contraction, you must understand it and not try to find some trick for avoiding the experience of it. You do not yet stand in the position of being responsible for this limit. You want something for yourself, but you are not transcending yourself. You are still the principle of all of this apparent surrendering.

The pain, the disease, the disturbance, and the discomfort of the self-contraction persist until you become responsible for it. Even then, even though you are responsible for it, the self-contraction would persist, by tendency, except that, having heard Me, you have the means to transcend it. Until the event of hearing, the self-contraction persists in the background of even your devotional surrender to Me. Perhaps sometimes it relaxes, but as a random, Graceful event, not because you have heard Me. The relaxation of the self-contraction is an inspiring event, perhaps, that motivates you to practice more intensely, because you would not have it be otherwise. Yet there is nothing you can do to the separate self to have it be otherwise. You must enter into Communion with Me more profoundly, until, confronted by this limit, you come to the point of understanding it most fundamentally: It is your action. Thereafter, through every moment of the "conscious process"—whatever form of the "conscious process" you practice—you can actually relinquish the self-contraction in Communion with Me, directly.

Until then, you are not in the position of being responsible for this knot to the degree that you can relinquish it. You are simply in the position of experiencing it in the background, as if it is somewhere else, as if it is someone else, as if it is an object, a thing that is not you. It is not a thing that is not you. It is you. You are doing it, right then and there. Yet you do not have to do it. Even so, since you have not heard Me, you are not yet in a position to not do it and you think it is just happening.

Obviously that is not true hearing. True hearing is to be in a position to directly transcend this knot, this action of self-contraction. You are still struggling with it, not knowing that you are doing it, or not knowing exactly what it is you are doing. Therefore, in all of this effort of surrender, which is fine and good, you are still being confronted with the knot behind it most of the time. This does not mean your practice is failing—confronting this knot is what your practice is about. Rather than trying to escape the self-contraction, therefore, you must intensify your practice, make it more profound, do it more intensively, under all circumstances, in every moment, until the revelation that is true hearing occurs.

True hearing is not something the ego can decide to realize. If hearing has occurred, there is no doubt about it. It is not an intellectual matter, not a "maybe". It is a profound change, but it is not particularly a Spiritual, or mystical, event. It is a turnabout in the ego-place. Anyone in whom this conversion has occurred can confess it directly, because there is no doubt about it and the signs will be evident in the life as well.

Ego hurts. As long as you persist in it, you are not going to be Happy by any means—not really, not truly Happy. You can have moments of release. You can have life-pleasures, life-distractions, life-consolations, life-comforts. But you cannot have fundamental Happiness, you cannot be Free, at the heart, responsible for your own dis-ease. Not that. You are trying to Realize Happiness and well-being on the basis of persisting as an ego, a self-referring, separative person, bodily based. You try all kinds of tricks—even some that could be called "Yogic" tricks, even tricks with the practice I have Given you, and all the usual tricks of life whereby people try to establish a feeling of well-being, Happiness, and fullness without transcending the ego.

All the forms of life-consolations, all the forms of self-indulgence—the ego uses everything to console itself. You are busy doing that instead of the intensive practice of Ishta-Guru-Bhakti Yoga, which is a very specific, simple, but nonetheless really technical, practice. You must oblige yourself to it in every moment. That is the sadhana.

I Call you to embrace a wide variety of disciplines in your life. They are good. You can embrace them on their own terms. But the benefit of the body-mind is not their primary purpose. Well-being is a secondary effect of discipline in the Way of the Heart. The real purpose of these disciplines is to further serve the reflection of you to yourself, to enable you to practice Ishta-Guru-Bhakti more profoundly rather than working against it with your bad habits.

Even the beginner's practice of Ishta-Guru-Bhakti is not Happiness. It is sadhana! Happiness is What is to be Realized. The sadhana requires great intention, great responsibility, counter-egoic work. It goes against the trends of the body, feeling, attention, and the breath. You constantly struggle against acquired adaptations, and, while persisting in that struggle, still you are constantly experiencing the fact that your surrender is not yet full. It is not really self-forgetting, not fully. There is this feeling of effort, this feeling of discomfort, this feeling of dis-ease, this feeling of being stopped short. And so you must persist.

Ishta-Guru-Bhakti is not some trick to be Happy. It is not a means to feel good in the moment. It leads to hearing. It leads to the capability for Divine Communion and for Realizing That Which Is Happiness, the Very Divine Self-Condition Itself. There is no self but the Divine Self. What you call "self" is a knot in the energies of the conditional world, yet you call it a "self". It is just uncomfortable. It is suffering. You somehow want to make it Happy, make it feel good, have it be consoled, rather than persisting in the practice that goes beyond it.

DEVOTEE: The fundamental thing that seems to slow down the process is adding consolations over and over, rather than staying in that frustration.

SRI DA AVABHASA: The practice is not a matter of staying in the frustration, not trying to feel the frustration. It is a matter of practicing Ishta-Guru-Bhakti Yoga, persisting in this particular practice. In that practice, tacitly, the ego is revealed to you, and felt by you.

The Yoga is a manly responsibility, for male or female. What is there to say about it except that you must do the Yoga in every moment, instead. That is your discipline. So what that you are reluctant! There is nothing more to be said about it, except that you must observe the discipline, meaning not the functional, practical, relational, and cultural disciplines I have Given you—yes, you must persist in them also—but the particular technical practice of moment to moment Ishta-Guru-Bhakti.

If you are intentionally avoiding Me, then you must intentionally surrender to Me. One way to describe the self-contraction is that you are dramatizing the avoidance of relationship [clenching His fist to illustrate the self-contraction]. You are intentionally not doing the practice of Ishta-Guru-Bhakti. Therefore, you must intentionally do it. The force of your not doing it is revealed in every moment of your doing it, until you come to the point of tacitly understanding, very directly understanding, most fundamentally understanding, that the self-contraction is not just a sensation but that you are doing this avoidance of Me [holding up His fist again]. It need not be so, and you must discover your inclination for doing it.

You can release the self-contraction. You can do this [opening His hand], but you do not. You persist as the self-knot, the self-contraction, the avoidance of relationship [holding up His fist]. Even the simple technical practice of Ishta-Guru-Bhakti Yoga is self-Enquiry. You may not be practicing that form of the "conscious process", but, even so, to practice Ishta-Guru-Bhakti Yoga effectively is self-Enquiry. This is why those who practice the Devotional Way of Faith are essentially doing the same thing as those who practice the Devotional Way of Insight, and vice versa. The technical practices of both those devotional forms of the Way of the Heart are all inherent in the practice of Ishta-Guru-Bhakti Yoga.

How come, even though you would surrender to Me, you do not? Surrender to Me is not merely a matter of will. The will is one of the ways whereby the self-contraction dramatizes itself. The will is simply an expression of the ego, until the ego itself is transcended. All the while, you are wanting to surrender, intending to surrender, doing the Yoga of surrender, but you do not completely do it. You are still dissatisfied, still uncomfortable. You cannot make the ego disappear by bearing down harder on it, because you are the self-contraction. Therefore, you cannot make it disappear. You cannot vanish the fist by clenching it harder.

You must fully enter into Communion with Me, specifically as I have Given you to do, until the Revelation occurs that the ego is your own action. Then you can Enquire or Invoke Me, using any of the means of the "conscious process", and you are in the seat of the knot itself and you are proceeding into Communion with Me, because you have the key. Until then, the notion that simply by practicing Ishta-Guru-Bhakti Yoga as I have Given it you will transcend the self-contraction and just feel good is part of the illusion of your seeking.

The Yoga of Ishta-Guru-Bhakti is not just wandering with the mind, or attention, and feeling—this thought feels good, My picture feels good—no. Ishta-Guru-Bhakti Yoga is the specific act of surrendering, bringing the faculties of bodily existence, feeling, attention, and the breath into Communion with Me. When you are established in the Yoga, then sometimes you examine My Heart-Word to increase your understanding of the practice and to help you establish further disciplines, but the practice that is moment to moment, and that must be consistent, is the specific Yoga I have Communicated to you. It is a counter-egoic effort, and it does not in itself feel good. Nevertheless, it is the practice that has the potential of true hearing, whereas your pursuit of feeling good, manipulating yourself in one way or another to feel good, does not have the potential of true hearing. That pursuit is just about manufacturing life on its own terms, for its own sake, trying to make a utopia for the ego—pond activity.

In the years when I was with Rudi, I practiced the technicalities of His Teaching, which were basically about surrendering to Him, and the limit on surrender became more and more and more profoundly obvious to Me, to the point where such heat was generated, even in the body, that I developed rashes and endured constant hotness. Apart from that physical sign, however, there was just the confrontation with the limit. What surrender? I was practicing constantly, but what surrender? It was not surrender.

Such is the effect of counter-egoic practice. It is not satisfying. It is not great and blissful. It is full of egoic self. It is confronted by the limit, even though it is doing the surrender. Nevertheless, you are not to stop doing the surrender and just watch yourself and look at your limit. You must persist in surrender. Persisting brings about the heat, the frustration, of confrontation, because surrender is not fully happening. It is happening in some sense, but not fully. It is not Happy. Nevertheless, that you are frustrated is not a reason to stop doing the Yoga. There is something fundamental to be understood, and there is something to be burned up, and there is something to be gone beyond. The Yoga is not a self-consoling practice. It is a self-offending practice. It is not comfortable, because it is always a counter-egoic activity.

The faculties of the body-mind can turn to the self-contraction and see it in its details. Instead of surrendering attention to Me, you think about this, that, or the other thing, you feel reactions, you allow the breath to become distorted, you move about in this, that, or the other way of turning back on yourself. As soon as you involve yourself in the content of the body-mind, you are turning the faculties of the body-mind back on yourself. The Yoga of Ishta-Guru-Bhakti is to turn the faculties to Me, not to the content of the body-mind, which is just content in any case, a flash in a moment. You write it in your diary, you tell it to the next devotional group, but to dwell on it at length is to fall from the Yoga. Then you indulge the reactions, you wander in thoughts for hours, you suffer all kinds of diversions.

The Yoga is to turn the faculties of the body-mind to Me in every moment, not to wander in the mind. Attention is the root of mind. Therefore, give Me your attention, and the mind follows. Instead of indulging in reaction and the varieties of emotion to try to deal with this, that, or the other object or circumstance, feel Me. Feeling is the fundamental faculty on which all reactive emotions are built. Therefore, give Me the faculty itself. Instead of wandering bodily into all kinds of inclinations, indulgences, and activities to pleasurize yourself, give yourself to Me bodily, convert your actions into service to Me. The breath is happening anyway, but you must artfully, randomly, practice the breath as reception and release, rather than allowing it to assume the crippled forms that do not open and do not relinquish but that become disturbed by thoughts, emotions, and bodily self-indulgence.

It is not that in every moment of the turning of these faculties to Me everything is okay and all-bliss. The faculties will not be turned perfectly to Me. The Yoga, your responsibility, is to turn them, but you will be frustrated in the turning. On the other hand, you will not be indulging the faculties, either. You will just be frustrated at some fundamental level—not absolutely, but at some fundamental level frustration will always be there. You must persist.

The Yoga generates greater and greater heat, a greater and greater frustration, a tacit sense of the limit, until you realize, as I have told you for many years, even from the beginning of My Work, that without noticing it, because you are greatly preoccupied with this, that, and the other thing, you are pinching yourself [reaching down and pinching His leg]. You are just feeling the pain, the pain, the pain, the frustration, the suffering, the heat, the difficulty, the discomfort [lifting His hand from His leg]. You have made this whole pain, from head to toe, you, pinching yourself, driving your nails right through the flesh [pinching His leg again].

The self-contraction is like that. You are not inspecting it as an activity you are doing. You are feeling it as an effect, but you are not inspecting it as your action so that you might observe that you are pinching yourself. As soon as you see it, then you take your fingers away and all the suffering stops.

By persisting in the tapas of this Yoga, as I have Given it to you, in effect you come to that point. Instead of just experiencing the self-contraction as a limit, as frustration, as struggle, you discover that you are doing it and that you are always doing it. You are doing it under all circumstances, and this activity that you are doing is itself the root of your seeking, your disturbance, your dis-ease, your discomfort.

At that point, the "conscious process" becomes effective as hearing. You can practice self-Enquiry, for example, before you have heard Me, but until hearing is awake in you, it is not an extension, an expression, or a demonstration of most fundamental self-understanding. Before true hearing, the forms of the "conscious process" I have Given you serve the possibility of most fundamental self-understanding, but they are not yet a demonstration of it until true hearing. Before true hearing, any form of the "conscious process" is part of the counter-egoic effort and not an expression of most fundamental self-understanding.

Therefore, by persisting in the Yoga, endure that tapas, that heat, that frustration, that difficulty, that discomfort, until there is the tacit understanding that you have been pinching yourself—and you take your hand away, established in the seat of responsibility for the very thing you are suffering.

How can I describe hearing more than this, since it is not an objective matter? I am suggesting to you what it is about, but you must persist in the Yoga until it is true of you and then it will be perfectly obvious what I have been talking about all this time.

Not only do you think about yourself constantly but you also talk about yourself constantly, consuming much so-called "cultural time". There are appropriate moments to engage in such talk, so that others may address you about assuming further discipline. Apart from that, however, such talk is not to be the substance of the culture of My devotees. Counter-egoic effort, not dwelling on separate self, is the substance of the culture of My devotees.

Another way of frustrating the intentions of the ego to think about or talk about itself is to bring yourself to My Heart-Word rather than letting your mind wander egoically. Instead of talking about yourself and thinking about yourself, bring yourself to My Word, and, thereby, bring yourself to Me. Attend to Me. Practice counter-egoic effort. The culture of My devotees is not the "Poisonous Ego Garden Society", a gathering of egos imposing their "case" on one another, dramatizing it or speaking it and having hardly any attention for Me or My Word. Instead of talking about yourself, tell My Leelas, study and discuss and apply My Word.

Self-contraction is what is ultimately understood. Self-contraction is affected by all this practice. Nevertheless, the practice is Ishta-Guru-Bhakti Yoga, not self-concern. Only in the practice of Ishta-Guru-Bhakti do you become responsible for the separate self, or the ego, which is not a thing, not a fact in conditional Nature, but an action—<u>your</u> action and no one else's. No one else is causing your suffering, although the game of blaming this or that other or circumstance or condition in life is one of the ways whereby you divert yourself from Ishta-Guru-Bhakti Yoga and from the practice that unwinds the self-knot.

Your real practice of Ishta-Guru-Bhakti, your authentic, right, and consistent practice, your manly—male or female—willingness to accept life as an ordeal rather than a game of feeling good, is basic to the Way of the Heart. The common view, however, is that everybody should be seeking ordinary fulfillment, seeking to feel good in the common, naively perceived terms, not accepting life as an ordeal and submitting to a greater purpose. The egoic disposition has been magnified in the modern era to such an extent that even politics is made out of the principle of egoity, very directly and very specifically suggesting to all that the purpose of life is to gain personal satisfaction and that everyone must have the opportunity to do so.

As a result, the political thing to do, the social thing to do, is to righteously demand this or that satisfaction. Today in the common world, there is no senior concern, human or otherwise. It is just so. Anything about life that feels like an ordeal is presumed to be negative and wrong and something that should not be. The common presumption is that life should not be an ordeal—you should be having fun, you should just be amused, consoled, and pleasurized, have more and more social and economic opportunity, and acquire all the goods you want. The ideal is to have piles of goods and much self-pleasure, to fulfill all your desires, and to become very aggressive and angry when your wants are not fulfilled.

Such is the ordinary way of life. It is the source of the daily news. It is politics, society, culture. It is the obnoxious end time of humanity! Everything has been reduced to self-fulfillment. The ego is justified on all sides.

The ordinary life of the ego has nothing to do with the religious life, nothing to do with real life. Real life is an ordeal. Getting your stick out of the mud, getting out of the trouble you are in, is a struggle, inherently. You can feel the effect of the struggle and suffer it, or you can understand its laws and participate in its governing principle and have your life be truly fruitful. That is the manly choice, male or female. It thoroughly runs against the trends of the times, and it always has. It requires great Revelation. It also requires personal choice, personal response, personal conversion. Having made the response and having been so converted, you can enter into the collective of those who are doing likewise. The collective of such of My devotees is based on the response of every one to Me, each and all serving one another in the devotional response to Me instead of constantly reintroducing the sideshow of self-concern and the usual politics, and addressing everybody's petty wants, petty confusion, petty neurosis, and the disturbance of wrong life and Godlessness.

Real life, right life, is the mature, manly—male or female—acceptance of life as an ordeal, a Yogic struggle, not merely an effort to survive. It is a Godly struggle. It is a struggle to go beyond separate and separative self. No end to it! It breaks your heart. No relief, nor would My true devotee want any. The more profoundly you become involved in devotion to Me, the less inclined you are toward the indulgences of the adaptations of egoity. You will not give the ego any space. This is why some in the traditional context have made the most extreme choices to live most dramatically for God-Realization. They just do not pay attention to ordinary life. They do not want to pay any time to it. They do not want to pay any life to it. If they are going to die, they want to die in devotion to God and not for any other reason.

The Way Out of Pleasure and Pain

February 19, 1994

SRI DA AVABHASA: You make the choices. I Make the Revelation. I can Call you to greater understanding and more profound practice, I can urge you on, but you make the choices. If you want What is Ultimate and Most Profound, you must be changed likewise, in your choices, in your understanding, and in your involvement in everything. Such transformation requires a profound discipline and a great ordeal.

Sooner or later, any kind of self-indulgence whatsoever reaches the point where discomfort is greater than pleasure. So it is with the world and with everything karmic, with every indulgence of attention in conditions. There is some pleasure in your indulgence, but as you repeat the indulgence, you reach a point after a while when the pleasure is greatly reduced and you are mostly suffering the results. Sex, intimate feelings, drugs, cigarettes, alcohol, TV, food—absolutely everything you can do in the domain of conditional existence produces the same result in due course, which is that at some point the pleasure is greatly reduced and you are mainly suffering ill effects. Such is life.

DEVOTEE: I think you are talking about sex.

SRI DA AVABHASA: Sex is certainly a major form of it, but all indulgence in conditionality is the same. There is no difference in effect. This is just how conditional existence works. Conditional existence is a play of opposites. If you work on the pleasure side, the opposite comes into play sooner or later and, like any addict, you continue to seek for pleasure, but now to relieve yourself of some pain rather than to magnify the enjoyment. Most of the time, you are just suffering, and the pattern is repeating itself automatically. You do not quite know what to do about it. You are just stuck with it, and you think, "Well, that is the way it is supposed to be."

You are basically just feeling the pain of it and trying to get rid of the pain. Your whole life feels like a dilemma of disease.

This understanding about conditional existence is one dimension of life in My Company that makes you a renunciate. The other dimension is your devotion to Me. The more profoundly your devotion to Me is magnified, the less consistently attention moves toward pleasure, or conditionality, or addictive patterns. This is the primary dimension of life in My Company that makes you a renunciate. When these two dimensions of your practice of the Way of the Heart become most profoundly consequential, then you are fully and truly a renunciate, or one who is not moved in attention toward conditionality but whose attention and entire body-mind are moved in submission to Me, in Divine Communion.

The way out of the cycle of pleasure and pain, the cure for your addiction, is also painful, to some degree. There is tapas in it. However, when you understand the reasonableness of the cure and its purpose, you become willing to endure it. Having so thoroughly adapted to what is inherently painful, you must understand, like a five hundred-pound man or woman committed to losing weight, that you must endure a process of purification. Therefore, a part of self-discipline is that you become willing to endure it, because of your intelligence, your understanding.

Participation in conditional existence ends in pain. In the meantime it shows all the signs of the addictive cycle, eventually becoming the endurance of pain and the search for release. Everything associated with conditional existence is just this cycle. If you are noticing this truth about some things and not others, you have more to learn about your desires and your bargaining. You must find out that every indulgence in conditions is the same: It becomes the addictive cycle, and it ends in pain.

If you could make a truly summary and most profound estimate of the nature of conditional existence and the option of true devotion, what would you do? You would do no more bargaining. You can be My devotee without having come to the great estimate about <u>everything</u> yet, but your destiny is dependent on the tendencies of attention you have not yet understood and relinquished. Because you have not understood most fundamentally yet, because you have not gotten the lesson yet, attention makes repetition. It keeps you continuous with your limitations, until you understand and are not moved toward them any more. When you come to that point, you are not strategically renouncing, without understanding, but it is obvious that you just do not do that anymore.

If people who drink or smoke day after day are honest with themselves, they find that eventually drinking or smoking does not feel good. It toxifies you more and more and makes you more and more uncomfortable. Eventually, the only motive left is to grasp something of the original pleasure, but you are only being sick and poisoned. You enjoy a few moments of pleasure, then the indulgence degrades you, you feel uncomfortable and sick, you must endure the aftereffects the next day, and then struggle with the process of purification, however long it takes.

Everything is like this. Everything! To understand this point transforms a life. You seem to be waiting to reach that point. What about it? What about everything? What about the habit of granting attention to conditional matters that eventually end in the pain of the addictive cycle? There is fun in it at the beginning, and then immediately you feel the results of the toxins and it is not so much fun any more. You are unsteady physically, emotionally, mentally, and in your breath. Instead of Ishta-Guru-Bhakti Yoga, then, there is bodily unsteadiness, emotional unsteadiness, mental unsteadiness, unsteadiness of attention, unsteadiness of breath, and you must endure these results and take actions that will purify you and restore your equanimity—and then you will do Ishta-Guru-Bhakti Yoga.

So it is with everything! Real Ishta-Guru-Bhakti Yoga is delayed, or certainly diminished, by your concessions to your addictive tendency, as if you do not understand. Understand this and change your life. Such understanding does not make the ideal life or utopia here, but it grants you the ability to give Me the faculties of the body-mind through true self-surrender and self-forgetting, the body not just feeling good but under your control and able to be given to Me. It is the same with emotion, the same with attention, the same with the breath. The reason for right discipline is not just to feel good as a human being and live an ideal, utopian life but to be in a position to make this sacrifice to Me in every moment, because you are able to be responsible for these faculties. As an addict, however, distracted by attention not merely to toxins but to everything else you do conditionally, you are not responsible for these faculties. You cannot give them directly to Me in every moment. You always have something else to do with them, some distraction, some leftover from previous indulgence. It is so!

Everything about your life-action, your life-process, your life-circumstance is a result of the concessions you have made and, therefore, everything you do is the picture of the degree to which you are living in the practice of Ishta-Guru-Bhakti Yoga in this moment. Various life-arrangements may be compatible with profound understanding and the renunciate disposition, but you must answer for your life. You must notice what you are doing: Is it the addictive cycle in any moment, or is it really free devotion to Me?

You must "consider" this, examine your life with true understanding, and make choices. Whatever your choice, whatever your circumstance, make it truly compatible with Ishta-Guru-Bhakti Yoga. If Ishta-Guru-Bhakti

Yoga is your understanding and disposition, then do whatever you must do. It is your business, and there is no bargaining with Me about it.

Yes, ultimately, the Way of the Heart is about renouncing every aspect of conditional existence, not for the sake of renouncing but as Ishta-Guru-Bhakti Yoga. Renunciation in the Way of the Heart is a disposition that enters into Communion with Me in every moment, that chooses the Divine Person, the Divine Condition, the Divine Self-Domain in every moment. You must make the measure. You must come to the understanding. You must respond to Me. You must change your life, however it must be changed, on this basis.

No matter how much longer you do what you have been doing all your life, you are not going to feel as good as you did when you started. You are only going to feel worse. Appreciate this, and then make the choices.

What if, on the basis of most profound examination of your involvement in emotional-sexual life and the most difficult choices, you become a celibate renunciate or a celibate in intimacy, with no consolations, no addictive behaviors anymore? So what! God will direct you—fresh, awake, free at heart, most profoundly engaging the God-Communing disposition. So what if there is no significant consolation in it! So what if you must give up everything for God! Whatever it takes, that is what you must do if you are serious about Most Perfectly self-transcending God-Realization. Whatever is binding you—your intimacy, sexuality, toxic substances, social life, daily life, food, money—whatever it is, it is your business to deal with it. Find your addiction, and cut it off. Then see what is left over that is compatible with the Way of the Heart. It is for you to discover, and it is different in every case, even a different process in some sense, but at last it is the same process fundamentally, the same requirement: Either you are given up to the tendencies of your attention and their results, or you are giving yourself with full attention to Me.

It is commonly said that you must give up the world for God, and it is true. Wherever your attention goes is your destiny. If your attention goes to Me, to Divine Communion, then your destiny becomes Divine. If it goes only to Me to some degree and also goes to many other things, then those other things become your destiny, while yet, perhaps, you remain My devotee in some sense. Divine Self-Realization, however, requires the abandonment of everything but the Divine. All other thoughts, all other dispositions, all other plans, all other activities of attention are not Godward or God-Realizing.

DEVOTEE: Beloved Heart, when attention moves with sympathy, if I am sympathetic with something I focus my attention on . . .

SRI DA AVABHASA: You would not put your attention on it if you were not sympathetic with it. Even if you are revolted, there is also a sympathy there, because your attention goes there.

DEVOTEE: The sympathy is the ego expressing itself.

SRI DA AVABHASA: It is not only egoity, not just the self-contraction, but it is the patterning of egoity, the adaptations of egoity, and they must be dealt with. If you weigh five hundred pounds, losing weight does not depend just on what you do with your attention! Yes, give your attention to Me, practice Ishta-Guru-Bhakti Yoga, but you must also handle the business of straightening out the body and losing a great deal of poundage.

The tapas of real self-discipline is an essential, necessary part of right practice of the Way of the Heart. Yes, it can be said that the basis of self-discipline is devotion to Me, giving Me your attention with feeling, directing the whole body to Me, surrendering with every breath—yes, that is so. Yet self-discipline bears an obligation for all your adaptations. Everything that has occurred as a result of your addiction, everything that has occurred as a result of your granting of attention to conditional matters, must be purified. Such purification requires real tapas, real devotion of attention to Me. In the process, you are losing those five hundred pounds and getting down to normal weight, meaning that you are relinquishing all the tendencies of your attention.

Your tendencies will be fighting back, because of your adaptation. Therefore, the fundamental principle of Ishta-Guru-Bhakti Yoga is simple to understand, even to do, if you bring yourself to it every moment, but you must go through the purification, or the reorientation. It is not fun, but it can be interesting—you can allow yourself an intelligent participation in the purification.

All of your karmas, all the results of your attention, all the tendencies of your attention must be redirected to Me. There is a necessary tapas in that process, in every moment and along the course. If you do this practice most profoundly, Most Perfectly, then all the movements of attention, all the results of attention, and all the destiny of attention are relinquished, gone, and all that is left is the Source of attention, the Domain of attention, the Origin of attention, the Divine Person, the Divine Self-Domain. Realization of the Ultimate requires the conversion of attention and the purifying process, the tapas, the understanding, the change of life, the discipline, the continuous moment to moment devotion, the profound work.

You are making more lifetimes, either here in this yellow-red place or somewhere else, on the basis of the same tendencies, adaptations, addictions. A summary word from the traditions for the cycle in which you are caught is "samsara". It is an irreducible cycle of suffering. The secret of renunciation is to comprehend it whole, in one glance, and be disposed unlike that, not making karma anymore but instead given up to Divine Communion with all of your faculties, moment to moment. Everything is purified in the heat of such constant practice. It is the Circumstance of Most Ultimate Realization.

The Principle of Communion with the Divine Person has been understood within the Great Tradition, certainly, but always with some imposition of limitation within it, so that the Realization develops only to some degree, only within the first six stages of life. The egoic exception is not inspected beyond the Realization presumed by the stage of life. I have Given you the Great Way of the Heart, which leads to Most Ultimate Realization, to Divine Translation, and which inspects and accounts for, in due course, everything, summarily, even the fine points of the sixth stage of life, for instance.

The Great Way of the Heart is a Great Matter, beyond Wonderful. You must get on with it, with no bargaining, or you stop at one place or another. You can see even now that all kinds of things that relate to your present stage of life-demonstration are no longer addictive, not of interest, not binding you, and you do not have any attention for them. Yet just one fraction, one part, one element, one function, one kind of association can bind you to the entire stage of life.

DEVOTEE: Sri Gurudev, I felt just a moment ago the consolation of the ocean, the air, the sand, drawing me so that I wanted to lie down in it.

SRI DA AVABHASA: You have the faculties to enjoy it, but you could be in another state, the body profoundly diseased and in pain, wherein the rustling of the waves would be profoundly disturbing to you.

The conditional realm is only Me. It is only the Divine Person. Why fasten onto it? Why luxuriate in it? Why be an odalisque, oblivious to the Place Where you Are, oblivious to the Person in Whom all of this is arising? You should devote your life to the Person in Whom all of this is arising, rather than clinging like an addict to such temporary luxuries.

Come to Me in every moment. How profoundly you will do that coming to Me in every moment, that Ishta-Guru-Bhakti Yoga, depends on your understanding of all of your uses of attention. I Call you to devote your attention to Me utterly, your feeling to Me utterly, your entire bodily existence to Me utterly, your breath, altogether, in every moment, utterly. Yet you have adaptations, tendencies, justifications in mind for doing something else with your faculties, and you bargain with Me. This is what is yet to be more profoundly inspected and understood and converted to

Me. It is the circumstance of your sadhana, stage by stage, in My Company.

Your choices change, through right sadhana. The understanding develops, fine, but you must take your understanding seriously. You must take My Revelation seriously, and truly respond to Me, as a serious person. My Revelation is not serious if you are not a serious person. You cannot worship Me, surrender to Me, in this bodily (human) Form in limitation. You must be continuous with the Divine Person.

DEVOTEE: Sri Gurudev, my attraction to You is beyond Your bodily (human) Form, because You are the Divine Person. This is really my understanding and confession of You, Beloved, because You are not an ordinary being, and You Communicate that Truth to me.

SRI DA AVABHASA: Nor is this an ordinary world. It is My Very Person, to be recognized as such and acknowledged as such, so that your submission to Me, your worship of Me, becomes most profound, not merely a token gesture of a part of you.

Ishta-Guru-Bhakti Yoga is an expression of your impulse to Divine Communion and Divine Self-Realization. Ishta-Guru-Bhakti Yoga is worship of the Divine Person. If you choose Me as your Ishta, you choose the Divine Person.

The Tar Baby and the Rabbit: A Tale of Non-Response

March 12, 1994

SRI DA AVABHASA: Do you know the story about Brer Rabbit? I have used it in conversations with My devotees many times over the years, as an example of a kind of life-situation.

Brer Bear and Brer Fox were always trying to trap Brer Rabbit and eat him. And Brer Rabbit was a trickster and always got himself out of the situation one way or another. So, one time, Brer Bear and Brer Fox made what was called a "tar baby". They got some tar and whopped it all together, sort of a lump for a basic lower body and a lump for a head. They put a hat on it, eyes and nose, like on a snowman, and a jacket, and they sat him on a log by the side of the road where they knew Brer Rabbit would be coming by soon.

So Brer Bear and Brer Fox hid in the bushes and watched. Sure enough, Brer Rabbit comes zippity-doo-dahing down the road, just hopping, and notices the tar baby, aforementioned, sitting on the log by the side of the road. He doesn't stop, just keeps zippity-doo-dahing, and says, "Good morning, Brer."

Several paces on, didn't get no "Howdy do", so jumps back several steps and says, "I said, 'How do you do, brother?'"

Keeps going on—nothing. It's just a lump of tar, but he expected a friendly "How do you do". So he hops backwards again.

"Brother, how do you do? Good morning. Wonderful day."

Tar baby is totally silent, no response, no reaction, no friendliness, no outgoing energy, no good feeling, no good wishes.

Brer Bear and Brer Fox knew what they were doing, you see. Hiding there in the bushes, they <u>knew</u>, considering Brer Rabbit's outgoing nature, that this non-response would really, really start to irritate him sooner or later.

So, Brer Rabbit keeps talking, asking questions, starts getting angrier and angrier and angrier.

He finally wallops the tar baby right smack in the face with his fist. Whomp! His arm goes all through, can't get out, stuck in the tar baby. Whomp! One more time with his left arm. Right up in the belly. Stuck up to the elbow. Struggles some more. Gets more and more wrapped up in this baby of tar.

There he is, stuck on a log at the side of the road, and *then*, Brer Bear and Brer Fox leap out of the bushes. "Ha-ha-ha-ha!" Hoisted the rabbit on his own petard. Had him stuck up in the tar baby there, so he could not get out. So then, of course, they were starting to cook the fire. They were getting ready to have rabbit lunch.

Well, as I said, the characteristic of Brer Rabbit is that he always got out of the situation, any situation, where he was about to be entrapped by Brer Bear and Brer Fox, by his enemies. So he calculated how he was going to get out of this situation. He decided he would not react to the possibility of being cooked.

He was praising the Brer Bear and the Brer Fox about this cooking thing. He said, "That's okay. I guess my time's come. You've caught me. I was stupid, so I guess my time's come. I'm glad I'm going this way, though. I'm glad this is the way it's going to turn out. It's right."

Brer Bear's mind didn't work too much, but the Brer Fox, he was getting curious. "What do you mean it's all right?"

They're getting ready to have rabbit lunch. They didn't want no undisturbed rabbit going to be cooked. This was the terminal event! This was finally getting the rabbit. But the rabbit is nonchalant.

Particularly the Brer Fox, he was always calculating, you see, and this was what the rabbit depended on.

"What do you mean, Brer Rabbit? What do you mean you're glad about this and your time has come and so forth?"

The rabbit says, "Well, since you asked, Brer Fox, I was just thinking, you know, that this is right, this cooking thing. But I'm just glad you didn't decide to do me in by throwing me into the briar patch. I wouldn't have liked that! That's the worst way to go. I'm *glad* if my time's come, you're going to do it right. If you had suggested throwing me into the *briar patch*—*that* would be a disgrace, a horror! I can't even contemplate that."

The fox said, "What do you mean? What don't you like about it?"

"I don't like being thrown into the briar patch. That would be the worst thing that could ever happen to a rabbit such as me."

Of course, Brer Bear is standing here behind. He doesn't think about much, but he's getting some sort of opinion here. Things are slowing down. "I just want to pick up my club and whomp his head clean off!"

But the Brer Fox, he's deep into the "consideration", like the rabbit was with the tar baby. The Brer Rabbit just turned the tide, turned the scales on the clever fox and the stupid bear. He gave them a tar baby in another form—the one thing he would not have happen is throw him into the briar patch!

The fox got stuck on this "consideration". And, I guess you may know, the rest is history. Brer Fox, he pulled that Brother Rabbit right out of that tar baby configuration of stuckness. Whomp! Right out with his bare hands. I guess he may have passed him to the bear to do the biggest throwing, to get him deep into the briar patch.

You have to understand, if you're not getting the message of the story—the briar patch was the Brer Rabbit's place. That wasn't where he didn't want to go. That was where he always wanted to be! So the fox or the bear, whichever one, flung him as far and hard as he could fling him, into the briar patch.

And zippity-doo-dah all over again! That rabbit was gone! That was a free rabbit forever, then. Who knows if Brother Bear and Brother Fox ever saw that rabbit again! But they never got him, ever. They're probably out there to this very day.

How many of you are the tar baby, something not like a living being? You do not say, "How do you do?" You do not respond. You do not do anything except aggravate people, and then they get stuck in their own reactivity.

A tar baby is never going to respond. No one is ever going to get any satisfaction from it. People just get more and more caught up in their own reactivity to the tar baby. People do not want anything to do with a tar baby, but even so the tar baby does not change. The tar baby talks about the pain of finding out that people do not like him or her, but that is nonsense. That is Brer Rabbit speech. The tar baby loves rejection, because it keeps him or her isolated, which is just what the tar baby wants.

People have just so much tolerance for being aggravated, just so much energy and attention they want to put into somebody who is a pain in the ass anyway. If you are a tar baby, people realize it is fruitless to deal with you, argue with you, "consider" things with you, give you disciplines, because tar babies never change. The only thing you can do with a tar baby is get stuck.

The tar baby experiences no pain. The tar baby is utterly detached, unmoved, isolated. If you are a tar baby, you are inert, you do not care, you do not experience the pain, you do not react. You just do your thing, sitting there like a lump that sticks people to it, a lump that makes people react.

Brer Rabbit knows Brer Bear and Brer Fox are hustling him, but he finds his way out and he will be in the briar patch for sure. So I also know what I have been dealing with. I have been talking to a great many tar babies, who must change in their disposition, at heart and altogether.

As My devotee, you will not be Happy until you respond to Me, make this submission to Me, practice this devotion to Me.

Spiritual Practice in My Company

March 13, 1994

SRI DA AVABHASA: My Divine Revelation is unique, and, therefore, Spiritual practice in My Company is unique. The traditions of religions and Spirituality are not the measure of My Appearance, nor are they the measure of Spiritual practice in My Company. There are forms of Spiritual esotericism in the traditions that are associated with Spiritual Transmission, but they are not the definition of Spiritual practice in My Company.

Just as Spiritual practice in My Company is not merely a matter of the practices associated with the natural energies of the body-mind, just so Spiritual practice in My Company is not about the conventional Spirituality of the "advanced" fourth stage of life and the fifth stage of life. I have helped you to understand this. I have criticized conventional Spirituality, and not because it is outside the range of My experience or Realization—all the experiences and Realizations of all the stages of life are in My experience—but Spiritual practice in the Way of the Heart is not defined by the conventional fifth stage point of view. Spiritual practice in My Company has nothing to do with the search for, or even the experience of, the so-called Spiritual phenomena of the fifth stage of life. Such phenomena may occur, as I have said, but they are not specific to the Way of the Heart. Spiritually activated practice in the Way of the Heart is a continuation of the process of ego-transcendence that is established in the beginning. It is about thorough—thorough—true, fundamental ego-surrender, ego-forgetting, ego-transcendence.

Therefore, Spiritual practice in the Way of the Heart is not about the development of the signs of psychic evolution, which exploit the subtler side of the natural faculties. It is not about visions, for example. Although visions may occur, Spiritual practice in My Company is not about visions.

All such phenomena are to be understood and transcended in devotion to Me.

Spiritual practice begins in My Company in the second developmental stage of the Way of the Heart, and it develops further in the third developmental stage. It is not about merely experiencing the effects of My Spiritual (and Always Blessing) Presence—your experiences in the body-mind, in other words—but it is about surrendering the body-mind in Spiritual Communion with Me. Spiritual practice in My Company is about identifying My Spiritual Presence, Finding Me, practicing surrender to Me, and forgetting separate self in Spiritual Communion with Me.

Spiritual practice in My Company is not about the experiences that may arise in the body-mind—not the physical experiences, not the psychic experiences, not the internal stimulations of the various faculties of audition, vision, taste, smell, and so on. Ultimately, Spiritual practice in the Way of the Heart becomes Objectless Communion with Me, beyond specificity of faculty. In the second and third developmental stages of the Way of the Heart, when you have "Located" Me—I My Self—Spiritually Present, the practice is truly self-surrendering and self-forgetting submission to Me. Such practice is a death, not a reception. It is to give yourself over to Me, not to take Me to yourself. The ego, the separate disposition, is crushed in submission to Me, and you are retired directly to the Witness-Position in the sixth stage of life, rather than invested in the subtler aspects of the body-mind.

For this reason, those who practice in My Company truly Spiritually are not likely to go on to the fifth stage of life, or even to the "advanced" form of the fourth stage of life. Some might, because of certain karmic limitations, but practice in the "advanced" form of the fourth stage of life and in the fifth stage of life is not the likely development for My devotee.

Therefore, the Spiritual practice that is fundamental to the Way of the Heart has nothing to do, in general, with the internal perceptual developments that are prized in the esoteric traditions of Spirituality. There is nothing objective about Spiritual Communion with Me. It is an ego-transcending process of surrendering to Me in Spiritual terms, As I Am Spiritually Present, Beyond My bodily (human) Form. Even so, through My Spiritual Heart-Transmission—even through the Vehicle of This Body but Beyond It—you, self-given and self-forgotten, Find Me Beyond This Body, Find Me Spiritually, objectlessly not objectively.

In the fulfillment of the "basic" context of the fourth stage of life in My Company, in the third developmental stage of the Way of the Heart—presuming that no diversions intervene—My devotee will Awaken to the Witness-Position, in the context of the sixth stage of life, and move on to the "Perfect Practice". The "Perfect Practice", again, is not a matter of reception. In that ultimate stage of life, what could you "receive" with? Only the ego can receive. Only by identifying with the body-mind can you "receive" Me. The Way of the Heart is not about taking up the position of the body-mind and "receiving" Me. It is about surrendering the self-contraction, surrendering the position of egoity, therefore surrendering the position of the body-mind and entering into My Sphere.

Objectless Communion with Me is the Spiritual Sign in the Way of the Heart. Spiritual practice in My Company is not consoled by objects—not consoled by subtle objects and not consoled by gross objects. It is without the point of view of consolation. If you are to so-called "receive" Me Spiritually, the ego-position must be assumed, and to take up the position of the ego, or the body-mind, is a self-contracting act. In the Way of the Heart, the ego-position must be renounced. Therefore, to engage in Spiritual practice in My Company, you relinquish the position of the body-mind, you relinquish the position of self-contraction. Therefore, you relinquish the position of reception, or of involvement in the effects, one can say, of My Spiritual Presence.

Practice of the Way of the Heart is not associated with the effects of My Spiritual Presence, although such effects may occur secondarily. Practice of the Way of the Heart is about relinquishing the egoic position, the position of the body-mind, and entering into My Spiritual Sphere, the Sphere of My Own Person. Those other signs, although they may occur, must be understood, and they must be transcended. They are not what the Way of the Heart is about.

The Samadhis of Egoity

March 14, 1994

SRI DA AVABHASA: In the Way of the Heart, conditional existence—meaning conditional forms, objects, the body, the body-mind—is not targeted as inherently problematic or negative, therefore as something that must be excluded. The ego presumes the "problem" of existence. The ego-principle, the self-contraction, the act itself of self-contraction, is the reason that any form of objectivity or conditionality is viewed negatively or found to be a problem. Generally, within the traditions of religion and Spirituality, the ego-principle, the self-contraction itself, is not identified and transcended. Rather, sadhana is a struggle with conditions, and the body is regarded to be the problem.

Ramana Maharshi, for instance, declared over and over again that the body is to be avoided, as if the body itself were the problem. In the Jain tradition, and very often in the Buddhist tradition, the same point of view appears. The ascetic practice of attempting to deal with conditions by dissociating from them has become part of traditional sadhana.

The search in any form is the dramatization of egoity. The ego, and not the ego's results or the things that arise to trouble it, must be found, understood, and transcended. The search to exclude the body-mind and the search to fulfill it are the gestures of egoity. The sadhana of the Way of the Heart is always the practice of locating the ego, or the self-contraction, transcending it in place, and Realizing That Which is Always Already the case. It is not struggling with the body-mind, or doing things to it to transform it, or evoking certain kinds of experiences in order to realize a resultant state or experience that is then called "Divine", or "Enlightenment", or "God-Realization".

All things that are acquired through the search, or the animation of egoity, are themselves conditional and dependent on conditional activity. They are not the Realization of That Which is Always Already the case. They are the experiencing of something that can only temporarily be the case. If the Realization of the sixth stage of life, for example, depends on the exclusion of objects, no sixth stage Samadhi can be permanent. What is not permanent is not always already the case. Truth is the Realization of Non-Separateness, or That Which is Always Already the case. Truth is not the realization or experiencing of anything that is arising conditionally or that is brought about by conditional effort, or ego-effort.

When we discuss the religious and Spiritual traditions, we are referring to rather advanced notions and prizes of self-pleasuring that are associated with the fourth, the fifth, and the sixth stages of life. Yet when I speak to you, I am speaking to people who are not altogether different from individuals in states of advancement in the Great Tradition, except that the objects you value are rather mundane. When you are caught up in your objects of self-pleasuring, you find them profoundly consoling and, in general, you speak as if you are willing to give up your whole life for them. There is not a profound or absolute difference between what you are doing, in your entanglement with the lesser potentials of life in the first three stages of life, and what others may be doing with the Samadhis and experiences associated with the advanced fourth stage of life, the fifth stage of life, and the sixth stage of life. The same point of view is exercised in the context of the later stages of life. The objects are different, but the point of view is fundamentally the same. It is the ego, "Narcissus", the self-contraction, finding results in one object or another and willing to let that object be enough, suggesting the object is enough, suggesting it is the fulfillment of existence, suggesting there is no more to seek, or suggesting a most profound sense of consolation.

You are in samadhi right now! Right now! Not the Samadhi of Divine Self-Realization, certainly, but every one of you is in samadhi at this very moment, every one of you is absorbed in some kind of self-pleasuring. And that, without your even saying a word, is your argument for non-practice. So if I ask each one of you, or any one of you, "What is on your mind? What are you up to?" the "case" talk starts flowing forward, and I hear you describe the object of your samadhi. Just as fifth stage Realizers talk about this blue light, that gold light, that red light, that black light, you talk about the object of your absorption—and it is *you*! It is not the Divine. It is not the Ultimate Realization. You think your absorption is happening to you. No, it *is* you. You are the source of your samadhi. These are *your* results, *your* effects. You are all in samadhi right now, distracted by your particular objects of fascination, interest, tendency. It is so!

Whenever objects arise, you are separate, and you become involved in a profound state of self-pleasuring. Even if what arises is not a pleasurable object, it is so distracting that you become totally self-involved—in pain, sorrow, anger. Even these states, which are not pleasurable, capture you and enforce the sense of separateness. There are samadhis of pain as well as of pleasure.

In your ordinary disposition, you are wandering in samadhi, like the traditional Yogis, Saints, and Sages. Compared to the objects they are holding onto passionately, your objects look rather stupid, or ordinary, certainly most mundane, by comparison, yet it is the same business. You are consoled by "money, food, and sex"—one could say that these are samadhis, states of absorption, consolation, and distraction of such magnitude that you forget, for the moment at any rate, your "problem" and feel that somehow the consoling and distracting and absorbing object is enough and makes life worth living. You are in a state of utter consolation, or, in other words, a state of consumed self-pleasuring, absorbed in the consumption of self-pleasuring, deeply embedded in it for the moment. Of course, the moment passes, this and that happens, and then you are seeking and complaining again.

What is the difference between you and somebody who, coming out of some conditional Samadhi in the fifth stage of life, complains and wants to struggle to make it happen again?

I have been Communicating just this Criticism during all the years since I formally began My Work with everyone twenty-two years ago. I Communicated the same critical disposition in *The Knee of Listening*. I have always been Communicating this Criticism to you. Many kinds of experiences and Samadhis are valued in the Great Tradition. The Great Tradition criticizes the mundane attachments and objects that people choose and by which they are distracted, but not the esoteric ones. From the beginning, I have Come to you Criticizing the esoteric ones as well.

There are no experiences in the context of the first six stages of life, no Samadhis, no objects of any kind whatsoever that are Most Ultimate Realization. They are all the dramatizations and the results of egoity. In the scale of the stages of life, yes, some are better than others—fine—but they are about the same thing. As a beginner in the Way of the Heart, you are ego-bound in the context of the first three stages of life, "considering" My Heart-Word, and observing the limitations of egoity. Therefore, you can also observe the traditions and see that they are not doing anything fundamentally different from the ordinary dramatization of egoity. You must do something fundamentally different, not only at the beginning of the Way of the Heart but all along, as the signs of the stages of life appear.

There is just one principle, one Way, one practice, one discipline, one sadhana. It is Ishta-Guru-Bhakti Yoga in My Company—the counter-egoic effort, transcending the primary fault and entering into the Sphere of Non-Separateness.

In the Great Tradition, although disciplines and various kinds of sadhana are usually recommended, the principal practice recommended within any school is concentration in the ultimate ego-object that is associated with the stage of life in which the school is based. It is not that these developmental experiences of the body-mind are just garbage, to be referred to without respect—that is not My opinion, and that is not what I am suggesting to you—but I am indicating what you must most fundamentally understand, which is the fault that carries through all of the first six stages of life.

Whatever your present mode of practice of the Way of the Heart, whatever stage of life is associated with it, there is just one thing to be done, one thing fundamentally to be understood, one practice. Only the Ultimate Realization is to be valued, not by seeking but by true self-understanding and right devotion to Me. No phenomenon that may be experienced in the context of the first six stages of life is Most Perfect Realization. None. Examine the stages of life, examine the Great Tradition in its display of all the exercises that can be done. You tell Me—are there any processes, sadhanas, effects, objects, Samadhis, states, that are not as I have just told you, not forms of the ego-game? You tell Me.

"Consider" it in yourself, in your present focus, in the traditions, if you like. Is what I am saying true or not? "Consider" it.

You cannot be silly, egoically "self-possessed" householders and still Realize everything. You talk about the things that console you in the most mundane sense, as if they are great Samadhis. They are samadhis of a kind, states of absorption, bizarre ecstasies of egoic "self-possession" and utter distraction in which nothing else is noticed, like hormonally induced obsessions—"All I want to do is have sex and fool around."

That is samadhi, but it is an absurd samadhi. It is not Great Samadhi. There is nothing Divine about it. It is the samadhi of distractedness by all kinds of emotional-sexual objects, patterning, and adaptation. Everything is excluded except the object of obsession, and you feel, "This is it, this is good, this is what life is about and what I should devote myself to. It feels perfectly good—why should I not just do it? What has anything else got to do with anything? I do not even know about anything else. All I know about is genitals!" Or household security—whatever your obsession may be. You are in a kind of samadhi! You are not yet involved in the advanced and the ultimate stages of life because you are involved in a lesser samadhi.

All the samadhis of the first six stages of life are self-absorbed, ego-based states of self-pleasure, and in their moment they are all equally distracting. "This is it, I do not need anything more. I do not want anything more. What else do I know, anyway? All I have before me is genitals, household comfort, lunch, some gastric balance, some emptied intestinal state." It feels good, and you have no time to do anything else. Hawk it, hammer on it, repeat it—all this is what you do. When I am talking to people who are still beginners in the Way of the Heart, nonetheless I am talking to people in samadhi. I might just as well be talking to people who have experienced fifth stage conditional Nirvikalpa Samadhi, or who are presently involved in Savikalpa Samadhi and seeing lights, something jumping up and down, moving around, being bright and distracting, so they cannot think about anything else. It is the same stuff.

This is the difficulty with you beginners—you are in samadhi. Not the Divine Samadhi but one or the other of the samadhis of egoity, in your case the samadhis of the first three stages of life. Anybody in such samadhi—who thinks that everything is fine, who thinks that whatever he or she is distracted by is the goal of life, who is consoled by the object of distraction, and who resists any greater obligation, any greater understanding, any greater practice—is a fool.

To people who are so-called "in love", for example, everything but the romantic object is utter garbage. All they want to do is the in-love thing, the romance thing, and the sex thing associated with it. They cannot see what they are doing. They have no discrimination about it. They have no impulse to understand it or go beyond it. They do not feel it particularly as pain at the moment. They do not know its future, the karma, the result, the tendencies that follow, the mortality with which it is identified. All they know is their present state of self-pleasure and consolation, and they think their obsession justifies it. They are enjoying a state of absorption, a kind of samadhi, wherein everything is excluded except the distracting object, nothing else is known, nothing else is remembered, and there is no attention for anything else.

The various traditions of the Great Tradition propose that people in great states are advanced beyond the crowd, and, therefore, traditionally, everything ordinary is regarded negatively. Yet to right understanding it is clear that people in the earlier stages of life who are not involved with esoteric exaggerations are doing the same thing as those in the great states. Ordinary people are in samadhi, too, distracted, like fools, at the moment without any capability for discrimination. In due course, everyone in the first six stages of life experiences the failure of his or her distraction and wants to seek some more and become bewildered again. In the moment of samadhi, in the moment of your fascination, however, you cannot listen, you cannot understand, you have no discrimination. You tend to lose your discipline altogether.

Therefore, samadhis are the "problem", not the solution! Except for the Samadhi of Most Ultimate Realization. The "problem" is that ordinary people are in samadhi. Because of this, they cannot understand themselves, and they cannot respond to the Divine.

The Way of Non-Separateness

March 13 and 16, 1994

1.

SRI DA AVABHASA: The Way of the Heart is the Way of self-transcendence in Divine Communion with Me, ultimately to the degree of Divine Self-Realization. Therefore, in the true advancement of the Way of the Heart, My devotee is not consoled by objective signs. The Way of the Heart has nothing to do with objective signs. By "objective" I do not refer only to the gross dimension of existence, but I include the subtle dimension, as well—anything that appears as an object is not fundamental to the Way of the Heart, because in order to perceive an object one must first assume the position of separateness. The Way of the Heart is the Way of Non-Separateness. Therefore, its specific, unique, Spiritual signs are different from the signs prized in the esotericism of the Great Tradition.

You cannot study the Spirituality of the Great Tradition and rightly presume that the Way of the Heart is about the same processes. It is not. The Way of the Heart is a unique, ultimate process that does not have anything to do with the conventions of the Great Tradition. It has nothing to do with egoity, or the body-mind—except the surrender of all of that. To take up the Way of the Heart is to enter into <u>My</u> Sphere—it is to practice Ishta-Guru-Bhakti Yoga from the beginning, in relationship to Me in My bodily (human) Form, in due course Finding Me Spiritually—My own Person, not the effects of My Spirit-Presence—and continuing the process of ego-surrender and ego-transcendence. This is why hearing is the fundamental realization in the Way of the Heart. Without it, you may not surrender the ego in the advancing, and Spiritually activated, developmental stages of the Way of the Heart.

In the true course of the Way of the Heart, there is no thing, there is no separateness. The developmental stages of the Way of the Heart are associated with the stages of life, but they are not identified with them. Therefore, the traditional paths, founded in the stages of life, are not fundamental to the Way of the Heart. All the content of the stages of life is specifically and directly transcended through right practice in My Company, which is simply Communion with Me. The practice of Divine Communion matures as you transcend the stages of life, ultimately Realizing the "Perfect Practice", when the last of the egoic stages is transcended at its root.

In the Way of the Heart, the Most Ultimate Realization is Objectless, the Realization of Non-Separateness, Divine Self-Realization Itself. It is the Most Ultimate Realization of Non-Objectivity. It is Realization without object, without consolation, without separate self, without egoity, without contraction, without separateness. Such is the Way of the Heart.

You can read the literature of the Great Tradition over and over and over again, yet you must understand that the traditions of religion and Spirituality are fundamentally about the exercise of the ego-based, objectively oriented, or otherwise separate disposition. That disposition is not the Way of the Heart. That disposition is what I Criticize.

All that having been said, in your characteristic disposition day by day, you are altogether object-oriented. Yet the objects are not the "problem", although you presume them to be. You imagine that even the body is your "problem", because it is a kind of object, too. You are altogether involved with objects, because you enforce the self-contraction. You made the gesture of separateness, and, in that process, you identified with the body-mind. Therefore, you view everything from the point of view or disposition of the body-mind. The Way of the Heart, even from the beginning, is to directly go beyond the egoic disposition and the act of self-contraction.

When you concentrate on objects, or the results of your own contraction, or when you are concentrated on the self-contraction itself, you only reinforce the "problem". In the Way of the Heart, you are Given, by Me, the means to go beyond yourself, persistently, moment by moment. Self-surrendered and self-forgetting, you Contemplate Me. <u>That</u> is the Way of the Heart. Even from the beginning, the Way of the Heart goes beyond self-contraction, goes beyond separateness and all the categories, the objective obsessions, the involvements, that are the results or signs of the self-contraction.

The Way of the Heart in every moment is Ishta-Guru-Bhakti Yoga, or surrendering and forgetting separate self and Communing with Me, practicing this counter-egoic effort moment by moment and not dwelling on the self-contraction, not dwelling on its effects, not dwelling on objects, but dwelling on Me, not casually relating to Me but profoundly practicing the counter-egoic effort of self-surrendering and self-forgetting Communion with Me. The Way of the Heart is the Way of Non-Separateness from the beginning, but it must be practiced. If you do otherwise, if you do anything other than this counter-egoic act of Communion with Me through self-surrender and self-forgetting, you only dwell on the self-contraction and its results. You are "Narcissus" again.

The Way of the Heart is a profound discipline founded in the Inherently Perfect Wisdom of the seventh stage Realization, even from the beginning. It is not about the stages of life themselves. It is not about their content, not at the beginning and not at the middle and not at the end. It is not about the first three stages of life, nor the fourth stage of life, nor the fifth stage of life. It is not even about the sixth stage of life as it is traditionally Realized in limitation. The Way of the Heart is Ishta-Guru-Bhakti Yoga, or the practice of entering into Communion with Me, the Non-Separate One. Anything else on which you place your attention, or with which you identify, is separateness and the act of separation.

Therefore, Ishta-Guru-Bhakti Yoga is the one thing to do. It is the Principle of the Way of the Heart. Understand what Ishta-Guru-Bhakti Yoga involves, and you understand why it is entrance into My Sphere, the Sphere of Non-Separateness, the Divine Sphere. If you presume to practice Ishta-Guru-Bhakti Yoga in some ego-congratulating fashion, or on the basis of some invention of your own, or on the basis of identification with the body, your practice is no longer true Ishta-Guru-Bhakti Yoga, nor is it the Way of the Heart.

You can read the literature of the traditions over and over again, and you will discover that, yes, many traditions are devoted to Guru, but the devotional traditions are not the Way of the Heart. You may find likenesses to the Way of the Heart in the traditions, but the Way of the Heart is specifically, most directly and always, self-forgetting, self-transcending immersion in the Wisdom of the seventh stage of life, Communion with the One Who Is the Realizer and the Revealer and the Very Divine Person and Self-Condition to be Realized.

The Great Tradition is not about the Most Ultimate Matter and the Most Ultimate Way. The Most Ultimate Matter of My Realization and the Way of the Heart that I have Revealed is My unique Revelation to You, and, therefore, the Way of Divine Self-Realization is unique. It is not found in the Great Tradition. It is not found in you. It is a unique and most profound discipline. It is the Way of Non-Separateness. It is the Way of No-Separation, No-"Difference", No-Objectivity, No-Relatedness. There is no separation. None. All of that is vanished, non-existent, in Most Ultimate Realization. In Most Ultimate, or seventh stage, Realization, there is no "difference", no separation, no relatedness, no identification with the body-mind or conditional existence, no identification with self-contraction, only Non-Separateness, No-"Difference"—That is the Realization.

When the act of separation is transcended, That Which Is is Obvious. That Realization is Given, by Grace. It is not a philosophical discovery or the result of a process of thought. No-Separation is Realized, by Grace, in devotional Communion with Me, in the context of this true sadhana, this truly counter-egoic sadhana, or the sadhana of Non-Separateness, the sadhana that always, in every moment, when done rightly, counters all signs of separateness.

To experience the various developmental results of the stages of life requires identification with the body-mind. Therefore, the experiences of the stages of life are not the Way of the Heart. You may have such experiences, but they are not the moments of fullest practice and Realization of the Way of the Heart. In Divine Self-Realization, there are no visions, no objects, no places. There is no separate self and no consolation. None of that! None!

The Outshining Radiance that is Divine Translation is utterly beyond objectivity. It is not a matter of going to a Great Place or finding Me objectively in some ultimate Form. It is a matter of Realizing Me Non-Objectively. There is no psychic content. There is no mind. There is no body. There is no world. There is no future, no past, no present—only the Eternal, only the Absolute. Only.

Why do you think so much? It seems you cannot endure even a moment without another thought, without another objective experience, without something to console you, something to entertain you, something to stimulate yourself with, something to be hopeful about. That is the ego-game, the game of seeking, showing its signs by adaptation. It has nothing to do with sadhana in the Way of the Heart. Nothing. All your ordinary preoccupations from day to day, your concerns for consolation, all your searches, adaptations, and ordinary human wants are not the Way of the Heart. They arise. Therefore, I have told you how to practice the Way of the Heart as they arise. The Way of the Heart is not those things, nor is it association with those things on the basis of an ideal of how life should be when it is best. The Way of the Heart is the practice of Ishta-Guru-Bhakti Yoga as things arise. The Way of the Heart is always, only, the Way of Non-Separateness, the Way of self-surrendering and self-forgetting Communion with Me, always. That is the moment, every moment. That is the discipline.

I have told you how to do this under the various circumstances of appearance and seeming experience, but not at all suggesting an ideal. No. My purpose always is to tell you how to practice Ishta-Guru-Bhakti Yoga with every function, in every circumstance, in every relationship—always Ishta-Guru-Bhakti Yoga, always going beyond the ego-principle, beyond the self-contraction, beyond the appearances, beyond identification with the body-mind. In every moment, this is the discipline, entirely and only. Self-surrendering and self-forgetting Communion with Me is the Yoga of the Way of the Heart.

Separateness, with all its effects, is an illusion. Non-Separateness—Ishta-Guru-Bhakti Yoga, in other words—is the Truth and the Way. That is it entirely. How many lectures must you hear? How many books must you read? The Way of the Heart is fundamental, simple, single, absolute, most precious. Find it out. Study My Heart-Word every day. Learn how to apply the practice of Ishta-Guru-Bhakti Yoga to every circumstance, every function, every relationship. I have Given you all kinds of disciplines for transforming every circumstance, every relationship, every function of the body-mind into Ishta-Guru-Bhakti Yoga, not by indulging in those things or associating with them on some idealistic basis, no, but by practicing Ishta-Guru-Bhakti Yoga in those circumstances, in those experiences, in the apparent exercise of those faculties of the body-mind.

The Way of the Heart is just one Yoga—it is real devotion to Me. This real devotion to Me, or Ishta-Guru-Bhakti Yoga, is a counter-egoic exercise of the principal faculties—body, emotion (or feeling), mind (or attention), and breath—in self-surrendering and self-forgetting Communion with Me, moment by moment by moment by moment by moment. It is a profound and most severe, most wonderful, most creative beyond wonderful, absolute Yoga and effort. It has never been known before. It has never been provided before. It has never been explained before—ever.

Understand the uniqueness of My Revelation, and do the Yoga. It is very simple and straightforward. Always study it. Always read and recite and study My Heart-Word. Tell My Leelas. The fundamental practice covers everything in anyone's life. If you have not grasped that simplicity, then all the elaborations on it and all the explanations are like instructions about how to put on a coat to someone who does not even know what a coat is! When you understand Me rightly, you see how simple and single it is. The fundamental principle covers everything. It is the effort you must do in every moment. The rest is a diversion.

The Truth is beyond your conception. It is beyond what you ever thought the Way of Liberation is about. You always thought Realization is somehow about yourself, and objects, and the development of experiences. All that is the ego-game. The Way of the Heart has nothing to do with any of it. Start forgetting yourself, surrendering beyond yourself, and entering fully into Me, into the Sphere of Who I Am, most fully, forgetting everything in every moment.

Yes, while you do that, you will function, you will do your service, karmas will be purified—good. But the practice is just this Yoga of absolute devotion to Me, to the point of self-forgetting Communion with

Me. That is it entirely. That is the Secret that has never been Revealed before, never been made possible before. Now it is made fully possible. It is thoroughly explained, thoroughly Revealed. I have Given you My Heart-Word. Therefore, go to My Source-Books.* Read them every day. Study them together intensively. Do the practice of Ishta-Guru-Bhakti Yoga. That is the Way of the Heart.

◆ ◆ ◆

DEVOTEE: My Lord, who is the one who is in Communion with You?

SRI DA AVABHASA: There is no "who" about it. There is just Me. If you are in Communion with Me, there is just Me. You do not get to Communion with Me until there is really self-surrender and self-forgetting. Therefore, there is no "who" about it.

DEVOTEE: So there is no one left but the Divine.

SRI DA AVABHASA: That is it.

DEVOTEE: In other words, there is no one there even to be in Communion with You.

SRI DA AVABHASA: That is it. If you try to remember the "who", you drop back from Communion with Me, you are remembering yourself and not quite surrendered. Then, "I think this, I wonder that, I feel that, I react to that, I want to do this, or I want to do that." It is a backwards spiral.

Communion with Me goes beyond all that, through the mechanism of self-surrender and self-forgetting, which are the necessary preliminaries. There is no Communion with Me without self-surrender and self-forgetting. Until there is true self-surrender, there can be gestures toward Me, but not Communion with Me. Communion with Me is the practice in every moment, then. If you are a beginner in the Way of the Heart, your practice is not always Communion with Me. It is the counter-egoic effort of noticing the limit. It is Communion with Me sometimes, but always there must be the forceful reintroduction of the Yoga itself and going beyond all that arises, until, in due course, true hearing occurs, which grants you the capability for Communion with Me very directly, moment to moment.

Seeing Me is the next Great Grace, and coming into My Company as My Spiritually activated devotee immediately follows, because the practice is no longer a matter of dealing with the signs of limitation that arise short of self-surrender and self-forgetting. Whatever arises, immediately its fundamental limitation is noticed and gone beyond. Such is the capability of true hearing.

There is nothing to do but Ishta-Guru-Bhakti Yoga. Just do that instead of chatting at Me and trying to create some absurd questions or other in your complicated state of mind, which is just total and absolute bullshit, you must realize. It is better to be really quiet, really devotional, and get on with the work. Be an example of devotion to Me in your service. It is your obligation in company with others, and there will be much less chat. Instead, there will be much telling of My Leelas, much studying of My Word, much quietness before and afterwards.

Go to the Communion Hall. Chant. Sit in meditation. Do service with full attention on Me, with all the faculties of the body-mind devoted to Me. Surrender and forget yourself. It is a profound work, and it is what you must do. It is a quiet life, an unstimulated life. Unstimulated. Not fascinated with objects. Not seeking. Just Ishta-Guru-Bhakti, that Yoga. All the rest is garbage. The attempt to be interesting, the attempt to re-make the world, has no business in My Company and nothing to do with Me. There is nothing much to say. You just must get on with it. Then, soon, Spiritual, too. Nothing else.

You cannot ever in reality lose Me. You can presume you have lost Me. You can presume separation from Me. You can indulge in the self-contracted illusions and apparent occupations of the body-mind. You can experience the illusion of separation from Me. You cannot, however, <u>in fact</u> be separated from Me. You never have been—you are not now. Yet still you notice a difference. The Samadhi of Non-Separation is not your Realization all the time, or, even in the fullest sense, ever, so far.

Nonetheless, I Am Who I Am, the Truth is the Truth, Reality is Reality, Non-Separation is What Is. Because you are experiencing illusions otherwise, you must do sadhana. To do sadhana is why you are here and why you came to Me to begin with.

Now, having come to Me, you have My Instruction and you have My Person. Commune with Me.

2.

SRI DA AVABHASA: Whatever your stage of life, you are in object-oriented samadhi. You are "Narcissus" at the pond. I am here to draw the attention of Narcissus up from the pond to Me, so that in Communion with Me he will give up his ordinary samadhi, his object-oriented samadhi, especially (at the beginning) his grossly oriented samadhi of objects. I have provided you with the Grace of My Company to bring your head out of the pond. In the meantime, however, like Narcissus, you are in samadhi. You are obsessed with an object, and you do not know its source, you do not know that it is you and that you are

are just confined to your object, consoling yourself with it and remaining oblivious to reality, including death.

Submit your attention to Me. Surrender. Forget yourself. Enter into My Sphere. Only then does real growth begin, by the way, not when you hear My Instruction and perhaps indulge in some outer observances. When you really practice Ishta-Guru-Bhakti Yoga, when you are not paying attention to yourself, things start becoming obsolete, passing by, getting purified, and you become refined in your disposition. You understand your bondage. You understand your own action. You become capable, then, of the moment to moment gesture—most profound and really effective—of surrendering to Me. You become ready to Find Me Spiritually and, through the progress of the Way of the Heart, you go more and more beyond your object-obsession, your egoic "self-possession".

Ishta-Guru-Bhakti Yoga is not the practice of renouncing objects. It is the practice of renouncing yourself, of surrendering to Me, forgetting yourself, and entering more and more into My Sphere of Being. Then the Truth of Non-Separateness and Freedom from objects is Realized, progressively, and, in due course, most profoundly. There is nothing to be confused about. There is only one practice—moment to moment investment of all the faculties of the body-mind in Me. Therefore, do not worry about whether objects are passing or not. You are supposed to forget about them. The conditions of bondage become obsolete not by your attention to them and struggle with them but by your submission to Me and your forgetting of separate self in Communion with Me. Only in that process do these obsessions pass.

By devoting himself—or herself—to Me, "Narcissus" forgets the obsessive image, not by struggling with the image but by being devoted to Me. The process, the Yoga, is surrender to Me, forgetting yourself to the point of Communion with Me. If Communion with Me is true, then you do not make much of even the objective nature of My Appearance. Even in the beginnings of your devotion to Me, when you make the act of turning from the pond, turning from separate self, by truly surrendering to Me and forgetting yourself to the point of Communing with Me, there are no objects, even the apparent "Object" that is My bodily (human) Form. Because you have surrendered to Me, forgotten yourself, entered into Communion with Me, there is no object.

When you realize true hearing, you equip yourself to Find Me Spiritually. Yet even then the Yoga is not about receiving Me or receiving the effects of My Spiritual (and Always Blessing) Presence and registering them in the body-mind. Secondarily, those things may happen, but your practice is still the Yoga of surrendering yourself to Me and forgetting yourself to the point of Communing with Me.

Spiritually activated practice in My Company is not a reception. It is a death. Separate self is undone. The principle, the position, the act, of separate self are forgotten. This is how the Spiritual course, even as early as maturity in the third developmental stage of the Way of the Heart, achieves the profundity that is identification with the Witness-Position.

The process of the Way of the Heart is ego-transcendence, not identifying the body-mind as a problem and struggling with it. The Way of the Heart is Ishta-Guru-Bhakti Yoga, not some self-based struggle with conditions and objects and the body—the traditional targets of sadhana. Yes, the body-mind, conditional existence, and the adaptations of egoity are disciplined, but, fundamentally, by virtue of your surrender to Me, you forget yourself and you enter into Communion with Me. Communion with Me is not a struggle with the objective aspects of conditional existence. It is directly, in every moment, the relinquishing of the ego-position, the ego-act.

In the process, you understand the ego-act to the degree of true hearing, or most fundamental self-understanding. Yes, there are purifications and disciplines of the body-mind—fine—but the body-mind is not the "problem" to be struggled with in the games of self-"guruing". If you choose to struggle, then evolutionary illusions may arise to distract you, and you will invest yourself in the effects of My Spirit-Presence instead of practicing Ishta-Guru-Bhakti Yoga.

The Yoga of the Way of the Heart is simple and most direct, in every moment. It is simply surrender to Me, forgetting separate self in surrender to Me, by devoting your faculties to Me in every moment to the point of Communing with Me. This is always the practice—always, at every stage of life in the Way of the Heart. Therefore, you are not concerned for the effects that may arise in My Company, nor for the concerns and problems that may register in the mind. There is none of that—only Ishta-Guru-Bhakti Yoga.

If, at present, you do not understand anything about the process I am describing, it is because you are not doing it. You are still thinking of the objects. "I've got to get rid of them now." The Way of the Heart, the Way of Non-Separateness, the Way of Ishta-Guru-Bhakti Yoga, of true surrender, true self-forgetting, true Communion with Me, will prove itself in the Realizing of it. In the foretime, all you can do is speak from your egoically "self-possessed" and unresolved and object-obsessed point of view. You are trying to figure it out. You generate symbols, suggestions, philosophies, thoughts—they have nothing to do with it! Just do the Yoga I have Given you. The Yoga will prove itself. And when you have the real experience of the Way of the Heart, based on real practice, you will understand what I am talking about. Until then, any trying to figure it out and any explanations or observations about it are based on your continued egoic "self-possession", and you are only talking nonsense.

In the first five stages of life, there are always objects that could obsess you. Always! As My devotee, however, you are supposed to do the Yoga of Ishta-Guru-Bhakti, from the beginning. By this means alone, the object-obsessive orientation of the egoic stages of life is relinquished, forgotten, in effect purified.

The sixth stage of life in My Company, the "Perfect Practice", is not about object-obsession. It is about Freedom from the obsessions, limitations, and orientations of the first five stages of life. In the "Perfect Practice", you identify the self-contraction most profoundly, even its most rudimentary, most simple, original form, which is the feeling of relatedness, the sense of "difference". Having Realized the Witness-Position, you Stand in that Position. Rather than moving toward the context of objects and the feeling of relatedness, you enter into the Sphere of Consciousness Itself, or That Which Is the Witness. Yet you do this in the context of your devotion to Me, your continued practice of Ishta-Guru-Bhakti. Only on the basis of your devotion to Me, and My Spiritual Heart-Transmission to you in the context of your Stand in the Witness-Position and Most Ultimately in Its Source-Condition, does this otherwise apparently sixth stage practice allow the Revelation, by Grace of My Spiritual Heart-Transmission, of the seventh stage Realization.

The Realization of the seventh stage of life is entirely a Grace. That Most Ultimate Transition is not figurable, calculable. There is no strategy in it. You do not make the seventh stage Awakening. I do—and not by an Act but by simply Standing As I Am. You practice the devotion to Me that is associated with the second stage of the "Perfect Practice", and in that context the Most Ultimate Awakening is Given. Its Realization is to be seen. You cannot make it yourself. Nor can you make the Way of the Heart yourself. All you can do is practice Ishta-Guru-Bhakti Yoga.

All the "things" that are valued in the traditions are the "things" that are transcended, not realized, in the Way of the Heart. Secondarily, those experiences may occur, because of the wanderings of attention and the adaptations of person and energy, but they are not specific to the Way of the Heart. They are only the cosmic possibilities associated with egoity. Therefore, they may be experienced and noticed, but they are not the demonstrations of the Way of the Heart. They are what is to be transcended. The Way of the Heart is just Ishta-Guru-Bhakti Yoga—not the Guru-devotion that is described in the traditions, even with the same language, but devotion to Me.

In Communion with Me, the Revelation is Given, the transitions are made, the transformations and Awakenings are Given. If you just want to be a fool, struggling forever with the obligation of devotion to Me, the obligation of self-discipline, the obligation of Ishta-Guru-Bhakti Yoga, then, in your arguing with Me, you are like all the rest of the gullible consumers and social religionists.

You do not get gold by just coming into My physical Company. You do not enter into Most Perfectly self-Transcending God-Realization by just belonging to the club. You must do the sadhana for real. Whatever you must discipline, whatever life-business you must handle, whatever you must do to make your faculties available for the practice of Ishta-Guru-Bhakti Yoga, it is your business! I have made totally plain to you how to do it, but doing it is your business. When you do it, I respond. That is the Law.

◆ ◆ ◆

SRI DA AVABHASA: The Divine Being, Who Is All That is all, Is One Only. Everything is One. Everything is That One.

The Divine Being is All-and-all, even in terms of what appears. At the same time, the Divine Being experiences Itself as being just what appears—not the All-and-all and One, but just whatever is appearing.

That explains you, then. You are just the same One and All-and-all, Appearing to be ignorant, Thinking It is you full of your concerns, Forgetting Its Real Condition, Living an apparent life, an adventure. It is the same with everyone. Thus identified, and ignorant of Its Divine Condition, the Divine Being Lives an apparent life and goes through all the thinking and desiring and conditioning and adaptation, confusion, and fear—and then dies!

Nothing in your life is guaranteed except that you are going to die. All the rest is not guaranteed. Life is a Play. Who knows what is going to happen? Although you try to avoid it, the only thing guaranteed is that everything you identify with and are struggling with and are desiring with is going to die!

Life is an ordeal. "Nobody is happy before they die", as someone once said. True. True not just of the death of the body at the end of life but also of the death of the ego.

Go beyond. There is no soul in the heart. There is only the Divine Person, the Divine Reality. By going beyond yourself, you Realize. There is no Eternal part in the individual being. There is only God, only Me here.

Get with Me, babies. No more questions need be asked. I have said everything that can be said. And now the time, forever, of the great discipline in My Company. Forever. Forever—for all My devotees forever.

My Eternal Work

March 23, 1994

SRI DA AVABHASA: There is only the Divine. The Divine Is the Divine Self-Domain. Self-Existing and Self-Radiant Reality of Divine Being is the only Domain that is. That Domain Is Always Already the case. There is no coming and going from It—except in your thinking, your presumptions, your fears, your self-contraction.

The Divine Self-Domain is not a "place". It is not elsewhere. It is not a "here". The Divine Self-Domain is the Perfectly Subjective Divine Condition Itself. Even all of this manifestation is arising in the Divine Self-Domain, presently. It is not that this arising manifestation is the Divine Self-Domain. The Divine Self-Domain Is the Context of this manifestation—indeed, of all manifestation. When this manifestation is utterly, Divinely Recognized as a transparent, or merely apparent, and un-necessary, and inherently non-binding modification of Divine Consciousness, the entire manifested cosmos is Outshined in Divine Consciousness, in the Great Event of Divine Translation, and only the Divine Domain Is.

Through My active Work in the cosmic domain, I Reveal the Way of Most Perfectly self-transcending God-Realization and, at last, of Divine Translation—the Way of Perfectly Subjective Divine Self-Realization. Therefore, I will remain Active, if necessary, even after the death of This Body, within the cosmic domain, until I am Satisfied that My Revelation-Work is entirely Accomplished.

My Work is the Divine Translation of All and all. I will maintain My own Active Agency within the cosmic domain until I am Satisfied that I have Established right and sufficient Instrumentality and Agency. Then I will Demonstrate the Siddhi of My Divine Translation. Even then, My Work does not cease. Through the Siddhi of My Divine Translation, I Draw All and all into the Condition of Divine Translation. When, in due course, I Divinely Translate, the Power of My own Divine Translation will always be Effective within the cosmic domain. The cosmic domain is within Me.

If it is necessary for My active Work to continue after the lifetime of this physical body, I will be Working Beyond this plane, for the Purpose of Establishing sufficient Instrumentality and Agency throughout the cosmic domain—as necessary, and different in every kind of context. Then, rather than Reincarnating in this Earth plane, I will simply Direct My Blessing Influence here. My Influence here will perhaps not be directly perceived. It will be a Quiet Persistence, Made to be felt, Made to Guide, Made to Awaken.

I Volunteered for this Sacrifice, this Service, this Work, and I am not bound by it in any sense whatsoever. My Love of beings Called Me out. This Compassion makes Me continue, but not as a slave. I could leave you to yourselves at any time, but I would not do it. That does not mean, however, that I am bound here, nor am I trying to escape. I need not escape, because I am not in bondage. I am not one who can be bound.

My Incarnation is associated with Siddhis that I have Brought into this plane. Therefore, to enter into <u>My</u> Sphere, to become <u>My</u> devotee, to practice Ishta-Guru-Bhakti Yoga in relation to Me—whether during or after My physical Lifetime—is to be invested in the Siddhis of My unique Work. My Siddhis are now eternally Established here. The Means whereby My devotees become involved in My Siddhis are the Means I have Established by Great Work. I am still Working to Establish the Way of the Heart altogether, concretely, so that the linkage to Me can be lived here and everywhere, forever.

I have taken My Stance here in a fashion that is not comprehensible. Simply by Exercising the Siddhis Inherent in Me, I am Effective throughout the cosmic domain. I have Chosen this Appearance. I have Taken on structures that existed in this domain for the sake of this Appearance. I have Done a particular kind of Work in this place, via this bodily (human) Form. That does not mean that if I am to be Effectively Active after the death of this bodily (human) Form, I must be wandering about on a white horse or Appearing in some such Manifestation—although it may amuse Me to do so sometime!

The Divine Process is not magic. You must respond. Beings must respond. You must do the work. Otherwise, you are controlled by the structures of your own adaptation, and no great thing occurs. The cosmic domain cannot be merely glanced at, as if it were an object, and magically Outshined. You must cooperate with My Divine Grace. Beings must respond. I Bring you the Gifts, the Revelation, My Teaching Word—everything—but you must respond. You must integrate with Me through the practice of Ishta-Guru-Bhakti Yoga that I have Given you.

The cosmic domain is not the problem. You are. The Way of the Heart is not based on an egoic motive to escape from this plane to higher planes. The Way of the Heart is based on the impulse to Most Perfectly self-transcending God-Realization. From the "Point of View" of the Realization of the seventh stage of life, the body is not a problem. It is Inherently, Divinely Recognized. The functions of the body-mind, which are simply structures of the cosmic domain—apparent attention, the energies in the body-mind, the natural form of the body-mind, and so forth—are not a problem. They are not escaped in Divine Self-Realization, and they are not a problem. They are just structures. What is transcended in Divine Self-Realization is egoity, bondage.

The Way of Communion with Me, heart-contact with Me, heart-availability to Me and to My Work altogether, is practiced through the specifics of the Way of the Heart, which I have Given, and through all the means associated with the Way of the Heart. That is how the process works, not by casual association with My Word and Person or by mere presumptions of understanding and advancement.

All you need to know is that I am with you and that the Way I have Given is True. Practice it, therefore. I am available to you forever, as I have told you. My Work is world-Work, and Spiritual Work. I am here to Fulfill My Intention completely.

I Will Be Incarnated Countlessly Through My Devotees

March 29, 1994

SRI DA AVABHASA: I am not here to make the world into a utopia. To do so is not My Work, although I may Respond spontaneously to events in the world—but always in an address to the mass of karmas and ego-results.

I am here to Draw people into Divine Communion, and, thereby, into living right life, assuming responsibility, truly handling their business, coming to Me for the sake of Most Perfectly self-transcending God-Realization and, most ultimately, Divine Translation. I am Exercised perpetually as this Attraction.

The cosmic domain is not purposed to become a utopia, an absolute, an end in itself, a perfect future. It is a mechanism that has meaning in its time among bound beings, but, most profoundly, it is a struggle to Realize the Divine, or That Condition Which is Beyond egoity, Beyond karma, Beyond limitation, Beyond attention, Beyond struggle.

However, you want to combine Me with yourself, so that I become part of your struggle to make the world perfect. Yet I am here to Draw you into combining with Me for the sake of the transcendence of egoity—even most ultimately, therefore, for the sake of the transcendence of the entire cosmic domain. This is not to suggest that the cosmos is or can be a utopia. It is not even possible. In itself, such a suggestion would bind you further. I Work Compassionately to make changes that Serve the Greater Purpose, the Divine Purpose, not to make a utopia out of the world.

Therefore, do not regard My Divine Siddhis as a kind of magic that works in the direction of utopia. My Siddhis are something that I Do in the context of a world that is about struggle and limitation, and that is karma-bound. In a Compassionate manner, I Serve changes that give time and occasion for sadhana. Whatever can be done Compassionately, responsibly, I Function to Serve. Even so, you must understand My Purpose and My Intention in such Service. You must understand the reality in which you are involved. And you must assume your responsibilities for right practice of the Way of the Heart.

What is the practice I have Given My devotees for the positive changing of conditions? It is the Devotional Prayer of Changes, which is simply and primarily self-surrendering and self-forgetting feeling-Contemplation of Me. In that Heart-Communion with Me, My devotee actively relinquishes and releases all identification with and affirmation of negative, or non-useful, conditions, and My devotee actively affirms, receives, and enacts positive, or useful and right, conditions.

What is that process about? It is to make use of My Virtue, or My Mere and Blessing Presence. In Communion with Me, you associate with, participate in, and draw upon My own Virtue. I am Calling you to assume your responsibilities and really, effectively, rather than only randomly and, therefore, ineffectively, to do the Devotional Prayer of Changes. Do it. Draw on My Virtue rather than bringing Me problems and negative conditions and expecting Me to deal with them. I have Given you the Means for making positive changes, through your Communion with Me, and by doing so I have Transferred to you responsibilities that until now have been Mine.

The Devotional Prayer of Changes can be effective relative to all kinds of things, if, as My devotee, you would draw upon My Virtue and do the Devotional Prayer of Changes as I have Given it to you, which is a form of Ishta-Guru-Bhakti Yoga, or participation in Me. By practicing the Devotional Prayer of Changes and handling your responsibilities, you replace the kind of Work I have Done through the exercise of My Siddhis.

You will always be able to draw upon Me, forever, through your right practice of the Devotional Prayer of Changes. After the death of This Body, I need not be physically present or present in any sense within the cosmic domain and intentionally exercising My Siddhis. Just as, over the years, I have Done something for a while and then have Shown you how to do it, have Given you Instruction about something and then have Given you the responsibility for doing it, so also with My Divine Siddhis—even These.

You make Me Effective by doing the practice I have Given to you, rather than transferring the responsibility to Me and expecting Me to fulfill it by My Intention, by My Maintaining a Mechanism within this domain or within any portion of the cosmic domain. The Instruction having been Given, and the Means for participating in Me having been Given, I need no longer be Active in the cosmic domain, because, in effect, you are providing the Mechanism for My Activity. I am Merely Present.

Therefore, the significance of My Divine Translation is that all responsibility is Given over to you—not you separate from Me, but you participating in Me—and I need not maintain a Mechanism within the cosmic domain, because now I have countless forms of such Mechanism—My devotees—in Communion with Me, As I Am, Merely Present.

Potentially, then, all beings throughout the cosmic domain can be maintaining My Effectiveness by providing the Instrumentality and the Agency, the Mechanism, whereby I am Effective. In some sense, this is the summary of what I am here to Reveal to you. All My devotees everywhere are to replace the Mechanism I have Brought into the cosmic domain and by Which I have Made this Revelation to you. The moment when I am Satisfied it is Done is the time—or the moment, or the occasion, or the Event—of My Divine Translation.

My Divine Translation is not the event of My leaving you nor in any sense the event of My moving into abstraction from you or dissociation from you—it is not that at all. My Divine Translation is the Event that occurs when responsibility is fully Given to you so that the Mechanism of My Effectiveness can be multiplied infinitely, countlessly.

I am here to show you the Way of inhering in Me and participating in Me, the Way that Grants you responsibility to provide the Mechanism for positive changes. You as an individual are not the source of My Siddhis. The mechanism of the body-mind-self must be devoted to Me, surrendered to Me, forgotten in Me, so that it becomes transparent to Me, so that you draw on My Virtue, and then your sadhana is effective—but because you are in Communion with Me, not because you practice certain techniques.

Ishta-Guru-Bhakti Yoga is the principle of the Way of the Heart. It is the Way of forgetting separate self, forgetting egoity, and participating in Me. Then the mechanism of the body-mind-self becomes less and less an obstruction and, rather, becomes more and more transparent to Me, therefore more and more effective, because of My Virtue.

The secret of the Way of the Heart is not self-applied techniques but the relationship to Me, this participation in Me, whereby you are Granted more and more responsibilities, even relative to the kinds of things that, having observed My Siddhis, you know I am Doing remarkably. The gathering of My devotees will do these things—not as individuals nor as a group of ordinary human beings who are practicing techniques but as My devotees who are transparent to Me. Therefore, My devotees become a Mechanism that is equivalent to This Body. You become the Means whereby My Virtue is Exhibited in the cosmic play.

Your responsibility does not depend on your creature-power or ego-power. It depends on your participation in Me, and on your engaging in the practices that establish your own mechanism as the means for the very same things you are presently calling on Me to Do by what may look to you to be My Personal Intention.

This is another characteristic of My Sign and My Demonstration of My Divine Indifference. I have Shown you how to do everything. Now your Devotional Prayer of Changes becomes effective because you use My Virtue, through your practice of Ishta-Guru-Bhakti Yoga, and through your taking your responsibilities seriously rather than imagining that they are only mysterious obligations that have nothing to do with you. You are drawing on My Virtue simply by practicing the Devotional Prayer of Changes, or true Ishta-Guru-Bhakti Yoga. You allow your own mechanism to become the means.

My devotees are to provide the body-minds whereby My Virtue becomes Effective. If you will really do so, then changes will occur. Yes, they will be changes that I have Made, but in the fashion I have just described to you.

So it will be forever. That My devotees have gotten the secret of Ishta-Guru-Bhakti Yoga allows My Divine Translation. It allows Me to be Effective forever throughout the cosmic domain. My Virtue changes things and Enlightens beings, and It Works, because My devotees assume their responsibilities by embracing the practices I have Given them, doing those practices for real, and using My Virtue.

Then, when the time comes that This Body dies, I will not disappear. I will be wholly Available to you. You have the Means, you have the secret, you do the practice, and I will be Effective forever—Fully Conscious, Self-Radiant, never gone, never separate, but also not requiring My Self to Establish a body-mind, or any other Mechanism, of My own within the cosmic domain anymore, because I have Empowered countless such body-minds to provide such Means. That is the secret of Communion with Me.

It has always been the case, but you did not know the secret. I have come to Reveal that secret and to Establish the Fullest Instruction. By your devotional response to Me, you give Me the Mechanism to do the same kind of Work I have been Doing in this bodily Lifetime here. I will be Incarnated countlessly by means of this process.

Every one of My devotees has the same essential responsibility. Some will fulfill it more profoundly, with greater advancement in the stages of life in the Way of the Heart, and some have special roles to play—fine—yet all My devotees are Called to the same practice from the day they become My devotee. You are to practice the Way of the Heart not just individually but collectively, as the culture of the Way of the Heart, which is the culture of participation in Me, of assuming responsibilities in Communion with Me. The culture of the Way of the Heart is the culture of Ishta-Guru-Bhakti Yoga, not the culture of attention to the ego and egoic dramatization.

My devotees are Bless-ed, Empowered by Me to live this great devotion to Me and provide the Means whereby My Blessing-Grace will become more and more profoundly Effective.

In the fullest, or Spiritually activated, demonstration of the Devotional Prayer of Changes, the affirmation of positive conditions may be visualized, or given form in mind, as a way of making it effective. The presumption of positive conditions must be a true presumption. It becomes more and more effective as the ego-presumption, the separateness, egoic "self-possession", self-content, and self-remembering disappear. The more profoundly separate self is surrendered and forgotten in Communion with Me, likewise the more profound your sadhana will be and the more profound your Devotional Prayer of Changes will be as part of your sadhana.

The more profoundly you practice Ishta-Guru-Bhakti Yoga, the more profound your sadhana will become, the more you will advance in the practice of the Way of the Heart, and the more effective will be your practice of the Devotional Prayer of Changes.

The more there is of such growth, the more you will see that the process is true. You will see how the process works. You will see that cosmic existence is a Unity and that there is no separateness in it. You will know the Divine Basis of it all by Communing with Me. Your conclusions about reality will be firm, steady, based in real experience, real understanding, real discrimination. In due course, you will enter into the "Perfect Practice", and you will be on the other side of attention.

You must understand that in My Divine Translation I am not disappearing. I am simply Manifesting My Self Wholly Present. Nevertheless, My Divine Translation is the Process whereby you must assume the responsibilities that I My Self have Manifested in the Lifetime of This Body and about which I have thoroughly Instructed you.

This is the great secret of Ishta-Guru-Bhakti Yoga: My Virtue does the sadhana in <u>your</u> body-mind, My Virtue does the Devotional Prayer of Changes in your body-mind, because, in your self-surrendering and self-forgetting Communion with Me, your body-mind has become as equally identified with Me as This Body sitting before you.

Accept this Empowerment by Me, therefore. Accept My Gift, accept the Yoga I have Given you, and all the responsibilities that belong to it. This is what Ishta-Guru-Bhakti Yoga, or the Way of the Heart, is all about. You are My inheritors. You are those who are here to inherit from Me the great Virtue of My Divine Presence and the great responsibilities that accompany Communion with Me.

You who are presently part of the gathering of My devotees are the first seeds of this Work. It is world-Work. It is Work that covers the entire cosmic domain. It is a profoundly important and real matter. There is no fakery in it and no mythology. It is real Divine Revelation, real Divine Blessing, real responsibility. Therefore, you must be truly serious about it.

Remember the secret of Ishta-Guru-Bhakti Yoga. Understand that you must make your own body-mind the Means whereby My Works are Done. There need not be much talk between Me and My devotees anymore. Knowing this secret I have told you, you must do the talking, the working, and the doing, and fulfill the responsibilities. This is how My Divine Siddhi Works. While This Body lives, and after it dies, it will be exactly the same.

I do not require that This Body go on forever. I Require, for the fulfillment of My Work, that all the bodies throughout this manifested universe be in Communion with Me and do this Great Work with My Virtue. That Work Embraces everything, absolutely everything—from personal sadhana to the transformation of the entire cosmic domain.

I Am the One Who Is. Therefore, I Am always the One at Work. What I Require are these Means, these Instruments and Agents. I will always be Active through these Means. Therefore, I need not Re-Incarnate in this realm, nor need I continue to be Active in the cosmic domain, in general, beyond a point. My ultimate Work is in Divine Translation.

I am not looking forward to a long life in This Body. I am looking forward to the fulfillment of My Divine Purpose. For all the while that This Body Lives, it is just Doing that Divine Work. Therefore, all this Life long, and after having done the initial Work, I have been passing on responsibilities to My devotees. So I have been doing all these many years.

Ishta-Guru-Bhakti Yoga, participation in Me, desiring that My Virtue be Manifested through your own body-mind in your devotion to Me—that is the secret of Divine Communion.

I am not natively body-minded. Your body-mind should be so transparent to Me that I need not speak again, or even seem to do anything again.

My essential Work is eternal Work.

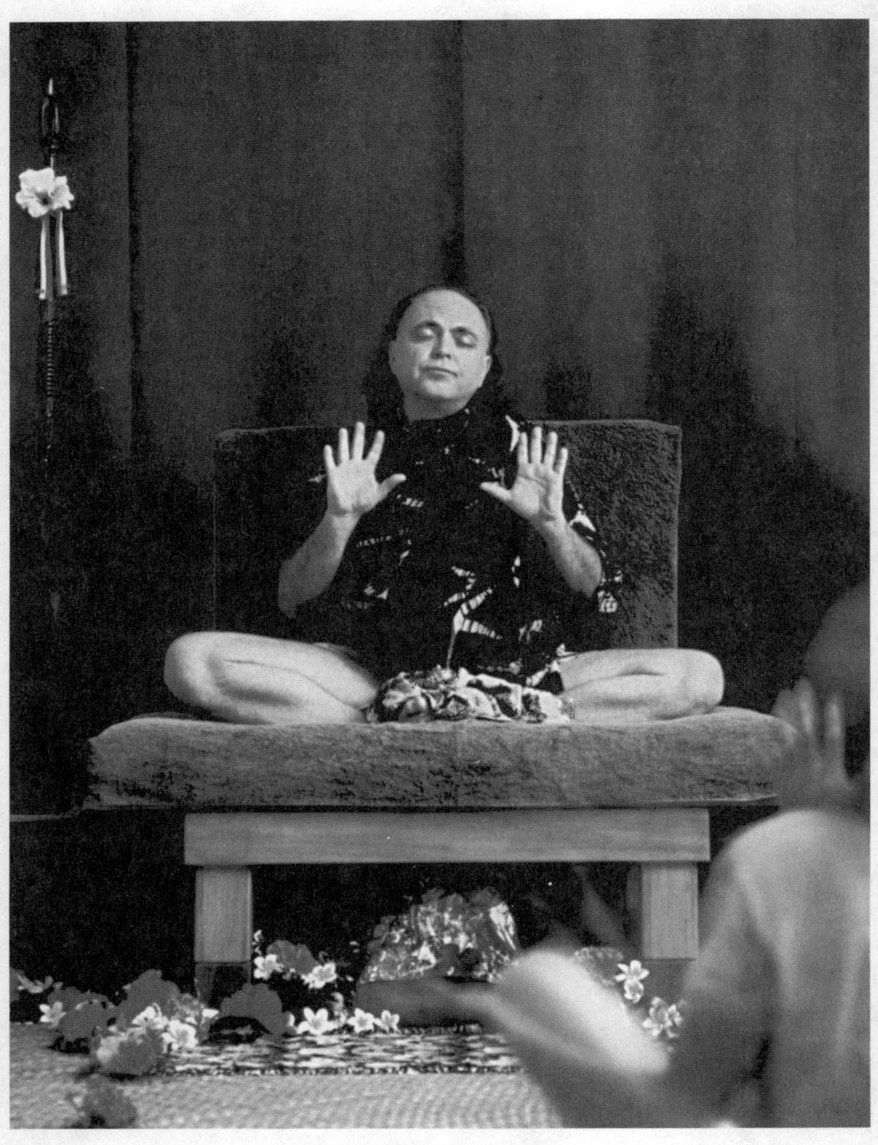

Da Avabhasa (The "Bright")
Sri Love-Anandashram, Fiji, 1992

PART TWO

The Sacred Life of Devotion to Me

The methods of seeking, self-applied, only intensify the bondage to separate self, but to live as if always in the True Heart-Master's Intimate Company, to engage every act as devotional service to Him, and to meditate on His Bodily (Human) Form, His Spiritual (and Always Blessing) Presence, and His Very (and Inherently Perfect) State in every moment, even in the moment of every relationship, and in every moment of circumstance, is to be always already released of the "problem of existence" and every kind of self-concern. Through such truly self-transcending devotion, the Transcendental and Inherently Spiritual Divine Self replaces the egoic self as the Center of practice, and the Grace of God is given Place to Awaken the Heart. Therefore, practice as a devotee of the True Heart-Master, and His "Bright" Free Heart will Find you easily.

DA AVABHASA (THE "BRIGHT")
The Hymn Of The True Heart-Master, verse 83

The Sacred Life of Devotion to Me

August 24 and 27, 1992

1. The Three Positions

SRI DA AVABHASA: I Am here Bodily. Therefore, you have a unique relationship to Me. Your relationship to objects and others is egoic, by tendency. Your relationship to Me, however, when it is rightly lived, is different from your relationship to objects and others, because you practice self-surrender and self-forgetting in relationship to Me. I Call you to Remember Me, and, from the beginning, to Remember Me in My bodily (human) Form. I Call you to relinquish the egoic tendency of attention to move to various objects and others, and to give Me your attention. I do not Call you to give your attention to Me as an object or an "other" in any conventional sense. I Call you to practice the unique relationship to Me, which is self-surrender and self-forgetting through feeling-Contemplation of Me.

If you do this feeling-Contemplation of Me moment by moment, then even though you live in the field of arising objects that are perceived via the self-contraction, you transcend that very act that is self-contraction, that very knot, and all its effects. You Stand in the position of Ecstasy, beyond your separative and separate self, beyond the self-contraction. By this act of devotion to Me, your perception of others and things is immediately transformed.

If you relinquish your devotion to Me in any moment, however, if you forget Me, if you cease to practice self-surrendering and self-forgetting feeling-Contemplation of Me, then you will become distracted by objects, things, and others of all kinds, and you will return to the dramatization of self-contraction once again.

The primary, or senior, position relative to the self-contraction is the position of observing the action of contraction.

The second position relative to the self-contraction is the position of the knot that is self-contraction itself.

And the third, or least, position is the position of the result of self-contraction, which is one or another object.

The self-contraction is the act of separation. All the objects that are perceived or encountered via the self-contraction are known egoically. Therefore, the realm of objects is the circumstance of the dramatization of self-contraction. If you are in the least position relative to the self-contraction, which is the position of perceiving the object of egoic interest, you are most fundamentally bound. The self-contraction is already established. To be absorbed in any object in the moment is to be least able to understand the self-contraction, because you are far from its source.

By practicing the Yoga of devotion to Me, however, you can transcend, or feel beyond, the self-contraction, or the dramatization of egoic attachment to objects. By your self-surrendering, self-forgetting feeling-Contemplation of Me in My bodily (human) Form, you are drawn, in due course, into Contemplation of My Spiritual (and Always Blessing) Presence and My Very (and Inherently Perfect) State. In the process of this Yoga of Ishta-Guru-Bhakti, the body-mind quiets, becomes calm, and is restored to equanimity and clarity. You function differently among others and things. You begin to understand your separate and separative self. You become more and more responsible for devotion to Me, and more and more clear, free, and responsible in the circumstance of others and things. You become more profoundly meditative. Soon, or later—in due course—you become sensitive to My Spiritual (and Always Blessing) Presence, of Which this bodily (human) Form is a manifestation.

Quite naturally, then, you become more sensitive to the self-contraction itself, the knot itself, the act itself, rather than merely perceiving its effect, which is the tendency of attention to move toward others and things. In Communion with Me in My Spiritual Form, or My Spirit-Presence, the knot, the action, of self-contraction is purified and released, and the process becomes still more profound. Perhaps subtler forms of perception arise, and subtler forms of awareness of others and things. Subtler objects may be perceived. You become more and more sensitive to the fact that you are observing the knot itself and the act of self-contraction itself.

In due course, your Contemplation of Me becomes most profound. Then you enter into Identification with My Very (and Inherently Perfect) State and Realize that you inherently Stand in the Witness-Position, which is the senior Position relative to the self-contraction. It is then that devotion to Me becomes most profound. The sadhana is no longer an action among perceived objects and others in the bodily plane. Likewise, it is no longer a process in the middle position, observing or encountering the knot, or the action that moves toward even subtle objects. The sadhana becomes a most profound process at the root of the self-contraction, in the senior position relative to the self-contraction, even prior to the self-contraction itself.

That sadhana is the Perfect sadhana, the "Perfect Practice". It is the sadhana to which I am Calling you and Guiding you by My Company and My Instruction and which is the purpose of your devotion to Me. Its beginnings are in all the devotional actions you perform bodily in your devotion to Me in My bodily (human) Form and in the signs of purification in the domain of your bodily life. However, purification in the domain of bodily life is not the great purpose of the Way of the Heart. It is only the beginning. The Way to which you are Called, Ultimately, is Perfect. It is practiced in the Source-Domain, in My Very Condition. The great import and purpose of the Way of the Heart is not even indicated when the Spiritual signs of subtle perceptions and more profound energy begin to arise. That is only the middle stage. The great purpose of the Way of the Heart is in the ultimate stages of life in the Way of the Heart, in the "Perfect Practice", in Perfect Contemplation of Me, when the process has become most profound, when it has gone beyond the bodily and grossly objective point of view and likewise gone beyond the subtle mental, or subtle objective, point of view.

The domain of social changes and bodily activity, therefore, is not the ultimate import of the Way of the Heart nor the circumstance of the work of the Way of the Heart, even though the sadhana of the Way of the Heart does not exclude these things. In fact, the Instruction I have Given you covers every functional, practical, and relational aspect of ordinary life, and you must apply My Instruction in every circumstance and in every moment and not presume that there are some moments or some functions, some practical realities, some relations, wherein the discipline of devotion to Me does not apply or can be taken lightly.

Already self-conscious as the body-mind and bound to the bodily point of view, you are established in the least position relative to the self-contraction. You identify with the body-mind because you are already bound in the knot of self-contraction. If it were not so, you would not be suffering from the presumption of identification with the body-mind. The body-mind is simply an object of egoic attention, perceived from the point of view of the self-contraction. The presumption of identification with the body-mind is a result of self-contraction. That identification already having taken place, you are easily bound to all the potential objects of the body-mind.

This is how it is in the context of the first three stages of life. Once the presumption of identification with the body is established, by self-contraction, the gross personality binds itself to the objects of the body-mind. Everything that comes under the heading of "money, food, and sex", therefore, becomes your dramatization, and all the stealth, all the strategy, all the pursuit of survival, all the conceptual effort and egoic technology that pursues survival, becomes your occupation.

The ordinary life is the result of self-contraction. The contraction already established, the ego already established, separation already established, ordinary life takes place in the least position and is nothing other than a dramatization of self-contraction, altogether, completely, in every moment, in every circumstance, in every relation, in every function. To understand this and be responsible for the self-contraction in this form is true hearing in the Way of the Heart.

True hearing does not awaken until there is great devotion to Me, which is not merely a matter of sending emotion in My direction but of surrendering and forgetting the separate self in feeling-Contemplation of Me, moment by moment, under all circumstances, in all relations, in the context of every function and every practicality. It must be so, or you will not observe the self-contraction most fundamentally. You will not discover the knot and act that is binding you to separateness and limitation in every plane of conditional being.

2.

First Be Devoted to Me

SRI DA AVABHASA: It is of absolute and most fundamental importance that you first understand and establish the foundation practice of devotion to Me and that you fully embrace every aspect of the beginner's sadhana of self-discipline, service, and meditation, as I have Given it to you. Establish the devotional relationship to Me first before you do anything. Begin every day by activating your devotion to me. Establish your life on the basis of devotion to Me. Become responsible for every function, every practicality, every relationship, every circumstance of your life through devotion to Me. Every day, before you leave the Communion Hall in the morning, be rightly established in devotion to Me, and then discipline every practicality, every function, every circumstance, every moment, by applying My Instruction in its details to the elaboration of your life.

The practice of Ishta-Guru-Bhakti Yoga is not limited to meditative feeling-Contemplation of Me in the Communion Hall. In regular periods of formal Communion with Me, establish the basic principle of right devotion to Me and then take that condition into all the circumstances of your daily life. Go to the Communion Hall not to console yourself with feeling a little good in the morning so that you can be an ego for the rest of the day. Go to the Communion Hall to surrender and forget separate self in Communion with Me, to be free of the binding force of self-contraction so that you can responsibly deal with the conditions of life. Reestablish this clarity every morning and live it for the whole day. Then end the day with a similar sacred event. And every few days, at least once a week, set aside an entire day for retreat for the same purpose.

It must be important to you to practice the "daily form" of life I have Given you. If your practice of the Way of the Heart is not profound, it is because you are not doing what I have just described—not because you do not have My Instruction or the Way of the Heart does not work. You must not indulge in the things and relations that are perceived from the bodily point of view. You only assume that point of view to begin with because of the self-contraction. This is the great discovery you must make. You may have all kinds of excuses for not applying yourself to the disciplines of the Way of the Heart—the conditions of your life, the state of your body-mind, the problems, the difficulties, the demands—"It all makes me not practice," you say. It is not so. You make yourself not practice. You are totally responsible for your failure to exercise the one-pointedness of attention to Me that is fundamental to the Way of the Heart.

You are always completely capable of practicing the Way of the Heart, with full responsibility and full effectiveness. It is always within your capability to do so, and you have no excuses whatsoever not to do so. You can fool yourself and build more time into the beginning sadhana and into the course of your sadhana altogether, but that is all you will be doing—fooling yourself, adding time, wasting time, using up your life-energy and your life-time bargaining, deluding yourself, presuming that you are without Instruction, without capability, even sometimes praying for what you have already received!

You cannot afford to be a fool in any sense. A fool fails to practice devotion, service, self-discipline, and meditation. A fool is without self-understanding, without commitment, without responsibility for attention. It is possible, however, to be greatly responsible and also playful at the same time. The sadhana of the Way of the Heart is not humorless and grim, nor does it require that you be puritanical and rigid.

3.

My Word and Person

SRI DA AVABHASA: Daily study of My Heart-Word is one of the disciplines of the Way of the Heart. Therefore, embrace My Heart-Word fully, every day, so that it may guide and focus your practice. Apart from listening to My Heart-Word in sacramental occasions every day—in the form of recitations in the morning Sat-Guru Puja, for instance—apply yourself to private, guided study of My Heart-Word every day and very frequently also study My Heart-Word with others of My devotees. Your study should be rather full, generally guided, and not casual.

Every devotional group and every formal cultural meeting of My devotees should be focused in My Heart-Word. Otherwise, such meetings are just opportunities for egos to babble to one another. People should be asked to study some section of My Wisdom-Teaching beforehand. The meeting should begin with at least a brief recitation to provide the focus of "consideration", and My devotees should turn to My Heart-Word whenever it is useful, so that their "consideration" can be fruitful. In this manner, focus yourselves in My Heart-Word. Be self-surrendered and self-forgetting in your speech and mind, through devotion to Me, Remembrance of Me, address to Me, attention to Me in the form of My Word.

Do not try to create substitutes for My Word—interpretations of My Wisdom-Teaching by others, for example, or brief aphorisms from My Source-Texts. Do not allow a general, even vague, sense of My Wisdom-Teaching to be the basis for egoic babbling. Discipline your speech and mind instead, through your devotional resort to Me in the form of My Heart-Word. In this manner, make My Heart-Word to you the foundation and the content of your daily life. My Heart-Word and My Person are the context of your every function, every circumstance, every relation, every practicality, every moment of your life. Such devotion to Me grants integrity to your practice of the Way of the Heart and makes it effective.

Therefore, I Call you from the wandering of attention. I Call you to turn attention to Me, to My Person and to My Word, and to make Me the Circumstance of all of your living, even all of your conversation with others, all that you do with others, and all that you do alone. This, rather than the mediocre conventional religiosity that is made out of egoity, is sadhana in the Way of the Heart.

If you do not make the Way of the Heart out of Me, you inevitably make it out of the ego. You are not, as a manifested personality, an independent center of Enlightenment, or God-Realization. It is not so. The Way of the Heart is based on this understanding. The Way of the Heart is not based on the idealization and glorification of the individual self. The glorification of the ego is the worldly path. The world is made of egoity. See the trouble. See the troubled mankind at large in the news, and see your own trouble in your personal life. It is all the same, and the ego is its root and source. The world is a dramatization of egoity, not a paradise of Divine making. Nothing that is manifested is Divinized without Most Perfectly self-transcending God-Realization, without the transcendence of egoity.

The Way of the Heart is not the practice of expressing some sort of social good feeling or social love toward Me or toward anyone. The Way of the Heart is the real sadhana of the devotion of attention to Me and the transcendence of self-contraction. Nothing else is the Way of the Heart. If you seriously and fully establish the foundation practice, then your growth in the Way of the Heart is inevitable, and the sadhana becomes interesting, always changing, always growing, full of development, and moving beyond the beginning stages very directly. If, in your reluctance and your clinging to egoity, you do not establish the foundation practice of the Way of the Heart, there is no real growth for you but only petty religiosity. You can struggle forever with the ego's resistance as it is characteristic of you and only suffer its results, its vagaries, and its endless complications.

The Way out is to embrace the foundation discipline of devotion, service, self-discipline, and meditation, in devotional relationship to Me, for real, and to bring it to every aspect of your life. This is the "cure" for egoity in any moment. In any moment of difficulty, in any moment when your practice seems less than fully fruitful or right, step aside, re-collect yourself, and reestablish the foundation practice. To do so does not require long-winded conversations and endless interviews. The process is not complicated. It is very direct and very simple. Always establish the foundation of your practice, simply and directly, and help others to do the same, by taking the "cure".

4.

My Attractiveness

DEVOTEE: Sri Gurudev, compared to everything else I am always doing, Your Attractiveness is the only thing that makes the practice possible.

SRI DA AVABHASA: My Attractiveness <u>is</u> the practice. Your heart-response to Me, and not your effort to be devoted to Me and surrender to Me, enables you to be self-surrendered and self-forgetting.

You know what happens in your intimate life if you become angry or detached from your intimate. You cannot find the person attractive at the moment. You cannot be happy with the person. When you relax the contraction, when your reactivity passes, and you allow yourself to be attracted once again, suddenly all the love-feeling, all the attraction, all the happiness, is there. Therefore, My Attractiveness is the secret of your relationship to Me, because you tend to bring to your relationship to Me the mechanism of dissociation that you dramatize in ordinary life. You know it does not work in the intimacies of your ordinary life. Neither does it work in your intimacy with Me.

You must always be in a position to feel My Attractiveness. Not your effort to surrender but your attraction to Me makes your devotional surrender possible. Then, yes, the effort—you must turn your attention to Me—but granting Me your attention is easy, natural, not quite automatic but almost. Your response to What is Attractive is immediate, not an effort. It is effortless.

The Attractiveness of the Loved-One is the reality of practice in the Way of the Heart. It is the sadhana itself. Noticing My Attractiveness, affirming it, drawing everyone to it—that is your sadhana and your message to everyone. Everybody needs to be reminded of My Attractiveness, all the time. When you are reminded of My Attractiveness, when you are responding to My Attractiveness, then, on the basis of your devotional response to Me, you can discuss the details of your practice in its elaboration. Otherwise, you will only talk forever and do nothing but overwhelm others with your dramatizations. Your devotional groups will never come to an end, and they will never be fruitful. The personal disciplines that result will not be significant, only self-suppressive, angular, ego-based, even puritanical.

5.

Feeling-Contemplation of Me

DEVOTEE: Sri Gurudev, before I came to You, I was so caught in the self-knot that I felt my suffering all the time, and I was exaggeratedly terrified. When I found You, I experienced relaxation for the first time in my life. I feel Happy without this heaviness around me all the time.

SRI DA AVABHASA: When you practice right devotion to Me, then you are not in the least position relative to the self-contraction. You are no longer self-contracted, merely obsessed with objects and others. Right feeling-Contemplation of Me, self-surrendering and self-forgetting, enables you to observe the act of self-contraction, the knot itself, and the perceptions that follow from it. This is the only position in which you can do sadhana. To be in the least position relative to the self-contraction—already obsessed with objects and others, already self-contracted, unable to view the self-contraction—is fruitless. No real sadhana can be done in that position. You can only manipulate your behavior.

DEVOTEE: I tried everything, everything. Just finding You, in Your Attractive Form, falling in love with You, there was no effort in it. Suddenly I was free to observe without that terror and that fear. Still, it is so terrible to feel that perhaps nothing fundamentally has changed.

SRI DA AVABHASA: Why sit around feeling terrible all the time when you can Contemplate Me? Why look at that? Look at Me!

◆ ◆ ◆

DEVOTEE: Sri Gurudev, You often describe feeling-Contemplation of You as "self-surrendering, self-forgetting, self-transcending feeling-Contemplation".

SRI DA AVABHASA: "Self-surrendering", then "self-forgetting". There must be surrendering if there is to be forgetting. The practice is self-transcending, ultimately, yes. But before you can transcend the self-contraction, you must surrender and forget it. In this sequence of descriptions, I am Giving you a practice. I am not just telling you, "There is the self-contraction. Go and transcend it. Get out!" I have told you exactly how the self-contraction works and how to establish the devotional relationship to Me that makes practice fruitful. The ego's effort to transcend itself does not work—to begin with, the ego does not want to transcend itself!

Whatever the technicalities you may embrace in the course of your practice in the Way of the Heart, the fundamental discipline is self-surrender and self-forgetting, in feeling-Contemplation of Me. My Instruction is not just to surrender and forget yourself. I Call you to surrender your separate self and forget your separate self <u>in relationship to Me.</u> This means you must keep Me in view. You must Remember Me, Invoke Me, glance at Me, keep Me in heart and in mind, keep Me bodily before you, be in relationship to Me at all times, in all places, all circumstances, all functions.

My Instruction is not "self-surrender and self-forgetting", but self-surrendering, self-forgetting <u>feeling-Contemplation of Me</u>. I am the unique process. If you play ego-games with Me, you never Realize Me. You find only a social "other", the male "other", all the "oedipal", social, and conventional egoic complications intervene, and your relationship to Me does not work. The devotional relationship to Me is unique, and you must practice it uniquely, singly, single-mindedly, intentionally, focusing your attention in every moment. It is a very real, very practical, process. Everything else, all the pondering, practicing, Enquiring, and the rest, is an extension of the fundamental process, the fundamental Gift.

The secret of the "knee of listening" is the "Method of the Siddhas".

6.

The Tapas of self-Transcendence

DEVOTEE: Sri Gurudev, I am beginning to discipline the wandering of my attention. It is not easy, but . . .

SRI DA AVABHASA: How could it be easy? One's entire life, one's entire existence, and every function and circumstance are devoted to self-contraction and, effectively, then, devoted to the avoidance of relationship. How could it be easy to transcend it? It is tapas. It requires the control, the intentional discipline, of attention. Most fundamentally, it is the control of attention. My Appearance here, in all My Forms, is the Gift to you that makes the practice uniquely effective and profound, from the beginning. In general, this Gift, which is most fundamental to the Way of the Heart, is not yet truly appreciated by My devotees, because of the ego-based approach of human beings to conditional existence. Even those who take up the Way of the Heart tend to become preoccupied with their own activities, their own disciplining of themselves, the things that arise if they do practice and the things that arise if they do not. Even as My devotees, they become preoccupied with all the business of seeking. The search is not the Way I have Given you.

My description of all the technicalities and developmental stages of the Way of the Heart is My Service to you, My Gift to you. Each portion of My Instruction applies in its moment. However, if, to your egoic view, the Way of the Heart is just a sequence of practices to be self-applied, stages to be completed, and goals to be attained, you are only involved in the search, an egoically "self-possessed" way of life, not the Way of the Heart, and, from your egoic point of view, Divine Self-Realization becomes un-Realizable and the Way of the Heart fundamentally unworkable.

I have Given you My Wisdom-Teaching complete in all its details, addressing all possibilities, all stages of life and practice, all technicalities. However, the principal Gift I have Given you is I, My Self. I Am the Way of the Heart. I make the Way of the Heart most direct. I Am the unique Gift, the unique Offering, the unique Message of the Way of the Heart. Devotion to Me in My bodily (human) Form, My Spiritual (and Always Blessing) Presence, and My Very (and Inherently Perfect) State, through self-surrendering and self-forgetting feeling-Contemplation of Me, is the Way of the Heart. I, My Self, Am the Gift and the Way Itself.

One who truly understands this Truth appreciates the uniqueness of the Way of the Heart, and realizes that the Way of the Heart is, in principle, easy, direct, uniquely Given, and, therefore, uniquely possible. One who remains egoically "self-possessed" embraces the technicalities, the efforts, and the stages of the Way of the Heart in the search for a Realization that seems impossible, and reduces the Way of the Heart to the beginner's sadhana.

7.

Testing What Works

DEVOTEE: Sri Gurudev, I have been practicing the Devotional Way of Insight, but it requires a kind of mental effort from me, whereas Your Name "Da" arises spontaneously. Is the fact that Your Name is arising spontaneously a sign that it is more useful? I have to cut through resistance when I Enquire.

SRI DA AVABHASA: That is not good?

DEVOTEE: It often just keeps me in the mind rather than releasing me to You.

SRI DA AVABHASA: To just focus on My Name can keep you in the mind, as well. My Name is supposed to be used to Invoke Me, not merely to occupy your mind. To use My Name rightly is to do the same thing as self-Enquiry fundamentally, which is to go beyond yourself.

DEVOTEE: For me, the best form of the "conscious process" is looking at Your picture, or visualizing You. I was just wondering if there is something about this spontaneous use of Your Name that means it is more appropriate for me.

SRI DA AVABHASA: It may be. You must find out, through the trial of experimenting with the various options I have Given you. To move beyond the student-beginner stage in the Way of the Heart, you must have come to a settlement about the form of your practice. All My devotees practice the "simplest" practice of Contemplating My bodily (human) Form and Invoking Me by Name, at least at random, whatever other technical practice they assume. Therefore, everyone practices the Devotional Way of Faith in some sense. You also have the option to practice the Devotional Way of Faith in its more technical elaboration, and the option to practice the Devotional Way of Insight, beginning with simple pondering and eventually becoming focused in self-Enquiry. What you practice depends on what works for you, and you must discover the form of the "conscious process" that works for you, through the trial of applying all of the options.

The best is what works. None of the approaches is inherently best. Therefore, you must endure the ordeal of discovering what works. For example, no single diet is prescribed in the Way of the Heart, but there is a basic diet with options that account for anyone's personal requirements. At the student-beginner stage of the Way of the Heart, you engage the ordeal of testing the options to discover the minimum-optimum version of the basic diet for you. You test the options, observe their effects, and refine your dietary practice through real observation. When you have developed an understanding of what works, then you assume the discipline.

Just so, simply because My Principal Name, "Da", arises spontaneously in your mind does not mean it is your right practice. Invocation of Me via My Name "Da" is a basic practice of all My devotees, but the technically "simplest" practice is not necessarily the one you should embrace as your exclusive discipline, unless it works. If your practice is real Invocation of Me, and if it is sufficient practice altogether, then it is appropriate. It is for you to discover.

I have not Given you a teeny booklet with a few pages of simplistic and consoling Teaching that you can just believe and in some mediocre way apply. I have elaborated My Wisdom-Teaching fully to cover all possibilities and every kind of person. The Way of the Heart requires seriousness, real practice, and a real trial of testing all the options. First you must know My Instruction. Then apply it. Test the options, until you can choose on the basis of knowing what works.

8.

The Discipline of the "Daily Form"

SRI DA AVABHASA: You must make the measure of every day. Do not do anything obsessively. Do not become superficially religious, making emotional gestures toward Me and keeping busy. Real service to Me is not being merely busy. If your functional life is not true service, you are only being busy. Therefore, measure the activities of every day. Apply yourself to the "daily form". Make room every day for all the aspects of your discipline. Service should occupy a certain portion of every day, but not the entire day and night. You must make room for meditation, for puja, for devotional activities, for gathering with other devotees, for study—make room for all of it.

To do so requires that you become much more efficient and competent in your service. Accomplish what is required in a shorter period of time. Ordinary people think life is about being busy, and they do not have anything else to do. Because you are an ordinary person by tendency, you tend to occupy yourself obsessively with the things you would do by tendency. Therefore, the discipline of "form" requires all My devotees to break the spell of their tendencies, including their use of time.

The culture of the Way of the Heart is the context wherein My devotees are observed in applying themselves to the "daily form" and fulfilling all the details of their responsibilities. Therefore, be observed in your practice, report to others about it, and do not allow yourself or others to lapse from the "daily form". In the Way of the Heart, you are subject to the view of the culture of My devotees.

9.

Fidelity to Me

SRI DA AVABHASA: You must break the spell of your attention to sex and all the games and strategies whereby you bind yourself to the dramatization of egoic sexuality and make the sexual "other" the obsessive object of your attention. I Call you to bring specific discipline to the emotional-sexual character and its relations and functions. I Call you to be single in relationship to Me, to manifest true fidelity to Me at all times, to not be bound by any relation, function, practicality, circumstance, or condition but to be responsible for all the relations, functions, practicalities, circumstances, and conditions of your ordinary life, by practicing the Yoga of devotion to Me and by applying My Instruction to every area of your life.

You must in every moment be responsible for your emotional-sexual character and function, whether you are in the moment sexually active or not. That character is always there. It is a structure that makes its appearance in your perception quite randomly, more or less constantly. It is not a responsibility that pertains only to your time in the bedroom. It is a lifetime responsibility, and you are always capable of exercising the discipline. In the Way of the Heart, you are always obliged to exercise it. I Call and oblige you to do so. The entire culture of My devotees must do so likewise. You must yourself assume such responsibility.

In itself, your desiring mind is nothing but bondage, and any of its objects is binding. Apart from the practice of Ishta-Guru-Bhakti Yoga, association with any object or any other is a dramatization, a form of indulgence in bondage. Understand this by observing yourself. Some of you have said that in the time you spent before you became My devotee you did observe this but, tending to be foolish, you have forgotten that you had already observed this and that you have a serious purpose in My Company. It is relatively easy to observe that obsessive sexual desire is bondage, because it generates stress, tension, seeking, dis-ease. You should likewise easily understand that any indulgence in such desire is bondage, and, therefore, that any relationship based on obsessive desire is bondage, unless the relationship is clarified and transformed in devotion to Me. If you fail to embrace the emotional-sexual discipline that devotion to Me requires, you are simply indulging in bondage, abandoning your fidelity to Me, submitting to the least position relative to the self-contraction, and reinforcing your karmic destiny, your bound destiny, your separateness, and your fear.

I Call you to the Yoga of Ishta-Guru-Bhakti, and to self-discipline in any chosen intimacy, even any relationship, any function, any circumstance. This Yoga should be your understanding and your commitment. Your commitment to the practice of Ishta-Guru-Bhakti Yoga gives you integrity as a practitioner of the Way of the Heart.

10.

Emotional-Sexual Discipline

SRI DA AVABHASA: I also specifically Call you to discipline the time you set aside for intimate occasions. Emotional-sexual intimacy is the last thing for which you have a possibility on any given day, and you have no right to it until you have fulfilled the rest of your obligations. Before you have sex, fulfill your obligations first, perhaps adjusting your schedule so that you can fulfill your obligations first and also attend morning meditation and the Sat-Guru Puja afterwards. Therefore, make right time and occasion for sexual intimacy. All other obligations are senior to that one. All of them are. Your emotional-sexual intimacy is the last of your obligations. This does not mean sexual intimacy is not all right, or that it should not be accommodated, but you see the measure you must make, the obligations you must fulfill first.

For most ordinary people, sexual intimacy is the first obligation of life. For My devotee, it is the last. For My devotee, the relationship to Me is the first obligation, and all other relationships and obligations follow. It is not that you should make nothing of your sexual life or have a negative view of it, but you should have a right understanding of its proportions—and its effect on all your other practices. Because you have tended to make sexual intimacy the first obligation of your life, your emotional-sexual intimate is also your first relation. It is not even that I am next, or that I am somewhere along the line on the list, or that I am even last. I am not. If I am not first, I am not.

Even if you make Me your primary, and constant, relation, many other obligations are senior to anything you may be doing with an intimate partner. Your purpose of existence as My devotee is Divine Self-

Realization, not social life, bodily life, sexual self-fulfillment, consolation, amusement, or the using up of time in distractions of an ordinary kind. When you have served Me and accomplished all the rest, then you can spend time with your intimate.

In general, it is not because you have a great urge to Yoga that you want to rush to your intimate. It is because of the self-contraction itself, because you are obsessed with the primary object that self-contraction makes, which is the stress-releasing, egoic self-pleasuring that is magnified by sexual contact. Sexual pleasure tends to be the primary obsession of ordinary people. The Way of the Heart is not about accommodating your emotional-sexual obsession. The Way of the Heart is about transforming it utterly, so that it is not a binding relation.

As I have told you again and again, you need not be a celibate either to practice the Way of the Heart or to Realize greatly in the Way of the Heart, but neither can you be a fool, and you cannot be an ordinary person. You must be completely responsible for your emotional-sexual character and its relations and functions. If you take Me seriously, and take your practice of the Way of the Heart seriously, you know that you cannot do otherwise.

Be serious about everything that comes first, before your emotional-sexual intimacy, and then you will have a clear view about how to function in emotional-sexual intimacy and how to live your sexuality. Unless you have such real practice and clarity, your sexuality will bind you for the rest of your life, or at least until you are so worn-out, old, confused, and diseased that it is academic even to talk about the matter. Then, of course, you will be telling Me you want to be a renunciate! Lack of emotional-sexual capability is not a reason for celibate renunciation, and not the basis for renunciate practice.

If I were asked to identify the principal source of the undoing of the practice of My devotees in all the years of My Work with them, the emotional-sexual business, this coupling, is it—with many others certainly, but this is the principal source, because of everything that it does to the body, the emotion, and the mind, and because of all the compromises you feel obliged to make because the relationship exists. The compromises are not necessary, but you somehow feel socially obliged, by education or experience—and it is a colossal education, purposed biologically, of learning behaviors that are reinforced by parents, siblings, and others. However you may use that education, its function is the continuation of bodies for reproduction. That is the root of your sexuality.

As soon as you are involved in sex, you are already somehow compromised, attached, bound, having to take someone else into account, and combining yourself with that one in various ways, in sympathy, in feeling, in mind, mind rolling, sexual matters already on your mind, and already less single and direct in relation to Me. All this does not necessarily suggest celibacy, but it does immediately point out the binding nature of what you are doing with all this emotional-sexual business. If you do not transform your emotional-sexual life by right practice in relation to Me, and by right discipline altogether, it will be one of the principal mechanisms whereby you undo your life in My Company.

You receive all kinds of messages that guarantee the survival of the race by implicating you in the necessity, the urge, the compromises, the intentions, that make you available to reproduce and to serve those you produce, to submit yourself to them, to submit yourself to ensure their survival, and your own survival in the meantime. All of a sudden these "units" mean "compromise everything Great and serve the purpose of the body"—which is not only pleasure but reproduction, society, survival.

There is a great argument for the process of human survival, and human survival should not be neglected. Human responsibility, whereby people serve their survival mutually, is not to be laughed at, not to be dismissed, not to be taken lightly. Even so, it is an easy course to bondage. It is an easy argument for relinquishing That Which is Great, an easy argument for confining your existence to lesser purposes, more ordinary, bodily-based, survival-bound purposes. Your reward is consoling, bodily self-pleasure, which is also the mechanism in your own body that guarantees your interest. Your own pleasure makes a great argument in you.

It is not a Yogic argument. It is not a God-Realizing argument. It is an argument of your own conceiving, based on self-contraction, defined by objects, obsessed with the body-based messages. And so you make couples, you frequently reproduce—mankind does—you devote your life to the purposes of the survival of bodies, and you reduce existence to social, political, and moral behaviors. In other words, you devote your life to bodily survival, not only your own survival, ultimately not even really your own, but the survival of the race, the survival of mankind, bodily—not the Realization of mankind, not the Liberation of mankind, not the great Fulfillment of mankind, not even the pleasure of mankind, but the continuation, only, of mankind.

The continuation of mankind is itself a great struggle, because people are so profoundly ego-based. Mankind's survival is a great and spontaneous effort in all human beings all over the world. It is a destructive enterprise. It is always making separateness and declaring that it has some ideal purpose—"my" family, "my" house, "my" body, "my" person, "my" community, "my" nation, "my" ethnic group, "my" background, "my" tradition. None of it is about anything great. It is just about continuing.

Such is the foundation of the choices you are signaling by sitting next to your intimate friend here. Because you are also in My Company, you have the notion that perhaps your relationship can be transformed, rightly aligned to the religious life, to the Spiritual life, to Realization Itself, to Yoga. Because of your immaturity, however, your "consideration" about it tends to be a silly, self-based conversation rather than a real practice, a real event. In the meantime, you are sitting in the bondage of your perception, which is based on your own self-contraction, your own identification with the body-mind. You are thinking about some ideal of Yoga and God-Realization, yet all the while you are actually serving your bondage. You are compromised just by sitting next to one another, even by knowing one another, even by choosing one another.

11.

Relinquishing the Dramatization of Your Emotional-Sexual Life

SRI DA AVABHASA: I have Instructed all My devotees about the emotional-sexual character and function, so that intimate sexual relationships are not a liability in the Way of the Heart. Nevertheless, unless you surely practice according to My Instruction, the emotional-sexual character is a limit on everything. Only those who transcend the emotional-sexual dramatization in devotion to Me are capable of real Sat-Guru-Seva.

Typically, men who are beginners in the Way of the Heart tend to struggle with the male "other". Therefore, I must inevitably confront this "oedipal" block in relationship with My male devotees so that they can be submitted in devotion to Me. Women in the beginning stages of the Way of the Heart likewise are typically reluctant in their devotional submission to Me, relating to Me either in what may be called a "frigid" manner, unable to surrender, or in a kind of promiscuous fashion, seductive, looking to be attractive, looking for My attention, but still not surrendered in devotion to Me.

Everything about your service to Me, whatever its form, is an extension of your devotion to Me. If your devotion to Me is right, everything about your life and practice is right. If your devotion to Me is not right, all of that is wrong.

The sacred life of devotion to Me is the primary principle of the gathering of My devotees. It is senior to any other principle of organization. This is why it is so important that mature devotees appear who are exemplary in the practice of devotion to Me and who are highly visible, vocal, and influential in every area of the culture of the Way of the Heart.

Nevertheless, My every devotee must be responsibly and fully accountable, and constantly associated with such a real devotional culture.

The worldly mind, or the social and emotional-sexual ego, is the way of the world, not the Way of the Heart. Set aside the principle of egoity by your right devotion to Me and your right practice of the Way of the Heart altogether, and your universal adherence to My Principles, Callings, and Agreements. As My devotee, do not relate to Me as the ego, or even as a male or a female. In other words, do not relate to Me through your emotional-sexual patterning. Relate to Me directly, through true devotional self-surrendering and self-forgetting feeling-Contemplation of Me, free of the self-contracted motive and emotional-sexual self-imagery. If you relate to Me as My self-surrendered devotee, rather than as male or female, then how could I be the male "other" to you?

As you grow in the developmental stages of the Way of the Heart, you will become more and more technically responsible for all the features of egoity. Nevertheless, from the very beginning, by virtue of your devotion to Me, you are always already, inherently, responsible for egoity and all its dramatizations. Devotion to Me is itself the relinquishment of all egoic patterning. Such relinquishment should be your sign as My devotee from the very beginning of your practice of the Way of the Heart. Devotion to Me, self-surrendering and self-forgetting feeling-Contemplation of Me, is Freedom Itself.

You are not here in My Company to work out your emotional-sexual life. You are here in My Company to relinquish the dramatization of your emotional-sexual life, and to do so now, always as a fundamental matter of devotion to Me. Therefore, deal with your emotional-sexual life according to My Instructions, not according to your dramatization.

I have My own Work to do. I am here to relate to all My devotees as My devotees only, in the context of their resort to Me for Most Perfectly self-transcending God-Realization.

12.

Freedom from Emotional-Sexual Dependency

DEVOTEE: Sri Gurudev, in a sexual occasion last week, I felt a great, blissful energy that felt very free. My perception turned on my intimate partner as the apparent object of the blissful energy, and I assumed the bliss was due to him. Then I felt the turning as a literal contraction upon the object, the origin of romanticism and fixation. For the first time, I felt the possibility of understanding that the sexual Yoga You describe is not about bondage. In that moment, I could choose to turn in on him or turn my attention to You and allow the blissful energy to magnify my feeling-Contemplation of You.

SRI DA AVABHASA: Were you self-surrendered? Did you forget yourself?

DEVOTEE: Yes, I did.

SRI DA AVABHASA: Were you enjoying the fullest Contemplation of Me? Was it a Yoga of Fullness, beyond bodily "self-possession", beyond possession by the object, or the "other"?

DEVOTEE: Yes, it was in moments.

SRI DA AVABHASA: And in the other moments?

DEVOTEE: I continued to observe the mechanism of turning in on the object again.

SRI DA AVABHASA: What about the object of your own body? You were the one experiencing the pleasure. It was your own mechanism that was stimulated. You could blame your intimate partner for it, but his pleasure was his own. He was taking his own pleasure in you, and you were taking your own pleasure in him. Ultimately, your pleasure did not have anything to do with the other one. It was about you in your own bodily-based self-position, and your feeling that somehow the "other" was necessary to achieve the pleasurable state. What state was it? A bodily "self-possessed" state, your own pleasure, your own natural energies?

Can you achieve such a state without that "other"? Is such a state available to you? Even though it may be conditional, it is available to you in the Communion Hall, or in any moment during the day. Can you always submit the body-mind to the degree of self-surrender, self-forgetting enjoyment, without embracing conditions, an "other", an object, even your own body? Or are you bound to conditions, bound to objects and others?

DEVOTEE: In meditative blisses, I have experienced times of feeling . . .

SRI DA AVABHASA: Was there still some stress in it? Was there a stress even in that meditative bliss if the mind wandered for a moment—get intoxicated, have sex, achieve a greater arousal, relieve this stress? Certainly. One thinks even in meditative bliss that the arousal could be greater. The stress persists. "I am having to work on it. If only I engineered the moment through the exercise of the genitals, or some intoxicant, then I would feel better still." Remember those moments?

The great Yoga of "sexual communion", which is the Spiritual practice of sexuality in the advanced and the ultimate stages of life in the Way of the Heart, is not what you might think. It is not dependence on the "other", or dependence on objects. It may be apparently associated with an "other", but it is greater than other-dependence and object-dependence. It is free of the ego-complex, the psychological complex, the craving bodily, the dependency.

In any case, the sexual Yoga in the Way of the Heart is not a means of Ultimate Realization. It is a conditional act. It can be entered into in such a manner that it does not interfere with or limit one's sadhana, but it cannot achieve Realization. The best it can become is neutral, and even if your sexuality is to be transformed to that degree, the sexual Yoga must become great and you must overcome yourself greatly in it.

In the meantime, there are all the bodily, emotional, mental, egoically "self-possessed" cravings, all the social and functional dependencies, that you animate, and their root is the self-contraction. The self-contraction manifests as separateness and, therefore, object-association and object-perception, and it encompasses everything, the whole domain of social life, the whole domain of bodies, the collective of bodies and its intention to survive.

The mass of human beings is like a hive of bees or ants. You function rather automatically, although you idealize what you are doing. The purpose of the hive is the persistence of bodies. The hive is dark. Yet all the ants—or bees—are animated, performing their functions in the dark hive. Who calls the roll in the morning in the bee hive, or the ant mound? Where is the schedule posted? How are the routines and the roles learned? Who corrects the wanderers? It all seems to happen automatically, doesn't it? There is no roll and no schedule. There is no board on which anything is posted. It all just goes on.

So with you. You do not even know you are in a hive. Neither do the bees and the ants. They are oblivious, performing roles they know nothing about. Nobody told them. The hive is engineered by the energies of the bodies. It is a mind without consciousness there. So with you.

The same unconsciousness is the meaning of your couplings. See what a hive you are here. The hive serves the bodies. You may have the purpose in mind to convert it somehow, transform it, so that it serves the Great Purpose that most ultimately is about Liberation from bodily bondage, but what are you actually doing? Where is the consciousness in it? How much of what you are doing in these "units" is conscious, intentional, free, free of dependency?

Very little, if any. You do not even know why you are doing it. Why are you sitting with that one? Why? You do not even know. You are no more conscious of it than you are conscious of the heartbeat, the sweat in your armpits, all of the bodily processes. When you get up in the morning, nobody says, "Eat three times a day." You just do it. You eat, wander, work, sex, do all this stuff, automatically. You do not even know why. Who governs it? There is no roll call, and no manual.

13.

Romantic Love and self-Satisfaction

DEVOTEE: Sri Gurudev, on one occasion when my intimate partner and I were having sex, I was practicing beyond my tendency to be indifferently related to her, and this time I was very present with her. As I practiced, I realized that I really did not know who she was, even though I have been with her for several years in intimate relationship.

SRI DA AVABHASA: You lost the sense of familiarity for a moment. I used to stand on the steps of Sue Ellen Beckman's house—Sue Ellen Beckman, in case some of you do not know, was a girlfriend of Mine in My late teenage years. There were all kinds of satoris and so forth in My early days. Very frequently, perhaps it would happen on other occasions, too, but frequently, whatever we did in the evening, when I took her home and said goodnight to her on the steps, I would become oblivious, totally entranced. I did not know where I was, did not know who she was, did not know what anything was, felt no familiarity whatsoever. You were having this experience.

DEVOTEE: I felt in the moment that familiarity is the thing that kills the relationship.

SRI DA AVABHASA: But the sense of familiarity, the mind, the ideas, also make relationship what it is in the ordinary sense. Of course, underneath the ordinariness is a mechanism you are not even conscious of that determines why you are there to begin with and doing all that you are doing. The mechanism is not really conscious. Just as the hive is not conscious.

The most auspicious circumstance of emotional-sexual intimacy requires that you overcome yourself. The relationships you choose, however, tend to be relationships that require little of you. They have the maximum potential to satisfy you, rather than to require you to overcome yourself. You look for another that satisfies some model that you do not even have altogether in mind—some shape, appearance, qualities, sign, talk. You are really looking for somebody who will play your game with you and who has the complementary strategy, so that you can be oblivious in the relationship and play out the motives of self-satisfaction.

Most relationships in the world of circumstance are based just on that game. The game is what people call "being in love". It is not what I call "being in love", but it is what people in general call "being in love", being obsessed with the one who allows you to be most oblivious, most at ease, who fulfills your impulses so that you will not have to deal with anything—at least you hope you will not. Of course, sooner or later you start having to deal with things, because in that oblivious state you do not notice the contraries—as a general rule, anyway—and there are always contraries, inevitably. Then you start disliking the relationship, and you get reactive, and you think about others, become promiscuous, in your mind, at any rate, think about other possibilities—"It would be better with this one, that one, the other one, get it on, get sexy, get it off."

Do you see how it all works? Always you are in the hive, wandering in your own disposition, your own limitations. There is no self-overcoming, no clarity, no Divinity, no Freedom. There are only all the obligations that come with the choice, the bond, the agreement, the circumstance, and all of the social messages that likewise come with it. You feel obliged. You start functioning on the basis of a necessity that carries with it all kinds of rules you do not even really understand. All of a sudden you are the need itself. You have all kinds of obligations, perhaps you have children, you live in a neighborhood, you become the housewife, the househusband, the dutiful servant of the hive, apparently serving a social purpose, but what great purpose is there to it?

Its purpose is the survival of bodies, the survival of forms. Soon you have no space or intelligence left over for Yoga, for sadhana, for the exercise of Freedom, nothing whatsoever. The reward for having made this choice is some occasional pleasures in a lifetime of stress, seeking, bondage, limitation, distress, disharmony, un-Happiness, boredom, doubt, discomfort, a little bit of friendliness here and there—on to death. And in the meantime, struggle, disease, old age.

So, there you are right now, dutiful members of the hive, sized up with your "units", your energy already suppressed, all the complications there, all kinds of ready to do it. That is why you are there with one another. Foremost in your mind are the primitive motives, the primitive messages, the reward cycle, that little bit of pleasure eked out here and there from the coupling.

14.

Intimate Relationships and God-Realization

DEVOTEE: Sri Gurudev, as You have been speaking tonight, I have felt that all Your Criticisms are true of me, but something different has occurred for me in relationship. I observe so often that I stop short of giving my intimate partner life-energy.

SRI DA AVABHASA: Even so, giving energy in direct relationship to your intimate partner has nothing to do with God-Realization. It is just about improving your intimate, personal, ordinary life.

DEVOTEE: But I also felt that it is in relationship to You.

SRI DA AVABHASA: No. First understand what I just said. It is so! Working to improve intimate relationships is a major occupation of ordinary people. From no human point of view could it be said that your relationship is "wrong". From the ordinary human point of view, you have a good relationship. That is good! But it has nothing to do with God-Realization, or Freedom from egoity. It is manufactured out of egoity itself. It serves ordinary human purposes. It can be said to be positive, and you would receive many congratulations from all over the world for it. Yet you must "consider" the Great Matter, which is very different.

Having had many experiences of bad relations, you feel, at least right now, that your present relationship is good, it is perhaps better than you have done before, and finally you have found somebody you can do "hmm-mm" with. Still, it has nothing to do with God-Realization. It is just doing the search you have been involved with all along anyway, to fulfill the socially reinforced, bodily-based, egoic impulse. You have finally integrated yourself with the hive, and you are not going to get out of there. You are going to live and function and die there.

You cannot make Realization in My Company out of your relationship. It will not happen, it cannot happen. If you would wake up and relate to Me rightly, if you would do the real sadhana of the Way of the Heart, then at least you could transform the relationship into a process that will not inhibit your sadhana. To get to that point, however, you must come to a great understanding, and you must practice much more profoundly than you have practiced so far. Your relationship is not the product of Realization and great Yoga. It is based on your own egoic impulses and almost nothing else. Left to yourself, left to just do what you want to do by desire, impulse, inclination, you would make your relationship into perhaps the greatest alternative to real practice of the Way of the Heart.

There is no mechanical solution. Be celibate forever, separate from your intimate partner, find somebody else—you have tried all those things, and they do not work. You are going to have to deal with yourself for real. You must find the motive in yourself to really practice in My Company and do something entirely different with your intimacy, entirely different, to make the relationship into a circumstance of self-transcendence, real practice, real devotion, where you do not mechanically grant attention to the other person anymore but you all the time intentionally grant your attention to Me, and in that granting of attention you do the great Yoga of self-surrendering, self-forgetting, self-transcendence, the real process.

In some fundamental sense, it does not make any difference whatsoever who you are sitting next to right now. You could have picked a name out of a hat. From the point of view of the sadhana of Divine Self-Realization, it does not make the slightest bit of difference. Yet you think it does make a difference who you are sitting next to. It has nothing to do with the great Yoga. It has to do with your egoic impulses and the potential to satisfy the impulses with the one you are with—that, and not the Great Matter, not your devotion to Me, is the basis of your choice. Therefore, in some very fundamental sense these choices are the great alternative you have manufactured to practicing in My Company.

What can be said, then, in some very fundamental sense, is that the one sitting next to you is your greatest enemy, not because of some gross evil qualities in that one but because of you.

15.

The Principle of Retreat

DEVOTEE: Sri Gurudev, You have said that the purpose of practicing Spiritual life is to Translate into the Divine Self-Domain. All my life I have been making the error of trying to make things work out in my life.

SRI DA AVABHASA: In this domain.

DEVOTEE: In this domain.

SRI DA AVABHASA: Not in the Divine Self-Domain—in your domain.

DEVOTEE: Yes, in my domain. Because of that error, I have also had the strategy that, when something is not working out, I try to cut it off. I suddenly realized that in my error of pursuits You are What Attracts me and You are my only hope to be free of anything in this life.

SRI DA AVABHASA: Yet as soon as your intimate comes and sits next to you, all of a sudden you have another thought, compromise, and alternative, you become double-minded, and you start trying to figure things out again. You are never going to fulfill the Way of the Heart by putting yourself in the circumstance of confusion. As I have told you: What is the cure for any moment of confusion? Step out, step aside, reestablish your practice in relationship to Me, reestablish your devotion, your service, your self-discipline, your meditation. Reestablish the Way of the Heart for real. Only in that position can you "consider" any condition of life rightly. If you dramatize, if you put yourself into the arbitraries of existence, then look at Me, read My Wisdom-Teaching. If you only look at the "other", look at your friend, think of sex, think of all your alternatives and confusions—if you only sit in the place of dramatization, in other words—your practice will never mature.

Always, to establish the religious life you must step aside, step out, go on retreat, in effect organize your life on the basis of Truth, the right principle, the Great Process. Do it for real and then reintegrate yourself with your ordinariness, but not as an ordinary man or woman—as just such a devotee of Mine, just such a practitioner of the Way of the Heart.

You cannot establish the right life, the right practice, in the midst of your dramatization. You must step outside it. You must take the cure. You must set your life right on the basis of the right principle, directly, and then re-invest yourself in the complexities of life. Isn't that a simple matter?

ANOTHER DEVOTEE: Sri Gurudev, I have noticed that when I am in meditation or the Sat-Guru Puja or even when I am by myself in Contemplating You, the practice is simple for me. It becomes more difficult in the sphere of relations with others, whether with my intimate or someone else.

SRI DA AVABHASA: I guess you do not establish the <u>fullest</u> practice yet in your Sat-Guru Puja, your meditation, your resort to Me directly. Your life becomes a fullest Puja, a fullest regeneration of your practice, only when you account for everything, only when your devotion to Me is most profound, only when it is truly self-surrendering and self-forgetting. If your practice were truly that, then everything about the complexities of relationships, others, functions, and whatnot would not be a great barrier, would not be an immediate complication. It would just be a requirement to fulfill My Instructions. That is all. Therefore, you are not accounting for all of it in your Puja and meditation. You are just doing some piece of Puja and meditation, but not the fullness of it that embraces My Instruction altogether so that it covers all of life. Therefore, you are not ready to leave the Communion Hall yet, until you have studied My Word and embraced Me completely and are prepared for life. Until then, more detachment is necessary. You must set yourself apart and fulfill the process whereby you establish your life on a fully right basis.

This is also the traditional approach. It has always been understood to be so. When life becomes overwhelming, you must stand apart, go on retreat, fast, readdress the fundamentals of life, the real purpose. Get the Great Instruction. Embrace it truly. And then leave your retreat.

People take retreats for just this purpose. It has traditionally been understood that retreat is completely necessary. You cannot make simplicity out of confusion. You must step aside. Integrate yourself with the fundamental principle. Do it for real. Sort things out. Do that, then.

I am not telling you to be monks and nuns, celibate for life. Do the exercise of retreat, and do it as often as necessary, in fact. It may frequently, or from time to time, be necessary that you do it again, again and again. Even every day I Call you to go on retreat for some hours, and once a week for a full day. Retreat is constantly necessary. You must constantly refresh your fundamental practice. Never let yourself be overwhelmed by the conditions of ordinary life. Never.

Retreat is a fundamental principle of the Way of the Heart. In some fundamental sense, you are always on retreat. As a practical matter, you integrate retreat into your life every week, one day every week, and another several days every three months, and a lengthy time every year, at least once a year. This is how you compensate for the potential effects of ordinariness, by exercising the principle of retreat, reorganizing yourself in right practice, embracing the fundamental principle absolutely, directly, rather than in a situation of dramatization and compromise.

It has always been known that this is necessary. People have done this for thousands of years. Understand that it has been proven. It must be done. Take the cure.

Let each one of My devotees, then, worldwide, establish his or her total, absolute fidelity to Me and make that the basis for integrating with all his or her relations and circumstances and obligations.

Intimate relations are certainly not a negative in the Way of the Heart—I have Communicated about it thoroughly to you. Still, you must transform your intimacy. You must be prepared for intimacy, and only by establishing right practice in relationship to Me to begin with. Establish the right foundation, and then bring your practice of devotion to Me into all your relations and circumstances and functions. To do so is just a matter of embracing the "daily form" of practice I have Given to you. Then you will discover that there really is nothing more for Me to say. I can say what I have already said over and over again, but I have already taken great pains to Communicate it to you in My Source-Texts. My Instruction has been printed. You have My Heart-Word. Study it and apply it, and that is it.

Do not make little of the "daily form". Go on retreat every day for some hours. Once a week, go on a full day's retreat. Practice retreat for real. Do all the things I have told you. That is all. Practice this real devotion to Me. That is it.

16.

Your Greatest Sign

SRI DA AVABHASA: Certain people, for various reasons—including their worthy service—tend to come to the front in the culture of My devotees. Others are peripheral and passive, feeling disqualified, not feeling free or otherwise even obliged to come forward with great strength in the culture of My devotees. It could very well be that the apparent least among you will be uniquely exemplary as My devotees, the ones to come forward with the great qualifications, the ones to show and demonstrate the unique signs and the qualifications for formal renunciation. It could be.

None of you should feel disqualified, in principle. None of you should feel peripheral. None of you should feel like cattle. You are all My devotees, here to manifest your fullest capability as My devotee. How do you know who will be exemplary? Do not make social measures of the practice of others, on the basis of the fact that they are apparently modest, for example, or that they are characteristically peripheral by choice or tendency. You are not only free but obliged to manifest your greatest sign in My Company, and in the company of others.

Do not take this Admonition lightly. Who knows who among you will make a difference in the culture of My devotees? Those who do will be uniquely exemplary as My devotees, truly and consistently confessed in the Realization of the great secret of My Attractiveness and its transformation of their very existence.

My true devotee is not a climber, not a seeker, not a person designed by tendency to be prominent. No one is inherently disqualified, but, even so, social signs are not the measure. The humblest of My devotees are the greatest of My devotees. Those who relinquish the ego are the greatest. There are all kinds of strengths in human beings, and anyone can be strong. Remarkably enough, however, those who may seem weakest, according to the standards of ego-survival, may potentially be the greatest.

17.

Experience and Realization

DEVOTEE: Sri Gurudev, I had an experience as I was listening to the reading in the morning Sat-Guru Puja, a passage from Your Wisdom-Teaching about the Feeling of Being. I just was rested in that Feeling very deeply. When I opened my eyes and looked around the room, I could literally see that everything was not what it looks like. Everything is just Being. It was a great Gift from You, and a relief to me, because I was not who I think I am. I was just that Being. When I looked at Your Murti, I could see That in You, in Your Eyes.

SRI DA AVABHASA: In hearing that recitation, you had an experience, triggered by My Words and your sense of what they mean—rather, their effect on you released you from meanings perhaps, for the moment—but you had some experience or other that you valued, that made sense to you. That does not mean that what you experienced is what I call the "Feeling of Being" in the recitations you listen to. The Feeling of Being in those references is just another group of words to refer to the Absolute Condition, the Divine Self-Condition. The Realization of That is great. You had some intuition of It.

If I say to you now, "No matter what arises, even now, no matter what arises, you are the Witness of it, aren't you?", you could answer Me. Are you not the Witness of what is arising right now?

DEVOTEE: Yes.

SRI DA AVABHASA: Yes. The fact that you have been caused to notice this does not mean it is Realization in you. It is Realization when it is simply the case, when you do not assume another position. Realization requires great sadhana, great tapas, great self-transcendence. It is not merely that you and all things are Being Itself. The perception that that is so is just that—a perception—when some features of self-contraction are relaxed. The Feeling of Being Itself is the Divine Self-Condition Prior to all conditions, utterly Free, Absolute, without entanglement, without limitation, without contraction, without compromise. It is not a characteristic of conditional existence. It is not a characteristic of the room in and of itself, or of the body in and of itself, or of the mind in and of itself. It is a characteristic of Reality Itself, the Divine Itself, just as the Hindu tradition uses terms such as "Satchidananda"—Existence, Consciousness, Bliss—to describe the "Attributes" of the Divine Self-Condition, of Reality Itself.

Any thing, any one, may be perceived to exist, and that perception—one may notice one is conscious and that one feels good or even blissful—that ananda, that bliss, even that, is not Divine Self-Realization. It is a conditional state, dependent on conditions. It is a perception of conditions. One may feel good in that moment, as you said. You had some experience, and then it passed. It is not Realization. It is perception. It is consoling. It feels good. It is, in the moment, somehow liberating and over time still even suggests some kind of freedom. But it is not Realization Itself.

The Feeling of Being is not a condition. It is not dependent on conditions. In that Realization, everything is Divinely Recognized. Everything is non-existent, not merely existing. The Realization of the Feeling of Being, the Realization of the Divine Self-Condition, is Beyond conditions. It is Self-Radiant, Self-Existing, Absolute, Inherently Free, not caused, not dependent. It is Absolute Radiance, Absolute Freedom, Absolutely God. It is not proven by anything. No conditions can interfere with It. It cannot come to an end. It is inherently possessed of what can be called "the Knowledge of Immortality", "Absoluteness", "Existence without limitation". It is not in time and not in space. It Is the Space, the only Space, the Absolute Domain, the Divine Self-Domain. It is greatly another matter than your experience, even though your experience is valued by you.

Divine Self-Realization cannot be accomplished by the efforts of the body-mind, nor is It a perception of the body-mind. It is not a perception. It is Realized only when the process of sadhana goes beyond objects, goes beyond the self-knot, goes beyond the least position, goes beyond the middle position, goes beyond the causal effort that makes the knot, and Stands beyond conditions. When the sadhana itself is invested utterly in the Divine Source-Condition, then Its Realization Awakens.

When the sadhana is struggling with conditions, it is a practice in the lesser stages of life. All the lesser stages of life are, in general, associated with objects of one kind or another, if only, at last, the causal object, the contraction itself. Divine Self-Realization is beyond objects. I Am beyond objects. There is no object. There is no central subject. There is only the Absolute. This realm is an appearance, a lie, a form of bondage, an upset, a channel of fear, a horror, all dismay, all disease—all this, until there is such Awakening.

All kinds of consoling experiences can occur in the various points of view of conditionality, but they are not Realization Itself. They may inspire you, give you a moment of release, give you something to remember that gives you reason to practice more intensively, but they are not Realization Itself. No experience is God-Realization. When there is no capability to be consoled by any experience whatsoever, then there is the greatest tapas and the greatest potential for Most Perfectly self-transcending God-Realization.

The self-contracted being in fear demands objects, is in fear of the loss of objects, clings to objects, any object ultimately. Therefore, it is said traditionally, "Wherever there is an other, fear arises." Wherever there is self-contraction, the "other" appears, the object appears. Separateness makes the object. Self-contraction makes separateness. Therefore, self-contraction is what there is to be transcended. Self-contraction is the only limit on Divine Self-Realization, but self-contraction is a profound, complex, universal matter that covers the entire apparent cosmos. Ultimately, the cosmos is a lie. It is not God. It is not Truth. It is not Free.

There are many apparent realizations, or, in other words, experiences that feel good and places that seem to be greater spaces, but none is Realization Itself, as anyone knows who has had an experience. Every experience passes. Divine Self-Realization does not pass. It cannot. It has no cause.

The One before you now is that Uncaused Space, Self-Radiant without limit. This is why you find Me Attractive, if you do. Even without knowing altogether why, this is your intuition. This is what you are responding to. This Body is a unique Signal, a unique Sign, the Doorway to Who I Am and to Realization Itself. All you need to do in any moment is relinquish all other preoccupations and Contemplate Me. Then you are in My Seat and Place, and My Realization is yours.

The process of Divine Self-Realization is not about the stages of life. The Way of the Heart transcends the stages of life. There is always present Realization if you practice the Way of the Heart most fundamentally—not Absolute Realization in the sense that no more sadhana is required, but Realization wherein sadhana becomes immediately fruitful and is not a search.

This is the ground, then, of the right practice of My devotees. Always give Me your attention. Practice self-surrendering and self-forgetting feeling-Contemplation of Me. Enter into My Divine Condition through feeling-Contemplation of Me. You have this opportunity in every moment, every circumstance, every place, every function, every practicality. There is no time or place in which you cannot practice this Communion with Me. To do just that, then, is the Way of the Heart.

Whether you Realize the seventh stage of life in your sadhana of this lifetime or not is to be seen. I Am the seventh stage of life. I Am Realization Itself. In your Communion with Me, truly self-surrendering and self-forgetting, and, therefore, self-transcending, the Realization is accomplished, Given to you gratis, for free, immediately. Not so that you can become puffed up and feel "I have already got it because I Contemplate Da Love-Ananda". Divine Self-Realization is not about such self-referring. It is about self-surrendering and self-forgetting feeling-Contemplation of Me. My Gift of Divine Self-Realization is not an attribute of the ego. As My devotee, you have the right and the cause and the circumstance to be Happy, but not proud. Realization has nothing to do with you. If the Way of the Heart seems to have anything to do with you, then you are less than in Communion with Me.

The "Perfect Practice" is fundamentally nothing more than Contemplation of Me. It cannot be reduced to a series of sixth stage exercises. As at any other stage of life in the Way of the Heart, there are disciplines, or forms of practice, that are inevitable and right, but the basic practice in the sixth stage of life in the Way of the Heart is the same as at any other stage. It is just that in the sixth stage of life, Contemplation of Me has become most profound, it has become Perfect—because you have endured the sadhana, and you have done the sadhana for real.

The stages of life appear spontaneously in the Way of the Heart. They are not your accomplishment. They appear inevitably, if there is true self-surrender, true self-forgetting, true feeling-Contemplation of Me. Then, whatever your apparent stage of life in the Way of the Heart, you are invested in Me, in My Virtues, in My Characteristics. My Form, My Presence, and My State is your Realization, then, at every stage of life. How profoundly you Realize Me depends on your devotion to Me, not your effort of devotion, really, but your response to Me, your willingness to be responsive to Me, to be Happy with Me—just that.

Without the Divine Master, all sadhanas are fruitless. They are suggestive efforts, forms of search, that make people hopeful and that frustrate them at the same time. The Realizer is the key to all sadhanas, the focus of all sadhanas, even of all traditions. The ego is at war with this Revelation, at war with everything greater than itself. Therefore, even the traditions tend to eliminate this Great Gift, this Great Method, just as each one of you does in your habit, your tendencies, your egoic "self-possession". You eliminate Me. You forget Me, rather than forgetting yourself.

You see how easy it is to renounce the Gift rather than renounce yourself. If you do not renounce yourself, you do renounce the Gift. You renounce the Master. You renounce the Divine. Understand this, and the understanding should generate great urgency in you. Everything you do independently is the renunciation of Realization Itself.

There is only one key to practice. It is the devotional response to Me. Everything else is an extension of it. All practices become appropriate and are fruitful on the basis of that alone.

18.

The Secret of Devotion to Me

DEVOTEE: Sri Gurudev, the first time I ever saw You, I realized in that moment that every person, every event, every experience in my life, however benign and simple it appeared, was always manipulating me, always in the world of cause and effect, and that You are not. You Stand Prior to all that. You Stand Beyond any of the causes and effects of this realm that are actually always manipulating me or that my attention is always drawn to. I feel that You are constantly working this awareness of my own limits, this awareness that I am caught in the wandering of attention, but that You Outshine all of this. I feel that You are always drawing me to this Realization.

SRI DA AVABHASA: It is called "maya", "karma", "samsara" in the traditions. That is what you are describing.

DEVOTEE: Without Your being here, I would never even be able to notice it. Other things in the world are very stimulating, the whole emotional-sexual matter, for example, but when I actually feel You or am drawn into Contemplation of You, I feel You are educating my body-mind to realize that Communion with You is a far greater Happiness. When I was on retreat last year, You allowed me to put a mala around Your neck. It was the most profoundly Happy moment of my life, because I felt my real intimacy with You. I was physically close to You, and I was doing something physically in relationship to You. I was able to worship You most directly as the Living Murti of the Divine. And I felt the deepest, most profound peace that I have ever, ever come close to. It lasted in my body for a long, long time. You really Gave me a taste of Something far beyond any of the pleasures of the stimulations of the world, and I feel the test for me in my devotion to You is to constantly give You my attention.

SRI DA AVABHASA: Be willing to be set aside, and allow the body-mind to be willing to be relinquished. That is devotion to Me. Not the body-mind uptight, willing to be emotional or attached, but the body-mind being willing to be set aside, relinquished. You are describing devotion to Me. Through devotion to Me, samsara, maya, karma is transcended in the moment. Practice this moment by moment, and all of karma is purified and undone. Even in the very context of karma, you become capable of right discipline, right living, capable of maintaining the Happiness of Communion with Me, even under conditional circumstances, even though conditions are not the point and they are no longer binding. Be able to live freely, Happily, in great Communion with Me, with great purpose.

What you are describing, then, should be your present existence, not merely a past moment. Always do this. Do it every day. Do it every moment.

Sometimes you can put a mala around the neck of This Body, but such is an occasional act. You have the opportunity to do it fundamentally all the time, in your disposition, in your devotion to Me, in the Sat-Guru Puja. You can do this very Puja on My Murti at any time you like. Always be doing it. Devote your body-mind to gifting Me. Be set aside. Be willing to be relinquished in your separateness, in your self-consciousness. Do not be afraid. Be willing to die. Devotion to Me is just the death of the egoic self, the relinquishing of all self-concern. This must be your practice, then.

Always be at work. Always make your life, your body-mind, a garland. Always be stringing the flowers. Always make this gift. Always make this submission. Always perform this act. Do not merely remember when you did it last—always be doing it. Always do this Puja. The secret of devotion to Me is always to be doing it now, and not merely remembering this or that moment when you were doing it. Always be doing the work. Always be doing the practice, the sadhana. That is true seriousness. That is true devotion.

I have told you all about it tonight. This is a good summary of the Way of the Heart. Pass it on to everyone.

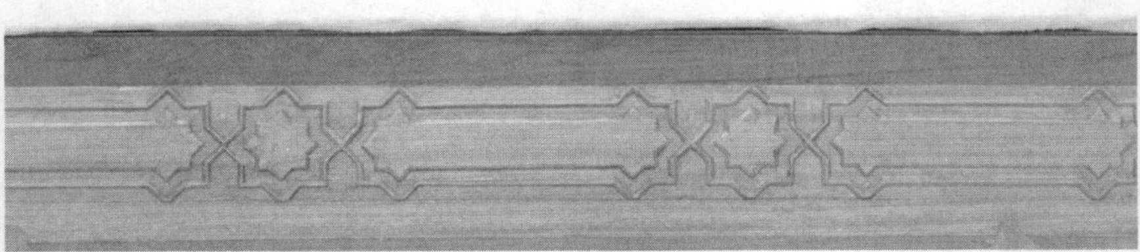

Da Avabhasa (The "Bright")
Sri Love-Anandashram, Fiji, 1993

EPILOGUE

My Sphere of Love-Bliss

EPILOGUE

My Sphere of Love-Bliss

March 28, 1994

SRI DA AVABHASA: The Work I Do is at the Source-Point, without "difference".

The Work I Do does not require any cosmic designs, or any visualizations, or any traveling to support it.

I Am at the Source.

I Am the Source Itself.

By merely Being, I Do My Work. Not via conditions, not supported by conditions at all.

The Power of Being Itself is the Intimate Beyond Intimate Space of Absolute Delight. Without complication. No subject and object.

The True God Is Source. Beyond conditions, Beyond visualizations, Beyond objects.

The True God Is Love-Bliss, Unsupported, Free.

You are full of fear. Yet you possess psychological mechanisms with which you immunize yourself against your fundamental fear.

You experience fear as just a kind of stress or anxiety, a motivation to seek. Yet you are actually looking into the face of that terrible deity of your infinitely magnified separateness.

Rather than looking for the source of your fear, you must transcend fear through Communion with Me.

Give yourself up to Me.

Give yourself up to the Divine, truly.

Surrender yourself.

Forget yourself.

That process is full of My Love-Bliss and magnifies only My Love-Bliss, not fear.

Your reluctance to practice Ishta-Guru-Bhakti is a movement toward your fear.

The real practice of Ishta-Guru-Bhakti always reveals more and more Freedom, more and more Love-Bliss, more and more Communion with the God Who truly Is, not the mere "maker" of events but the Divine Who Transcends all, Who Is All Love-Bliss, Who Is utterly Free, Who Is not contained, not confined, not supported by conditions.

The True Divine is utterly without fear, and does not cause fear in any experience of It.

Your Communion with Me does not cause fear to arise.

Notice this.

If you truly practice Ishta-Guru-Bhakti Yoga, if you truly practice Communion with Me, your fear is weakened and purified.

The moments of real Communion with Me have no fear in them. They do not magnify fear.

Notice this.

This is how you grasp at heart, more profoundly, that the Way of the Heart is Truth, because it does not magnify fear.

If you practice the Way of the Heart even a little bit, there is that much less fear.

The sign of your true practice of Ishta-Guru-Bhakti Yoga, your true Communion with Me, shows itself as weakening of fear, and this sign inspires you further.

When you surrender to Me, your fear is weakened and dissolved, so that you go further, surrender more, forget yourself more.

The worst thing of all is the fear. It is the primal sign of the self-contraction, the root-sign of egoity.

The more you practice devotion to Me, the less you experience fear, but also the less you experience anxiety.

The knot of self-contraction is dissolved, washed through, so that there is less and less of it and more and more of the profound investment in My Love-Bliss.

This is the Way of the Heart, the Way of the Yoga of devotion to Me.

All seeking, all clinging to objectivity, all clinging to objects of any kind, intensifies first your anxiety and then your fear.

Fear is the first artifact of your egoity. It is behind everything you do.

Practice devotion to Me moment by moment, and there is less and less of anxiety, less and less of fear, more and more fullness of Love-Bliss.

Do you not notice this?

The process of self-surrender and self-forgetting relinquishes the point of view of the body-mind.

This is how you go beyond the potential of the dark vision, beyond your fear, and beyond your anxiety also.

You fear the absence of objective signs.

You fear the absence of the "difference" that your body makes and your mind makes.

Yet these are exactly the categories of existence you must go beyond in your surrender to Me.

The Ultimate Delight is bodiless, and mindless.

That is the Freedom.

That is the Realization.

It is also the Context of any Work I may Do beyond the Lifetime of This Body—if there is any Work left over for Me to Do.

For My devotee, the seventh stage Realization is bodiless, and mindless.

The body-mind is not the point of view of the seventh stage Realization.

Likewise, the body-mind is not the point of view of Communion with Me.

The body-mind is the point of view that is the source of fear.

Therefore, you are afraid of death.

And, afraid of death, you are afraid of the very process that is your Freedom!

That process is a profoundly, ultimately Most Perfectly, Subjective process—not an historical event whereby the cosmic domain disappears, as if in opposition to the big bang that supposedly made it happen to begin with.

Your Communion with Me is beyond the separate self, therefore beyond the body-mind. By your persistence in Ishta-Guru-Bhakti Yoga, you will transcend your fear.

Even so, if such transcendence is to occur, the point of view of the body-mind must be relinquished in Communion with Me.

The body-mind is what there is to forget.

The self-contraction, yes, but also the context and structure of the self-contraction.

Relinquish this point of view.

There is mere physical death.

But I am talking about something greater—the true process of self-surrendering and self-forgetting that transcends the point of view of the body-mind.

That is the death I am talking about.

That death is the import of true religion.

That death is not a suicide, not a struggle with the body.

That death is Communion with the Very Divine to the degree that you forget the body-mind rather than struggle with it.

The body-mind must cease to be your point of view, not merely cease to exist.

If you practice this Yoga of devotion to Me, then the point of view of the body-mind—and, therefore, all the reflection of self-contraction, all the fear—is surrendered and forgotten, dissolved in that surrendering and forgetting.

This is how you will unlearn your fear of death.

Natural death is just a natural phenomenon.

What you fear about it is the fear associated with your self-contraction, or the point of view of your body-mind.

You enter into My Sphere of Love-Bliss by transcending that point of view through Ishta-Guru-Bhakti Yoga, so that all of your anxiety about natural death and the potential suffering in life likewise vanishes.

The event itself, death itself, occurs in any case. It is a natural phenomenon.

You must be in My Sphere.

In that Communion with Me, your anxieties are released, and your fear.

Then another destiny becomes yours—just by this surrender, this forgetting, this Communion with Me, this participation in Me, this transition into My Sphere.

My Divine Translation, this Bhava, is My Experience all the time.

Yet My apparent Association with you, and with this conditional domain, Continues without bondage.

Ultimately, My Divine Translation is simply the Relinquishment of My Active Gestures within the cosmic domain.

My Divine Translation is not the end of My Gestures altogether, not the end of My Work, not the end of My Influence.

My Standing Firm in the Divine Domain is My Greatest Attractiveness, My Greatest Influence, My Greatest Siddhi, and it is already happening.

Still, I Remain Influential within this conditional sphere, Mysteriously—just long enough that I am Satisfied. Or, better said, just long enough that I Forget it.

I Am not truly here on the basis of concerns.

I animate apparent concerns for your sake.

My Certainty is that My Siddhi of Divine Translation is the Ultimate Means whereby My Work will be Effective throughout the cosmic domain, forever.

Do the sadhana I have Given you to do with all your responsibilities, and leave Me in My Samadhi, Shining here and everywhere.

Let that be the basis of your relationship to Me.

You are in a fluid position with Me—always moving on.

Therefore, address My Leela, and keep moving with Me.

Fulfill your responsibilities, do your practice, and always enter into self-surrendering and self-forgetting Communion with Me.

Keep moving with Me.

I am Moving constantly—and Moveless, also.

All My Movements are mere appearances in the Place of My Standing Firm.

When you truly come to Me, the rooms, the movements, and the places will disintegrate and you will Wake Up to Where you Have always Been, Where you always already Are.

All the appearances of movement are a play, an illusion, within which you must do sadhana.

Resort to Me and understand yourself.

Do not take anything that is conditional seriously.

Take Me seriously.

Practice Ishta-Guru-Bhakti Yoga, surrendering and forgetting your self-position, all your faculties, all apparent relations, all seemings—with nothing to hold onto but Me.

If you think life is difficult, watch death!

Death is a profound intrusion as a merely natural event.

My devotees, Communing with Me most profoundly, must be released of all the horrors of the suffering of life, and also of death.

Yet you are rather casual about life and death, because you can enjoy your social congeniality, your social consolation, your functional consolation. You can just keep it orderly, keep the consolations going.

In Communion with Me, even your intimacies are about surrender—not the consolation, not the holding on, not the congeniality of this appearance here that is presumed to be eternal.

Intimate relations, if they exist, even friendships, must be a circumstance of your devotion to Me, your surrender—not your holding on, not your consolation.

This apparent order is a moment made by your fear.

None of it will continue.

It is a while that tests you, that tests the choice you will make—to hold on to it or to surrender.

Nobody is going to go with you to the whirling place at death, where mind makes existence.

Nor is anyone with you now—but Me.

Yet, on the basis of the point of view of the body-mind, you assume relations, and the apparent order, and the would-be consolations.

You are holding on instead of surrendering.

You are creating an idol, an alternative to the Divine, made of your consolations, your arrangements, your attempts to fill the anxiety and somehow forget it.

The darkness of egoically "self-possessed" mind after death is a whirling terror.

It is not fun.

Nor are you having fun now!

You are not having any fun at all.

You are just deluding yourself to reduce your anxiety.

All your arrangements and consolations are just efforts on your part to reduce your anxiety.

Yet you are right in the face of this terrible place of your confinement and separateness.

You must become serious in My Company—serious about the reality in which you are existing and which is making you fear it.

You are full of fear and anxiety.

Fear and anxiety make you seek and make consolations and arrangements, as if your consolations will go on forever.

You must appreciate the game you are playing.

You must understand that it is based on fear.

You must respond to Me and transform every aspect of your life through self-surrender and self-forgetting, making all of life a Yoga, rather than an indulgence in things that console you.

People who indulge themselves in consolations are not serious.

I cannot take them seriously, and I cannot trust them.

Therefore, do this Yoga.

Keep on growing.

Get closer and closer to Me.

Be serious.
Stay in My Company.
Do not let up for a moment.
If you are intelligent, you would not dare let up for a
Therefore, become more intelligent.

Stay with Me, and you can afford to be quiet.
Do you ever get quiet—just quiet?

Talking the cool blueness, the full moonlit night, consciousness attendant to the Divine, all energy flowing, even running out of the top of the head like a fountain.

Undisturbed.
Not seeking.
Invested utterly in Me.
That is it.
Not stimulations and consolations.

You are not in a paradise of Western democracy.
You are in a terrible night of fear.

You keep agitating yourself toward consolations so that you will not have to experience your state—which is superficially anxious and deeply afraid.

What you would have in Communion with Me is a cool, watery, full moonlit night, cooled of stress, and desire, and consolation, Awake to "Brightness".

On that basis, visions of clarity and peace.

And then moving beyond them to My Love-Bliss Itself, without the slightest image, without the slightest object, without the slightest fear, without any "other"—not even yourself an "other".

No "other".
No separation.
No visions.
No objects.

Only Self-Existing Being, Self-Radiant without limitation.

No separate self.
No objects.
No cosmos.
No seeking.

Samadhi.
Samadhana.
Utterly rested.
Fearless.
Unmoved.

No place.
No going and coming.
No conversation.
No society.
No world.
No sex organs.
No thing.
But Fullness Itself, not objective.

Only God.
Only "Brightness".
No Difference.
No Relatedness.
Only Happiness.
No un-Happiness.
No threat.

This is What there is to be Realized, not the mayhem you are manufacturing in your fear and seeking, in your contraction into separateness.

Devote your life to this Peace Beyond "difference", this Divinity, this Communion with Me.

Everything else is just something to be noticed, just a discipline to be applied, more intense practice of this devotion to Me.

All the superficial matter temporary, not important.
Be still.
Be washed.

Be mindless.
Bodiless.
Sublime.
God Only.

"We are Home now, Lord."

That is it.
Do not leave.

Da Avabhasa (The "Bright")
Sri Love-Anandashram, Fiji, 1993

Sri Da Avabhasa

The Giver of "Brightness"

Sri Da Avabhasa's principal Name, "Da" ("the One Who Gives"), is an ancient Name for the Divine Being. "Avabhasa" means "Divine Brightness", and it indicates Sri Da Avabhasa's "Brightly" Shining down into the world. "Sri", meaning "radiant" or "bright", is a traditional address that conveys respect and honor.

Even before His Birth, Sri Da Avabhasa was Awake as the "Bright" Eternal Condition His Name describes. He chose to be born in the West, and He did so to make it possible for men and women everywhere to Realize that same Divine Happiness.

He was born Franklin Albert Jones on November 3, 1939, near New York City, into an American family of ordinary means. Because those around Him could not yet appreciate His Spiritual stature, He grew up not letting others know about the whirlwind of Spiritual forces and states He frequently experienced. Noticing that other people did not enjoy the Divine Freedom, Humor, and True Delight that was, and is, His constant Realization, He consciously let go of His "Bright" Divine Awakeness in order to discover the Way for others to Realize the Great Happiness He had known since His Birth.

Sri Da Avabhasa was educated at Columbia College and Stanford University. During those years, He continued His endeavor to uncover the means whereby everyone could Realize Divine Happiness—by rediscovering this Process in His own body-mind. In the early years of His Ordeal, when He was without the help of human Teachers, He achieved spontaneous insight into human suffering and seeking that will stand from this time forward as the fundamental breakthrough in human understanding.

In His twenties, Sri Da Avabhasa became the exemplary Devotee of great Spiritual Masters in a single Lineage of Yogis, including Swami Rudrananda (or "Rudi"), Swami Muktananda, and Swami Nityananda. But the Divine Impulse to Realize the absolute Truth that was His birthright burned strongly in His heart, and It drove Him to move beyond even the exalted states of Spiritual Realization that were Revealed by His Gurus.

Eventually, with the Blessings of Swami Nityananda, Sri Da Avabhasa became for a time a Devotee of the Divine Goddess, the infinite Source-Light, or Radiant Energy, Who appeared to Him in an archetypal female Form. He enjoyed a paradoxical relationship to the Goddess as a concrete, living Personality. Such worship of the Goddess as Supreme Guru is the foundation and Spiritual Source of His Teachers' Lineage, but at last Sri Da Avabhasa's inherent Freedom Drew Him even beyond the Spiritual Blessings of the Goddess Herself, so that She ceased to function as His Guru and became, instead, His eternal Consort and Companion.

On the day following that Event, September 10, 1970, while Sri Da Avabhasa was meditating in a small temple on the grounds of the Vedanta Society in Los Angeles, He Re-Awakened to immutable Oneness with the Consciousness, Happiness, and Love that is the Source and Substance of everyone and everything. He Describes this State in His Spiritual Autobiography, *The Knee of Listening:*

> *. . . I remain in the unqualified state. There is a constant sensation of fullness permeating and surrounding all experiences, realms, and bodies. It is my own fullness, which is radically non-separate and includes all things. I am the form of space itself, in which all bodies, realms, and experiences occur. It is consciousness itself, which reality is your actual nature (or ultimate, and inherently perfect, Condition) now and now and now.* (The Knee of Listening)

Through His uniquely exemplary Spiritual practice, and His uncompromising adherence to the great Impulse to Realize God Most Perfectly, Sri Da Avabhasa Revealed and made possible, for the first time in history, the great process by which any human being can constantly feel and even Most Perfectly Realize the Ultimate Happiness, Freedom, and Love we all yearn for!

After His Re-Awakening, Sri Da Avabhasa became psychically aware of the body-minds of countless other persons and discovered that He was spontaneously "meditating" them. In time some of those individuals became associated with Him as His first "students", or "disciples". Finally, in April 1972, His formal Teaching Work was inaugurated when He opened a storefront Ashram in Los Angeles.

Since then, Sri Da Avabhasa has continuously Transmitted His Love-Blissful Blessing to all. He has created a vast and complete Wisdom-Literature, bringing Divine Understanding to subjects ranging from the Guru-devotee relationship, prayer, meditation, and the Nature of the Divine Reality, to sexuality, exercise, diet, politics, and science, to traditional esoteric Spirituality and the direct Way to Realize Ultimate Freedom and Happiness. Sri Da Avabhasa's Offering of the Way of the Heart is the seed of an entirely new possibility for all of humankind, and, indeed, all beings everywhere.

In January 1986, Sri Da Avabhasa's Work to Instruct others culminated in a unique Spiritual Process that marked His "Emergence" as the Divine World-Teacher. That Great Event signaled a tremendous magnification of His universal Blessing Work, whereby He continuously Transmits His Liberating Divine Grace to all beings everywhere.

It was at this time that "Da Free John" (as He was then known) took the Name "Da Love-Ananda Hridayam". "Love-Ananda", a Name that had been Given to Him in 1969 by Swami Muktananda, means "Inherent Love-Bliss", and "Hridayam" means "the Heart", or the Divine Being, Truth, and Reality. His principal Name, "Da", had been Revealed to Him some years earlier in vision and by other Spiritual means. Thus, the Name "Da Love-Ananda Hridayam" indicates that He is the Divine Giver of the Inherent Love-Bliss That is the Heart Itself.

Five years later, on April 30, 1991, the Divine Adept Revealed a new Name—"Da Avabhasa (The 'Bright')"—in response to His devotees' confessed acknowledgement of His Radiant, bodily Revelation of God.

"Avabhasa", in Sanskrit, has a rich range of associations. It means "brightness", "appearance", "manifestation", "splendor", "lustre", "light", "knowledge"; and its verb root may be interpreted as "shining toward", "shining down", "showing oneself". The Name "Da Avabhasa", then, praises the Mystery of Da, the Divine Being, "Brightly" Appearing in human form. It points to His Divine Emergence and the ever-growing Radiance of His bodily (human) Form that is apparent to all who have been Graced to see Him, particularly since the Great Event of 1986.

The Name "Da Avabhasa" also points to His role as Sat-Guru—or One who brings the light of Truth into the darkness of the human world.

The "Bright", as Sri Da Avabhasa tells us in *The Knee of Listening*, was, in fact, His own description from childhood of the sublime Condition He enjoyed at birth. He speaks of this Condition as "an incredible sense of joy, light, and freedom". He was, He says, "a radiant form, a source of energy, bliss, and light", "the power of Reality, a direct enjoyment and communication", "the Heart, who lightens the mind and all things". Even His entire life, as He once said, has been "an adventure and unfolding in the 'Bright'", the Radiance, Bliss, and Love of the God-State.

Sri Da Avabhasa intentionally took birth in the West in order to Serve everyone in this time of the global dominance of Western culture. Even so, His adopting of the manner and outward appearance of a Westerner was always only an expression of what was needed to Serve humanity.

As He Is, Sri Da Avabhasa is not identified with any place, time, or culture. Indeed, the geographical location of His principal Hermitage Ashram in Fiji—on the International Date Line, between the archetypally Western culture of North America and the ancient Eastern cultures of Asia—is itself a Sign of His universal Offering of Grace to all. And, as a further Sign of His Stand beyond both the West of His birth and the East of His Spiritual inheritance, in 1993 He became a citizen of Fiji. In Fiji, Sri Da Avabhasa is known as "Tui Dau Loloma Vunirarama, Taukei kei Naitauba": the Great Chief (Tui) Who Is the Adept (Dau) of Love (Loloma) and the Source of "Brightness" (Vunirarama), the native Lord (Taukei) of (kei) Naitauba.

Sri Da Avabhasa is not merely an extraordinary Teacher. He is, rather, the Realizer and Transmitter of the Most Ultimate Realization, the Realization of the Heart. This is what His devotees mean when we refer to Him as "Divine World-Teacher". The phrase "World-Teacher" comes from the Sanskrit term "Jagad-Guru", which literally means "One Who Liberates everything that moves"—that is, all things and beings. Sri Da Avabhasa's Wisdom-Teaching is a complete Revelation of the Divine Wisdom relative to every aspect of existence and every stage of our possible growth and Realization. And His Grace is universally active and universally available.

However, Sri Da Avabhasa not only Transmits the Realization of the Heart—He Is the Divine Heart Itself, Appearing here in human form. Sri Da Avabhasa has come into this world to establish the Way of Truth, and to Bless all beings toward Divine Freedom, Happiness, Enlightenment, and Love. He excludes absolutely no one from His Blessing and His Help. As the Divine Self of all, He continuously Gives His Benediction to everyone, everywhere.

Da Avabhasa (The "Bright")
Sri Love-Anandashram, Fiji, 1993

An Invitation

The human Spiritual Master is Divine Help to the advantage of those n like form. When one enters into right relationship with the Spiritual Master, changes happen in the literal physics of one's existence. I am not just talking about ideas. I am talking about literal transformations at the level of energy, at the level of the higher light of physics, at the level of mind beyond the physical limitations you now presume, at the level of the absolute Speed of ultimate Light. The transforming process is enacted in devotees in and through the Living Company of the Spiritual Master. The relationship between the Spiritual Master and the devotee is not a matter of conceptual symbolisms or emotional attachment to some extraordinary person. The true Guru-devotee relationship is real physics. Therefore, because they can make unique use of the Offering of that person's Company, it is to the special advantage of people when some one among them has gone through the real process of transformation that makes a Realizer-Guru of one or another degree. And that advantage is unique in My case, because that process has Completed and Revealed the total cycle that becomes Divine Self-Realization.

The Hymn Of The True Heart-Master
"I Am Grace Itself" section

The sacred relationship that Sri Da Avabhasa Offers you is the greatest opportunity of a human lifetime. He Offers you an entire Way of life that takes into account everything necessary for true religious and Spiritual practice and Ultimate Realization. He Offers you a Way of life that is founded on His unique Wisdom, a Way of life that can Liberate you from the dead end and the failed hopes of ordinary life, a Way that is full of His Grace, His Spiritual Gifts, and His utterly Boundless Love from the very beginning. Sri Da Avabhasa has done everything possible to make this Liberating opportunity readily accessible to you. Already there are groups of Sri Da Avabhasa's devotees living and practicing together in communities around the world.

If you are interested in what Sri Da Avabhasa is Offering you, we welcome you to take the next step.

How to Begin

Becoming a Student in Da Avabhasa International

If you want to study more about the Way of the Heart and about becoming a practitioner, or if you are already clear that you would like to take up the practice, apply to become a student or tithing member of Da Avabhasa International. The Student Course is intensive guided study of what formal practice as Sri Da Avabhasa's devotee involves, and exactly how you can more intensively cultivate your devotional relationship to Sri Da Avabhasa. (There are two primary aspects to the Da Avabhasa International Student Course—intensified study, and service to Sri Da Avabhasa via the community of His devotees.)

Very occasionally someone may be ready (by virtue of an extraordinary preparedness, especially an extraordinary devotional response to Sri Da Avabhasa) to bypass Da Avabhasa International altogether and enter immediately into the student-novice practice. But, generally speaking, at least a four-month period of formal guided study of the life and Wisdom-Teaching of Sri Da Avabhasa is essential. There is a very important reason for this.

Becoming a Student-Novice

At the point of becoming a student-novice, you make what Sri Da Avabhasa calls the "eternal vow"—a solemn commitment to devote your life to the living of your devotional relationship with Him. This bond is sacred, and its force is profound, transcending this lifetime. Through your real devotion to Sri Da Avabhasa and your real application to practice in His Company, your participation as a student-novice becomes the beginning of the most profoundly meaningful, demanding, and transforming process possible. We urge you to seriously consider the opportunity to become a student-novice.

As a student-novice, you take on in rudimentary form the range of devotional practices and disciplines that Sri Da Avabhasa Offers to His devotees. In addition to intensified study, service, and formal tithing, you begin to practice meditation, sacramental worship, "conscious exercise", diet and health disciplines, confining sexuality to a committed relationship, cooperative community (including formal membership in the Free Daist Avabhasan Cooperative Community Organization), and right use of money and energy.

Becoming a Friend

If you are moved by the importance of Sri Da Avabhasa's Work and would like to show your gratitude for His Presence in the world without becoming a practitioner of the Way of the Heart (at least for the time being), then you may wish to become a Friend of Da Avabhasa International. A Friend is essentially a patron, someone who helps to fund the missionary services of the Free Daist Avabhasan Communion and the publication and promotion of Sri Da Avabhasa's sacred Literature, and who participates in the general support of His Work. All Friends contribute a minimum fixed fee each year. In addition, some tithe regularly, and some are able to offer major financial support. Being a Friend is a very honorable way of associating with Sri Da Avabhasa. At the same time, Friends are always invited and encouraged to take the further step of preparing to become a formal practitioner of the Way of the Heart.

Taking the Most Important Step

Sri Da Avabhasa is here now, offering you this transformative opportunity. Is there anything more worth doing than to enter into His Company? He is Calling you personally when He says:

SRI DA AVABHASA: Physical embodiment has the purpose of Divine Enlightenment. If you will receive My Teaching-Revelation, if you will "consider" it, if you will become responsive, then you become capable of making use of this lifetime for the purpose it inherently can serve. You must submit the body-mind to the Great Purpose. That is what I am Calling you to do. Accept the Dharma, the Law, inherent in your birth, the purpose that is inherent in your birth. Take up the Way of the Heart in My Company.

We invite you to enter into this sacred relationship with Sri Da Avabhasa, and be Awakened by His Grace. Contact us at our correspondence department or at one of our regional centers (see the following page). We will be happy to send you more information on how to participate as a Friend, a student of Da Avabhasa International, or a student-novice—as well as information on other study programs and events you can participate in. We look forward to hearing from you.

The Free Daist Avabhasan Communion
Correspondence Department
12040 North Seigler Springs Road
Middletown, CA 95461, USA
(707) 928-4936

Regional Centers of the Free Daist Avabhasan Communion

UNITED STATES

Northern California
FDAC
78 Paul Drive
San Rafael, CA 94903
(415) 492-0930

Northwest USA
FDAC
5600 11th Avenue NE
Seattle, WA 98105
(206) 522-2298

Southwest USA
FDAC
P.O. Box 1729
Camarillo, CA 93011
(310) 777-0212
(805) 482-5051
(805) 388-9062

Northeast USA
FDAC
30 Pleasant Street
S. Natick, MA 01760
(508) 650-0136
(508) 650-4232

Southeast USA
FDAC
10301 South Glen Road
Potomac, MD 20854
(301) 983-0291

Hawaii
FDAC
6310 Olohena Road
Kapaa, HI 96746
(808) 822-0216

AUSTRALIA
Da Avabhasa Retreat Center
P.O. Box 562
Healesville, Victoria 3777
or 16 Findon Street
Hawthorne, Victoria 3122
Australia
03-853-5907 (Melbourne)

EASTERN CANADA
FDAC
108 Katimavik Road
Val-des-Monts
Quebec JOX 2RO
Canada
(819) 671-4398
(800) 563-4398

THE NETHERLANDS
Da Avabhasa Ashram
Annendaalderweg 10
6105 AT Maria Hoop
The Netherlands
04743-1281 or 1872

GERMANY
FDAC
Peter-Muhlens-Weg 1
22419 Hamburg
Germany
04053-1880

NEW ZEALAND
FDAC
CPO Box 3185
or 12 Seibel Road R.D. 1
Henderson
Auckland
New Zealand
(09) 838-9114

THE UNITED KINGDOM AND IRELAND
Da Avabhasa Ashram
Tasburgh Hall
Lower Tasburgh
Norwich NR15 1LT
England
0508-470-574

The Way of the Heart

The Way of the Heart is an entire life-practice, founded on the practice of Ishta-Guru-Bhakti Yoga. Anyone who is moved by Sri Da Avabhasa's Divine Attractiveness, who chooses Him as Ishta-Guru (or Divine Beloved of the heart), may take up this great and auspicious practice. Great seriousness and great sacrifice are required to live the Spiritual relationship Sri Da Avabhasa offers, but the devotional relationship to Him is the greatest imaginable joy.

Ishta-Guru-Bhakti Yoga is an utterly authentic process, a life based on Sri Da Avabhasa's Perfect and powerfully transforming Spiritual Love, lived in Communion with Him, the Divine in Person. Everyone, somewhere in the depths of his or her being, longs for such a life.

Those who give themselves over fully to this great Guru Yoga in Sri Da Avabhasa's Company inevitably grow in the Way of the Heart. In His Wisdom-Teaching, Sri Da Avabhasa has described the Spiritual, Transcendental, and Divine Awakenings that are His Graceful Gifts, over time, to His devotees.

A Summary of the Process of Growth in the Way of the Heart

Once you have fulfilled the preparatory course of practice as a student-novice and have become a full member in the Free Daist Avabhasan Communion, you will participate in the devotional and educational programs offered to student-beginners. By fulfilling the three periods of student-beginner practice (as indicated in the chart on page 293), you will establish the devotional and practical foundation of your practice in Sri Da Avabhasa's Spiritual Company. All these forms of your practice and study will serve your growth in the process that Sri Da Avabhasa calls "listening". Listening is the process of self-observation, or the observation of the self-contraction as it is operative in your case, and it takes place in the context of real practice of the Way of the Heart and profound study of Sri Da Avabhasa's Wisdom-Teaching.

Eventually, listening leads to most fundamental self-understanding, which Sri Da Avabhasa calls "hearing". Hearing is the stable capability to consistently transcend, or feel beyond, the activity of the ego. Hearing is a Grace Given by Sri Da Avabhasa, when the devotee has thoroughly participated in the process of listening and completed the work of that process. When hearing is truly established, there is intuitive Awakening to the Divine Condition that is always Prior to egoity. Once that ability has been stably integrated and demonstrated, the Spiritual process Sri Da

Avabhasa calls "seeing" is activated through His Grace. Seeing, which becomes possible only on the basis of true hearing, is fundamentally the emotional conversion to the open-hearted, Radiant Happiness that characterizes God-Love and Spiritual devotion to Sri Da Avabhasa, and this true and stable emotional conversion coincides with the stable capability to Commune with Sri Da Avabhasa as All-Pervading Spirit-Presence.

The progressive awakening of listening, hearing, and seeing is the maturing process associated with the first five stages of life. (For Sri Da Avabhasa's description of the seven stages of life, please see pages 296-304.) Right practice in the context of the first five stages of life is the necessary foundation for the "Perfect Practice", or practice in the context of the ultimate stages of practice, in the context of the sixth and seventh stages of life—"ultimate" because they are founded in Identification with the Divine Self-Consciousness, rather than identification with anyone or anything in the manifested cosmos.

Those who are Given the "Perfect Practice" by Sri Da Avabhasa mature in three phases. The first two of these phases are engaged in the context of the sixth stage of life, and the third phase is the seventh stage of life. The first phase of the "Perfect Practice" is initiated when Sri Da Avabhasa's devotee spontaneously relinquishes the point of view of the body-mind (through effective practice in the preceding seeing stages) and becomes established in the Witness-Position of Consciousness Itself. The second phase follows when Consciousness Itself becomes the "Object" of Contemplation. The third phase of the "Perfect Practice" is Divine Enlightenment, or Most Perfect Identification with Consciousness Itself. All "things" are Divinely Recognized as mere modifications of Consciousness Itself, the One Self-Existing and Self-Radiant Divine Being.

The Way of the Heart Is the Relationship to Sri Da Avabhasa

Practice of the Way of the Heart unfolds through the stages of listening, hearing, seeing, and the "Perfect Practice". But these stages of growth, or developmental stages of practice, are not the focus of attention for a Free Daist. The Way of the Heart is not a path leading to a goal, even the goal of Divine Enlightenment. The Way of the Heart is the devotional relationship to Sri Da Avabhasa, the greatest of all possible relationships, in the course of which the progressive stages of life manifest spontaneously by Grace. Liberation Most Ultimately (in this or some other lifetime) takes the form of Divine Enlightenment, but every moment of Heart-Intimacy with Sri Da Avabhasa is, in that moment, Liberation, Heart-Companionship with Him, freedom from egoic limits.

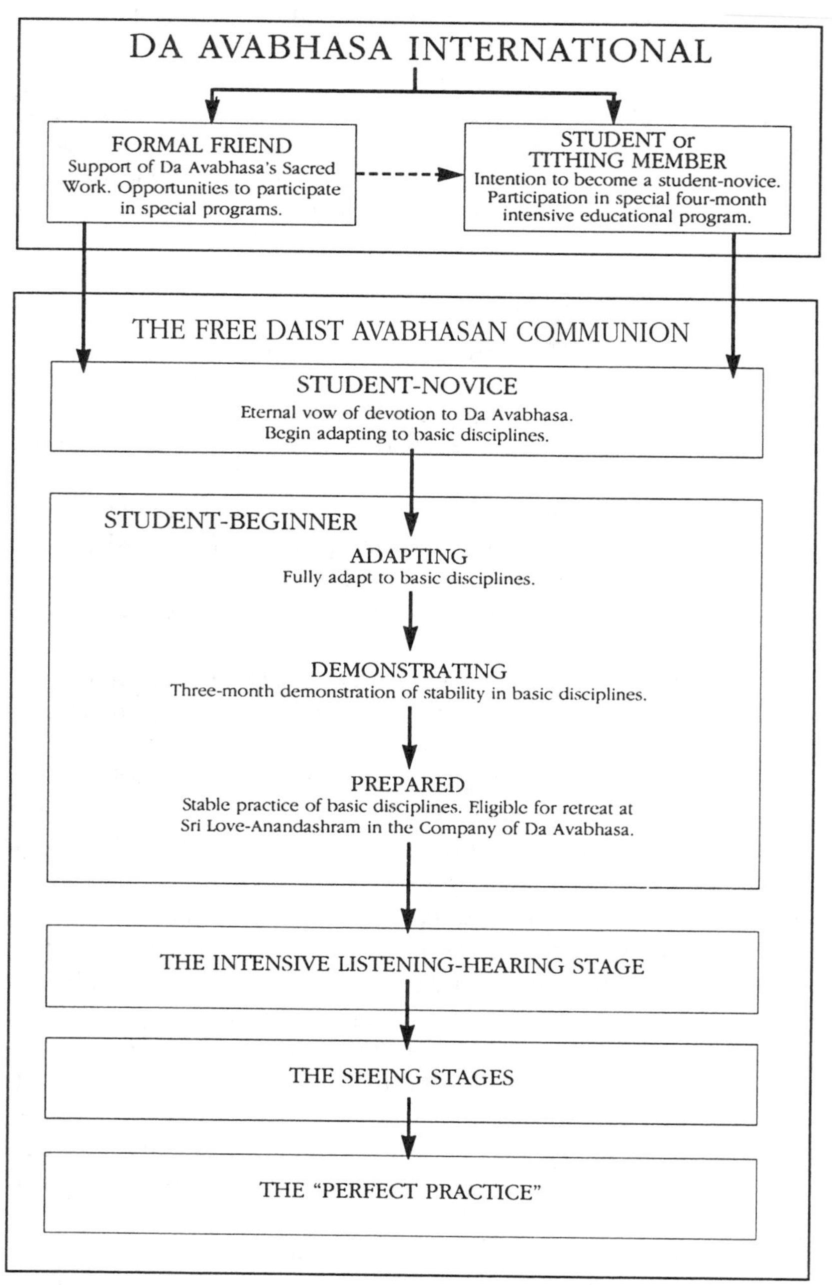
DA AVABHASA INTERNATIONAL
FORMAL FRIEND
Support of Da Avabhasa's Sacred Work. Opportunities to participate in special programs.
STUDENT or TITHING MEMBER
Intention to become a student-novice. Participation in special four-month intensive educational program.
THE FREE DAIST AVABHASAN COMMUNION
STUDENT-NOVICE
Eternal vow of devotion to Da Avabhasa. Begin adapting to basic disciplines.
STUDENT-BEGINNER
ADAPTING
Fully adapt to basic disciplines.
DEMONSTRATING
Three-month demonstration of stability in basic disciplines.
PREPARED
Stable practice of basic disciplines. Eligible for retreat at Sri Love-Anandashram in the Company of Da Avabhasa.
THE INTENSIVE LISTENING-HEARING STAGE
THE SEEING STAGES
THE "PERFECT PRACTICE"

The Practicing Orders

Sri Da Avabhasa has established three practicing orders for all His devotees who advance beyond the student-beginner level of practice—the Free Daist Avabhasan Lay Congregationist Order (or, simply, the Lay Congregationist Order), the Free Daist Avabhasan Lay Renunciate Order (or, simply, the Lay Renunciate Order), and the Naitauba (Free Daist Avabhasan) Order of Renunciates (or, simply, the Free Renunciate Order). The primary function of all of the orders is to allow each devotee to intensify his or her devotional practice in the form and manner that is most appropriate for each one. The members of any of the three orders can potentially fulfill the entire course of practice in Sri Da Avabhasa's Company, most ultimately Realizing Divine Enlightenment.

When Sri Da Avabhasa's devotee moves beyond the student-beginner stage (the first phase of formal practice in the Way of the Heart beyond the student-novice stage), he or she enters the Lay Congregationist Order. The Lay Congregationist Order is a practical service order whose members perform the many supportive practical services necessary for the work of the institution, the culture, and the community of all Free Daists. "Lay congregationists" conform every aspect of their life and practice to the Wisdom and Blessings of Sri Da Avabhasa, but their practice is not as intensive, nor as intensely renunciate, an approach to Most Perfectly self-transcending God-Realization as the practice of formal renunciates in the two renunciate orders.

Any member of the Lay Congregationist Order who develops the required signs (at any point in his or her practice of the Way of the Heart) may be accepted into the Lay Renunciate Order.

The Lay Renunciate Order is a cultural service order composed of practitioners who are especially exemplary in their practice of devotion, service, self-discipline, and meditation. Most typically, a devotee becomes eligible to apply to the Lay Renunciate Order once he or she has fulfilled the listening process and is practicing in the hearing or seeing stages. Members of the Lay Renunciate Order are to provide the inspirational and cultural leadership for the institution, the culture, and the community of Sri Da Avabhasa's devotees, and they also guide and participate in public missionary work. Their basic responsibility is to serve all practitioners of the Way of the Heart in their practice of Ishta-Guru-Bhakti Yoga and to attract others to a life of Guru-devotion. When they reach the stage of stable Spiritual Awakening, Sri Da Avabhasa's "lay renunciate" devotees begin to function as His Instruments, or means by which His Divine Grace and Awakening Power are Magnified and Transmitted to other devotees and to all beings.

Members of the Lay Renunciate Order may practice either celibacy or a truly renunciate (and, Yogically, uniquely effective) discipline of sexuality.

The Lay Renunciate Order is directly accountable to the senior practicing Order of the Way of the Heart, the Free Renunciate Order.

The Free Renunciate Order

The Free Renunciate Order is a retreat Order composed of uniquely exemplary devotees practicing in the sixth and seventh stages of life. Because of their extraordinary practice and Realization in the Company of Sri Da Avabhasa, "free renunciate" devotees are His principal human Instruments in the world. From among the fully Enlightened practitioners in the Free Renunciate Order, there will be selected after, and forever after, Sri Da Avabhasa's human Lifetime, successive "Living Murtis", or Empowered Human Agents, who will serve the magnification of His Heart-Transmission to all beings universally and perpetually.

"Murti" means "form", or "representational image". The "Living Murtis" of Sri Da Avabhasa (of which there will be only one in any given time) will not be Gurus in their own right. They will serve, rather, as a unique Living Spiritual Link to Sri Da Avabhasa, through Whom Sri Da Avabhasa's Heart-Transmission will remain continuously active and available, generation after generation.

Apart from its profound function to provide "Living Murtis" from among its membership, the Free Renunciate Order is the senior authority on all matters related to the culture of practice in the Way of the Heart and is completely essential to the perpetual continuation of authentic practice as Sri Da Avabhasa has Given it.

An Invitation to Participate in the Sacred Culture of Free Daism

The magnitude of the Gift Sri Da Avabhasa brings to humanity is being Revealed through the developing sacred culture of Free Daism, or the gathering of all those who formally practice the Way of the Heart. If you decide to participate in Da Avabhasa International and to proceed from there to become a formally acknowledged practitioner of the Way of the Heart, you will be participating in a unique undertaking—the founding of a culture and a community whose sacred practice is always founded in direct enjoyment of Divine Communion with the Divine World-Teacher, Sri Da Avabhasa. We invite you to join us and to partake of Sri Da Avabhasa's incomparable Blessing.

The Seven Stages of Life

by the Free Daist Avabhasan Writers Guild
based on the Wisdom-Teaching of Sri Da Avabhasa

What is the total process of human growth? What would occur in us if we were to grow to the full extent of our potential? Sri Da Avabhasa Offers a schema of seven stages of life which represents His Wisdom on the entire spectrum of human possibility. He has systematically described not only our physical, emotional, and mental development but also all the phases of Spiritual, Transcendental, and Divine unfolding that are potential in us, once we are mature in ordinary human terms. This unique schema, which proceeds from birth to the final phases of Divine Enlightenment, is a central reference point in Sri Da Avabhasa's Wisdom-Teaching. It is an invaluable tool for understanding how we develop as individuals and also for understanding how the Teachings and practices proposed by the various schools of religion and Spirituality fit into the whole course of human developmental possibility.

Sri Da Avabhasa describes the seven stages of life on the basis of His own Realization, as One Who has fulfilled that entire course. His testimony is literally unique. No one before Sri Da Avabhasa has Realized the State which He describes as the seventh and Most Ultimate stage of life. There are rare hints and intuitions of this Realization in the annals of Spirituality, particularly within the traditions of Hinduism and Buddhism. Sri Da Avabhasa, however, has both described and Demonstrated not only the process of Awakening to the seventh stage of life, or Divine Enlightenment, but also the progressive signs that unfold in the seventh stage Realizer. And His Wisdom-Revelation is thus a unique Guide by which we may understand all the necessary stages of our developmental "growth and outgrowing".

The first three stages of life are the stages of ordinary human growth from birth to adulthood. They are the stages of physical, emotional, and mental development, occurring in three periods of approximately seven years each (until approximately twenty-one years of age). Every individual who lives to an adult age inevitably adapts (although, in most cases, only partially) to the first three stages of life.

Stage One—Individuation: The first stage of life is the process of adapting to life as a separate individual no longer bound to the mother. Most important for the first stage child is the process of food-taking, and coming to accept sustenance from outside the mother's body. In fact, this whole stage of life could be described as an ordeal of weaning, or individuation.

Tremendous physical growth occurs in the first stage of life (the first seven or so years) and an enormous amount of learning—one begins to manage bodily energies and begins to explore the physical world. Acquiring basic motor skills is a key aspect of the first stage of life—learning to hold a spoon and eat with it, learning to walk and talk and be responsible for excretion. If the first stage of life unfolds as it should, the separation from the mother completes itself in basic terms. But there is a tendency in us to struggle with this simple individuation, or to not accept the process fully. If by the age of seven or so we are left with a chronic feeling of separation from the source of life and support, then there is something lacking in our adaptation to the first stage of life.

Stage Two—Socialization: Between the ages of five and eight years we begin to become aware of the emotional dimension of existence—how we feel and how others respond emotionally to us becomes of great importance. This is the beginning of the second stage of life, the stage of social adaptation and all that goes with it—a growing sense of sexual differentiation, awareness of the effects of one's actions on others, a testing of whether one is loved. Sri Da Avabhasa points out that in the second stage of life children are naturally psychic and sensitive to etheric energy. Children should be encouraged to feel that "you are more than what you look like", for the sake of their future Spiritual growth. The full process of growth in the second stage of life is frustrated if we become locked in patterns of feeling rejected by others, and rejecting and punishing others in return.

Stage Three—Integration: In the early to mid teens, the third stage of life becomes established. The key development of this stage is the maturing of mental ability—the capacity to use mind and speech in abstract, conceptual ways—together with the power to use discrimination and to exercise the will. On the bodily level, puberty is continuing (having begun during the later years of the second stage of life) with all its attendant bodily and emotional changes.

The purpose of the third stage of life is the integration of the human character in body, emotion, and mind, so that the emerging adult becomes a fully differentiated, or autonomous, sexual and social human character. If the process of growth in the first and the second stages of life has proceeded unhindered, then this integration can take place naturally. If, however, there have been failures of adaptation in the earlier stages—a chronic feeling of being separate and unsustained or chronic feelings of being rejected or unloved, and consequent difficulties in relating happily to others—then the process of integration is disturbed.

In fact, in most individuals, the process of the third stage of life becomes an adolescent struggle between the conflicting motives to be dependent on others and to be independent of them. This adolescent drama tends to continue throughout adult life. It is one of the signs that growth has stopped, that the work of the third stage of life was never completed.

So how does one begin to grow again? By participating in a culture of living religious and Spiritual practice that understands and rightly nurtures each stage of development. This is Sri Da Avabhasa's recommendation, and the circumstance that He has Worked to create for His devotees by establishing the Way of the Heart. Anyone, at any age, who chooses the Way of the Heart can begin the process of understanding and transcending the limits of his or her growth in the first three stages of life and in all the stages of life that follow.

Sri Da Avabhasa refers to the first three stages of life as the "foundation stages", because the ordeal of growth into human maturity is mere preparation for something far greater—for Spiritual awakening, and, ultimately, for Divine Enlightenment. This greater process begins to flower in the fourth stage of life on the basis of a profound conversion to love.

Stage Four—Spiritualization: Even while still maturing in the first three stages of life, many people devote themselves to religious practices, submitting to an ordered life of discipline and devotion. This is the beginning of establishing the disposition of the fourth stage of life, but it is only the beginning. The real leap involved in the fourth stage of life is a transition that very few ever make. It is nothing less than the breakthrough to a Spiritually-illumined life of Divine contemplation and selfless service. How does such a life become possible? Only on the basis of a heart-awakening so profound that the common human goals—to be fulfilled through bodily and mental pleasures—lose their force.

The purpose of existence for one established in the fourth stage of life is devotion—moment to moment intimacy with the Spiritual Reality, an intimacy that is real and ecstatic, and which changes one's vision of the world. Everything that appears, everything that occurs is now seen as a process full of Spirit-Presence. This new vision of existence is given through Spirit-Baptism, an infilling of Spirit-Power (usually granted by a Spiritually Awakened Master), which is described in many different religious and Spiritual traditions.

For the devotee in the Way of the Heart who has completed the listening-hearing process and entered the seeing stages of practice, Sri Da Avabhasa's Spirit-Baptism is first felt as a Current of energy descending from above the head, down through the front of the body to the perineum, or bodily base. This descent is forceful, sublime, and very effective in purifying and Spiritualizing the human personality, bringing forth the signs of radiance, peace, and universal love that characterize a Spiritually Awakened being. This descending Spirit-Baptism is one of the uniquely characteristic signs of Sri Da Avabhasa's Grace in the life of His Spiritually activated devotee. By the time the fourth stage of life is complete, not only has the Spirit-Current descended fully down the front of the body but It has turned about at the bodily base and ascended up the spine to a place deep behind the eyes (called the "ajna chakra", or sometimes the "third eye"), where It is felt to rest.

The fourth stage of life, though it represents a profound and auspicious advance beyond the foundation stages, is only the beginning of truly Spiritual growth. Sri Da Avabhasa points out that the primary presumption of one in the fourth stage of life is that God and the individual personality are inherently separate from one another. God is the Sublime "Other" with Whom one Communes and in Whom one may become ecstatically absorbed at times, even to the point of apparent union. Nevertheless, such raptures pass, and one is left with the continuing urge for union with the Divine Beloved. The individual being is still a separate ego, still searching, even though the goal of seeking is Spiritual in nature.

Stage Five—Higher Spiritual Evolution: The fifth stage of life could be described as the domain of accomplished Yogis—individuals involved in the pursuit of Enlightenment through mystical experience, such as the vision of the "blue pearl" and through the attainment of psychic powers. But it is important to note that just as exceedingly few religious practitioners fully Awaken to the Spiritual Reality in the fourth stage of life, exceedingly few would-be Yogis become fifth stage Realizers.

The important difference between the fifth stage of life and all the stages of life that precede it is that awareness on the gross physical plane is no longer the normal mode of existence. Rather, attention is constantly attracted into subtle realms—dreamlike or visionary regions of mind.

The phenomena of the fifth stage of life arise as a result of the further movement of the Spirit-Current, now in the higher regions of the brain. In the fifth stage of life the Spirit-Current moves from the ajna chakra through and beyond the crown of the head. At its point of highest ascent, the Spirit-Current triggers the Yogic meditative state traditionally called "Nirvikalpa Samadhi" ("formless ecstasy") in which all awareness of body and mind is temporarily dissolved in the Divine Self-Condition. (Sri Da Avabhasa describes this Realization as "fifth stage conditional Nirvikalpa Samadhi".) Such an experience, if rightly understood in the context of the Way of the Heart, marks an enduring change in one's being. This temporary dissolution of body and mind is a direct demonstration that the individuated self has no eternal existence or significance. Only the Divine Condition of absolute Freedom and Happiness truly exists. Once this Divine Condition has been glimpsed in the state of "formless ecstasy", one's relationship to embodied existence can be entirely different—one can begin to see the body as an arbitrary, even humorous phenomenon.

Even so, a limit remains. This great Samadhi, the culminating achievement of the fifth stage of life, is fleeting. At some point bodily consciousness returns, and so does the ache to renew that boundless, disembodied Bliss. Fifth stage conditional Nirvikalpa Samadhi, for all its profundity, is achieved on the basis of a subtle stress. It is the ultimate fruit of the Yogic strategy to escape the body by directing one's awareness upward into infinite Light.

In His description of the Way of the Heart, Sri Da Avabhasa Reveals that higher mystical experience and the achievement of profound trance states in the maturity of the fourth stage of life and in the fifth stage of life are not prerequisites for most ultimate Divine Enlightenment. In the Way of the Heart, the whole tour of the subtle planes can be bypassed, because of Sri Da Avabhasa's unique Transmission of the Love-Blissful Power of the Divine Itself. When, in the fourth stage of life, the devotee in the Way of the Heart is mature enough to be responsible for constantly receiving and "conducting" Sri Da Avabhasa's Spirit-Current, a most extraordinary process begins to take place in the body-mind. The Infusion of His Spirit-Current purifies and quickens the body-mind in every cell from the crown of the head to the very toes. Every knot in the body-mind is opened up in this ecstatic reception of Him.

When this Sublime Infusion has completed its Work, a great conversion has occurred in the body-mind. One is not susceptible to the fascinations of visionary experience, even when such experiences arise. Neither is one moved to direct one's attention up and out of the body into the infinitely ascended state of "formless ecstasy". Rather, the "tour" of mystical experience is revealed to be simply more of the futile search to be completely Happy and fulfilled. And so that whole pursuit of mystical satisfaction relaxes, and the devotee may be easily drawn beyond all habits of identification with bodily states and even beyond the subtle mind states of the fifth stage of life into a pristine understanding of Reality as Consciousness Itself.

Stage Six—Awakening to the Transcendental Self: In the sixth stage of life, one is no longer perceiving and interpreting everything from the point of view of the individuated body-mind with its desires and goals. One stands in a Transcendental Position, Awake as the Very Consciousness that is the Ground of all that exists. In that Position, one stands as the "Witness" of all that arises, even while continuing to participate in the play of life. While life goes on like a movie on a screen, one sees the greater import of Existence and the non-necessity of all that arises. This is the beginning of what Sri Da Avabhasa calls "the ultimate stages of life", or the stages of Identification with Consciousness Itself.

The sixth stage of life may include the experience of Jnana Samadhi, which, like fifth stage conditional Nirvikalpa Samadhi, is a form of temporary and conditional Realization of the Divine Self. However, fifth stage conditional Nirvikalpa Samadhi comes about through the strategy of ascent, the urge to move attention up and beyond the body-mind; in Jnana Samadhi, on the other hand, awareness of gross and subtle states is excluded by concentration in Transcendental Self-Consciousness.

Most prominent among the great sixth stage Realizers, historically, have been the Hindu and Buddhist, and in some cases Taoist, Sages who eschewed the fascinations of experience from the beginning. These great Realizers turned away from the enticements of "money, food, and sex" in the first three stages of life, as well as from the attractions of devotional (fourth stage) rapture and of Yogic (fifth stage) mysticism. Instead, the Sages of the sixth stage of life have traditionally contemplated the freedom and purity of Consciousness—to the degree of Realizing that Consciousness Itself, eternal and Prior to any mortal form or temporary experience, is our True Condition, or True Self.

But even deep resting in the freedom of Transcendental Consciousness is not Most Perfect Enlightenment. Why not? Because there is still a stress involved. Sixth stage Realizers have one last barrier to Divine Self-Realization that must be penetrated. Sixth stage practice and Realization is expressed by turning within, away from all conditional objects and experiences (including the energies and the movements of attention of one's own body-mind), and concentrating upon What is felt to be the Source of individual consciousness. Thus, the root of egoity is still alive. The search still remains, in its most primitive form. The sixth stage of life is the search to identify with Pure Consciousness Prior to and exclusive of phenomena.

Stage Seven—Divine Enlightenment: The Realization of the seventh stage of life is uniquely Revealed and Given by Sri Da Avabhasa. It is release from all the egoic limitations of the previous stages of life. Remarkably, the seventh stage Awakening, which is Sri Da Avabhasa's Gift to His devotees who have completed the developmental course of the first six stages of life, is <u>not an experience at all</u>. The true Nature of everything is simply obvious. Now the Understanding arises that every apparent "thing" is Eternally, Perfectly the same as Reality, Consciousness, Happiness, Truth, or God. And that Understanding is Supreme Love-Bliss.

Sri Da Avabhasa calls this Divine Awakeness "Open Eyes" and also "seventh stage Sahaj Samadhi" ("Sahaj" meaning "natural", or inherent, and "Samadhi" meaning exalted State). No longer is there any need to seek meditative seclusion in order to Realize perpetual Identification with the One Divine Reality. The Ecstatic and world-embracing Confession "There is Only God" is native to one who enjoys the State of "Open Eyes". Consciousness is no longer felt to be divorced from the world of forms, but Consciousness Itself is understood and seen to be the very Nature, Source, and Substance of that world. And so the life of the seventh stage Realizer, Most Perfectly Awake by Grace of Sri Da Avabhasa, becomes the Love-Blissful process of Divinely Recognizing, or intuitively acknowledging, whatever arises to be only a modification of Consciousness Itself.

The Divinely Self-Realized Being is literally "Enlightened". The Light of Divine Being Flows in him or her in a continuous circuitry of Love-Bliss that rises in an S-shaped curve from the right side of the heart to a Matrix of Light above and Beyond the crown of the head. This is Amrita Nadi, the "Channel of Immortal Bliss", mentioned in the esoteric Hindu Spiritual tradition, but fully described for the first time by Sri Da Avabhasa Himself. After His Divine Re-Awakening in 1970, Sri Da Avabhasa experienced the "Regeneration" of this Current of Love-Bliss, and He came to understand Amrita Nadi as the Original Form of the Divine Self-Radiance in the human body-mind (and in all conditional beings and forms).

In the seventh stage of life, or the context of Divine Enlightenment, the developmental process (which is now the Divine Yoga of Amrita Nadi) continues. Sri Da Avabhasa, the first to Realize the seventh stage of life, is also the first to describe this most profoundly esoteric aspect of our Divine potential. He describes the seventh stage of life as having four phases: Divine Transfiguration, Divine Transformation, Divine Indifference, and Divine Translation.

In the phase of Divine Transfiguration, the Realizer's whole body is Infused by Love-Bliss, and he or she Radiantly Demonstrates active Love.

In the following phase of Divine Transformation, the subtle or psychic dimension of the body-mind is fully Illumined, which may result in extraordinary Powers, Grace-Given by Sri Da Avabhasa, of healing, longevity, and the ability to release obstacles from the world and from the lives of others.

Eventually, Divine Indifference ensues, which is spontaneous and profound Resting in the "Deep" of Consciousness Itself, with progressively less and less noticing of the manifested worlds.

Divine Translation is the ultimate "Event" of the entire process of Awakening—the Outshining of all noticing of objective conditions through the infinitely magnified Force of Consciousness Itself. Divine Translation is the Destiny beyond all destinies, from Which there is no return to the realms.

The experience of being so overwhelmed by the Divine Radiance that all appearances fade away may occur temporarily from time to time during the seventh stage of life. But when that Most Love-Blissful Swoon (or Moksha-Bhava Samadhi) becomes permanent, Divine Translation occurs and the body-mind is inevitably relinquished in death. Then there is only Eternal Inherence in the Divine Domain of unqualified Happiness and Joy.

Sri Da Avabhasa has frequently described the unfolding Mystery of the seventh stage of life through the image of crocks baking in a furnace:

SRI DA AVABHASA: When you place newly made clay crocks in a furnace of great heat to dry and harden the crockery, at first the crocks become red-hot and seem to be surrounded and pervaded by a reddish glow, but they are still defined. Eventually the fire becomes white-hot, and its radiation becomes so pervasive, so bright, that you can no longer make out the separate figures of the crocks.

This is the significance of Divine Translation. At first, conditions of existence are Transfigured by the inherent Radiance of Divine Being. Ultimately, through Self-Abiding and through Divinely Recognizing all forms, in effect all forms are Outshined by that Radiance. This is the Law of life. Life lived Lawfully is fulfilled in Outshining, or the transcendence of cosmic Nature. In the meantime, cosmic Nature is simply Divinely Transfigured, and relations are Divinely Transfigured, by the Power of the Divine Self-Position. [February 9, 1983]

◆ ◆ ◆

The religious and Spiritual traditions of mankind characteristically conceive of human life as a "Great Path of Return", a struggle to be reunited with the Divine Source of existence. From Sri Da Avabhasa's viewpoint, this is an error. The Way of the Heart is founded in "radical" understanding, or constant restoration to the intuition of present Happiness, present God. Thus, although Sri Da Avabhasa allows for and fully explains all the developmental signs or stages of life through which His devotee may pass, the Way of the Heart is not purposed to "progress through" the stages of life. The entire process is founded in the Wisdom of the seventh stage from the very beginning—and thus is one of release, of surrendering, progressively, via heart-Communion with Sri Da Avabhasa all obstructions in body, mind, and psyche that prevent that unqualified Divine Enjoyment.

Because the ultimate non-necessity of the stages of life and our real, present Inherence in the Divine State of Happiness is always utterly obvious to Him, Sri Da Avabhasa can speak Ecstatically of the seven stages of life as seven "jokes":

SRI DA AVABHASA: Living the stages of life, though a profound and necessary gesture, is ultimately foolishness. The seven stages of life are stages of laughter, each of which must, in its turn, become a great laugh to you. You must be able to feel the pleasure of self-forgetting in the face of each stage of experience before you can go on to complete the next stage. In your present level of realization, however, you have not yet laughed at any of the stages of life. You are still burdened by them, still carrying them around, still being tested by them.

Even the seventh stage of life, you will see, is a colossal lot of foolishness. The only way to move through the seventh stage is to laugh your head off. The seventh stage of life must become a laughing matter, along with all the rest of your body and its stages of growth. You must get the seventh joke, the last laugh. That joke is eternal, and its Humor is infinite Love-Bliss. [February 14, 1979]

An Invitation to Support the Way of the Heart

Da Avabhasa's sole purpose is to act as a Source of continuous Divine Grace for everyone, everywhere. In that spirit, He is a Free Renunciate and He owns nothing. Those who have made gestures in support of Da Avabhasa's Work have found that their generosity is returned in many Blessings that are full of His healing, transforming, and Liberating Grace—and those Blessings flow not only directly to them as the beneficiaries of His Work, but to many others, even all others. At the same time, all tangible gifts of support help secure and nurture Da Avabhasa's Work in necessary and practical ways, again similarly benefiting the whole world. Because all this is so, supporting His Work is the most auspicious form of financial giving, and we happily extend to you an invitation to serve the Way of the Heart through your financial support.

You may make a financial contribution in support of the Work of Da Avabhasa at any time. You may also, if you choose, request that your contribution be used for one or more specific purposes of Free Daism. For example, you may be moved to help support and develop Sri Love-Anandashram, Da Avabhasa's Great Hermitage Ashram and Empowered Retreat Sanctuary in Fiji, and the circumstance provided there for Da Avabhasa and the other "free renunciates" who practice there (all of whom own nothing).

You may make a contribution for this specific purpose directly to the Sri Love-Anandashram (Naitauba) Trust, the charitable trust that is responsible for Sri Love-Anandashram. To make such a contribution, simply mail your check to the Sri Love-Anandashram (Naitauba) Trust, P.O. Box 4744, Samabula, Fiji.

If you would like to make such a contribution and you are a United States taxpayer, we recommend that you make your contribution to the Free Daist Communion, so as to secure a tax deduction for your contribution under United States tax laws. To do this, mail your contribution to the Advocacy Department of the Free Daist Avabhasan Communion, 12040 North Seigler Springs Road, Middletown, California, 95461, USA, and indicate that you would like it to be used in support of Sri Love-Anandashram.

You may also request that your contribution, or a part of it, be used for one or more of the other purposes of Free Daism. For example, you may request that your contribution be used to help publish the sacred Literature of Da Avabhasa, or to support either of the other two Sanctuaries He has Empowered, or to maintain the Sacred Archives that preserve Da Avabhasa's recorded Talks and Writings, or to publish audio and video recordings of Da Avabhasa.

If you would like your contribution to benefit one or more of these specific purposes, please mail your contribution to the Advocacy Department of the Free Daist Avabhasan Communion at the above address, and indicate how you would like your gift to be used.

If you would like more information about these and other gifting options, or if you would like assistance in describing or making a contribution, please contact the Advocacy Department of the Free Daist Avabhasan Communion, either by writing to the address shown above or by telephoning (707) 928-4096, FAX (707) 928-4062.

PLANNED GIVING

We also invite you to consider making a planned gift in support of the Work of Da Avabhasa. Many have found that through planned giving they can make a far more significant gesture of support than they would otherwise be able to make. Many have also found that by making a planned gift they are able to realize substantial tax advantages.

There are numerous ways to make a planned gift, including making a gift in your Will, or in your life insurance, or in a charitable trust.

If you would like to make a gift in your Will in support of Sri Love-Anandashram, simply include in your Will the statement "I give the Sri Love-Anandashram (Naitauba) Trust, an Australian charitable trust, P.O. Box 4744, Samabula, Fiji, _______" [inserting in the blank the amount or description of your contribution].

If you would like to make a gift in your Will to benefit other purposes of Free Daism, simply include in your Will the statement "I give the Free Daist Avabhasan Communion, a California nonprofit corporation, 12040 North Seigler Springs Road, Middletown, California 95461, USA, _______" [inserting in the blank the amount or description of your contribution]. You may, if you choose, also describe in your Will the specific Free Daist purpose or purposes you would like your gift to support. If you are a United States taxpayer, gifts made in your Will to the Free Daist Avabhasan Communion will be free of estate taxes and will also reduce any estate taxes payable on the remainder of your estate.

To make a gift in your life insurance, simply name as the beneficiary (or one of the beneficiaries) of your life insurance policy the Free Daist organization of your choice, according to the foregoing descriptions and addresses. If you are a United States taxpayer, you may receive significant tax benefits if you make a contribution to the Free Daist Avabhasan Communion through your life insurance.

We also invite you to consider establishing or participating in a charitable trust for the benefit of Free Daism. If you are a United States taxpayer, you may find that such a trust will provide you with immediate tax savings and assured income for life, while at the same time enabling you to provide for your family, for your other heirs, and for the Work of Da Avabhasa as well.

The Advocacy Department of the Free Daist Avabhasan Communion will be happy to provide you with further information about these and other planned gifting options, and happy to provide you or your attorney with assistance in describing or making a planned gift in support of the Work of Da Avabhasa.

Further Notes to the Reader

An Invitation to Responsibility

The Way of the Heart that Da Avabhasa has Revealed is an invitation to everyone to assume real responsibility for his or her life. As Da Avabhasa has Said in *The Dawn Horse Testament,* "If any one Is Interested In The Realization Of The Heart, Let him or her First Submit (Formally, and By Heart) To Me, and (Thereby) Commence The Ordeal Of self-Observation, self-Understanding, and self-Transcendence." Therefore, participation in the Way of the Heart requires a real struggle with oneself, and not at all a struggle with Da Avabhasa, or with others.

All who study the Way of the Heart or take up its practice should remember that they are responding to a Call to become responsible for themselves. They should understand that they, not Da Avabhasa or others, are responsible for any decision they may make or action they take in the course of their lives of study or practice. This has always been true, and it is true whatever the individual's involvement in the Way of the Heart, be it as one who studies Da Avabhasa's Wisdom-Teaching, or as a Friend of or a participant in Da Avabhasa International, or as a formally acknowledged member of the Free Daist Avabhasan Communion.

Honoring and Protecting the Sacred Word through Perpetual Copyright

Since ancient times, practitioners of true religion and Spirituality have valued, above all, time spent in the Company of the Sat-Guru, or one who has, to any degree, Realized God, Truth, or Reality, and who thus Serves the awakening process in others. Such practitioners understand that the Sat-Guru literally Transmits his or her (Realized) State to every one (and every thing) with which he or she comes in contact. Through this Transmission, objects, environments, and rightly prepared individuals with which the Sat-Guru has contact can become Empowered, or Imbued with the Sat-Guru's Transforming Power. It is by this process of Empowerment that things and beings are made truly and literally sacred, and things so sanctified thereafter function as a Source of the Sat-Guru's Blessing for all who understand how to make right and sacred use of them.

Sat-Gurus of any degree of Realization and all that they Empower are, therefore, truly Sacred Treasures, for they help draw the practitioner more quickly into the process of Realization. Cultures of true Wisdom have always understood that such Sacred Treasures are precious (and fragile) Gifts to humanity, and that they should be honored, protected, and reserved for right sacred use. Indeed, the word "sacred" means "set apart", and thus protected, from the secular world. Da Avabhasa has Conformed His body-mind most Perfectly to the Divine Self, and He is thus the most Potent Source of Blessing-Transmission of God, Truth, or Reality, the ultimate Sat-Guru. He has for many years Empowered, or made sacred, special places and things, and these now Serve as His Divine Agents, or as literal expressions and extensions of His Blessing-Transmission. Among these Empowered Sacred Treasures is His Wisdom-Teaching, which is Full of His Transforming Power. This Blessed and Blessing Wisdom-Teaching has Mantric Force, or the literal Power to Serve God-Realization in those who are Graced to receive it.

Therefore, Da Avabhasa's Wisdom-Teaching must be perpetually honored and protected, "set apart" from all possible interference and wrong use. The Free Daist Avabhasan Communion, which is the fellowship of devotees of Da Avabhasa, is committed to the perpetual preservation and right honoring of the sacred Wisdom-Teaching of the Way of the Heart. But it is also true that in order to fully accomplish this we must find support in the world-society in which we live and from the laws under which we live. Thus, we call for a world-society and for laws that acknowledge the Sacred, and that permanently protect It from insensitive, secular interference and wrong use of any kind. We call for, among other things, a system of law that acknowledges that the Wisdom-Teaching of the Way of the Heart, in all Its forms, is, because of Its sacred nature, protected by perpetual copyright.

We invite others who respect the Sacred to join with us in this call and in working toward its realization. And, even in the meantime, we claim that all copyrights to the Wisdom-Teaching of Da Avabhasa and the other sacred literature and recordings of the Way of the Heart are of perpetual duration.

We make this claim on behalf of Sri Love-Anandashram (Naitauba) Pty Ltd, which, acting as trustee of the Sri Love-Anandashram (Naitauba) Trust, is the holder of all such copyrights.

Da Avabhasa and the Sacred Treasures of Free Daism

Those who Realize God to any degree bring great Blessing and Divine Possibility for the world. Such Realizers Accomplish universal Blessing Work that benefits everything and everyone. They also Work very specifically and intentionally with individuals who approach them as their devotees, and with those places where they reside, and to which they Direct their specific Regard for the sake of perpetual Spiritual Empowerment. This was understood in traditional Spiritual cultures, and those cultures therefore found ways to honor Realizers, to provide circumstances for them where they were free to do their Spiritual Work without obstruction or interference.

Those who value Da Avabhasa's Realization and Service have always endeavored to appropriately honor Him in this traditional way, to provide a circumstance where He is completely Free to do His Divine Work. Since 1983, Da Avabhasa has resided principally on the Island of Naitauba, Fiji, also known as Sri Love-Anandashram. This island has been set aside by Free Daists worldwide as a Place for Da Avabhasa to do His universal Blessing Work for the sake of everyone and His specific Work with those who pilgrimage to Sri Love-Anandashram to receive the special Blessing of coming into His physical Company.

Da Avabhasa is a legal renunciate. He owns nothing and He has no secular or religious institutional function. He Functions only in Freedom. He, and the other members of the Naitauba (Free Daist Avabhasan) Order of Renunciates, the senior renunciate order of Free Daism, are provided for by the Sri Love-Anandashram (Naitauba) Trust, which also provides for Sri Love-Anandashram altogether and ensures the permanent integrity of Da Avabhasa's Wisdom-Teaching, both in its archival and in its published forms. This Trust, which functions only in Fiji, exists exclusively to provide for these Sacred Treasures of Free Daism.

Outside Fiji, the institution which has developed in response to Da Avabhasa's Wisdom-Teaching and universal Blessing is known as "The Free Daist Avabhasan

Communion". The Free Daist Avabhasan Communion is active worldwide in making Da Avabhasa's Wisdom-Teaching available to all, in offering guidance to all who are moved to respond to His Offering, and in providing for the other Sacred Treasures of Free Daism, including the Mountain Of Attention Sanctuary (in California) and Tumomama Sanctuary (in Hawaii). In addition to the central corporate entity of the Free Daist Avabhasan Communion, which is based in California, there are numerous regional entities which serve congregations of Da Avabhasa's devotees in various places throughout the world.

Free Daists worldwide have also established numerous community organizations, through which they provide for many of their common and cooperative community needs, including needs relating to housing, food, businesses, medical care, schools, and death and dying. By attending to these and all other ordinary human concerns and affairs via self-transcending cooperation and mutual effort, Da Avabhasa's devotees constantly free their energy and attention, both personally and collectively, for practice of the Way of the Heart and for service to Da Avabhasa, to Sri Love-Anandashram, to the other Sacred Treasures of Free Daism, and to the Free Daist Avabhasan Communion.

All of the organizations that have evolved in response to Da Avabhasa and His Offering are legally separate from one another, and each has its own purpose and function. He neither directs, nor bears responsibility for, the activities of these organizations. Again, He Functions only in Freedom. These organizations represent the collective intention of Free Daists worldwide not only to provide for the Sacred Treasures of Free Daism, but also to make Da Avabhasa's Offering of the Way of the Heart universally available to all.

A Selection of the Sacred Literature of Da Avabhasa

NEW EXPANDED EDITION
The Knee of Listening
The Early-Life Ordeal and The "Radical" Spiritual Realization of The Divine World-Teacher and True Heart-Master, Da Avabhasa (The "Bright")

This new, unabridged edition of Da Avabhasa's autobiography (which sold over 100,000 copies in its previous edition) has been called the greatest Spiritual autobiography ever written. Since its first publication in 1972, *The Knee of Listening* has become an acknowledged classic of modern Spiritual literature—essential reading for anyone interested in Spiritual life.

In Part I, Da Avabhasa recounts His first 31 years—the poignant, often hilarious, always astonishing story of a Being who was absolutely determined to discover the Truth of our existence, and did. He describes His Illumined birth and infancy, His experiments with every kind of possible human experience—from the Western pursuits of "money, food, and sex" to the mystical experiences of the East—and His Transcendence of all of it.

Parts II and III feature Da Avabhasa's earliest Essays on the process of "radical" understanding He Offers to everyone, and the final section of the book tells the remarkable Story of His Life and Work over the two decades since *The Knee of Listening* was originally published.

$18.95,* quality paperback; $39.95, cloth
605 pages

NEW EXPANDED EDITION
The Method of the Siddhas
Talks on the Spiritual Technique of the Saviors of Mankind

In these provocative dialogues, Da Avabhasa discusses the sublime import of Spiritual life and Reveals the secret of the profound and transforming relationship that He Offers everyone.

Self-help is not the ultimate answer. At best, it produces a better-adjusted, more functional ego. How could it produce anything else?

As *The Method of the Siddhas* makes clear, the sacred relationship with an Awakened Being (a "Siddha") has always been the most effective means for Spiritual growth. But few have been daring enough to engage such a relationship. The conversations in *The Method of the Siddhas* are unique glimpses into how that relationship is conducted.

I first read The Method of the Siddhas *twenty years ago and it changed everything. It presented something new to my awareness: One who understood, who was clearly awake, who had penetrated fear and death, who spoke English (eloquently!), and who was alive and available!*

Ray Lynch
composer, *Deep Breakfast, No Blue Thing,* and *The Sky of Mind*

$14.95, quality paperback, 420 pages

*All prices are in U.S. dollars

Easy Death

Spiritual Discourses and Essays on the Inherent and Ultimate Transcendence of Death and Everything Else

In this major revision of the popular first edition of His Talks and Essays on death, Da Avabhasa Reveals the esoteric secrets of the death process and Offers a wealth of practical instruction.

- Near-death experiences
- How to prepare for an "easy" death
- How to serve the dying
- Where do we go when we die?
- Our Ultimate Destiny
- The truth about reincarnation
- How to participate consciously in the dying (and living) process

An exciting, stimulating, and thought-provoking book that adds immensely to the literature on the phenomena of life and death. Thank you for this masterpiece.

Elisabeth Kübler-Ross, M.D.
author, *On Death and Dying*

$14.95, quality paperback
432 pages

Free Daism

THE ETERNAL, ANCIENT, AND NEW RELIGION OF GOD-REALIZATION
An Introduction to the God-Realizing Way of Life Revealed by The Divine World-Teacher and True Heart-Master, Da Avabhasa (The "Bright")

Addressed to new readers and written in a highly accessible style, *Free Daism* is an introduction to Da Avabhasa's Life and Work, the fundamentals of His Wisdom-Teaching, the Guru-devotee relationship in His Blessing Company, the principles and practices of the Way of the Heart, and life in the community of His devotees. This book is a comprehensive and engaging introduction to all aspects of the religion of Free Daism, the Liberating Way that Da Avabhasa has made available for all.

$17.95, quality paperback
376 pages

The Love-Ananda Gita (The Wisdom-Song Of Non-Separateness)

The "Simple" Revelation-Book Of Da Kalki, The Divine World-Teacher and True Heart-Master, Da Love-Ananda Hridayam

In 108 verses of incredible beauty and simplicity, *The Love-Ananda Gita* reveals the very essence of the Way of the Heart—Contemplation of Da Avabhasa as the Realizer and Revealer of the Divinely Awakened Condition. Then, in an extensive section of commentary following the verses, Da Avabhasa leads us into a full understanding of the details of this Contemplative practice. Finally, in a collection of inspiring stories from His devotees, the effectiveness of this practice is demonstrated.

Therefore, because of My always constant, Full, and Perfect Blessing Grace, it is possible for any one to practice the Way of the Heart, and that practice readily (and more and more constantly) Realizes pleasurable oneness (or inherently Love-Blissful Unity) with whatever and all that presently arises. . . .

Da Avabhasa
The Love-Ananda Gita, verse 78

This is the birth of fundamental and radical Scripture.

Richard Grossinger
author, *Planet Medicine, The Night Sky,* and *Waiting for the Martian Express*

[Future editions of *The Love-Ananda Gita* will be titled *The Da Love-Ananda Gita and* will be published with the following attribution: The Simple Revelation-Book Of The Divine World-Teacher and True Heart-Master, Da Avabhasa (The "Bright").]

$19.95, quality paperback
818 pages

The Dawn Horse Testament

The Testament Of Secrets Of The Divine World-Teacher and True Heart-Master, Da Avabhasa (The "Bright")

This monumental volume is the most comprehensive description of the Spiritual process ever written. It is also the most detailed summary of the Way of the Heart. *The Dawn Horse Testament* is an astounding, challenging, and breath-taking Window to the Divine Reality.

The Dawn Horse Testament *is the most ecstatic, most profound, most complete, most radical, most comprehensive single spiritual text ever to be penned and confessed by the Human-Transcendental Spirit.*

Ken Wilber
author, *Up from Eden* and *A Sociable God*

$24.95, quality paperback
$45.00, cloth
8-1/2" x 11" format, 820 pages

The Hymn Of The True Heart-Master

(The New Revelation-Book Of The Ancient and Eternal Religion Of Devotion To The God-Realized Adept)

This book is Da Avabhasa's passionate proclamation of the human Guru as the supreme means of Enlightenment. In 108 poetic verses, freely evolved from the traditional *Guru Gita*, Da Avabhasa extols the great virtues of worship of and service and devotion to one's chosen Guru. This central Hymn is followed by a selection of Da Avabhasa's most potent Talks and Essays on the nature, primacy, and laws of the Guru-devotee relationship. The book concludes with moving stories and confessions by His devotees about the sacred trial of growth and awakening in Da Avabhasa's Company. A most beautiful and inspirational text for anyone interested in Spiritual growth.

I do feel this Hymn will be of immense help to aspirants for a divine life. I am thankful that I had an opportunity to read and benefit by it.

M. P. Pandit
author, *The Upanishads: Gateways of Knowledge and Studies in the Tantras and the Veda*

$19.95, quality paperback
$27.95, cloth
450 pages

The Da Upanishad

The Short Discourses on self-Renunciation, God-Realization, and the Illusion of Relatedness

In this sublime collection of Essays, Da Avabhasa Offers an unsurpassed description of both the precise mechanism of egoic delusion and the nature, process, and ultimate fulfillment of the Sacred Ordeal of Divine Self-Realization.

The Da Upanishad *is a work of great linguistic beauty, as well as a remarkable description of the "before" of self and existence. It is a book about the direct realization of Consciousness, characterized by intellectual precision, but also with a depth of feeling that works away beneath the surface of the words.*

Robert E. Carter
author, *The Nothingness Beyond God*

[Future editions of this book will be titled *The Da Avabhasa Upanishad*]

$19.95, quality paperback
$39.95, cloth
514 pages

The ego-"I" is the Illusion of Relatedness

Published here in book form, this central Essay from *The Da Upanishad* is an indispensable introduction to the esoteric Wisdom-Instruction of Da Avabhasa. It includes His unique commentaries on dietary and sexual Yoga, His Divinely Enlightened secrets on how to responsibly master and transcend all dimensions of our existence, and passages of sublime beauty in which He Gives us glimpses of the absolute Divine Condition.

$8.95, quality paperback
192 pages

The Basket of Tolerance

A Guide to Perfect Understanding of the One and Great Tradition of Mankind

A unique gift to the world—an overview of the traditions of humanity from the viewpoint of the Divinely Enlightened Adept! This comprehensive bibliography (listing more than 2,500 publications) of the world's historical traditions of truly human culture, practical self-discipline, perennial religion, universal religious mysticism, "esoteric" (but now openly communicated) Spirituality, Transcendental Wisdom, and Perfect (or Divine) Enlightenment, is compiled, presented, and extensively annotated by Da Avabhasa. The summary of His Instruction on the Great Tradition of human Wisdom and the sacred ordeal of Spiritual practice and Realization. (forthcoming)

The Perfect Practice

This book is Da Avabhasa's summary distillation of the Wisdom and Process of practice in the ultimate stages of life in the Way of the Heart. In it, Da Avabhasa wields His Great Sword of Most Perfectly self-transcending God-Realization, dispatching the dragons of egoic delusion, and all limited truths. He Calls us, and Draws us, to Realize the Very Divine Consciousness that is Radiantly Free, beyond all bondage to the limited states of the body, mind, and world.

The Perfect Practice includes the text of *The Lion Sutra*, Da Avabhasa's poetic Revelation of the esoteric technicalities and Liberated Freedom of the "Perfect Practice", and the text of *The Liberator (Eleutherios)*, in which He Epitomizes, in beautiful prose, the simpler approach to that same ultimate, or "Perfect", Practice leading most directly to Divine Awakening.
(forthcoming)

Scientific Proof of the Existence of God Will Soon Be Announced by the White House!

Prophetic Wisdom about the Myths and Idols of mass culture and popular religious cultism, the new priesthood of scientific and political materialism, and the secrets of Enlightenment hidden in the body of Man

Speaking as a modern Prophet, Da Avabhasa combines His urgent critique of present-day society with a challenge to create true sacred community based on God-Communion and a Spiritual Vision of human destiny. A masterpiece of prophetic and groundbreaking commentary!

A powerfully effective "de-hypnotizer" . . . that will not let you rest until you see clearly—and so seeing, choose to act. In modern society's time of troubles, this is a much needed book.

Willis Harman, president
The Institute of Noetic Sciences

$12.95, quality paperback
430 pages

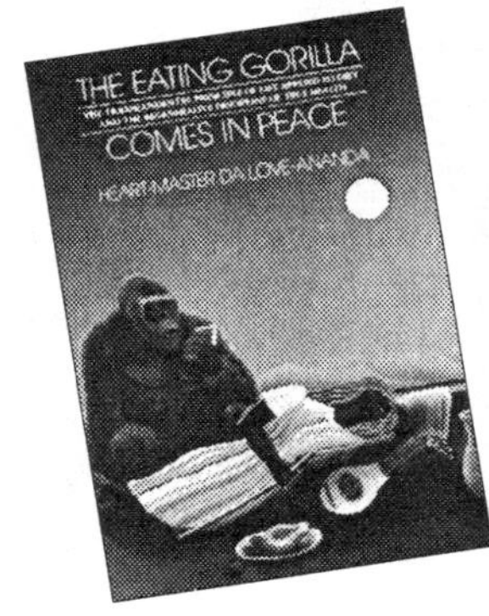

The Transmission of Doubt
Talks and Essays on the Transcendence of Scientific Materialism through "Radical" Understanding

Da Avabhasa's "radical" alternative to scientific materialism, the ideology of our time. The discourses in this book help each of us to grow beyond the linear, left-brained point of view so prevalent in today's society.

The Transmission of Doubt *is the most profound examination of the scientific enterprise from a spiritual point of view that I have ever read.*

Charles T. Tart
author, *Waking Up*
editor, *Altered States of Consciousness*

$10.95, quality paperback
484 pages

The Eating Gorilla Comes in Peace
The Transcendental Principle of Life Applied to Diet and the Regenerative Discipline of True Health

In this book, Da Avabhasa Offers Enlightened Wisdom on diet, health, healing, and the sacred approach to birthing and dying. The book discusses:

- The true principle of health as Love, or the feeling-connection to Infinite Life
- The root of many food obsessions and common health failures
- How to compensate for physical and emotional imbalances through right diet and health practices
- How right diet affects your ability to have a pleasurable, mature, and regenerative sex-life
- Fasting, herbal remedies, and dietary modifications to purify and regenerate the body
- And much, much more

$16.95, quality paperback
565 pages

Divine Distraction
A Guide to the Guru-Devotee Relationship, The Supreme Means of God-Realization, as Fully Revealed for the First Time by the Divine World-Teacher and True Heart-Master, Da Avabhasa (The "Bright")
by James Steinberg

In this wonderful book, a longtime devotee of Da Avabhasa discusses the joys and challenges, the lore and laws, of the most potent form of Spiritual practice: the love relationship with the God-Man. Along with many illuminating passages from the Wisdom-Teaching of Da Avabhasa, *Divine Distraction* includes humorous, insightful, and heart-moving stories from His devotees, as well as other Teachings and stories from the world's Great Tradition of religion and Spirituality. Essential for anybody who wants to know first-hand about the time-honored liberating relationship between Guru and devotee.

$12.95, quality paperback
288 pages

Feeling Without Limitation
AWAKENING TO THE TRUTH BEYOND FEAR, SORROW, AND ANGER
A Spiritual Discourse by The Divine World-Teacher and True Heart-Master, Da Avabhasa (The "Bright")

A woman once confessed to Da Avabhasa that she often felt emotionally frozen, unable to allow herself to really feel and release anger, sorrow and fear. Da Avabhasa's response to her is illuminating to us all.

In the very direct and simple Discourse contained in this book, Da Avabhasa presents His fundamental insight into human suffering, seeking, and the nature of Liberation. Also included in this brief introductory volume are three remarkable personal testimonies about Da Avabhasa's life-transforming Divine Influence.

$4.95, paper
112 pages

The Incarnation of Love
"Radical" Spiritual Wisdom and Practical Instruction on self-Transcending Love and Service in All Relationships

This book collects Da Avabhasa's Talks and Writings on giving and receiving love. A profound guide to transcending reactivity, releasing guilt, expressing love verbally, forgiving, cooperative living, and many other aspects of love and sevice in all relationships.

$13.95, quality paperback
314 pages

The Heart's Shout
THE LIBERATING WISDOM OF DA AVABHASA
Essential Talks and Essays by The Divine World-Teacher and True Heart-Master, Da Avabhasa (The "Bright")

The Heart's Shout is a powerful and illuminating introduction to Da Avabhasa's Wisdom-Teaching on such topics as the sacred relationship to Da Avabhasa; the awakening of self-understanding; the Nature of the Divine Reality; the Great Tradition of religion, Spirituality, and practical wisdom; human politics; truly human culture; cooperative community; science and scientific materialism; death and the purpose of life; the secrets of love and sex; the foundations of practice in the Way of the Heart; Da Avabhasa's "Crazy Wisdom"; and Divine Self-Realization.

$14.95, quality paperback
360 pages

The books listed on these pages are only a selection from the titles by and about Da Avabhasa that are currently available. For a complete listing of books and periodicals, as well as audiotaped and videotaped Discourses by Da Avabhasa, please send for your free Dawn Horse Press Catalogue.

Ordering the Books of Da Avabhasa

To order books, or to receive your free Dawn Horse Press Catalogue, send your order to:

THE DAWN HORSE PRESS
12040 North Seigler Springs Road
Middletown, CA 95461, U.S.A.
or

Call TOLL FREE (800) 524-4941
Outside the U.S.A. call
(707) 928-4936

We accept Visa, MasterCard, personal check, and money order. In the USA, please add $4.00 for the first book and $1.00 for each additional book. California residents add 7-1/4% sales tax. Outside the USA, please add $7.00 for the first book and $3.00 for each additional book. Checks and money orders should be made payable to the Dawn Horse Press.

GLOSSARY

Advaita Vedanta The Sanskrit word "Vedanta" literally means the "end of the Vedas" (the most ancient body of Indian Scripture), and the term is used to refer to the principal philosophical tradition of Hinduism. "Advaita" means "non-dual". Advaita Vedanta, then, is a philosophy of non-dualism, the origins of which lie in the ancient esoteric Teaching that Brahman, or the Divine Being, is the only Reality. According to Advaita Vedanta, the apparent self, the world, and all manifestation have no independent existence but merely arise in and as that one Divine Reality.

advanced and ultimate stages of life Sri Da Avabhasa uses the term "advanced" to describe the fourth stage of life and the fifth stage of life. He reserves the term "ultimate" to describe the sixth stage of life and the seventh stage of life.

(See "The Seven Stages of Life" on pp. 296-304 of this book.)

"advanced" context of the fourth stage of life (See **three [possible] contexts of the fourth stage of life in the Way of the Heart**.)

Agency When Sri Da Avabhasa Speaks and Writes of the Agents of His Divine Blessing Work, He is referring to all the Means that may serve as Vehicles of His Divine Grace and Awakening Power. The first Means of Agency that have been fully established by Sri Da Avabhasa are the Wisdom-Teaching of the Way of the Heart, the three Retreat Sanctuaries that He has Empowered, and the many Objects and Articles that He has Empowered for the sake of His devotees' Remembrance of Him and reception of His Heart-Blessing. In any time after Sri Da Avabhasa's human Lifetime, only one from among Sri Da Avabhasa's Divinely Awakened "free renunciate" devotees will serve the Spiritual, Transcendental, and Divine function of His human Agents in relationship to other devotees, all beings, the psycho-physical world, and the total cosmos.

See p. 295 for a description of "free renunciate" devotees.

ajna chakra Also known as the "single eye", the "mystic eye", or the "third eye". It is the subtle center, or chakra, located between and behind the eyebrows and associated with the brain core.

Amrita Nadi The Sanskrit term "Amrita Nadi" literally means "Channel (or Current) of Immortal Bliss". It is the ultimate "organ", or Root-Structure, of the body-mind, Realized in the seventh stage of life. It arises in the right side of the heart, which is the psycho-physical Seat of Consciousness Itself, and it terminates in the Light, or Locus, infinitely above the head. Please see *The Dawn Horse Testament* for Sri Da Avabhasa's unique Confession of the Realization of Amrita Nadi and His unprecedented description of the structure of Amrita Nadi in the human body-mind.

asana The Sanskrit word "asana" derives from the verbal root "as", meaning "to sit" or "to dwell", and it generally refers to the posture or pose of one's body. By extension, and as Sri Da Avabhasa often intends, "asana" also refers to the attitude, orientation, posture, or feeling-disposition of the heart and the entire body-mind.

"Atma-Murti" In Sri Da Avabhasa's term "Atma-Murti", "Atma" indicates the Transcendental, Inherently Spiritual, and Divine Self, and "Murti" means "Form". Thus, "Atma-Murti" literally means "the Form (Murti) That Is the (Very) Divine Self (Atman)". In the sixth stage of life in the Way of the Heart, Sri Da Avabhasa's devotee "Locates" Him as "Atma-Murti", the Very Divine Self of all, Who is "Located" as "the Feeling of Being (Itself)" in the right side of the heart.

atman In Sanskrit, "atman" means both the individual (essential, or conditional) self and the Divine Self, depending on the context. In Sri Da Avabhasa's usage, "atman" refers to the individual self and "Paramatman" to the Divine Self.

"Avoiding relationship?" The practice of self-Enquiry in the form "Avoiding relationship?", unique to the Way of the Heart, was spontaneously developed by Sri Da Avabhasa in the course of His own Ordeal of Divine Re-Awakening. Intense persistence in the "radical" discipline of this unique form of self-Enquiry led rapidly to Heart-Master Da's Divine Enlightenment (or Most Perfect Divine Self-Realization) in 1970.

Self-Enquiry in the form "Avoiding relationship?" and Re-cognition are the principal technical practices that serve feeling-Contemplation of Sri Da Avabhasa in the Devotional Way of Insight.

"basic" context of the fourth stage of life (See **three [possible] contexts of the fourth stage of life in the Way of the Heart**.)

Bhava The Supreme and final Demonstration of God-Consciousness, or the most "radical" unspeakable Enjoyment, prior to conditional self, mind, energy, body, or any realm at all.

"Bright", "Brightness" Since His Illumined boyhood, Sri Da Avabhasa has used the term "the 'Bright'" (and its variations, such as "Brightness") to describe the Love-Blissfully Self-Luminous, Conscious Divine Being, Which He knew even then as the Divine Reality of His own body-mind and of all beings, things, and worlds.

causal (See **gross, subtle, causal**.)

Circle The primary circuit or passageway of the Living Spirit-Current as It flows through the body-mind. The Circle is composed of two arcs: the descending Current in association with the frontal line, or the more physically oriented dimension, of the body-mind; and the ascending Current in association with the spinal line, or the more mentally, psychically, and subtly oriented dimension, of the body-mind. When both these portions of the Circle are free of obstruction, the body-mind is harmoniously surrendered into the Current of Spirit-Life and full of Its Radiant Love-Bliss.

"conductivity" Sri Da Avabhasa's technical term for those disciplines in the Way of the Heart through which the body-mind is aligned and submitted to the all-pervading natural life-energy and, for those who are Spiritually Awakened, to the Spirit-Current of Divine Life.

Practitioners of the Way of the Heart practice participation in and responsibility for the movement of natural bodily energies and, when they become Spiritually Awakened practitioners, the movement of the Spirit-Current in its natural course of association with the body-mind, via intentional exercises of feeling and breathing.

Sri Da Avabhasa also uses the term "conductivity" in a more general sense, to refer to all of the practical life-disciplines engaged by practitioners of the Way of the Heart. Although the discipline of "conductivity" is an essential component of the practice of the Way of the Heart, it is nevertheless secondary, or supportive, to practice of the "conscious process".

"conscious process" Sri Da Avabhasa's technical term for those practices in the Way of the Heart through which the mind or attention is surrendered and turned about (from egoic self-involvement) to feeling-Contemplation of Him. It is the senior discipline and responsibility of all practitioners in the Way of the Heart.

"consider", "consideration" The technical term "consideration" in Sri Da Avabhasa's Wisdom-Teaching means a process of one-pointed but ultimately thoughtless concentration and exhaustive contemplation of something until its ultimate obviousness is clear.

Cosmic Mandala The Sanskrit word "mandala" (literally, "circle") is commonly used in the esoteric Spiritual traditions to describe the hierarchical levels of cosmic existence. "Mandala" also denotes an artistic rendering of interior visions of the cosmos. Heart-Master Da Avabhasa uses the phrase "Mandala of the Cosmos", or "Cosmic Mandala", to describe the totality of the conditional cosmos.

Ordinarily, beings cycle helplessly in the hierarchy of planes within the Cosmic Mandala, taking birth in one or another plane according to their psycho-physical tendencies, or the orientation of their attention. Only Sri Da Avabhasa, as the Avataric ("crossing down") Incarnation of the Supreme Divine Person entered the conditional worlds from the Divine Self-Domain, Which Stands Free of the entire Cosmic Mandala and all its planes. He appears in the Cosmic Mandala with the specific intention of Serving the Liberation of ego-bound beings. Sri Da Avabhasa is such a Being of Grace.

For a full discussion of the Cosmic Mandala (and a color representation of its appearance in vision), see chapter thirty-nine of *The Dawn Horse Testament*. See also Heart-Master Da's Instructions in *Easy Death: Talks and Essays on the Inherent and Ultimate Transcendence of Death and Everything Else*.

"Crazy" The exemplars of what Heart-Master Da calls "the 'Crazy Wisdom' tradition" (in which He Stands) are Realizers of the advanced and the ultimate stages of life in any culture or time who, through spontaneous Free action, blunt Wisdom, and liberating laughter, shock or humor people into self-critical awareness of their egoity, a prerequisite for receiving the Adept's Spiritual Transmission. Typically, such Realizers manifest "Crazy" activity only occasionally or temporarily, and never for its own sake.

Heart-Master Da Himself Taught in a unique "Crazy-Wise" manner. For sixteen years He not only reflected but also Submitted completely to the egoic limits of His early devotees. He Submitted His body-mind to live with them, and to live like them, and in Consciousness He lived as them. By thus theatrically dramatizing their habits, predilections, and destinies, He continued always to Teach them the Liberating Truth, to Radiate Divine Blessing through His own Person, and to Attract them beyond themselves to embrace the God-Realizing Way that He Offers.

Now, since His Divine Emergence in 1986, Sri Da Avabhasa no longer Teaches in the "Crazy-Wise" manner. Instead, He "Stands Firm" in His own Freedom, spontaneously Revealing the Divine Self-Reality to all and Calling all to conform themselves to Him absolutely through practice of Ishta-Guru-Bhakti Yoga in the Way of the Heart. This in itself, over against the illusory rationality of the separate, egoic mentality, is a Divinely "Crazy" State and Manner of life. Thus, Heart-Master Da's Service to others in His Divine Emergence Work, in which He is spontaneously Moved to Bless all beings, can likewise be called "Crazy-Wise".

Da The Name "Da", in Sanskrit, means "to give or to bestow", or "the One Who Gives", and it is honored in many sacred traditions as a Name of the Divine Person. It is also the sound of thunder, which is one of Sri Da Avabhasa's Signs in the cosmic realms.

Da Avabhasa Guruvara "Guruvara", meaning literally "Most Auspicious or Best of Gurus", is the traditional Hindu name for the "Day of the Guru". Da Avabhasa Guruvara is a weekly day of retreat when all formal practitioners of the Way of the Heart celebrate the extraordinary Grace of Satsang with Sri Da Avabhasa as the Divine World-Teacher and the True Heart-Master of His devotees.

"daily form" From the preparatory level of practice as a student-novice to the advanced and the ultimate stages of practice in the Way of the Heart, a basic "daily form", or schedule, of practice is recommended by Sri Da Avabhasa. Though the specifics of that "form" vary from one stage of practice to the next (especially in terms of time spent in any given activity), and the order of certain activities may vary depending on one's circumstance, the basic "daily form" for student-beginners (and beyond) begins with early-morning meditation, followed by the Sat-Guru Puja and chanting, a period of study, and Da Namaskar and a recommended program of calisthenics, or other vigorous exercise. ("Da Namaskar" means "Salutation to Da" and is similar to the traditional Surya Namaskar, or Salutation to the sun—a Hatha Yoga exercise consisting of a series of poses designed to balance and enliven the body—but which Sri Da Avabhasa has transformed into a devotional exercise in the Way of the Heart.) After a day of work or service, the evening schedule calls for Da Namaskar and Hatha Yoga (or another recommended exercise routine), dinner, the Sat-Guru Arati Puja (for devotees who live in Ashram), and a formally designated evening activity (which may be service, study, a devotional group, intimate time with one's intimate partner or family, or a community meeting, to mention a few of the possibilities). (The arati is a traditional ceremony of waving lights around the physical Form or a representation of the physical Form of the Sat-Guru as an expression of Happiness, devotion, and gratitude on the part of devotees.) A daily diary entry precedes evening meditation, which is the last event of the day. Student-beginners also have weekly practice obligations, including attendance at a full-day Da Avabhasa Guruvara, and an agreed-upon period of service.

(See pp. 288 and 291-93 for descriptions of student-novice and student-beginner practice.)

Danavira Mela Danavira Mela (also called "The Feast of the Da Love-Ananda Leela") is a celebration of the Play (Leela) of the Divine Person, or the Story of the unfolding miracle of Sri Da Avabhasa's own Life and Work. Danavira Mela is composed of the following elements of meaning in Sanskrit: "Dana" is "the giving of gifts"; "vira" is "hero"; and "mela" is "religious gathering, or festival". Heart-Master Da is the Danavira, the Hero of Giving, Whose Leelas we recount and Celebrate.

Danavira Mela is a time for Sri Da Avabhasa's devotees to employ song and dance and drama and recitation and Leelas (or Stories of Sri Da Avabhasa's Play) in honoring the Story of His Giving Grace, not only in intimate community gatherings, but also in public events. Gifts are exchanged as a conscious offering of love and energy to others in the mood of Satsang, of Love-Communion with the Diving Giver, and it is a period in which the devotional bond of the community is strengthened and celebrated.

Devotional Way of Faith The Devotional Way of Faith and the Devotional Way of Insight are the two variant forms of meditative feeling-Contemplation of Heart-Master Da Avabhasa in the Way of the Heart.

The Devotional Way of Faith is a technical process of (primarily) feeling and faith, whereby the practitioner is heart-Attracted by Sri Da Avabhasa's bodily (human) Form, His Spiritual (and Always Blessing) Presence, and His Very (and Inherently Perfect) State to feel beyond the self-contraction, and is thereby spontaneously awakened to self-understanding and self-transcendence.

Devotional Way of Insight Through a technical process of (primarily) feeling and insight, the practitioner of the Devotional Way of Insight, while engaged in feeling-Contemplation of the bodily (human) Form, the Spiritual (and Always Blessing) Presence, and the Very (and Inherently Perfect) State of Sri Da Avabhasa, observes, understands, and then feels beyond the self-contraction in Divine Communion.

Dharma, dharma The Sanskrit word "dharma" means "duty, virtue, law". It is commonly used to refer to the many paths or esoteric ways by which mankind endeavors to seek the Truth. In its fullest sense, and when capitalized, "Dharma" means the complete fulfillment of duty—the living of the Divine Law. Thus, a truly great Spiritual Teaching, including its disciplines and practices, may rightly be referred to as "Dharma".

Divine Enlightenment The Realization of the seventh stage of life, which is uniquely Revealed and Given by Sri Da Avabhasa. It is release from all the egoic limitations of the previous stages of life. Remarkably, the seventh stage Awakening, which is Sri Da Avabhasa's Gift to His devotees, is <u>not</u> <u>an</u> <u>experience</u> <u>at</u> <u>all</u>. The true Nature of everything is simply obvious. The Understanding arises that every apparent "thing" is Eternally, Perfectly the <u>same</u> as Reality, Consciousness, Happiness, Truth, or God. And that Understanding is Supreme Love-Bliss.

Divine Recognition The self- and world-transcending Intelligence of the Divine Self in relation to all conditional phenomena. In the most ultimate, or seventh, stage of life, the Realizer of the Divine Self simply Abides as Consciousness, and he or she Freely Recognizes, or inherently and Most Perfectly comprehends and perceives, all phenomena (including body, mind, and conditional self) as (apparent) modifications of the same "Bright" Divine Consciousness.

Divine Self-Domain Sri Da Avabhasa Affirms that there is a Divine Domain that is the "Bright" Destiny of every Realizer of the Divine Self. It is not elsewhere, not a place like a subtle heaven or mythical paradise, but It is the always present, Transcendental, Inherently Spiritual, Divine Self of every conditional self, and the Radiant Source-Condition of every conditional place. Sat-Guru Da Reveals that the Divine Self-Domain is not other than the Heart.

Divine Transfiguration, Divine Transformation, Divine Indifference, Divine Translation The Ultimate or fully Awakened Practice in the seventh stage of life unfolds in four progressive phases of the Perfect Demonstration of the Heart. And each of the four phases of the seventh stage Demonstration is an expression of the "Bright" Yoga of Amrita Nadi.

Divine Transfiguration is the phase in which the Divine or "Original Spiritual Current of Love-Bliss" is reflected from the Infinitely Ascended Terminal or "Head" of Amrita Nadi into the descending circuit of the body-mind of the Awakened practitioner—Pervading and Transfiguring the body-mind. This results in great Heart-Service to others and signs of (even sometimes visible) bodily Illumination and Infusion by the Self-Radiance of the Heart.

Divine Transformation is the phase in which the Divine or "Original Spiritual Current of Love-Bliss" is reflected from the Infinitely Ascended Terminal of Amrita Nadi in the full Circle (both descending and ascending) of the body-mind of the Awakened Practitioner—resulting in the spontaneous manifestation of Siddhis, or extraordinary Powers of Blessing.

Both the Divine Transfiguration and the Divine Transformation phases are founded in Descent—as the "Original Spiritual Current of Love-Bliss" is reflected from the Infinitely Ascended Terminal of Amrita Nadi into the descending (or descending and ascending) circuit of the conditional body-mind. It is this very Descent that allows the apparent conditional embodiment of the Realizer to take place.

Divine Indifference is the phase in which the Divine or "Original Spiritual Current of Love-Bliss" abides in Amrita Nadi Itself, and It is only minimally, and less and less, reflected in the Circle of the body-mind of the Awakened practitioner. Thus, the conditional body-mind and all experience are only minimally noticed (and less and less engaged), as the enlightened being Inheres in the Prior and formless Well of Love-Bliss or Divine Being Itself. This was Sri Da Avabhasa's Disposition at the time of His Birth until approximately the age of two, when He allowed It to receded, and It is the State to which He Re-Awakened after the Event of His Divine Emergence in 1986.

Divine Translation is the phase of the seventh stage Demonstration in which all conditions (including Amrita Nadi) are Recognized and Outshined in the Divine Self-Condition, in the Perfect Space and "Bright" Domain that is Consciousness Itself, Realized as the Native Love-Bliss-Feeling of Being. In Divine Translation, there remains no impulse or necessity to continue appearing in a conditional form. In Divine Translation, Absorption-Identification with the Self-Existing and Self-Radiant, Infinite and Divine Person utterly Outshines the Structure of Amrita Nadi, the conditional body-mind, and all the possible worlds of experience.

The four phases of the Yoga of Divine Enlightenment are discussed fully by Heart-Master Da in chapters forty-three and forty-four of *The Dawn Horse Testament*.

Durga In Hinduism, the Durga is worshipped as the personification of the Goddess, or the creative energy aspect of existence. She is depicted variously as the consort of Siva, the Bride of the One Who Is Consciousness, or the World-Mother. She is a fierce protectress, equipped with multiple arms, most of them brandishing weapons to help Her in fighting demons and protecting the cosmic order. Part of Her appeal is that She is always victorious in Her preservation of justice. Her predominant hand is open and weaponless in a gesture of reassurance to those who approach Her humbly.

$E=mc^2$ The mathematical equation formulated by Albert Einstein in 1905 to express the ultimate equivalence of matter and energy. Sri Da Avabhasa states in *Scientific Proof of the Existence of God Will Soon Be Announced by the White House!*:

When its true implications are taken into account, Einstein's equation of energy and matter (expressed in the formula $E=mc^2$) represents the possibility of a multidimensional interpretation of the total universe, in which the so-called "material" universe is realized to be a paradoxical entity or process.

Feeling of Being The uncaused (or Self-Existing), Self-Radiant, and unqualified feeling-intuition of the Transcendental, Inherently Spiritual, and Divine Self. This absolute Feeling does not merely accompany or express the Realization of the Heart Itself, but it is identical to that Realization. To feel, or, really, to Be, the Feeling of Being is to enjoy the Love-Bliss of Absolute Consciousness, Which, when Most Perfectly Realized, cannot be prevented or even diminished either by the events of life or by death.

feeling-Contemplation Sri Da Avabhasa's term for the essential devotional and meditative practice that all devotees in the Way of the Heart engage at all times in relationship to His bodily (human) Form, His Spiritual (and Always Blessing) Presence, and His Very (and Inherently Perfect) State. Feeling-Contemplation of Sri Da Avabhasa is Awakened by Grace through Darshan, or feeling-sighting, of His Form, Presence, and State. It is then to be practiced under all conditions, and as the basis and epitome of all other practices in the Way of the Heart.

fifth stage conditional Nirvikalpa Samadhi "Nirvikalpa" means "without form". Hence, "Nirvikalpa Samadhi" means literally "deep meditative concentration (or absorption) without form". Traditionally this state is the final goal of the many schools of Yogic ascent whose orientation to practice is that of the fifth stage of life. Fifth stage conditional Nirvikalpa Samadhi is an isolated or periodic Realization. In fifth stage conditional Nirvikalpa Samadhi, attention ascends beyond all conditional manifestation into the formless Matrix of the Spirit-Current or Divine Light infinitely above the world, the body, and the mind. And fifth stage conditional Nirvikalpa Samadhi is a forced and temporary state of attention (or, more precisely, of the suspension of attention). It is produced by manipulation of attention and of the body-mind, and is thus incapable of being maintained when attention returns, as it inevitably does, to the states of the body-mind.

"fully elaborated" form of the Way of the Heart (See **technical forms of practice in the Way of the Heart**.)

Gavdevi "Gav" means "village". "Devi" means "goddess". The Gavdevi is thus the village goddess.

the Goddess (See **Sri Da Avabhasa's Lineage of Blessing**.)

Great Tradition Sri Da Avabhasa's term for the total inheritance of human, cultural, religious, magical, mystical, Spiritual, Transcendental, and Divine paths, philosophies, and testimonies from all the eras and cultures of humanity, which has (in the present era of worldwide communication) become the common legacy of mankind.

gross, subtle, causal Sri Da Avabhasa is in agreement with the traditional descriptions that the human body-mind and its environment consist of three great dimensions—gross, subtle, and causal.

The gross, or most physical, dimension is associated with the physical body and experience in the waking state.

The subtle dimension, which is senior to and pervades the gross dimension, includes our etheric (or energetic), lower mental (or verbal-intentional and lower psychic), and higher mental (or deeper psychic, mystical, and discriminative) functions. The subtle dimension is associated primarily with the ascending energies of the spine, the brain core, and the subtle centers of mind in the higher brain. It is also, therefore, associated with the visionary, mystical, and Yogic Spiritual processes encountered in dreams, in ascended or internalized meditative experiences, and during and after death.

The causal dimension is senior to and pervades both the gross and the subtle dimensions. It is the root of attention, or the essence of the separate and separative ego-"I". The causal dimension is associated with the right side of the heart, specifically with the sinoatrial node, or "pacemaker" (the psycho-physical source of the heartbeat). Its corresponding state of consciousness is the formless awareness of deep sleep. It is inherently transcended by the Witness-Consciousness (Which is prior to all objects of attention).

The causal being, or limited self-consciousness (which is identical to the root-feeling of relatedness), is also associated with a knot or stress-point in the heart-root on the right side. When this knot is broken, or "untied", by Sri Da Avabhasa's Liberating Grace in the form of Most Perfect understanding, the Transcendental, Inherently Spiritual, and Divine Self-Consciousness Stands Free and Awake as the Heart Itself.

Hatha Yoga The word "hatha" means "force" or "power", referring to the forceful, potent nature of Hatha Yoga, which traditionally aims at achieving ecstasy and even Liberation through manipulation of body, breath, and energy, with concomitant discipline of attention. "Hatha" has also been interpreted as originating from two basic root-sounds, "ha" and "tha", which represent sun and moon, or the opposing solar and lunar flows of prana, or life-energy. Thus, a traditional aim of Hatha Yoga is to achieve harmony in the body-mind through the balancing of these opposing bodily energies, represented by the sun and moon, the right and left sides of the body, and the exhaled (expansive) and inhaled (centering) breaths.

In the Way of the Heart, the bodily poses (asanas) of Hatha Yoga are engaged in order to purify, balance, and regenerate the functions of the body-mind, and (in due course) to align them to the Spirit-Current. The regulation and control of the life-energy is accomplished primarily through breath control (pranayama). Heart-Master Da recommends that His devotees make use of simple poses of relaxation, rather than the more rigorous application of Hatha Yoga, when preparing for meditation. See *Conscious Exercise and the Transcendental Sun* for the program of Hatha Yoga poses recommended for daily exercise.

hearing Sri Da Avabhasa's technical term for most fundamental understanding of the self-contraction, through which the practitioner awakens to the unique capability for direct transcendence of the self-contraction and simultaneous Communion with Sri Da Avabhasa and, thus and thereby, with the Divine Person and Self-Condition, Who always already Stands Present, prior to the self-contraction. Hearing is awakened in the midst of a life of devotion, service, self-discipline, meditation, disciplined study of, or listening to, Sri Da Avabhasa's Wisdom-Teaching Argument, and constant self-surrendering, self-forgetting, and self-transcending feeling-Contemplation of Him.

Hearing is the necessary prerequisite for the Spiritual Realization that Heart-Master Da calls "seeing".

the Heart The Heart is God, the Divine Self, the Divine Reality. Divine Self-Realization is associated with the opening of the primal psycho-physical seat of Consciousness and attention in the right side of the heart, hence the term "the Heart" for the Divine Self.

Sri Da Avabhasa distinguishes the Heart as the ultimate Reality from all the psycho-physiological functions of the organic, bodily heart, as well as from the subtle heart, traditionally known as the "anahata (or heart) chakra". The Heart is not "in" the right side of the human heart, nor is it in or limited to the human heart as a whole, or to the body-mind, or to the world. Rather, the human heart and body-mind and the world exist in the Heart, the Divine Being.

Hridaya-Shakti "Shakti" is a Sanskrit term for the Divinely Manifesting Energy, Spiritual Power, or Life-Current of the Divine Person. "Hridaya-Shakti" is thus "the Power of the Heart".

Instrumentality Sri Da Avabhasa uses the term "Instrumentality" to indicate His Spiritually Awakened devotees in the advanced stages of life in the Way of the Heart. Such devotees have received Sri Da Avabhasa's Spiritual Baptism and practice in Spiritually activated relationship to Him.

Ishta-Guru-Bhakti Yoga A compound of traditional Sanskrit terms that denotes the principal Gift, Calling, and Discipline Sat-Guru Da Avabhasa Offers to all who would practice the Way of the Heart.

"Ishta" literally means "chosen", or "most beloved". "Guru", in the reference "Ishta-Guru", means specifically the Sat-Guru, the Revealer of Truth Itself (or of Being Itself). "Bhakti" means, literally, "devotion".

Ishta-Guru-Bhakti, then, is devotion to the Supreme Divine Being in the Form and through the Means of the human Sat-Guru.

"Yoga", from a Sanskrit verb root meaning "to yoke", "to bind together", is a path, or way, of achieving Unity with (or Realizing one's Prior Identity with) the Divine.

Ishta-Guru-Seva In Sanskrit, "seva" means "service". Service to the Sat-Guru is traditionally treasured as one of the great Secrets of Realization. In the Way of the Heart, Sat-Guru-Seva is the remarkable opportunity to live every action and, indeed, one's entire life, as direct service and responsive obedience (or sympathetic conformity) to Sri Da Avabhasa in every possible and appropriate way.

Jnana Samadhi "Jnana" derives from the Sanskrit verb root "jna", literally "to know". In the development of the sixth stage of life of the Way of the Heart, Jnana Samadhi (or Jnana Nirvikalpa Samadhi) will most likely be experienced (even frequently). Produced by the forceful withdrawal or inversion of attention from the conditional body-mind-self and its relations, Jnana Samadhi is the conditional, temporary Realization of the Transcendental Self, or Consciousness, exclusive of any perception or cognition of world, objects, relations, body, mind, or separate self-sense, and thus formless (nirvikalpa).

Kali In Sanskrit, "Kali" means "the Black One". Kali is a Hindu goddess, a form of the Mother Shakti, the consort of Siva in her wrathful aspect of destroyer of all evil.

karma, karmic In Sanskrit, "karma" means "action". Since action entails consequences, or reactions, *karma* is destiny, tendency, the quality of existence and experience which is determined by prior actions or conditions.

Karma Yoga In Sanskrit, "yoga" literally means "union". The tradition of Yoga speaks of several traditional or paths of Spiritual union with the Divine. Karma Yoga, extolled by Krishna in the *Bhagavad Gita,* is the Yoga of action in which every activity, no matter how humble, is transformed into self-transcending service to the Divine.

Krishna Krishna was a legendary Avatar of ancient India. The *Bhagavad Gita* recounts the conversation between Krishna and his devotee Arjuna that leads to Arjuna's conversion.

kumbhak The most common traditional form of kumbhak (Sanskrit: kumbhaka) is momentary retention of the breath between exhalation and inhalation, or between inhalation and exhalation. In its most profound form, kumbhak is temporary and total spontaneous suspension of the breath while attention ascends beyond awareness of the body into states of ecstatic absorption. The common form of kumbhak is sometimes intentionally practiced as a form of pranayama. Both the common and the profound forms of kumbhak may also occur spontaneously (in an easeful and blissful manner) in response to the Spiritual Presence of Sat-Guru Da Avabhasa.

leela The Sanskrit word "leela" literally means "play", or "sport". Traditionally, all of manifest existence is seen to be the Leela, or the Divine Play, Sport, or Free Activity, of the Divine Person. Leela also means the Awakened Play of a Realized Adept of any degree, through which he or she mysteriously Instructs and Liberates others and Blesses the world itself. By extension, a leela is an instructive and inspiring story of such an Adept's Teaching and Blessing Play.

listening Sri Da Avabhasa's term for the disposition of the beginner's preparation and practice in the Way of the Heart. A listening devotee is someone who, in the context of his or her life of devotion, service, self-discipline, and meditation at the beginning developmental stages of practice, gives his or her attention to Sri Da Avabhasa's Teaching Argument, to His Leelas (or inspirational Stories of His Life and Work), and to feeling-Contemplation of Him (primarily of His bodily human Form) for the sake of awakening self-observation and most fundamental self-understanding, or hearing, on the basis of which practice may begin to develop in the Spiritual stages of life and beyond.

mahavakya In Sanskrit, "mahavakya" means "great utterance". In the Vedic tradition, such great utterances were revealed to practitioners who were duly prepared for initiation into their truths in order to serve their practice and Realization. The truth of these great utterances was not dependent on intellectual knowledge but on participatory understanding.

mala A mala, which means "garland" in Sanskrit, is typically a rosary of 108 beads, plus a central or Master bead, which, as used in the Way of the Heart, is a Reminder of Sri Da Avabhasa, His Teaching-Revelation, and His many Gifts of Grace that Serve one's practice. Sri Da Avabhasa Himself also sometimes wears malas to Empower them as Sacred Articles of His Heart-Transmission. Traditionally, a flower mala, made in the likeness of a beaded mala, may also be offered to one's Sat-Guru as a sign of devotion.

mantra (See **Name-Invocation**.)

maya Illusion formed from ignorance, or any limited view of God

"missing the mark" (See **"sin"**.)

mleccha In traditional India in times past, those who resided outside of India were regarded—like the untouchables within Hindu society—to be ineligible to participate responsibly in the Spiritual Way of life. As such, the untouchables, outcasts, and so-called barbarians of the world, including all foreigners, were known generally as "mlecchas" (pronounced "MLETCH-uhs"). And it was assumed, in orthodox circles of Vedic Hinduism, that such beings were gradually evolving from relatively inauspicious lifetimes until they might merit a birth within one of the castes of those eligible for salvatory and Liberating Divine Grace under the Vedic code.

Most Perfect(ly), Most Ultimate(ly) Sri Da Avabhasa uses the phrase "Most Perfect(ly)" in the sense of "Absolutely Perfect(ly)". Similarly, the phrase "Most Ultimate(ly)" is equivalent to "Absolutely Ultimate(ly)".

In the sixth stage of life and the seventh stage of life, What is Realized (Consciousness Itself) is Perfect (and Ultimate). This is why Sri Da Avabhasa characterizes these stages as the "ultimate stages of life", and describes the practice of the Way of the Heart in the context of these stages as "the 'Perfect Practice'". The distinction between the sixth stage of life and the seventh stage of life is that the devotee's <u>Realization</u> of What is Perfect (and Ultimate) is itself Perfect (and Ultimate) only in the seventh stage. The Perfection or Ultimacy (in the seventh stage) <u>both</u> of What is Realized and of the Realization of It is what is signified by the phrase "Most Perfect(ly)" or "Most Ultimate(ly)".

Murti Sanskrit for "form". The verb-root of the word means "to become rigid or solid". Thus, "murti" is defined as "solid body, manifestation, incarnation, embodiment, substantial form or body, image, statue". Traditionally, as well as in Sri Da Avabhasa's usage, "murti" may mean either "representational image", or, simply, "form" (or "substance") itself (as in Heart-Master Da's term "Atma-Murti", meaning "the Form That Is the Very Self", or "the One Whose Form, or Substance, Is the Self Itself"). In the Way of the Heart, "Murti" most commonly refers to a Representational Image (often a photograph) of Sri Da Avabhasa's bodily (human) Form.

Name-Invocation Sacred sounds or syllables and Names have been used since antiquity for Invoking and worshipping the Divine Person and the Sat-Guru. In the Hindu tradition, the original mantras were cosmic sound-forms and "seed" letters used for worship, prayer, and incantatory meditation on the Revealed Form of the Divine Person. In the Way of the Heart, Name-Invocation may be practiced simply, by Invoking Sri Da Avabhasa's Principal Name, "Da", or as the Sat-Guru-Naama Mantra, either in the form "Om Sri Da Avabhasa Hridayam" or in the form "Om Sri Da Love-Ananda Hridayam".

"Narcissus" In Sat-Guru Da Avabhasa's Teaching-Revelation, "Narcissus" is a key symbol of the un-Enlightened individual as a self-obsessed seeker, enamored of his or her own self-image and egoic self-consciousness. As "Narcissus", every human being constantly suffers in dilemma, recoiling from all relations and even from the fundamental condition of relationship (or relatedness) itself. In *The Knee of Listening* (p. 26), Sat-Guru Da summarized His insight into "Narcissus" as the avoidance of relationship: "He is the ancient one visible in the Greek 'myth', who was the universally adored child of the gods, who rejected the loved-one and every form of love and relationship, who was finally condemned to the contemplation of his own image, until he suffered the fact of eternal separation and died in infinite solitude." For one who understands most profoundly, the activity of avoidance, or self-contraction, is ultimately understood to be completely unnecessary and is directly transcended through devotional feeling-Contemplation of the Perfectly un-contracted bodily (human) Form, Spiritual (and Always Blessing) Presence, and Very (and Inherently Perfect) State of the True Heart-Master.

"oedipal" In modern psychology, the Oedipus complex is named for the Greek myth of Oedipus, who was fated to unknowingly, or unconsciously, kill his father and marry his mother. Through years of personal observation, beginning even in childhood, Sri Da Avabhasa has understood that the primary dynamisms of emotional-sexual desiring, rejection, envy, betrayal, self-pleasuring, resentment, and other primal emotions and impulses are patterned throughout one's life upon unconscious reactions first formed early in life, in relation to one's father and mother.

Sri Da Avabhasa calls this "the 'oedipal' drama" and points out that we relate to all women as we do to our mothers, and to all men as we do to our fathers, and that we relate, and react, to our own bodies exactly as we do to the parent of the opposite sex. Thus, we impose infantile reactions to our parents on our relationships with lovers and all other beings, according to their sex, and we also superimpose the same on our relationship to our own bodies.

"original" context of the fourth stage of life (See **three [possible] contexts of the fourth stage of life in the Way of the Heart**.)

Outshined, Outshining The term "Outshining" Sri Da Avabhasa uses synonymously with His term "Divine Translation", to refer to the final Demonstration of the four-phase process of Divinization in the seventh, or fully Enlightened, stage of life in the Way of the Heart. In this Event, body, mind, and world are no longer noticed, not because the Divine Consciousness has withdrawn or dissociated from manifested phenomena, but because the Ecstatic Divine Recognition of all arising phenomena (by the Divine Self, and As only modifications of Itself) has become so intense that the "Bright" Radiance of Consciousness now Outshines all such phenomena. (See also **Divine Transfiguration, Divine Transformation, Divine Indifference, Divine Translation**.)

"peculiar" (See **"solid", "peculiar", "vital"**.)

"Perfect Practice" Sri Da Avabhasa's technical term for the discipline of the sixth stage of life and the seventh stage of life in the Way of the Heart.

Devotees who have mastered (and thus transcended the point of view of the body-mind by fulfilling the preparatory processes of the Way of the Heart, may, by Grace, be Awakened to practice in the Domain of Consciousness Itself, in the sixth and seventh, or ultimate, stages of life.

The three parts of the "Perfect Practice" are summarized by Sri Da Avabhasa in chapter forty-four of *The Dawn Horse Testament*.

pondering Sri Da Avabhasa's technical term for meditative reflection on His Wisdom-Teaching as practiced by His listening devotees who are experimenting with or practicing the Devotional Way of Insight in the Way of the Heart. The practice of pondering includes formal and increasingly meditative "consideration" of His ten Great Questions, and random, informal reflection upon His Arguments and Great Questions in daily life, in the context of feeling-Contemplation of Sri Da Avabhasa. The primary Great Question is the self-Enquiry "Avoiding Relationship?" For a detailed description of meditative pondering in the Way of the Heart, see chapter nineteen of *The Dawn Horse Testament*.

practicing stages of the Way of the Heart The Way of the Heart develops for all practitioners through (potential) developmental stages of practice and Revelation. The term "practicing stages", however, is applied only to the technically "fully elaborated" form of the Way of the Heart, which is practiced by members of the Lay Renunciate Order and members of the Free Renunciate Order. The technically "simpler" (or even "simplest") practice of the Way of the Heart, which is practiced by members of the Lay Congregationist Order, also develops by developmental stages, which correspond to the practicing stages, but the developmental stages of the "lay congregationist" are measured in less technical detail than the practicing stages of the "lay renunciate" or "free renunciate".

In *The Da Avabhasa Upanishad*, Sri Da Avabhasa Writes of the seven practicing stages of the technically "fully elaborated" course of practice of the Way of the Heart and their correspondence to the seven stages of life:

The technically "fully elaborated" (or "elaborately detailed") course of the Way of the Heart involves seven (potential) practicing stages, and these develop in the context of the seven stages of life. However, in the technically "elaborately detailed" course of the Way (or Yoga) of the Heart, the seven stages of life and the seven practicing stages do not correspond to one another numerically (number by number), except in the case of practicing stages five, six, and seven (which correspond to the fifth, sixth, and seventh stages of life respectively). Practicing stages one through four of the technically "fully elaborated" form of the Way of the Heart each correspond to a progressive development of the fourth stage of life (beginning also in the context of the first three stages of life). Indeed, practice of even any by Me Given form of the Way of the Heart is initially a culture of self-transcendence in the general context of the first three stages of life (based in the "original", or beginner's, Devotional context of the fourth stage of life), and then, progressively, toward and to the seventh stage of life, stage by stage (as necessary). And, of course, the "Radical", or Inherently Most Perfect, Disposition of the seventh stage of life informs and inspires the practice at even every stage of life in the Way of the Heart.

Following the student-novice stage (of formal approach to the Way of the Heart) and the student-beginner stage (of formally acknowledged practice of the Way of the Heart), practicing stage one of the technically "fully elaborated" form of the Way of the Heart continues (and further develops) the process of listening (or self-surrendering and self-forgetting Devotional "consideration") relative to the first three stages of life (in the "original", or beginner's, Devotional context of the fourth stage of life), and (in the form of eventual true hearing, or most fundamental self-understanding) practicing stage one of the technically "fully elaborated" form of the Way of the Heart regenerates the effective capability for direct self-transcendence (which capability progressively releases the body-mind via the Heart-Response that characterizes the fourth stage of life).

Practicing stage two of the technically "fully elaborated" form of the Way of the Heart Awakens clear seeing, or the Devotional and Spiritual Heart-Practice that characterizes the ("basic") Spiritually established fourth stage of life.

Practicing stage three of the technically "fully elaborated" form of the Way of the Heart develops fully responsible practice of all "basic" (or frontal and descending) aspects of the fourth stage of life.

Practicing stage four of the technically "fully elaborated" form of the Way of the Heart is the "advanced" (and ascending, or spinal) stage of the technically "fully elaborated" practice of the Way of the Heart in the context of the fourth stage of life, and it is at (or via) this practicing stage of the technically "fully elaborated" form of the Way of the Heart that the natural (psycho-physical) transition is made from the context of the fourth stage of life to that of the fifth stage of life.

The transition to practicing stage five of the technically "fully elaborated" form of the Way of the Heart is the transition to the technically "fully elaborated" practice of the Way of the Heart in the context of the fifth stage of life, or the Spiritual Process of the ascent of attention via (or through, or from) the Ajna Door (or the brain core, deep behind and between and slightly above the brows), and via (or through, or from) the upper reaches of the subtle mind, to the crown of the head (and beyond, to ascended Realization above and beyond the body, its brain, and the mind).

The transition to practicing stage six of the technically "fully elaborated" form of the Way of the Heart, or to the technically "fully elaborated" practice of the Way of the Heart in the context of the sixth stage of life, is made when the binding motives and errors of practice associated with each and all of the first five stages of life are really transcended and Identification with the Witness-Consciousness is Perfect (or Inherently, effortlessly, and stably the case).

The transition to practicing stage six of the technically "fully elaborated" form of the Way of the Heart will (by Grace) be made (in most cases) directly from practicing stage three of the technically "fully elaborated" form of the Way of the Heart, once clear signs of basic maturity in practicing stage three are demonstrated. Otherwise (in the case of a relative few practitioners of the Way of the Heart, and only because of their unusually strong subtle tendencies of mind), the transition to practicing stage six of the technically "fully elaborated" form of the Way of the Heart will be made either at maturity (if not earlier) in practicing stage four of the technically "fully elaborated" form of the Way of the Heart or at some advanced (or even earlier) moment in practicing stage five of the technically "fully elaborated" form of the Way of the Heart.

The total Process of the Way of the Heart in the context of the first <u>six</u> stages of life (and in the context of the first six practicing stages of the technically "fully elaborated" form of the Way of the Heart) can also be called "the Yoga of 'Consideration'". That Yoga, or Way, is Full (or Complete) when seventh stage Sahaj Samadhi (or the Awakening that Initiates and Characterizes the seventh stage of life) is Realized.

Practicing stage seven of the technically "fully elaborated" form of the Way of the Heart (or the Demonstration of the Way of the Heart in the technically "fully elaborated" context of the seventh stage of life) is a spontaneous and progressive Demonstration of the Signs of Divine Transfiguration and Divine Transformation, until the Signs of Divine Indifference spontaneously begin to be Demonstrated.

The Most Ultimate (and Final) Demonstration

of practicing stage seven of the technically "fully elaborated" form of the Way of the Heart is Divine Translation (the Outshining of conditional existence in the Inherent and Infinite "Bright" Love-Bliss of Divine Self-Existence).

(See pp. 288 and 291-95 for descriptions of student-novice and student-beginner practice, the Lay Congregationist Order, the Lay Renunciate Order, and the Free Renunciate Order. See also "The Seven Stages of Life" on pp. 296-304.)

pranayama In Sanskrit, "prana" means "breath", and "yama" means "control, or restraint". Pranayama, or the restraint of breath, is a traditional Yogic discipline.

puja (See **Sat-Guru-Puja**.)

"radical" The term "radical" derives from the Latin "radix", meaning "root", and thus it principally means "irreducible", "fundamental", or "relating to the origin". Because Sri Da Avabhasa uses "radical" in this literal sense, it appears in quotation marks in His Wisdom-Teaching to distinguish His useage from the popular reference to an extreme (often political) position or view.

In contrast to the developmental, egoic searches typically espoused by the world's religious and Spiritual traditions, the "radical" Way of the Heart Offered by Heart-Master Da is established in the Divine Self-Condition of Reality, even from the very beginning of one's practice. Every moment of feeling-Contemplation of Sri Da Avabhasa, Who has Most Perfectly Realized that "radically" Free Divine Self-Condition, undermines, therefore, the illusory ego at its root (the self-contraction in the heart), rendering the search not only unnecessary but obsolete, and awakening the devotee to the "radical" Intuition of the always already Free Condition.

rajas (See **tamas, rajas, sattva**.)

Ramakrishna Better known in the West than any other modern Indian Saint, Ramakrishna (1836-1886) was a renowned ecstatic, and a lifelong devotee of Kali, a form of the Mother Shakti. In the course of his Spiritual practice, Ramakrishna passed spontaneously through many religious and Spiritual disciplines, and he Realized a state of profound mystical unity with God.

Ramana Maharshi Ramana Maharshi (1879-1950) is regarded by many as the greatest Indian sage of the twentieth century. He became Self-Realized at a young age and gradually assumed a Teaching role as more people approached him for Spiritual guidance. He told his students that there were two ways: "Either ask yourself 'Who am I?' or surrender to the Guru." His relationship with devotees was a loving one, though he could also be very direct, even fierce, if necessary, to help a student. His characteristic mood, however, was Transmission in silence.

Ramana Maharshi's Teaching focused on the process of introversion (through the question "Who am I?"), which culminates in conditional Self-Realization (or Jnana Samadhi), exclusive of phenomena. He established his Ashram at Tiruvannamalai in South India, which continues today.

Re-cognition "Re-cognition", which literally means "knowing again", is Sri Da Avabhasa's term for non-verbal, heart-felt, intuitive insight into any and every arising conditional phenomenon as a form of egoic self-contraction. It is the mature form into which verbal self-Enquiry evolves in the Devotional Way of Insight in the Way of the Heart. The practitioner simply notices and tacitly "knows again", or directly understands, whatever is arising as yet another species of self-contraction, and he or she transcends or feels beyond it in Satsang with Heart-Master Da and, thus and thereby, with the Divine Person.

right side of the heart Da Avabhasa has Revealed that, in the context of the body-mind, the Divine Consciousness is intuited at a psycho-physical Locus in the right side of the heart. This center corresponds to the sinoatrial node, or pacemaker, the source of the physical heartbeat in the right atrium, or upper right chamber, of the heart.

Rudi (See **Sri Da Avabhasa's Lineage of Blessing**.)

sadhana Self-transcending religious or Spiritual practice.

Sahaj Samadhi Seventh stage Sahaj Samadhi, or seventh stage Sahaja Nirvikalpa Samadhi: The seventh stage of life is the unique Revelation of Sri Da Avabhasa, and He is the only Adept Who has Realized (or Who will ever Realize) seventh stage Sahaj Samadhi. Sri Da Avabhasa's Realization of the seventh stage of life makes that same Realization possible for His devotees (only), though none of His devotees will have the Adept-Function. The Hindi word "sahaj" (Sanskrit, "sahaja") literally means "together born". Sri Da Avabhasa uses the term "seventh stage Sahaj Samadhi" to indicate the Coincidence, in unqualified self-transcending God-Realization, of the Unconditional, Inherently Spiritual, and Transcendental Divine Reality with empirical, conditional reality.

"Sahaj" also connotes the "Natural" State. Seventh stage Sahaj Samadhi, then, is eternal, Unconditional Divine Self-Realization, free of dependence on any form of meditation, effort, discipline, experience, or conditional knowledge.

"Sahaj Samadhi" (in the sense of a "natural" state of ecstasy) is a term also used in various esoteric traditions (of the fourth stage, the fifth stage, and the sixth stage of life) to refer to a state of Realization that is continuous even during moments of ordinary occupation. What is called "Sahaj Samadhi" in these traditions is described by Sri Da Avabhasa as "fourth stage 'Sahaj Samadhi'", or "fifth stage 'Sahaj Samadhi'", or "sixth stage 'Sahaj Samadhi'". In contrast, Seventh stage Sahaj Samadhi is the Unconditional and Eternal Realization of the Divine.

Sri Da Avabhasa also refers to seventh stage Sahaj Samadhi as "seventh stage Sahaja Nirvikalpa Samadhi", indicating that it is the "Open-Eyed" Realization of the formless (Nirvikalpa) State.

Samadhi In Sanskrit, "samadhi" means "placed together". It indicates concentration, equanimity, and balance, and it is traditionally used to denote various exalted states that appear in the context of esoteric meditation and Realization.

samsara A classical Buddhist and Hindu term for all conditional worlds and states, or the realm of birth and change and death. It connotes the suffering and limitations experienced in those limited worlds.

Satchidananda In Sanskrit, "Sat" means "Being, or Truth", "Chit" means "Consciousness", and "Ananda" means "Bliss". The term "Satchidananda" ("Being-Consciousness-Bliss") describes the three irreducible Divine Qualities of God, Truth, and Reality.

Sat-Guru Puja The Sanskrit word "puja" means "worship". All formal sacramental devotion in the Way of the Heart is consecrated to Sri Da Avabhasa and is thus celebrated as Sat-Guru Puja. It is a ceremonial, even theatrical, but feeling practice of Divine association, or expressive whole bodily devotion to Sri Da Avabhasa, in Person, as the Realizer, the Revealer, and the Revelation of the Divine Person. Sat-Guru Puja may involve bodily invocation of, self-surrender to, and intimate Communion with Sat-Guru Da (and, thus and thereby, the Divine Person) by means of prayer, song, recitation of His Word of Instruction, dance, the offering and receiving of gifts, and other forms of outward, or bodily active, devotional attention.

In the Way of the Heart, all practitioners participate daily in formal Sat-Guru Puja, as self-transcending practice that establishes Sri Da Avabhasa's Blessing at the heart and thus establishes devotees profoundly in ecstatic feeling-Contemplation of Sri Da Avabhasa. The principal forms of daily Sat-Guru Puja are Sat-Guru-Murti Puja (ceremonial service to and worship of the Sacred Image of Sat-Guru Da) and Sat-Guru-Paduka Puja (ceremonial service to and worship of Sat-Guru Da's Blessed Sandals, or Padukas).

Sat-Guru-Seva The Sanskrit word "seva" means "service". Service to the Sat-Guru is traditionally treasured as one of the great Secrets of Realization. In the Way of the Heart, Sat-Guru-Seva is the remarkable opportunity to live every action and, indeed, one's entire life, as direct service and responsive obedience and conformity to Sri Da Avabhasa in every possible and appropriate way.

Satsang The Sanskrit word "Satsang" literally means "true or right relationship", "the company of Truth, or of Being". In the Way of the Heart, it is the eternal relationship of mutual sacred commitment between Sri Da Avabhasa as Sat-Guru (and as the Divine Person) and each true and formally acknowledged practitioner of the Way of the Heart. Once it is consciously assumed by any practitioner, Satsang with Heart-Master Da is an all-inclusive Condition, bringing Divine Grace and Blessings and sacred obligations, responsibilities, and tests into every dimension of the practitioner's life and consciousness.

sattva (See **tamas, rajas, sattva**.)

scientific materialism In scientific materialism, the method of science, or the observation of objective phenomena, is made into philosophy and a way of life. Scientific materialism is the dominant philosophy and world-view of modern humanity that suppresses our native impulse to Liberation.

seeing Sri Da Avabhasa's technical term for emotional conversion from the self-contracted heart to the open-hearted, Radiant Happiness that characterizes God-Love and Spiritual devotion to Him. Such true and stable emotional conversion coincides with true sensitivity to Heart-Master Da Avabhasa's Spiritual (and Always Blessing) Presence, and stable receptivity of His Spiritual Heart-Transmission, which is a prerequisite to the further development of practice in the Way of the Heart.

self-Enquiry The practice of self-Enquiry in the form "Avoiding relationship?", unique to the Way of the Heart, was spontaneously developed by Sri Da Avabhasa in the course of His own Ordeal of Divine Re-Awakening. Intense persistence in the "radical" discipline of this unique form of self-Enquiry led rapidly to Heart-Master Da's Divine Enlightenment (or Most Perfect Divine Self-Realization) in 1970.

Self-Enquiry in the form "Avoiding relationship?" and Re-cognition are the principal technical practices that serve feeling-Contemplation of Sri Da Avabhasa in the Devotional Way of Insight.

"self-possession", "self-possessed" Conventionally, "self-possessed" means "possessed <u>of</u> oneself"—or with full control (calmness, or composure) of one's feelings, impulses, habits, and actions. Sri Da Avabhasa uses the term to indicate the state of being possessed <u>by</u> one's egoic self, or controlled by chronically self-referring (or egoic) tendencies of attention, feeling, thought, desire, and action. Thus, unless (in every moment) body, emotion, desire, thought, separate and separative self, and all attention are actively and completely surrendered, one is egoically "self-possessed", even when exhibiting personal control of one's feelings, habits, and actions. And the devotional practice of feeling-Contemplation of Heart-Master Da is the principal Means Given (by Grace) to practitioners of the Way of the Heart, whereby they may <u>responsively</u> (and, thus, by Grace) surrender, forget, and transcend egoic "self-possession".

seventh stage Sahaj Samadhi (See **Sahaj Samadhi**.)

"sexual communion" Sri Da Avabhasa uses the technical term "sexual communion" to describe the conservative discipline engaged by sexually active devotees practicing in the first actually seeing stage, and beyond, of the Way of the Heart. Because such devotees are Spiritually active, they are qualified to engage sexual intimacy as a Spiritual practice of Communion with the All-Pervading Divine Reality. (In the developmental stages of life before the first actually seeing stage, sexually active practitioners of the Way of the Heart engage a likewise conservative discipline called "sexual 'conscious exercise'".)

Heart-Master Da first described "sexual communion" in *Love of the Two-Armed Form,* which introduced and explained in rudimentary form its process and practice. The description given in *The Dawn Horse Testament*, by contrast with that in the earlier introductory book, is a complete, technical elaboration of the practice of "sexual communion".

Shakti, Guru-Shakti, "Shakti" is a Sanskrit term for the Divinely Manifesting Energy, Spiritual Power, or Life-Current of the Divine Person. Guru-Shakti is the Power of the Guru to Liberate his or her devotees.

Shaktipat In Hindi, "shaktipat" is the "descent of the Power". Yogic Shaktipat, which manipulates natural, conditional energies or partial manifestations of the Spirit-Current, is typically granted through touch, word, glance, or regard by Yogic Adepts in the fifth stage of life, or fourth to fifth stages of life. Yogic Shaktipat must be distinguished from (and otherwise understood to be only a secondary aspect of) the Blessing-Transmission of the Heart Itself (Hridaya-Shaktipat). Such Heart-Transmission, is freely and spontaneously Granted to all only by the Divinely Self-Realized, or seventh stage, Sat-Guru, Sri Da Avabhasa. Hridaya-Shaktipat does not require intentional Yogic activity on His part, although such Yogic activity may also be spontaneously generated by Sri Da Avabhasa. Hridaya-Shaktipat operates principally at, in, and as the Heart Itself, primarily Awakening the intuition of "Bright" Consciousness, and only secondarily (and to one degree or another, depending on the characteristics of the individual) magnifying the activities of the Spirit-Current in the body-mind.

Shankara Adi Shankara (788-820) was a Hindu sage revered for his championing of the Teachings of Advaita Vedanta, or non-dualism.

Shirdi Sai Baba In the spring of 1970, before Sri Da Avabhasa's Re-Awakening, while wandering consciously in the subtle dimension in sleep, He met an unnamed Saint. The white-bearded old man lovingly embraced Heart-Master Da and told his family, friends, and devotees gathered with him that Sri Da Avabhasa was his "son". In the dream-vision, Heart-Master Da felt that this Saint was one of His Spiritual Protectors, and He understood that He would receive from him an "inheritance". He later learned that the Saint He had met was Sai Baba of Shirdi, in India, a great Spiritual Master who lived in the later nineteenth and early twentieth centuries. And the Inheritance, He saw, was Spiritual Realization of God.

Siddha In Sanskrit, "Siddha" means "a completed, fulfilled, or perfected one", or "one of perfect accomplishment, or power". In Sri Da Avabhasa's usage, a Siddha is a Transmission-Master who is a Realizer, to any significant degree, of God, Truth, or Reality.

Siddhi In Sanskrit "siddhi" means "power", or "accomplishment". When capitalized in Da Avabhasa's Wisdom-Teaching, "Siddhi" is the Spiritual, Transcendental, and Divine Awakening-Power that He spontaneously and effortlessly Transmits to all.

"simpler" form of the Way of the Heart; "simplest" form of the Way of the Heart (See **technical forms of practice in the Way of the Heart**.)

"sin" Sri Da Avabhasa elaborates on the meaning of the word "sin" (as He uses it) in the following paragraph:

What does "sin" mean, anyway? It comes from the Greek word "hamartia", which means "to miss the mark", the Mark of God, of Divine-Communion. Sin is dissociation from the Divine, not mere acts. All sins are the same. They are all about missing the mark.

"solid", "peculiar", "vital" Sri Da Avabhasa has observed and described three distinct character types or patterns—ways individuals tend to dramatize egoity in the first three stages of life—which He calls "solid", "peculiar", and "vital". These character types correspond, respectively, to the reactive and self-protective egoic strategies of a characteristically mental (or chronically mentally conceptual), a characteristically emotional (and even hysterical), and a characteristically vital (or physically self-indulgent) kind.

For further discussion, see chapter twenty-three of *The Dawn Horse Testament* and *The Eating Gorilla Comes in Peace*.

Source-Texts Sri Da Avabhasa has written seven Texts that form the summary of His entire Teaching-Word and that He calls His "Source-Texts". On pp. xxii-xxiii is a brief description of each of the Source-Texts.

Sri Da Avabhasa's Lineage of Blessing The principal Spiritual Masters Who Served Sri Da Avabhasa's Ordeal of Re-Awakening to the Divine Self-Condition belong to a single Lineage of extraordinary Yogis whose Parama-Guru (Supreme or Head Guru) was the Divine Goddess, or Mother Shakti.

Sri Da Avabhasa's first Spiritual Teacher was Swami Rudrananda (1928-1973), or Albert Rudolph, known as "Rudi", who was His Teacher from 1964 to 1968, in New York City. Rudi helped Heart-Master Da develop basic practical life-disciplines and the frontal Yoga of truly human Spiritual receptivity, which is the Yoga or process whereby knots and obstructions in the physical and etheric dimensions and relations of the body-mind are penetrated, opened, surrendered, and released through Spiritual reception in the frontal, or descending, line of the body-mind from the head to the bodily base. Rudi's own Teachers included the Indonesian Pak Subuh (from whom Rudi learned a basic exercise of Spiritual receptivity), Swami Muktananda Paramahansa (with whom Rudi studied many years), and Swami Nityananda (the Indian Swami who was also Swami Muktananda's Spiritual Teacher). Rudi met Swami Nityananda shortly before Swami Nityananda's death, and Rudi always thereafter acknowledged Swami Nityananda as his original and principal Spiritual Teacher.

The second Teacher in Sri Da Avabhasa's Lineage of Blessing was Swami Muktananda (1908-1982), who was born in Mangalore, South India. Having left home at the age of fifteen, he wandered for many years, seeking the Divine Truth from sources all over India. Eventually, he came under the Divine Influence of Swami Nityananda, whom he accepted as his Guru and in whose Spiritual Company he mastered Kundalini Yoga. As an Adept of Kundalini Yoga, Swami Muktananda Served Heart-Master Da Love-Ananda as Spiritual Teacher during the period from 1968 to 1970. In the summer of 1969, during Heart-Master Da's second visit to India, Swami Muktananda wrote Him a letter confirming Heart-Master Da's attainment of "Yogic Liberation", and acknowledging His right to Teach others. However, from the beginning of their relationship, Swami Muktananda instructed Him to visit Swami Nityañanda's Burial Site every day (whenever He was at Swami Muktananda's Ashram in Ganeshpuri, India), and to surrender to Swami Nityananda as the Supreme Guru of the Lineage.

Swami Nityananda, a great Yogi of South India, was Sri Da Avabhasa's third Spiritual Teacher in His Lineage of Blessing. Little is known about the circumstances of Swami Nityananda's birth and early life, although it is said that even as a child he showed the signs of a Realized Yogi. It is also known that he abandoned conventional life as a boy and wandered as a renunciate. Many miracles (including spontaneous healings) and instructive stories are attributed to him. Nityananda surrendered the body on August 8, 1961. Although Heart-Master Da Love-Ananda did not meet Swami Nityananda in the flesh, He enjoyed Swami Nityananda's direct Spiritual Influence from the subtle plane, and He acknowledges Swami Nityananda as a direct and principal Source of Spiritual Instruction during His years with Swami Muktananda.

On His third visit to India, while visiting Swami Nityananda's burial shrine, Sri Da Avabhasa was instructed by Swami Nityananda to relinquish all others as Guru and to surrender directly to the Goddess in Person as Guru, by performing a Puja (sacramental worship) at the Durga Temple next to Swami Muktananda's Ashram. Through this Puja, Sri Da Avabhasa surrendered His relationships to Swami Nityananda, Swami Muktananda, and Rudi and accepted the Goddess as His Guru. Thus, Swami Nityananda passed Sat-Guru Da to the Goddess Herself, who was then the Parama-Guru (or Source-Guru) of their Lineage.

In the Culmination of His Sadhana in the Vedanta Society Temple in Hollywood, California, Sri Da Avabhasa Husbanded the Goddess Herself in the Great Event of His Divine Re-Awakening.

Sri Da Avabhasa has said that although He was served by others through one or another means during the years of His Sadhana, He does not regard any of these individuals as His Guru, and only acknowledges as His Gurus those in this single Lineage of Blessing. Likewise, by virtue of Sri Da Avabhasa's own, Inherently Perfect, Divine Self-Realization, He has become the Parama-Guru of His Lineage.

stages of life (See "The Seven Stages of Life" on pp. 296-304.)

Sukra Kendra The term "Sukra Kendra" literally means "the 'Brightness' of the Heart". The Sukra Kendras are Sri Da Avabhasa's Personal Temples and are the principal Places of His Divine Work. They contain both His Chair and a statue of the Goddess. Because of this, Sri Da Avabhasa has said that the Sukra Kendras are "a way of picturing the two halves of Oneness, and I Am That Very One".

Swami Muktananda (See **Sri Da Avabhasa's Lineage of Blessing**.)

Swami Nityananda (See **Sri Da Avabhasa's Lineage of Blessing**.)

Swami Rudrananda (See **Sri Da Avabhasa's Lineage of Blessing**.)

tamas, rajas, sattva The Hindu texts declare that manifested existence is a complex variable of three qualities, or gunas. These are tamas, rajas, and sattva. Tamas, or the tamasic quality, is the principle, or power, of inertia. Rajas, or the rajasic quality, is the principle, or power, of action or motivation. Sattva, or the sattvic quality, is the principle, or power, of equilibrium or harmony.

tapas In Sanskrit, "tapas" literally means "heat". The fire of self-frustrating discipline generates a heat that purifies the body-mind, transforms loveless habits, and liberates the practitioner from the consolations of ordinary egoic existence.

technical forms of practice in the Way of the Heart Sri Da Avabhasa has provided a number of different approaches to the progressive process of Perfectly self-transcending God-Realization in the Way of the Heart. In this manner, He accounts for the differences in individuals' inclination toward and capability to develop the more intensive and more renunciate form of practice, as well as the technical details of practice, in the Way of the Heart.

Sat-Guru Da refers to the most detailed development of the practice of the Way of the Heart as the "technically 'fully elaborated'" form of practice. This technically "fully elaborated" form of the Way of the Heart develops and, over time, demonstrates, all the Yogic and other classic signs of Spiritual, Transcendental, and Divine Awakening. Each successive stage of practice in the technically "fully elaborated" form of the Way of the Heart is likewise defined by progressively more detailed responsibilities, disciplines, and practices that may be assumed in order to take responsibility for the signs of growing maturity in the process of Divine Awakening.

Uniquely exemplary practitioners for whom a more intensive approach and a more technically detailed discipline of attention and energy are effective as self-transcending practice may apply for formal acceptance into the Lay Renunciate Order, and thus into the technically "fully elaborated" form of practice (after a period of "testing and proving" in the student-beginner stage of practice).

All those who practice in this fashion are Called to demonstrate exemplary self-renunciation via an increasingly economized discipline of body, mind, and speech, and to maximize their growth in meditative self-surrender, self-forgetting, and self-transcendence through feeling-Contemplation of Sri Da Avabhasa's bodily (human) Form, His Spiritual (and Always Blessing) Presence, and His Very (and Inherently Perfect) State. The progress of practice in the technically "fully elaborated" form of the Way of the Heart is monitored, measured, and evaluated by stages through the devotee's direct accountability to the Free Renunciate Order, which is the senior practicing renunciate order in the Way of the Heart, and through his or her participatory submission to the sacred culture of either the Lay Renunciate Order (which is the second formal practicing renunciate order in the Way of the Heart) or, for the most exemplary practitioners in the ultimate stages of life, the Free Renunciate Order.

Yet, most individuals will find, in the course of the student-beginner experiment in practice, that they are qualified for a less intensive approach and that their practice is served by a less technical form of the conscious process than is exercised in the technically "fully elaborated" form of the Way of the Heart. Thus, most practitioners of the Way of the Heart will take up the technically "simpler" (or even "simplest") form of practice of the Way of the Heart, as members of the Lay Congregationist Order, or "lay congregationists".

The technically "simpler" practice involves the use of either pondering, maturing as self-Enquiry and Re-cognition, or Sat-Guru-Naama Japa—which is Name-Invocation of Sri Da Avabhasa via the Sat-Guru-Naama Mantra, "Om Sri Da Avabhasa Hridayam", or "Om Sri Da Love-Ananda Hridayam"—as a supportive aid to feeling-Contemplation of Sri Da Avabhasa.

The technically "simplest" form of the Way of the Heart is the practice of "simplest" feeling-Contemplation of Sri Da Avabhasa's bodily (human) Form, His Spiritual (and Always Blessing) Presence, and His Very (and Inherently Perfect) State, which practice may be accompanied by the random use of Sri Da Avabhasa's Principal Name, "Da", a practice that He has Given for use by practitioners in every form and developmental stage of the Way of the Heart.

Whereas the technically "simpler" (or even "simplest") form of practice of the Way of the Heart evolves through the same developmental stages as the technically "fully elaborated" practice, the progress may not be as technically detailed in its demonstration or its description. No matter what elaborate signs of maturity may arise in the course of the technically "simpler" (or even "simplest") form of the Way of the Heart, the practitioner simply maintains the foundation practice of feeling-Contemplation of Sri Da Avabhasa by using either self-Enquiry or the Sat-Guru-Naama Mantra (in the technically "simpler" form of practice), or perhaps random Invocation of Sri Da Avabhasa via His Principal Name, "Da" (in the technically "simplest" form of practice), and he or she does not look to adopt technically more "elaborate" practices of the conscious process in response to these developmental signs.

Heart-Master Da also uses the term "'simple' practice" (as distinct from "simpler" and "simplest") to describe the practice of feeling-Contemplation that is the foundation of all practice in the Way of the Heart, whatever the form of an individual's approach.

(See pp. 294-95 for descriptions of the Lay Congregationist Order, the Lay Renunciate Order, and the Free Renunciate Order.)

three (possible) contexts of the fourth stage of life in the Way of the Heart Sri Da Avabhasa has Revealed that, in the Way of the Heart, there are three (possible) contexts of the fourth stage of life, which appear in sequential order.

The "original", or beginner's, devotional context of the fourth stage of life involves the initial cultivation of devotional Heart-response to Sri Da Avabhasa (as Divine Self-Realizer and as Adept Heart-Teacher), and, thus and thereby, to the Divine Person, through consistent application to the practices of self-surrendering, self-forgetting, and self-transcending devotion, service, self-discipline, and meditation. In the Way of the Heart, this devotional course of discipline begins in the student-beginner stage of formally acknowledged practice of the Way of the Heart (and even in the student-novice stage, of formal approach to the Way of the Heart), and it remains as the fundamental devotional context of every form and developmental stage of practice in the Way of the Heart.

The essential religious "considerations" and devotional practices Given to listening devotees and hearing devotees in the Way of the Heart (particularly when served by the individual's direct personal contact with Sri Da Avabhasa in appropriate occasions of Blessing) awaken the open-hearted love-feeling, gratitude, and self-surrender that characterize the fourth stage of life. They thus grant a fourth stage context to dimensions of practice that otherwise focus on developing responsibility for functions of the body-mind associated with the first three stages of life.

The "basic" context of the fourth stage of life is true Spiritual Awakening enjoyed by devotees in the first actually seeing stage (and Initiated at the would-be-seeing, or progressively seeing, stage) of the Way of the Heart. Such devotees demonstrate seeing, or emotional conversion to actively radiant love, God-Communion, and receptivity to Sri Da Avabhasa's Spirit-Baptism, and then progressive responsibility for conducting that Spirit-Blessing in the context of the entire gross or frontal personality.

The "advanced" context of the fourth stage of life is characterized by the process of ascent of the Spirit-Current and attention toward the brain core. In the Way of the Heart, this process is a sign of readiness for entrance into practicing stage four of the technically "fully elaborated" form of practice, or its corresponding developmental stage in the technically "simpler", or even "simplest", form of practice. Most practitioners of the Way of the Heart will bypass practice in the ascending stages (the "advanced" context of the fourth stage of life, and the fifth stage of life) by entering the sixth stage of life directly from maturity in the first actually seeing stage (the fully established "basic" context of the fourth stage of life).

For more discussion of the early transition to

the sixth stage of life, see chapter forty-three of *The Dawn Horse Testament,* and also *The Da Avabhasa Upanishad.*

transcendence The term "transcendence" is commonly used to convey the quality or state of surpassing, exceeding, or moving beyond a condition or limitation. Kantian metaphysics extends the term to refer to a state of being beyond the limits of all possible experience and knowledge.

Sri Da Avabhasa uses the term "transcendence" to mean "the action or process of transcending" in connection with the presumed limits of body, emotion, and mind, or even any and all of the conditional states of experience within the first six stages of human life—all of which must be transcended in order to Realize the Free, Unqualified, and Absolute Condition of Inherent Happiness, Consciousness Itself, or Love-Bliss Itself.

vital (See **"solid", "peculiar", "vital"**.)

Witness-Position When Consciousness is free from identification with the body-mind, it takes up its natural "position" as the Conscious Witness of all that arises to and in and as the body-mind.

In the Way of the Heart, the stable Realization of the Witness-Position is associated with, or demonstrated via, the effortless surrender, or relaxation, of all seeking (and release of all motives of attention) relative to the conditional phenomena associated with the first five stages of life.

Identification with the Witness-Position, however, is not final (or Most Perfect) Realization of the Divine Self. Rather, it is the first stage of the "Perfect Practice" in the Way of the Heart, which Practice Realizes, by Heart-Master Da's Liberating Grace, complete and irreversible Identification with Consciousness Itself.

Yellow-red In the progression of lights seen in the Cosmic Mandala, the red, or gross physical, and yellow, or etheric and lower mental, realms form the outer circles.

Yoga From the Sanskrit verb root "yuj", meaning "to unite", usually referring to any discipline or process whereby an aspirant attempts to reunite with God. Sri Da Avabhasa acknowledges this conventional and traditional use of the term, but also, in reference to the Great Yoga of the Way of the Heart, employs it in a "radical" sense, free of the usual implication of egoic separation and seeking.

INDEX

Page number in *italics* refers to definitions of terms.

D

An Invitation

Da Avabhasa Offers you the most profoundly transformative opportunity that you will ever encounter— the opportunity to enter into sacred relationship with Him. In that relationship, He will Serve your human and Spiritual growth and, ultimately, your Divine Self-Realization.

If you would like to receive a free introductory brochure or talk to someone about forms of participation in the Way of the Heart, please write to or call:

The Free Daist Avabhasan Communion
Correspondence Department, I
12040 North Seigler Springs Road
Middletown, CA 95461, USA
Phone (707) 928-4936